Henry and Beezus

Henry

and

Beezus

By BEVERLY CLEARY

Illustrated by LOUIS DARLING

A YEARLING BOOK

Published by
Dell Publishing
a division of
The Bantam Doubleday Dell Publishing Group, Inc.
666 Fifth Avenue
New York, New York 10103

The trademark Yearling® is registered in the U.S. Patent
and Trademark Office.

ISBN: 0-440-43295-2

Printed in the United States of America
Reprinted by arrangement with William Morrow & Company, Inc.

May 1979

20 19 18

CW

Contents

1. RIBSY AND THE ROAST   9

2. HENRY GETS RICH   39

3. THE UNTRAINING OF RIBSY   75

4. HENRY PARKS HIS DOG   104

5. BEEZUS MAKES A BID   128

6. HENRY'S BARGAIN BIKE   148

7. THE BOY WHO ATE DOG FOOD   168

Henry and Beezus

CHAPTER ONE

Ribsy
and the Roast

HENRY HUGGINS stood by the front window
of his square white house on Klickitat Street and
wondered why Sunday afternoon seemed so much
longer than any other part of the week. Mrs. Huggins was reading a magazine, and Mr. Huggins,
puffing on his pipe, was reading the funnies in
the Sunday *Journal*.

Henry's dog, Ribsy, was asleep in the middle
of the living-room rug. As Henry looked at him,
he suddenly sat up, scratched hard behind his
left ear with his left hind foot, and flopped down
again without even bothering to open his eyes.

Henry pressed his nose against the windowpane and looked out at Klickitat Street. The only person he saw was Scooter McCarthy, who was riding up and down the sidewalk on his bicycle.

"I sure wish I had a bike," remarked Henry to his mother and father, as he watched Scooter.

"I wish you did, too," agreed his mother, "but with prices and taxes going up all the time, I'm afraid we can't get you one this year."

"Maybe things will be better next year," said Mr. Huggins, dropping the funnies and picking up the sport section.

Henry sighed. He wanted a bicycle now. He could see himself riding up and down Klickitat Street on a shiny red bike. He would wear his genuine Daniel Boone coonskin cap with the snap-on tail, only he wouldn't wear the tail fastened to the hat. He would tie it to the handle bars so that it would wave in the breeze as he whizzed along.

"Henry," said Mrs. Huggins, interrupting his thoughts, "please don't rub your nose against my clean window."

"All right, Mom," said Henry. "I sure wish something would happen around here sometime."

"Why don't you go over to Robert's house? Maybe he can think of something to do," suggested Mrs. Huggins, as she turned a page of her magazine.

"O.K.," agreed Henry. Robert's mother said they couldn't give the white mice rides on Robert's electric train any more, but maybe they could think of something else. "Come on, Ribsy," said Henry.

Ribsy stood up and shook himself, scattering hair over the rug.

"That dog," sighed Mrs. Huggins.

Henry thought he had better leave quickly. As he and Ribsy started down the front steps, Robert came around the corner.

"What's up, Doc?" said Robert.

"Hi," responded Henry.

"My dad said maybe if I came over to your house, you could think of something to do," said Robert.

The boys sat down on the front steps. "Here comes old Scooter," observed Robert. The two boys watched the older boy pumping down the street on his bicycle. He was whistling, and not only was he riding without touching the handle bars, he even had his hands in his pockets.

"Hi," said Scooter casually, without stopping.

"Big show-off," muttered Robert. "I bet he takes that bike to bed with him."

"He sure thinks he's smart," agreed Henry. "He's been riding up and down all afternoon. Come on, let's go around in the back yard, where we won't have to watch old Scooter show off all day. Maybe we can find something to do back there."

Ribsy followed at the boys' heels. Unfortunately, the back yard was no more interesting than the front. The only sign of life was next door. A large yellow cat was dozing on the Grumbies' back steps, and there was smoke coming from the barbecue pit.

Robert looked thoughtful. "Does Ribsy ever chase cats?"

"Not that old Fluffy." Henry, understanding what was on Robert's mind, explained that Mrs. Grumbie sprinkled something called Doggie-B-Gone on her side of the rosebushes. Ribsy disliked the smell of it and was careful to stay on his side of the bushes.

Robert was disappointed. "I thought Ribsy might . . ."

"No such luck," interrupted Henry, looking at his dog, who had settled himself by the back steps to continue his nap. Henry picked a blade of grass and started to blow through it when the

squeak-slam of the Grumbies' screen door made him look up. "Jeepers!" he whispered.

Stepping carefully over Fluffy, Mr. Hector Grumbie walked down the back steps. He was wearing a chef's tall white hat and an immense white apron. *What's cooking?* was written across the hat, and on the apron was printed a recipe for *Bar X Ranch Bar-B-Q Sauce*. Mr. Grumbie carried a tray full of bowls, jars, bottles, and what appeared to be bunches of dried weeds.

"Is he really going to cook?" whispered Robert.

"Search me," answered Henry. The two boys edged closer to the rosebushes that divided the two yards.

"Hello, Mr. Grumbie," said Henry.

"Hello there, Henry." Mr. Grumbie crossed the lawn and set the tray on the edge of the barbecue pit in the corner of his yard. He peeled a small object which he put into a bowl, sprinkled with salt, and mashed with a little wooden stick. Then he broke off pieces of the dried weeds and mashed them, too.

Henry and Robert exchanged puzzled looks.

"Need any help, Mr. Grumbie?" asked Henry.

"No, thank you." Mr. Grumbie poured a few drops of something into the mixture.

"Is that something that's supposed to be good to eat?" asked Robert. Mr. Grumbie didn't answer.

"What's that stuff in the bowl?" asked Henry.

"Herbs and garlic," answered Mr. Grumbie. "Now run along and play, boys. I'm busy."

Henry and Robert did not move.

"Etta!" called Mr. Grumbie to his wife. "I forgot the vinegar." He coughed as a breeze blew smoke in his face.

"I'll go get it for you," offered Henry, but his neighbor ignored him.

Squeak-slam went the screen. Mrs. Grumbie stepped over Fluffy and walked across the yard with a bottle in her hand. "Hector, can't we take your friends out to dinner instead of going to all this trouble?" she asked, as she fanned smoke out of her eyes.

"This is no trouble at all." Mr. Grumbie added a few drops of vinegar to the mixture in the bowl.

Henry thought Mrs. Grumbie looked cross, as she said, "Hector, why don't you let me cook the meat in the house? It would be so much easier and then we could bring it outside to eat."

"Now, Etta, I know what I'm doing." Mr. Grumbie poured a few drops from another bottle and mashed some more.

"But I don't like to see you spoil the flavor of a perfectly good piece of meat with all that seasoning. It would be different if you really knew how to cook." Mrs. Grumbie frowned, as she swatted at a bug circling over the sauce.

Mr. Grumbie frowned even more. "Anyone who can read a recipe can cook."

Mrs. Grumbie's face turned red, as she clapped

the bug between her hands, and said sharply, "Oh, is that so? What about the time you cut up tulip bulbs in the hamburgers because you thought they were onions?"

"That," said Mr. Grumbie, even more sharply, "was different."

Mrs. Grumbie angrily fanned smoke with her apron. "Just remember when we try to eat this mess you're fixing that it wasn't my idea. Even if the recipe is any good, the meat will probably be burned on the outside and raw inside. Smoke will get in our eyes and we'll be eaten alive by mosquitoes and . . ."

Mr. Grumbie interrupted. "Etta, we won't argue about it any more. I invited my friends to a barbecue and we're going to have a barbecue."

Henry and Robert were disappointed. They hoped the Grumbies would argue about it a lot more.

Then Mr. Grumbie looked at the recipe printed

on his apron. Because he was looking down at it, the words were upside down for him. "What does it say here?" he asked, pointing to his stomach.

Henry and Robert could not help snickering.

"Now, boys, run along and don't bother us. We're busy," said Mrs. Grumbie.

"Come on, Robert." Henry turned away from the rosebushes. He felt uncomfortable around Mrs. Grumbie, because he thought she didn't like him. At least, she didn't like Ribsy and that was the same as not liking Henry. He didn't want to make her any crosser than she was already, although secretly he couldn't see why she minded Ribsy's burying a bone in her pansy bed once in a while.

Henry tried standing on his hands just to show Mrs. Grumbie he wasn't paying any attention to what she was doing. Then he heard someone coming up his driveway. It was his friend Beezus and her little sister Ramona, who lived in the next

block on Klickitat Street. Beezus' real name was Beatrice, but Ramona called her Beezus, and so did everyone else. Beezus was carrying a baton and Ramona was riding a shiny new tricycle.

"Whoa!" yelled Ramona to her tricycle. Then she got off and tied it to a bush with a jumping rope.

"Hello," said Beezus. "See my baton."

The boys examined the metal rod, which was about two and a half feet long with a rubber knob at each end.

"What are you going to do with it?" asked Henry.

"Twirl it," said Beezus.

"I'll bet," scoffed Robert.

"I am too," said Beezus. "I take lessons every Saturday. By June I'll be good enough so I can twirl it in the Junior Rose Festival parade, and some day I'm going to be a drum majorette."

"June is only a couple of months away," said Henry, wondering what he would do in the parade this year. "Let's see you twirl it."

Beezus held the baton over her head and started to turn it with her right hand. It slipped from her fingers and hit her on the head.

"Boi-i-ing!" shouted the two boys together.

"You keep quiet," said Beezus crossly.

"Let me try," said Henry.

"No," answered Beezus, whose feelings were hurt.

"I didn't want to anyway." Henry started across the yard. "Come on, Robert, let's climb the cherry tree."

"All right for you, Henry Huggins!" shouted

Beezus, as the boys scrambled up through the branches. "I'm going home. Come on, Ramona, untie your horse."

But Ramona had seen Ribsy and she began to pat him on the head. Ribsy groaned in his sleep and sat up to scratch. Suddenly he was wide awake, sniffing the air.

"Wuf!" said Ribsy.

Henry could tell by the sound of the bark that Ribsy was excited about something. He peered out through the leaves of the cherry tree, but could see nothing unusual in his back yard. He saw Ribsy stand up, shake himself, and trot purposefully toward the Grumbies' back yard, with Ramona running after him.

Henry looked across the rosebushes and groaned at what he saw. On a platter beside the barbecue pit was a large piece of raw meat. The Grumbies were nowhere in sight.

"Here, Ribsy! Come here, boy!" called Henry

frantically, but Ribsy did not stop. "Catch him, Beezus!"

Ramona, who was trying to follow Ribsy through the rosebushes, shrieked.

"Hold still," directed Beezus, struggling with her little sister. "I can't get you loose from all these thorns when you wiggle that way."

"Come on, we better be getting out of here." Henry slipped and slid down the tree. "I bet the rain washed off the Doggie-B-Gone."

"I guess we better," agreed Robert cheerfully. After all, Ribsy wasn't his dog.

Henry hit the ground and tried to run through the rosebushes. Thorns clawed at his jeans and held him fast. "Here, Ribsy," he yelled. "Here, Ribs, old boy!"

Ribsy jumped for the roast.

With one desperate jerk, Henry tried to free himself from the roses. The thorns dug deeper into his legs.

Ribsy sank his teeth into the meat and pulled it to the ground.

Mr. Grumbie came through the back door with an armload of kindling. "Hey, stop that dog!" he yelled, dropping the wood on his toe. "Ow!" he groaned, as he started toward Ribsy and stepped on Fluffy's tail.

An ear-splitting yowl brought Mrs. Grumbie to the back porch. "Fluffy," she cooed, "did the man step on the precious pussycat's tail?"

Ribsy paused to take a firmer grip on the roast.

"If that cat hasn't any more sense than to sleep on the steps . . ." snapped Mr. Grumbie. "Hey, make that dog come back here!"

"Oh, my goodness!" exclaimed Mrs. Grumbie, when she saw what had happened. "Here, Ribsy, here, Ribsy!"

That was just what Ribsy needed to make him start running. He didn't like Mrs. Grumbie. He

knew she sprinkled Doggie-B-Gone on the shrubbery to keep him away.

With one final yank and the sound of ripping
cloth, Henry jerked away from the bushes.

"Tackle him," yelled Robert, who was still trying to untangle himself from the thorns.

Henry flung himself at his dog, but Ribsy raced
on. Henry picked himself up off the Grumbies'
driveway and ran after him.

Around the Grumbies' house he ran and on
down Klickitat Street. He could hear Robert's and
Mr. Grumbie's feet pounding down the sidewalk
after him.

"Ribsy!" yelled Henry.

"Hey, come back here," shouted Robert.

"Stop thief!" bellowed Mr. Grumbie, holding
onto his tall white hat with one hand.

Doors and windows began to open. "What's
cooking, Grumbie?" someone called out.

Henry heard his mother say, "Oh, that dog!"

"Henry!" shouted Mr. Huggins.

"Go get 'em, Grumbie," yelled the man across the street.

Mr. Grumbie paused for breath. "Somebody head him off," he directed.

Ribsy ran into the street. A car turned the corner.

"Ribsy," wailed Henry, afraid to look.

"Hey, look out," warned Robert.

The car slammed on its brakes. Ribsy ran back to the sidewalk.

If only Henry could put on a burst of speed and make a really good flying tackle. But no matter how fast he ran, Ribsy was just out of his reach. He glanced over his shoulder and saw that Mr. Grumbie's face was red and he had lost his hat.

"Come . . . here . . . sir!" panted Mr. Grumbie. He wasn't used to running. Then his footsteps grew slower and slower until they stopped altogether.

. Henry ran on, with Robert close behind. Their friend Mary Jane came out of her house and started down the sidewalk toward them. If only she would stop Ribsy.

"Catch him!" yelled Henry.

When Ribsy was only a few feet from Mary Jane, he dropped the meat on the sidewalk. Here was her chance. "Get it, Mary Jane," Henry shouted, with almost all the breath he had left. "Get the meat!"

Mary Jane stood staring at Ribsy.

"Pick up the meat, you dope!" yelled Robert.

Still Mary Jane did not move. Ribsy waited until Henry was almost within tackling distance before taking a firm grip on the roast and starting to run again.

"Mary Jane," panted Henry, "head him off."

Mary Jane stepped aside and Ribsy ran on. Henry felt as if he could not move another step.

"Why didn't you grab the meat?" he demanded, as he paused to catch his breath.

"You could have caught him if you wanted to," accused Robert.

"I couldn't either stop your dirty old dog," said Mary Jane. "Can't you see I'm wearing my Sunday School dress?"

"Mary Jane, you give me a pain." Henry glared at her.

"You're a poet and don't know it," said Mary Jane, twirling around to show off her full skirt.

Robert and Henry looked at one another. Girls!

Robert clutched Henry's arm and pointed in the direction from which Ribsy had come. "Look!"

A police dog, a fox terrier, and a sort of a collie were running down Klickitat Street toward Ribsy. Now there would be a dog fight, and the roast would be torn to pieces, and the two big dogs would chew up Ribsy. They would probably chew the fox terrier, too, and Henry knew the lady who owned him was very particular about keeping him out of dog fights. Henry would be blamed because the big dogs bit the little dog and . . . Suddenly Henry found he was too tired to do much of anything. He picked up a clod of dirt and threw it at the dogs as they passed him. "Beat it," he said, but he didn't bother to shout. He knew it was no use.

"Boy, a dog fight!" Robert was delighted. "This is going to be keen."

"Aw, keep quiet," said Henry. Robert wouldn't feel that way if Ribsy were his dog. The sort of collie was gaining on Ribsy, and the police dog was not far behind. Poor Ribsy! Henry shut his eyes. He couldn't stand seeing Ribsy chewed to pieces.

"Gangway everybody!" It was Scooter's voice. Leaning over his handle bars and pumping as hard as he could, he tore down the street behind the three dogs. He passed Henry and Robert and,

swerving to avoid the dogs, caught up with Ribsy.
He didn't stop for the curb, but rode right over it
with a tremendous bump. Then he flung himself
off the bicycle and on top of Ribsy before the
dog knew what was happening.

Ribsy dropped the meat and Scooter snatched
it. He sprang on his bicycle, wheeled around in
the middle of the street, and started back toward

the Grumbies' house, holding the meat above his head with one hand. The three other dogs and Ribsy all chased after Scooter, barking and growling as they jumped up and tried to snap at the meat.

Eluding them all, Scooter pedaled triumphantly back down Klickitat Street. "Hi," he said briefly to Henry and Robert, as he passed them.

"Hey, give me that meat," demanded Henry. Scooter ignored him.

"How do you like that!" said Robert. "He sure thinks he's smart."

Henry ran after Scooter, who pedaled even faster. Henry put on a burst of speed. So did Scooter. So did the dogs. Henry could hear the neighbors laughing. He tried to run faster, but Scooter stayed just out of his reach.

When Scooter reached the Grumbies' house, he handed the meat to its owner. "There you are, Mr. Grumbie," he said.

Mr. Grumbie took the battered roast. "Thank you, Scooter. That was mighty quick thinking on your part."

"It wasn't anything," said Scooter modestly. "It was easy to catch up with him on my bike."

The other dogs lost interest and ran away, but Ribsy continued to whimper and jump for the meat. Then even he gave up and sat panting, with his long pink tongue hanging out.

Poor Ribsy, thought Henry. He wanted that meat so much. Maybe he's tired of horse meat. Henry wished he dared to pet his dog, even though he had been cross with him.

"He's a dumb dog," said Scooter. "It's a good thing I came along and saved him from those other dogs when I did."

"I think you're mean, Scooter McCarthy," said Beezus. "Poor Ribsy."

"Why don't you go home?" said Henry to Scooter.

"Now, children," said Mrs. Huggins. Then she said to Mrs. Grumbie, "You must let us buy you another roast. Henry can help pay for it out of his allowance. He knows he is supposed to keep his dog out of your yard."

"Gee, my mother says roasts are expensive," said Scooter.

"You keep quiet." Henry scowled at Scooter. Why was Scooter always around when things happened to him? "Jeepers, I'm sorry, Mrs. Grumbie," said Henry. "I don't know what got into Ribsy. He was just hungry, I guess."

"He always is," observed Mr. Huggins.

Meat markets were closed on Sunday, but Henry knew that the delicatessen counter in the Supermarket was open. "Delicatessens have wienies, don't they?" he asked. "I could run down to the Supermarket and get some for you, if you'd like."

"I could go faster on my bike," said Scooter.

Mrs. Grumbie smiled. "Thank you, Henry. That won't be necessary. I think we'll go out to dinner." She looked at Mr. Grumbie, who had started toward the house with the roast. "Just between you and me," she whispered, "I don't think the meat would have been fit to eat with that sauce Mr. Grumbie was going to put on it." Then she called to her husband, "Hector, what are you going to do with that dirty piece of meat?"

"I suppose he might as well have it," said Mr. Grumbie reluctantly. "Not that he deserves it." He threw the remains to Ribsy.

Mrs. Grumbie paused in the doorway. "Henry, I'm going to bake cookies tomorrow. If you'll stop by on your way home from school tomorrow, I'll give you some."

"Thank you, Mrs. Grumbie," answered Henry. She seemed almost glad Ribsy had stolen the roast. At least, she wasn't cross any more.

"Here, Ribsy, it isn't time for you to eat yet." Henry tugged at the roast, but Ribsy hung on and growled. "Come on, Dad, give me a hand."

Mr. Huggins took hold of the meat and together they got it away from Ribsy. "I'll put it in the refrigerator for him," said Mr. Huggins, "and I'll have a talk with you later."

"Aw, gee, Dad," protested Henry. "I wasn't doing anything."

"You wanted something to happen, didn't you?" said Mr. Huggins, as he carried the meat into the house.

Henry did not answer. He just sighed and sat down on the steps. Why did these things always have to happen to him, anyway? Robert sat down beside him while Ramona sat on the grass beside Ribsy. Scooter picked up his bicycle. Beezus began to practice twirling her baton again.

"That was pretty exciting, wasn't it?" asked Robert. "It isn't often something happens around here on Sunday."

"I suppose so," said Henry, with no enthusiasm at all.

"It sure was a good thing I caught that dog of yours when I did," boasted Scooter.

Henry glared. "You think you're smart, don't you?"

"Well, somebody had to stop him." Scooter threw his leg across his bicycle.

"You just wait till I get my bike," said Henry.

Both boys looked interested. "Aw, you aren't going to get a bike," said Scooter. "You're just saying that."

"I am too going to get a bike," insisted Henry. "And it's going to be a better bike than yours. You just wait and see."

"When are you going to get it, Henry?" asked Robert.

"Never mind when." Henry tried to look mysterious. "You just wait and see."

"You're just saying that," repeated Scooter.

"He is not." Beezus flipped her baton and almost caught it before it fell to the grass. "If Henry says he's going to get a bicycle, he's going to get one. So there!"

"Ha," said Scooter, and pedaled down the street.

"Are you really going to get a bike?" asked

Robert and Beezus at the same time, when Scooter had gone.

"Sure, I'm going to get one." Henry tried to sound as if he meant it. He had to get a bike now. He just had to, that was all. He would start a bicycle fund right away. Of course, he had to think about paying for the roast first, but with all that beef in the refrigerator, he wouldn't have to buy horse meat for Ribsy at the Lucky Dog Pet Shop for a couple of weeks. The money he saved on horse meat would start his bike fund. He'd get that bicycle yet.

CHAPTER TWO

Henry Gets Rich

ONE day after school Mrs. Huggins asked Henry to run down to the market for a pound of ground round steak. On the way home he decided to cut through the vacant lot to see if he could find a coke bottle to turn in at the Supermarket for pennies to add to his bike fund. He was careful to keep the meat out of Ribsy's reach.

While Henry was looking for bottles, Ribsy, barking excitedly, bounded off into the bushes. Because it was so unusual for his dog to leave a package of meat, Henry followed to see what he was chasing. It was only a neighborhood cat, but when Henry started back to the path, he noticed a piece of gray cardboard with printing on it, sticking out of the bushes. He stopped to see what it was.

"Wow!" exclaimed Henry. Thrown carelessly in a hollow, and half hidden by weeds, was a pile of boxes. On the end of each box was printed the words *Double Bubble Gum.*

Telling himself the boxes were probably empty, Henry hastily hid the meat in a bush out of his dog's reach before he eagerly ripped open one of the boxes. It was full of pink balls the size of a marble. Henry popped one into his mouth, bit through the sugar coating, chewed vigorously, and then blew a rubbery pink bubble. It really was bubble gum!

Henry opened several other boxes and found them full of gum too. He couldn't take time to count the balls, but there must have been two hundred, maybe even three hundred, in each box. He counted the boxes. There were forty-nine, all

full of bubble gum. Forty-nine times three hundred was . . . Well, it was a terribly big number.

Henry couldn't believe it. Forty-nine boxes of bubble gum, and three hundred balls in each box! It was enough to last the rest of his life. He would never have to park his gum again. He was rich!

Then Henry began to think. He knew he was rich only if he could get the gum home without being seen by the other boys and girls. That was not going to be easy. He took the pound of ground round steak out of the bushes and picked up two boxes of gum. "Come on, Ribsy," he said and ran home as fast as he could.

Henry tossed the package of meat onto the drain board in the kitchen and stowed the gum under his bed in his own room. Then he ran down Klickitat Street toward Beezus' house. He was careful to slow down when he saw her in the yard.

"Hi," said Henry, as if he had all the time in the world.

"Hello, Henry," said Beezus, gathering a handful of tulip petals and tossing them into the air so they fell over her in a pink shower. Her little sister Ramona was sitting on an apple box at the edge of the sidewalk.

"Say, Beezus," said Henry casually, "could I borrow your red wagon for a little while?"

"What for?" asked Beezus, looking much too interested.

"Oh, just an errand," said Henry.

"Can I go?" asked Beezus.

"No." Henry hid his impatience. "It's just some work I've got to do."

"Then you can't borrow it," said Beezus, and gathered another handful of petals.

Henry saw that this was a situation that must be handled carefully. "I'll give you a piece of bubble gum." He blew a bubble for her to admire.

"O.K.," agreed Beezus. "Give it to me and I'll get the wagon."

Henry knew she had him there. He hadn't put any loose gum in his pockets. He should have known better than to ask a favor of a girl, anyway. "I'll give it to you when I get back," he said.

Beezus was firm. "Not unless I go too."

Henry saw Scooter riding toward them on his bicycle and knew he had to act fast. He didn't want old Scooter hanging around asking questions. "O.K.," he agreed quickly. "You can go, but just remember I've got double dibs on what I'm going to bring home."

When Henry and Beezus returned from the back yard with the red wagon, Scooter was no longer in sight, but Ramona was still sitting on the apple box.

"Come on, Ramona," said Beezus, taking an old panda bear out of the wagon. "We're going with Henry."

"No," said Ramona.

Henry was growing anxious. What if Scooter

decided to cut through the vacant lot? "Jeepers, Beezus, we've just got to hurry. It's awfully important. If we don't get where we're going, we might be too late."

"Ramona," coaxed Beezus, "can't you play that game some other time?"

"What game?" asked Henry. He couldn't see that Ramona was playing any game.

"She's playing she's waiting for a bus," explained Beezus.

Henry groaned. It was the dumbest game he had ever heard of. "Doesn't she know it isn't any fun just to sit on a box?" he asked, looking nerv-

ously up and down the street. If only he could be sure no one else had discovered his gum!

"Sh-h," whispered Beezus. "She thinks it's fun and I don't want her to find out it isn't. It keeps her quiet." Then she said to her little sister, "If you get in the wagon, Henry and I'll pull you and you can pretend you're riding on the bus."

Henry was relieved that this idea pleased Ramona, who climbed into the wagon. He and Beezus ran down the street pulling the wagon behind them. When they came to the path through the vacant lot, Beezus pushed the wagon and Henry pulled. If only no one else had discovered Henry's treasure!

"Gee whillikers!" said Beezus in a hushed voice, when she saw what they had come for. "Are all those boxes really full of gum?"

"They sure are," said Henry, gathering an armload.

Beezus began to help. "And is it all yours?"

"Sure. I found it and said I had double dibs, didn't I?" said Henry. "But just to be sure, I've got to get it home before the other kids see it."

Beezus was a sensible girl who understood the importance of this, and she began to work faster. She lifted Ramona out of the wagon. Ramona yelled. "Here, chew this," said Beezus, poking a piece of gum into her mouth.

When Beezus and Henry had all the gum loaded onto the wagon, Henry took off his jacket and spread it over the boxes. Then they pulled their cargo home as fast as Ramona could run.

"Whew!" breathed Henry, when they turned into his yard. Now that the gum was on his property, no one could come along and say he had dibs on it too. He flung himself down on the front steps. "Come on," he said. "Let's chew."

Beezus helped herself to a ball of gum and crunched through the sugar coating. Henry added a ball to the one he already had in his mouth.

Ramona, too young to be an expert, smacked noisily. Henry gave Ribsy a piece. Looking puzzled, the dog tried to bite into it. The ball rolled around in his mouth until he spat it out on the grass and looked reproachfully at Henry.

Beezus admired the size of the bubbles Henry blew with a double wad, so she tried a second ball. Henry tried a third.

Then Robert came down the street. "What's up, Doc?" he asked.

"Look." Henry blew a bubble the size of a tennis ball. When it broke with a satisfying pop, he had difficulty getting the gum back into his mouth, because it stuck to his chin. "Have a piece. Have two pieces," he said, when he was able to talk.

"Wow!" Robert stared at the wagonload of gum. He lost no time in putting two pieces into his mouth.

The group chewed busily until Mary Jane appeared. "Henry Huggins, where did you get that gum?" she demanded.

"Have a piece." Henry ignored her question as he extended a box of gum to her.

"No, thank you," said Mary Jane. "My mother says chewing gum is vulgar." She watched the others chew until she could stand it no longer. "If you don't mind," she said, "I think I will try just one piece."

Henry pulled a bubble back into his mouth. "Sure, help yourself."

The first time Mary Jane tried to blow a bubble, she blew the gum out of her mouth onto the grass.

"No, that's not the way," said Henry, offering her another piece. "Flatten it with your teeth and poke your tongue into it before you blow."

After a little practice Mary Jane blew small, ladylike bubbles.

Then Scooter came pedaling down the street

on his bicycle. He stopped when he saw the group on the steps. "Say, Huggins, when are you going to get that bike?"

Henry blew an extra-large bubble before he answered. "You just wait and see."

Scooter whistled with amazement. "Say, where'd you get all that?"

"None of your beeswax," said Henry through his wad.

"How about letting me have a piece?" asked Scooter.

"Nope," said Henry.

"Aw, come on," coaxed Scooter.

"Nope." Henry was pleased that he had something Scooter wanted.

Scooter thought a minute. "I'll let you ride my bike to the corner and back if you'll give me a piece."

This put a new light on the matter. "Let me ride around the block," bargained Henry.

"O.K." Scooter got off his bicycle.

"Just one piece. Robert, you watch my gum while I'm gone." Henry picked up the bicycle. He wished he weren't so wobbly at riding, because he knew he would never hear the last of it if he took a spill in front of Scooter. He stepped on the high pedal with his left foot, threw his right leg across the seat, and found the other pedal with his right foot. The bike was too large for him, and he teetered from one side of the walk to the other before he got started.

Then Henry began to enjoy himself. This was the life! And if Scooter let him ride around the block for one piece of gum, there was no telling what he could get with the rest of the gum.

Henry started to make plans. He would use the gum the way the Indians used wampum. He would take some to school and see what the other boys and girls offered him. Why, they would probably even give him money for the gum. If he sold it for less than the store did, say two balls for a penny, he would get rid of it in no time and have the money for his bike fund. He'd show old Scooter yet!

The ride around the block was much too short. When he laid the bike on the lawn, Beezus said, "Henry, I need my wagon. I've got to take Ramona home. She's got gum in her hair."

"Sure," said Henry. "Here's a box of gum for letting me use the wagon."

"A whole box?" exclaimed Beezus gratefully. "Gee, thanks, Henry. I never expected this much."

As Beezus and her little sister left, Mr. Huggins pulled into the driveway and got out of his car. "Hello, kids," he said. "What's all this?"

When Henry explained, his father laughed and quickly estimated the total amount of gum. "Forty-nine boxes of three hundred balls each is . . . let's see . . . fourteen thousand seven hundred balls of gum. Quite a lot, isn't it?"

Even Scooter looked impressed until Mr. Huggins said, "How do you know there isn't something wrong with it?"

Four wads of gum were promptly spat into the shrubbery. Henry discovered his jaws were very tired. Come to think of it, there *was* something funny about all that gum lying around in a vacant lot.

"Or maybe it's stolen goods," suggested Mr. Huggins. "There must be some reason why it was dumped in the lot."

"Receiving stolen goods is pretty bad, isn't it?" asked Scooter.

"Aw, keep quiet," said Henry. "Gee, Dad, what do you think I better do?"

"Suppose I phone the police and ask them about it," suggested Mr. Huggins.

"O.K." Henry knew it was the right thing to do, but he didn't see how he could give up all that valuable gum. Not after his idea for building up his bike fund. And besides, it would really be something to show the kids at school.

After Mr. Huggins talked to the police, who said they would let him know what they found out about the gum, Henry spent an anxious evening. He stacked the boxes neatly under his bed, just in case he could keep them. Then he found he didn't feel much like reading or working on his model plane, so he wandered around the house, drumming his fingers on the windowpanes and waiting.

Finally Mrs. Huggins put down her knitting and said, "Henry, for heaven's sake, can't you light some place?"

Henry flung himself into a chair. "Gee, Mom, do you think they'll phone or drive up in a squad car?"

As if in answer to his question, the telephone rang. Henry held his breath while his father answered. "Yes," said Mr. Huggins. "Yes . . . yes

. . . I see. . . . It is? . . . Oh . . . yes. . . .
Thank you for letting us know."

"What did they say, Dad? What did they say?"
demanded Henry.

"The gum was thrown away by a man who
owned a lot of gum machines and is going out of
business," answered Mr. Huggins.

"I get to keep it then, don't I, Dad?"

Mr. Huggins smiled. "The police say there's no
reason why you shouldn't keep it."

"I was afraid of that," sighed Mrs. Huggins.
"Henry, how do you get mixed up in these
things?"

"Boy, oh, boy!" Henry gloated. "Wait till I tell
the kids at school!"

The next morning Mrs. Huggins didn't have to
tell Henry to hurry. He and Ribsy left for school
fifteen minutes early. On the way Henry chewed
a couple of balls out of the box he was carrying,
so he could show off some really good bubbles.

As soon as he reached Glenwood School, boys and girls began to crowd around him. "Did you get to keep all that gum Mary Jane said you found in the lot?" they asked.

"Sure I got to keep it," said Henry, disappointed at having his surprise spoiled. If that wasn't just like a girl, especially Mary Jane. "I'm going to sell it two for a penny."

The boys and girls knew a bargain when they saw one. "I'll take four," said Joey.

"Give me two," said Peter.

Some of the children did not have money with them, but Henry said they could bring it the next day. He opened charge accounts by writing their names and the amounts they owed on the margin of a comic book he had in the hip pocket of his jeans. By the time the second bell rang, Henry had twenty-two cents coming to him. Boy, oh, boy, he thought. This is even better than I expected.

By noon the news of Henry's treasure had spread throughout the school, and boys and girls from other rooms crowded around to buy the bargain gum. Henry was so busy selling that Beezus offered to write down the names of those who were going to bring their money the next day. By the time school was out, Henry had fifty-one cents in real money and forty-three cents written in his comic book. That was almost a dollar for his bike fund. Besides that, he had four marbles, a yo-yo, and six comic books.

And that was not all. Joey chose him to be the next blackboard monitor, Kathleen said she was going to invite him to her birthday party, six boys wanted to sit beside him in the cafeteria at noon, and Roger rode him home on his bicycle.

The next day Henry left even earlier and took another box of gum to school. He found business more complicated, because he not only had to sell gum and write down the names of the boys and girls who would bring their money the next day, he had to cross off in his comic book the names of those who had remembered to bring the pennies they owed him. He was glad when Beezus arrived and helped him keep the transactions straight.

At first, the boys and girls who were chewing Henry's gum were careful to chew only when Miss Bonner wasn't looking, but after a while they forgot to be careful. Then she said unexpectedly, "Henry, tell the class what mark of punctuation should go at the end of the sentence I have written on the blackboard."

Taken by surprise, Henry quickly shifted his

quid of gum to his cheek. "A period . . . uh . . . I mean a question mark," he said.

"I think, Henry," said Miss Bonner, "that if you throw your gum in the wastebasket, we shall all have much less trouble understanding you."

Feeling foolish, Henry walked to the front of the room and threw his wad of gum into the empty metal wastebasket. When it landed with a loud *clonk*, the whole class tittered.

"And now," said Miss Bonner, "I want everyone in the room who has gum in his or her mouth to throw it into the wastebasket."

Sheepishly, half a dozen boys and Beezus walked to the wastebasket and discarded their gum.

Miss Bonner looked around the room. "Robert," she said sternly. "George." The two boys slouched to the wastebasket.

After recess Miss Bonner marched another procession of gum chewers to the wastebasket. Although she didn't say much, Henry decided she looked pretty cross.

When Henry carried his gum out to the playground at noon, he found to his surprise that no one wanted to buy. Nearly everyone was already chewing and blowing.

"Maybe if you cut the price you could sell more," suggested Beezus.

"I guess I'll have to," said Henry. "I'll try four for a penny."

Business picked up after that, but when Henry went home after school, he wasn't sure how much money he had. He actually had thirty-one cents in his pocket, but when he tried to figure out the accounts in the comic book, he had to give up. Some of the boys who had forgotten to bring their money had charged more gum. Some had paid, but he had forgotten to cross off their names. Anyway, the comic book was getting so ragged and dirty, and the pencil marks so smudged, that it was impossible to read anything. Tossing the book into the fireplace, Henry decided he could remember how much Roger and Peter and a few more owed. He would just have to hope the others paid him.

The next morning when Henry was about to start to school with a box of gum, Beezus rang the doorbell. She handed Henry her box of bubble gum. "Mother says I have to give this back to you," she said.

"What for?" asked Henry.

"Because of Ramona. She gets into the gum and chews it and gets it stuck in her hair. The only

way Mother can get it out is to cut it out with the scissors. Ramona looks pretty awful with her hair all different lengths, and Daddy says if this keeps up she'll be bald before long." Beezus looked apologetic. "Anyway, I'm kind of tired of chewing gum."

When they reached the playground, Henry found business slow; everyone was already chewing gum. But when Henry cut the price to ten balls for a penny, he made several sales.

"Do you have any flavors beside cinnamon-peppermint or whatever it is?" asked Joey.

Henry had to admit he did not.

"Oh," said Joey, and went away.

Henry tried to think what stores did when they wanted to sell something. He knew they had sales, they advertised, and they gave away free samples. Henry had tried gum sales and he couldn't think of a good way to advertise, so he decided to try free samples. Although a dozen children crowded around him for samples, the demand was not as large as he had expected.

Then Roger, who owed Henry four cents for gum, approached him and asked for a free sample. Henry wasn't sure whether he should give gum to someone who owed him money, but since he had given it to the others, he gave Roger a piece. Roger put it in his pocket.

"How about that four cents you owe me for eight balls of gum you bought yesterday?" asked Henry.

"I forgot it," said Roger. "And anyway, how come you're giving gum away today when you sold it yesterday?"

"Well . . ." Henry didn't like to admit that no one was interested in his gum.

"Yes," said Peter, joining in the conversation. "I don't see why I have to pay you. You're giving it away now."

"I wasn't giving it away yesterday and the day before," said Henry. "I was selling it, so you owe me money."

"I do not." Peter blew a bubble that popped.

"You do too," said Henry, feeling confused.

The bell rang, and they started toward their classroom. Henry noticed Peter and Roger talking to each other. Then they gathered a bunch of children around them outside the door. They talked earnestly together until Miss Bonner herded them into the room.

Now what are they up to? thought Henry. He worried about it all through social studies and arithmetic. Somehow, things didn't seem to be turning out the way he had planned. He was secretly pleased when Miss Bonner made Peter throw his gum in the wastebasket.

When recess came, Henry was surprised at the number of boys and girls who suddenly wanted free gum. He had almost as big a crowd around him as he had had on the first morning. He began to enjoy himself again.

Then Roger and Peter called to him. "Hey, Henry, can we see you a sec?"

"Sure," said Henry, stepping away from the others.

"Here's the gum I owe you." Roger handed Henry eight balls of bubble gum.

"Mine, too." Peter held out four balls.

"Hey, now wait a minute," protested Henry. "That's not fair."

"It is too," said Roger. "We bought gum from you and now we're returning it instead of paying for it."

"But you chewed it," objected Henry. "I saw you, and Miss Bonner made you throw it in the wastebasket."

"This gum hasn't been chewed, has it?" asked Peter.

Henry had to admit it hadn't.

"Then why can't we return it, like in a department store?" demanded Roger.

Baffled, Henry took the gum. Something was wrong some place, but he couldn't figure out what. He did know one thing, that was sure There went six cents out of his bike fund.

Then Mary Jane ran up to Roger and Peter. "Did he take the free samples we collected for you?" she asked.

"Well, how do you like that!" exclaimed Henry. "That's cheating, that's what it is."

"It is not," said Mary Jane. "You gave us the gum and if we want to give it to someone else, that's our business."

Henry looked glum. He supposed it was her business. Mary Jane was one of those annoying girls who were always right. The worst of it was, now he couldn't expect the others to pay. Henry was actually glad when the bell ended recess, even though he knew spelling came next.

That day no one chose Henry to be a monitor, and only Robert sat with him in the cafeteria. He heard Kathleen say she thought she wouldn't invite any boys to her birthday party.

After lunch, when the class was settled with its readers, the room door opened and Miss Mullen, the principal, entered. She whispered to Miss Bonner and then turned to the class. "Boys and girls," she announced, "I want to talk to you for a few minutes this afternoon. We have a problem at Glenwood School that we all should discuss."

Now what? thought Henry. Probably running in the halls again or writing on the building with chalk.

Miss Mullen looked around the room. Then she said, "That problem is gum."

Henry felt his neck and ears grow hot. He was sure everyone in the room was looking at him.

Miss Mullen continued. "There has been more gum chewing than usual at Glenwood School in the last few days. I wonder if someone can tell me why it is not a good idea to chew gum in school."

The class was silent.

"Can't someone give me a reason?" she asked. "Henry Huggins, why do you think it is not a good idea to chew gum in school?"

Henry's ears felt as if they were on fire. He hadn't known Miss Mullen even knew his name. "Uh . . ." he said. Why couldn't he think of something to say? "Well . . ." He had to think of something. "It . . . uh . . . well . . . uh . . . I guess it is . . . lots of trouble for teachers to make kids throw it in the wastebasket." The words came out in a rush. At least, he had said something.

"That is an excellent reason," said Miss Mullen. "Chewing gum wastes valuable time. Who else can give me a reason?"

One of the girls timidly raised her hand and

said, "Sometimes it gets stuck on the floor and things."

"Splendid," said Miss Mullen. "I was hoping someone would mention that, because our janitor tells me he has spent most of his time in the last few days scraping gum off the floors and desks."

The class began to feel less shy and was suddenly full of reasons why gum should not be chewed in school.

Then Mary Jane raised her hand and said, "Miss Mullen, I know where the gum is coming from."

Leave it to old tattletale Mary Jane, thought Henry. And after I showed her how to blow bubbles, too.

Miss Mullen said, "That isn't important, Mary Jane. What is most important is that so many boys and girls have been chewing gum in school."

What a relief! At least, Miss Mullen wasn't going to point him out in front of everyone.

Miss Mullen smiled at the class. "Now that we have talked about our problem, I wonder how many boys and girls have decided not to chew gum in school any more."

Thirty-five hands shot into the air. "Splendid," exclaimed the principal. "I knew I could count on Miss Bonner's room to co-operate."

When Miss Mullen left, Roger whispered across the aisle to Henry, "Now see what you've done."

"Aw, keep quiet," answered Henry out of the corner of his mouth, as he bent over his reader. He knew one thing. Even though the class forgot its promise in a few days, he wouldn't be able to sell any gum around Glenwood for a long time.

After school he wasted no time in finding Mary Jane. "Tattletale!" he yelled.

"Pooh to you," answered Mary Jane, with her nose in the air. "Everybody's tired of your old gum anyway. It's all that funny cinnamon-peppermint flavor."

"Come on, Ribsy," said Henry to his dog, who had been waiting under the fir tree. He popped a ball of gum into his mouth, chewed, and blew a halfhearted bubble that broke with a little *spip*. He spat out the gum. Somehow, he didn't enjoy cinnamon-peppermint flavor any more.

When Henry reached home, he threw his jacket and Daniel Boone cap onto a chair and went straight to the refrigerator. "Hi, Mom!" he said to Mrs. Huggins, who was frosting a chocolate cake. "That sure looks good."

"You may lick the bowl when I'm finished." Mrs. Huggins swirled the icing in a pattern on the cake. "And by the way, I want to talk to you."

With a swipe of his finger, Henry wiped a drop of frosting from the edge of the bowl. It was peppermint-flavored.

"Henry, your hands aren't very clean," said his mother. "It's about those boxes of gum you have under your bed. How do you expect me to run the vacuum cleaner in your room? Why don't you give the gum to your friends? I'm sure they'd be glad to have it."

Henry sighed. That was all his mother knew about his friends. Suddenly he found it made his jaws tired just to think about all those boxes and boxes of gum. He didn't want to think about it. Gum—ugh!

"O.K., Mom," he agreed. "I'll get rid of it. And don't bother saving the bowl for me to lick."

Henry and Ribsy went out onto the front porch. As Henry was wondering how he would get rid of the gum, Scooter rode by and called out, "Miss Mullen was sure on the warpath because of your old gum. She went to every room in the school. I bet you caught it."

"I did not," said Henry. "And anyway, what do I care?" That's right, he thought, what do I care?

He had saved over a dollar for his bike fund, even if he couldn't expect to collect from the rest

of the people who owed him money. Not only had
he earned some bike money, he had been famous
for a few days, too. And for once in his life he had
chewed all the gum he wanted. So had his friends.
More than they wanted.

It did not take Henry long to make up his mind.
"Come on, Ribsy," he said, and ran down the
street to Beezus' house.

When Beezus and her little sister came to the
door, Henry stared at Ramona. "Jeepers!" he exclaimed. "What happened to her?" Almost all the
hair was cut off the left side of her head. The right
side was jagged.

"Doesn't she look awful?" asked Beezus. "After

Mother cut the gum out of her hair, she got hold of the scissors and cut it herself. She says she wants to be bald like our Uncle Jack."

Henry groaned. Now probably everyone would say this was his fault. It certainly was funny the way he kept getting into trouble just because of a bunch of old gum. He would be glad when he saw the last of it. "Say, Beezus," he said, "could I borrow your red wagon again? I'm going to take that gum back to the lot and dump it where I found it."

"Sure, you can borrow it," answered Beezus. "Come on. I'll help."

CHAPTER THREE

The Untraining of Ribsy

ONE Saturday afternoon Henry was sitting on the front steps amusing Ribsy by throwing a stick for him to retrieve. Every time Henry tossed the stick out onto the lawn, Ribsy bounded after it, brought it back, and dropped it at Henry's feet. Then Ribsy wagged his tail and waited for Henry to throw the stick again. Henry decided that since his dog was so smart about fetching sticks, he would teach him to bring his father's slippers or something useful.

While Henry and Ribsy were playing, Scooter McCarthy rode up on his bicycle and tossed the

Huggins' copy of the *Journal* onto the grass. "Say, Huggins," he said, "I'm going to Scout Camp during Easter vacation next week and I wondered if you knew anybody I could get to take my paper route while I'm gone."

Henry tossed the stick for Ribsy again. "I'll take it, Scooter. I've always wanted to deliver papers."

Scooter looked doubtful. "Aw, you're not old enough."

Henry knew that *Journal* carriers had to be eleven years old, but he said, "It wouldn't matter for three days, would it? It would still be your route and I'd just be a substitute. Aw, come on, Scoot. Let me do it."

"You don't have a bike," said Scooter, "and I could only pay a dollar."

"I could walk," said Henry. "And it's all right about the dollar, too." He wouldn't admit it to Scooter, but he thought a dollar would be a lot of money to add to his bike fund all at once. "Please,

Scooter. I won't make any mistakes or anything."

"I've got some pretty cross customers on my route," warned Scooter. "That old Mrs. Jones phones the *Journal* office if just one teeny corner of her paper gets in the mud, and Mrs. Green gets mad if I throw the paper in her flower boxes. You've got to be careful when you deliver papers."

"I could do it," said Henry. "I'd be real careful. Honest, I would."

"We-l-ll." Scooter thought a minute. "All right. You can take the route, but you better not get me in trouble. I'll give you a list of customers next week."

"Gee, thanks, Scooter," said Henry gratefully.

Jeepers, another dollar for his bike fund! Henry made up his mind he'd do such a good job delivering papers that Scooter would want him to take the route when he went away during summer vacation. Then he would really make some money for the fund. He could see himself walking down

Klickitat Street throwing papers onto porches
with an experienced flip of his wrist. Still better,
he pictured himself riding down the street on a
shiny red bike with his snap-on raccoon tail floating from the handle bars. Boy, oh boy, he was getting closer to that bike all the time.

Then he noticed the tightly rolled *Journal* lying
on the lawn. That gave him an idea. Instead of
training Ribsy to fetch his father's slippers, he
would teach him to bring in the paper every night.
"Fetch, Ribsy," he said. "Fetch the paper."

Ribsy sat thumping his tail on the lawn.

"Aw, come on." Henry picked up the paper and
held it under Ribsy's nose. Then he threw it. Still
Ribsy sat. He was used to fetching sticks, not newspapers. He turned and chewed at a flea on his
back.

"Come on, you old dog." Henry showed Ribsy
the paper again. Ribsy glanced at it and settled
himself with his nose on his paws. Henry threw

the paper half a dozen times, but Ribsy paid no attention. Thinking how silly he must look, throwing a paper and fetching it himself while his dog watched, Henry held the *Journal* behind his back. With his other hand he picked up the stick. "Ribsy, look," he ordered.

At the sight of the stick Ribsy sprang to his feet. "Wuf," he said, wagging his tail expectantly.

Henry pretended he was going to throw the stick. Instead, he tossed the paper. Before he knew the difference, Ribsy bounded after it and caught it in his mouth.

When the dog dropped the paper at his feet, Henry patted him. "Good dog, Ribsy," he said. "Good old Ribsy."

Ribsy wriggled, and wagged his tail with delight. The next time Henry threw the paper, he sprang to fetch it. "Good dog," Henry said approvingly. "I guess you're just about the smartest dog around here."

The next day was Sunday. Henry, who always woke up earlier than his mother and father, decided to read the funnies in the *Journal,* which was delivered early on Sunday morning. He tiptoed out to the porch, expecting to pick up the paper as he always did. Instead, he stood staring in horror at what he saw. There was not just one *Journal* on the door mat. There was a whole pile of them. Ribsy sat beside the papers, wagging his tail and looking pleased with himself.

Henry groaned. "Did you pick up all these and

bring them here?" he asked Ribsy in a whisper.

Thump, thump, thump. Ribsy wagged his tail. Then he stood up and wagged his whole body.

"You old dog," muttered Henry crossly, as he counted the papers. There were seventeen *Journals* on his door mat. Fortunately, the *Oregonian* carrier was late this morning. What if Ribsy had collected two kinds of newspapers and piled them on the door mat?

Seventeen *Journals!* Henry wondered how he could ever face Scooter. And now he wouldn't get to earn the dollar. He wouldn't get to deliver papers when Scooter went to camp during summer vacation. But worst of all was the way Scooter would behave after this. He would never, never forget that Henry's dog had got him in trouble with his *Journal* customers.

Henry scowled at Ribsy, who looked puzzled because he hadn't been praised for retrieving all those papers. Henry knew he had to think of something, and fast, too. Then he remembered that Klickitat Street was the beginning of Scooter's route, and because it was so early, Scooter was probably still delivering papers.

"Come on, Ribsy," he ordered, hurrying into his room. There he pulled on jeans and a sweater over his pajamas and shoved his feet into sneakers. He shut Ribsy in the room, grabbed the papers on the porch, except for one copy which he tossed into the living room, and ran down the street as fast as he could to Scooter's house.

No one on Klickitat Street was up at that hour, and Henry was relieved to see the blinds still down on Scooter's house. He tiptoed up the front steps and, after looking uneasily up and down the street and listening for sounds from within the house, laid the sixteen *Journals* on the door mat. Then he ran home as fast as he could.

After entering as quietly as he could, Henry threw himself on his bed with a gasp of relief. No one had seen him! Scooter would never know how the sixteen papers found their way back to his door mat. The dollar for the bike fund was safe.

Henry felt unusually cheerful after his narrow escape and was enjoying a second helping of hot cakes when the doorbell rang. Mr. Huggins answered it, and Henry heard Scooter say, "Here's your paper, Mr. Huggins. I'm sorry it was late."

Holding his breath, Henry looked at the breakfast table, strewn with the Sunday *Journal.*

Mr. Huggins said, "There must be some mistake, Scooter. We have our paper."

"You have?" Scooter sounded surprised. "You're the only people on Klickitat Street that have one."

"Henry, where did you find the paper this morning?" asked Mr. Huggins.

"On the door mat." Well, he *had* found it on the door mat. His father didn't ask what else he had found, did he?

"It sure is funny," repeated Scooter. "I know I

delivered all the papers, but . . . well, thanks anyway, Mr. Huggins. It sure is funny."

Jeepers, thought Henry. Now he had done it. Why hadn't he thought of putting his own paper on Scooter's door mat along with the others? Now Scooter would get suspicious and might figure out what had happened.

Mr. Huggins folded back the sport section. "Isn't it funny that Scooter's papers should disappear from Klickitat Street?" he remarked to no one in particular. "When I used to deliver papers when I was a kid, I had a lot of trouble with dogs stealing them."

Henry looked sharply at his father, but Mr. Huggins appeared to be interested in the paper. "What did you do about it?" asked Henry, as if he were just making polite conversation.

"Sprinkled red pepper on the papers for a while until the dogs learned to leave them alone," answered Mr. Huggins, pouring himself another cup of coffee.

After breakfast Henry waited until his mother had finished the dishes. Then he quietly found the can of red pepper and an old newspaper and called Ribsy out into the back yard, where he was sure Scooter couldn't see him.

He rolled the paper, sprinkled it with red pepper, and threw it out on the grass. Ribsy ran over to it, stopped, and sniffed. He walked all the way around the paper, sniffing. Then he rolled it over with his paw before he picked it up carefully by one end and dropped it at Henry's feet. He wagged his tail and looked pleased with himself.

"You old dog," said Henry crossly.

Ribsy jumped up on Henry and looked so eager that Henry couldn't help petting him. "What am I going to do with you, anyway?" he asked. Then he sprinkled pepper on the paper again and tossed it onto the grass. Ribsy bounded after it. Again he sniffed, and rolled the paper with his paw before he picked it up and carried it to Henry.

Henry had a feeling that although pepper might work with other dogs, it wasn't going to work with Ribsy. Anyway, he couldn't follow two paper boys around and sprinkle pepper on every single paper they delivered, could he? And then there was the *Shopping News* besides. He would spend all his bike fund buying pepper.

Henry sat down to think of another way to untrain Ribsy. He couldn't keep the dog shut in the house alone very long, because he would howl and scratch on the door to get out. Mrs. Huggins didn't like scratches on her woodwork, and the neighbors didn't like to hear Ribsy howl. He couldn't tie the dog up, either. It never took Ribsy long to chew through a rope or leash.

Henry tried to think what Ribsy didn't like. He didn't like to have his tail pulled. Henry thought about pulling his tail every time he picked up a paper, but that would hurt Ribsy. Ribsy didn't like the egg he was supposed to eat once a week so he would have a glossy coat, but Henry didn't see how he could give him an egg every time he stole a paper. Henry couldn't think of anything else Ribsy didn't like except baths. Ribsy was really a very agreeable dog.

While Henry was still trying to think of a way to untrain Ribsy, he heard Scooter calling. He quickly put the pepper and the paper inside the back door and ran around the house. What would he say if Scooter guessed?

"Hi! Sure is funny how you got a paper when nobody else on this street did, isn't it?"

"Yeah," said Henry, wondering how he could change the subject.

"And you know what?" asked Scooter.

"What?" said Henry, knowing very well what.

"I know I delivered those papers, and when I

got home I found sixteen papers on my porch."

"Jeepers!" Henry did his best to look surprised. Why couldn't a fire engine or something come down Klickitat Street right now? He heard the jingle of Ribsy's license tag. The dog trotted around the corner of the house and, after scratching, settled himself at Henry's feet. Then he suddenly sat up and looked toward the Grumbies' house next door.

Henry looked too, and what he saw gave him a terrible sinking feeling in his stomach. There in plain sight on the front steps lay the Grumbies' *Oregonian.*

Ribsy jumped to his feet, and Henry knew he had to do something in a hurry or Ribsy would retrieve the Grumbies' paper before Scooter's very eyes. Shuddering at the thought of what would happen if he did, Henry hastily grabbed his dog around the neck.

"Good old Ribsy," he said, hanging on tight.

Ribsy squirmed. Henry wished as hard as he. could that Scooter would go home.

"If anything happens to the papers tomorrow afternoon, I guess I better not go to Scout Camp," said Scooter. "If I lose my route, I won't have the money to go to camp during summer vacation."

Henry didn't answer. He was too busy trying to hang onto Ribsy without looking as if he were holding him. Ribsy strained toward the Grumbies' paper. Henry turned the dog's head in the opposite direction, but the minute he let go, Ribsy whimpered and tried to get at the paper.

"What's the matter with that dog, anyway?" asked Scooter. "Why don't you let him go?"

"He doesn't want to go," said Henry. "Do you, Ribsy?"

Ribsy whimpered and struggled to get out of Henry's arms. Henry couldn't see why Scooter had to hang around so long, anyway. Why couldn't he go home?

Henry tried not to look at the paper on the Grumbies' front steps, but it was all he could think about. Then the Grumbies' front door opened, and Mr. Grumbie, wearing his bathrobe and slippers, walked sleepily out on the porch, picked up the paper, and went into the house again.

Ribsy relaxed and Henry let go of him. Whew! That was close. Henry looked anxiously up and down the street to see if he could see any other papers. Instead he saw Beezus and her little sister Ramona.

The two girls stopped in front of Henry's house. Beezus had a handful of waxed paper. Ramona had a red plastic water pistol. She looked at Scooter, aimed, and shot a stream of water into his face. "You're dead," she announced.

"I am not, and you cut that out." Scooter wiped his face with his sleeve.

"Ramona, stop that or I'll have to take the pistol away from you," ordered Beezus. "Henry, come on over to the park with us. I've got a bunch of bread wrappers to sit on when we slide on the slides."

"O.K.," said Henry promptly, more because he wanted to get away from Scooter than because he wanted to go to the park. Still, it was a long time since he had waxed the slides by sitting on a bread wrapper. "Here, Ribsy," he called.

Ribsy bounded out of the shrubbery with his license tag jingling. In his mouth was a *Shopping News,* yellow with age, which he dropped at Henry's feet. Henry didn't have the courage to look at Scooter. Ribsy bounded into the bushes and came out with another old paper. Then he stood wagging his tail and looking at Henry.

"I thought so, Henry Huggins," said Scooter accusingly. "I thought you knew something about my papers disappearing."

"Well, maybe . . ." Henry didn't know what to say. Now he really was in trouble. A stream of

water from Ramona's pistol hit him in the eyes. "Aw, cut it out," he said, wiping his face. As if he didn't have enough trouble without a little kid shooting him with a water pistol!

"I bet you trained that mutt of yours to steal papers." Scooter was really angry. "I suppose you're going to let him steal my papers all the time and make me lose my route."

"No, he won't," promised Henry. "I'll untrain him . . ."

"You better untrain him," interrupted Scooter angrily. "And I'm going to find somebody else to take my route while I'm gone, too. I have enough trouble with papers getting in the mud and stuff, without having your old mutt going around stealing them."

"You got the papers delivered again this morning before anybody complained, didn't you?" asked Henry.

"Yes, because I started extra early in the first place, that's why. But what about tomorrow, when I have to deliver them after school?"

That was just what Henry had been asking himself. What about tomorrow? He had to think of something fast if he didn't want to lose a dollar from his bike fund. "I'll tell you what, Scooter. You make me a list of your customers and I'll deliver the papers tomorrow night free of charge. And if I do it right and Ribsy doesn't take any, I get to deliver the papers while you're gone. How about it?" Henry waited anxiously for Scooter's answer.

"That's fair," said Beezus.

Scooter scowled and thought over Henry's offer. "O.K.," he said at last. "Maybe that way you'll be sure to untrain him."

"It's a deal," said Henry. Now all he had to do was figure out how to keep Ribsy from stealing papers.

Scooter started home and then turned back. "But just you remember, if you make me lose my route, I'll, I'll . . . Well, I'll do something."

While the two boys were arguing, Robert had joined the group in the front yard. "Scooter is pretty mad, isn't he?" he asked. "I'm glad I'm not in your shoes."

"Yeah." Henry looked at the papers at his feet. "Jeepers, how am I going to get Ribsy untrained by tomorrow afternoon? Nothing I try works."

"It's easy," said Robert. "You've got to make him afraid of what he steals. Hit him with a paper a few times and he'll get the idea."

"I'll try," said Henry, "but I bet it won't work with Ribsy."

"Don't hit him too hard," begged Beezus.

Ribsy came trotting across the lawn with an old paper in his mouth. When he dropped it at Henry's feet, Henry picked it up and rapped him on the head with it. He didn't hit hard enough to hurt, but just hard enough so he would get the idea. Ribsy was delighted. He growled a pretended growl and grabbed the paper. Henry hung on and so did Ribsy. Wagging his tail, the dog growled and tugged. Henry managed to yank the paper away.

This time he hit Ribsy harder. Ribsy gave a joyful bark and sprang at the paper. He snatched it from Henry and worried it. Then he settled down to chew it to pieces.

"See what I mean?" said Henry. It was bad enough to have a dog that stole papers, but it was worse to have one that chewed them to bits. Henry could see Klickitat Street strewn with chewed-up *Journals* and he tried to picture what Scooter would do. Whatever it was, he didn't like to think about it.

After school the next day Henry joined Ribsy, who was waiting under the fir tree, and ran home with his dog as fast as he could. Then he changed into his after-school clothes, fixed himself some bread and peanut butter, and, after shutting Ribsy in his room, went out on the front porch to wait for Scooter.

In a few minutes Robert joined him. "Thought of anything yet?" he asked.

"No," admitted Henry. "I shut Ribsy in the house, but he won't stay there long."

Ribsy appeared at the window with his front feet on the sill. He whimpered and scratched at the glass with one paw.

"Go away," ordered Henry.

Ribsy ran to the front door, where Henry could

hear him scratching on the wood. Then Mrs. Huggins opened the door and said, "Henry, you'll just have to keep this dog outdoors with you."

"O.K., Mom," answered Henry, looking at Robert. "See what I mean?"

Then Beezus and her little sister Ramona joined

the boys on the steps. Ramona promptly shot Robert with her water pistol. "You're dead!" she shouted.

Robert wiped his face with his sleeve. "I am not dead. I can't be dead if I'm not playing, can I?"

Then Scooter appeared, lugging a bundle of newspapers which he threw down on the walk in front of Henry's house. He handed Henry a list of addresses. "Be sure you remember about Mrs. Green's flower boxes," he said. "And I better not get any complaints about missing papers tonight or any other night."

"You won't," said Henry, but he didn't sound very sure about it.

Ramona fired a shot at the departing Scooter. Beezus said, "Come on, we'll help you."

Keeping a wary eye on Ramona's water pistol, the other three began to roll newspapers. Henry was so busy watching the pistol that he forgot to watch Ribsy. Before he knew it, the dog had snatched a paper and had begun to worry it to pieces.

"Ribsy!" yelled Henry. "Drop that!"

Ribsy shook the paper harder. Henry grabbed one end of the paper. Ribsy hung on.

Then Ramona raised her water pistol and aimed. A stream of water hit Ribsy in the face. "You're dead!" shouted Ramona, and Ribsy dropped the paper. Looking puzzled, he backed away and shook himself.

"Hey! Did you see that?" Henry jumped up and tripped over the papers in his excitement. "Ribsy dropped the paper! Ramona made him drop the paper. Do it again, Ramona."

"No," said Ramona.

"Aw, come on," coaxed Henry. "Beezus, make her shoot Ribsy again. This has just got to work."

"No," said Ramona.

Scooter came riding down the street on his bicycle. "You started delivering my papers yet?" he asked.

"In a minute," said Henry. "You just wait. Everything's going to be all right."

"It better be." Scooter looked threatening as he

rode away. "And you better get going," he yelled back.

Henry ran into the house and found his own plastic water pistol. After loading it at the kitchen sink, he ran outdoors and threw a paper at Ribsy. When the dog picked it up, Henry let him have a stream of water right in the face. Ribsy dropped the paper and backed away. Looking puzzled and embarrassed, he shook himself.

"It works!" shouted Henry. "It really works! I'm going to get Ribsy untrained after all." He ran into the house again and filled his army-surplus canteen with water, in case he needed to reload his pistol.

Beezus and Robert had the papers rolled and stuffed into the canvas bag, which Henry now lifted over his head. The *Journals* were heavier than he expected. "Come on," he said. "Let's go."

By then Beezus had succeeded in getting the

water pistol away from Ramona. "I'll help you keep Ribsy covered," she said.

Henry threw a *Journal* onto the lawn of the first house on the list. Ribsy bounded after the paper, but the minute he opened his mouth to pick it up, Henry and Beezus shot him with two streams of water. Looking surprised and unhappy, Ribsy backed away from the paper and shook himself.

The next time Henry threw a paper, Ribsy approached it cautiously. The instant he touched it, Beezus and Henry opened fire. This time Beezus shot from the hip.

"You're dead!" shrieked Ramona. Ribsy decided he wasn't interested in the paper after all.

The third time Henry threw a paper, Ribsy ignored it. He was too busy sniffing a bush even to look at it.

"Good dog," said Henry, bending over to pet him. The weight of the papers in the canvas bag nearly tipped him over.

Ribsy wagged his tail. "Good old Ribsy," said Henry proudly. Ribsy was untrained at last.

When the children returned after delivering all the papers without a single mistake, they found Scooter waiting on the front steps. "How many did your mutt run off with?" he wanted to know.

"He isn't a mutt and he didn't run off with any,"

boasted Henry. "He wouldn't touch a paper. See?" Henry tossed his own copy of the *Journal* onto the grass. Ribsy looked the other way.

"I guess I did a pretty good job of delivering papers," bragged Henry. "You won't get any complaints tonight."

"That's right," agreed Beezus. "I checked every address on the list with him just to make sure."

Scooter threw one leg over his bicycle.

"And I get to deliver papers while you're away, don't I?" Henry was thinking of his bike fund again, now that Ribsy was untrained.

"Sure," said Scooter, "if you don't think it's too hard work for a kid without a bike."

"You just wait," said Henry. "I bet I get that bike sooner than you think."

"Ha," said Scooter, pedaling down the street.

"You're dead!" shrieked Ramona, squirting her pistol with deadly accuracy.

CHAPTER FOUR

Henry Parks
His Dog

ONE Friday after school Henry was fixing himself a snack of bread, peanut butter, and straw-
berry jam when the doorbell rang.

"Come in, Beezus," he heard his mother say.

As Henry went into the living room, he held
up his bread and licked the jam that had run
down his wrist. Beezus and her little sister Ramona each held a gnawed cabbage core. They
had stopped eating because they were too polite
to eat in front of people.

Beezus handed Henry a newspaper clipping.
"I thought maybe you'd like to see this."

"Bikes for Tykes," was the headline. "Lost Bicycles up for Sale Tomorrow."

"Hey, maybe you've got something." Henry
read faster.

"Enough bicycles—some hundred or more—
have been found by the police this past year to
equip half a company of soldiers, and tomorrow
at ten A.M. they go up for auction at the Glenwood police station."

This was Henry's chance. "Hey, Mom, look!
Isn't an auction where somebody holds up something and everybody says how much he'll pay
for it and the one who says the most gets it?"

"Yes, it is," answered Mrs. Huggins, as she read the clipping.

"Boy! I've got four dollars and fourteen cents saved. I bet I can get a bike for that much." Henry pictured a hundred soldiers riding by on bicycles —and one of those bicycles was meant for him. He'd show old Scooter yet.

Mrs. Huggins looked doubtful. "I wouldn't be too sure," she advised. "After all, there must be some reason why the bicycles haven't been claimed. If you lost a bicycle you'd try to get it back, wouldn't you?"

"Yes," agreed Henry, who was sure most of the bicycles belonged to rich boys who had so many bikes they didn't miss one when they lost it. "But I can go, can't I, Mom?"

"Yes, it won't hurt to try," said Mrs. Huggins, "but don't be too disappointed if you don't get a bicycle."

"And I can go with you, can't I?" asked Beezus eagerly.

"Well . . ." Henry didn't want to bother with Beezus. He wanted to go early and look the bicycles over. If he could get a good one, he would ride it in the Rose Festival parade in a couple of weeks and really show it off.

"Of course you may go, Beezus," said Mrs. Huggins. "Henry will be glad to take you."

"Isn't it pretty far for Ramona to walk?" asked Henry. "It's about ten blocks. Long blocks, too."

"Oh, no. Ramona never gets tired," said Beezus. "Daddy says he wishes sometimes she would, but she never does. Come on, Ramona. See you in the morning, Henry." Gnawing on their cabbage cores, the girls left.

"Aw, Mom," said Henry, "why did you have to go and say they could come with me? I don't want to drag a couple of girls around all morning."

"Now, Henry," said his mother firmly, "Beezus was nice enough to come and tell you about the auction, and it won't hurt you to let her go with you."

"Oh, all right," muttered Henry.

"Why, Henry, you and Beezus used to play together so nicely. Don't you like her any more?"

"She's all right, I guess. She's just a girl, is all," said Henry, thinking of the shiny red bicycle he was going to buy the next day. Maybe Beezus would forget to come.

But Beezus did not forget. The next morning after breakfast Henry found the two girls sitting on the front steps waiting for him. When Henry and Ribsy came out of the house, Beezus started down the walk. Ramona stood still until Beezus went back and made a winding motion behind her little sister. Then Ramona walked along beside her.

"She's pretending she has to be wound up like

a toy before she can walk, and I forgot to wind her," explained Beezus.

Henry groaned. Girls thought of the dumbest things. He tried to keep ahead of them so people wouldn't think they were walking together. Ribsy trotted beside him.

"Henry Huggins, you wait for us!" said Beezus. "Your mother said we could go with you and if you don't wait I'll tell on you."

"Well, come on then," answered Henry crossly, anxious for a glimpse of that red bicycle before anyone else got there.

Suddenly Ramona stopped. Beezus wound her up again and they went on. "She ran down," explained Beezus.

Girls! Henry was disgusted. It seemed to him that it had taken half the morning to go three blocks. He saw a couple of other boys walking in the same direction, and he wondered if they were going to the auction too. He began to walk faster.

Then Henry saw Mrs. Wisser, a friend of his mother's, coming toward him. The sight of three more boys coming along on the other side of the street made Henry hope she wouldn't stop him long.

"Well, if it isn't Henry Huggins," she exclaimed. "And Beatrice."

"Hello, Mrs. Wisser," said Henry and Beezus politely.

"My, Henry, how you have grown! And you're getting to look more like your father every day. I was telling your mother only yesterday that every time I see you, you look more like your father."

Another boy hurried down the street. Was every boy in town going to the auction? Henry smiled as politely as he could at Mrs. Wisser and looked uneasily in the direction of the police station. The best bikes would be gone, he was sure, by the time he got there. Maybe he could find an older bike that just needed a little paint or something. He had plenty of time before the parade to fix it up. He tried not to show how impatient he felt.

"Don't you think he looks more like his father every day?" asked Mrs. Wisser of Beezus.

"Yes, I guess he does," said Beezus. She had also noticed the boys going in the direction of the police station, but she felt she should say something. "Especially the way his hair sticks up," she added.

Henry gave her a disgusted look.

"And is this Ribsy?" asked Mrs. Wisser. "Nice doggie."

Ribsy sat down and scratched. Thump, thump, thump went his hind leg on the sidewalk

"And this must be Ramona. How are you, sweetheart?"

Ramona was silent.

"What a pretty dress you're wearing," said Mrs. Wisser. "And it has a pocket, too. Do you have something in your pocket?"

"Yes," said Ramona.

"Isn't she sweet?" said Mrs. Wisser to Beezus. "What do you have in your little pocket, dear?"

Ramona poked her fist into her pocket and pulled out a fat slimy garden slug, which she held out to Mrs. Wisser.

"Oh," gasped Mrs. Wisser. "Oh!"

"Ramona, throw that thing away," ordered Beezus.

Henry couldn't help grinning, Mrs. Wisser looked so horrified.

"Well . . . I must be running along," said Mrs. Wisser.

"Good-by, Mrs. Wisser," said Beezus and Henry. Ramona put her slug back in her pocket, Beezus wound her up again, and they went on.

Until they reached the Glenwood shopping district, Henry almost thought girls were good for something after all. Then Ramona stopped in front of the Supermarket. "I'm hungry," she announced.

"Come on, Ramona," coaxed Beezus. "We're in a hurry."

"I'm hungry," repeated Ramona.

Henry groaned. He knew they couldn't go any

farther until Ramona had something to eat. That was the kind of little girl she was.

"I have a quarter," said Beezus. "I better get her something."

"O.K.," agreed Henry reluctantly. "I could stand something myself." Then Henry noticed a sign on the door of the market. It said *No dogs allowed in food stores.*

"Lie down, Ribsy," he ordered, as he went through the swinging door.

On the next swing of the door Ribsy came in too. "Sorry, sonny," said a clerk. "You'll have to take your dog outside."

"Beat it," said Henry to his dog. Ribsy sat down. "Come on, you old dog," said Henry, seizing his pet by the collar and dragging him out onto the sidewalk.

Henry hurried back into the market and was trying to decide between a bag of Cheezy Chips and a box of Fig Newtons when the clerk said,

"Say, sonny, I thought I told you to get that dog out of here."

Once more Henry dragged Ribsy out. This time he dug into his pocket and pulled out a piece of heavy twine. He tied one end to Ribsy's collar and fastened the other end securely to a parking meter. "Now don't you chew the twine," he said, before he went back into the store. He chose the Cheezy Chips and stood impatiently behind Beezus in line at the cashier's counter.

Finally they were out on the sidewalk again, where they found Ribsy busy chewing the twine. Beezus had to stop and find several lions in the animal-cracker box she had bought, because Ramona wanted to eat all the lions first. Henry felt it was pretty useless to try to go any place with a couple of girls. But maybe he would get there in time to find a bike in fairly good condition with just a few spokes missing.

"Hey, Henry!" It was Robert calling.

Henry, who was trying to untie Ribsy from the parking meter, saw Scooter pedaling his bicycle slowly down the sidewalk while Robert jogged along at his side.

"Bet you're going to the bike sale," said Scooter. "We're going just to watch."

"What's that paper under Ribsy's collar?" asked Robert.

"What paper?" said Henry. Sure enough, there *was* a paper under Ribsy's collar. Henry pulled it out and unfolded it as the other children crowded around.

Scooter was first to understand. He shouted with laughter. "It's a parking ticket. Ribsy got a parking ticket!"

The children all laughed. "Don't be dumb," said Henry. "Everybody knows dogs don't get parking tickets."

"Sure it's a ticket," said Scooter. "See, it says *Notice of traffic violation* across the top, and *vio-*

lation means he's done something wrong, doesn't it?"

"Did you put a penny in the meter?" asked Robert.

"That's right. Did you put a penny in the meter when you parked your dog?" laughed Scooter.

"I didn't know leaving a dog on the sidewalk counted as parking," said Henry, looking at the meter. "See! The red thing doesn't show and there's still sixteen minutes left from whoever put the money in before."

"Maybe there was a car here and Ribsy got a ticket for double parking," said Scooter, guffawing again.

Beezus handed Ramona another lion. "That's all the lions. You'll have to eat camels now." Then she said to Henry, "Maybe it was a mistake."

"How could it be a mistake?" asked Scooter. "It was under Ribsy's collar, wasn't it?" He looked at the ticket again. "See, it says here that you have violated a code. The policeman has written the number of the law you broke. I know, because my dad explained it to me once when he got a ticket. Maybe you have to put in more money to park dogs."

"Maybe they'll put Ribsy in jail," suggested Robert.

"No they won't," said Henry. "You never heard of them putting a car in jail, did you? This is the same thing."

"That's right," agreed Scooter, and laughed. "Maybe they'll put you in jail."

"What do you suppose they'll do, Henry?" asked Beezus anxiously.

"I don't know. I guess I'll have to pay a fine." Henry stuffed the ticket in his pocket.

"My dad knows a man who knows the mayor," said Robert. "Maybe he could do something about it."

"No, I'll have to take it out of my bike money," said Henry. "Say, Scoot, how much did your dad pay when he got the ticket?"

"A dollar, I think," said Scooter. "No, I guess it was two."

There went at least a dollar from Henry's bike fund. Maybe two. Two dollars plus a dime for Cheezy Chips. Take that from four dollars and fourteen cents and he had two dollars and four cents left for a bike—that is, if he ever got to the auction and if there were any bikes left when he did get there. Maybe he could get a good sturdy frame and pick up a couple of wheels some place.

"You could ask at the police station," suggested Beezus.

Why hadn't he thought of that before? "Hey, kids, let's go," said Henry. He didn't have to untie the twine. Ribsy had chewed it in two.

Scooter pedaled slowly and the others ran along

beside him. Even Ramona ran. Eating all the lions out of the animal-cracker box made her forget she had to be wound up.

Henry worried about the ticket. What was wrong with leaving Ribsy outside the Supermarket? He couldn't take him in, so he had to leave him out, didn't he? And if he didn't tie him, he wouldn't stay out, would he? It must be a mistake. It had to be. If only he could get to the station and find out before the auction.

"Wow!" exclaimed Henry, when they finally turned a corner and came to the Glenwood police station. The steps of the building swarmed with children. The driveway beside the station was crammed with boys and girls, and grownups, and dogs, too. Other children perched on the fence between the driveway and the apartment house on the other side. More children were getting out of the cars that jammed the streets.

"I'll go with you to see about the ticket," Beezus

told Henry. Scooter and Robert decided they would try to find a place on the fence.

When Henry made his way through the crowd on the steps, he found a policeman blocking the door. "Around to the side of the building, kids," he said. "The auction is out in the driveway and no one is allowed to go through the station."

"But I just wanted to ask . . ." said Henry.

"Run along, everybody," directed the police-man.

"But . . ." said Henry.

"Sorry," said the policeman.

"Come on." Beezus tugged at Henry's sleeve. "It's started already. You can ask afterward."

"But I won't know how much money I can spend," protested Henry, as he followed Beezus. When they reached the driveway, Henry tried to worm his way through the crowd. Maybe he could get to the back door of the police station and ask about his ticket there.

"Hey, quit shoving," ordered a boy.

"Yes, we were here first," said another. "Who do you think you are?"

"We'll never make it to the back door in time. There must be other policemen around some place." Henry was worried, because he could hear the auctioneer's voice and knew that bicycles were being sold.

"What am I bid for this bicycle?" Henry heard faintly above the noise of the crowd. He knew he had to get his ticket straightened out pretty soon, or he might as well go home and forget the whole thing.

"There's a policeman," exclaimed Beezus. "Over there by the fence."

When Henry, the two girls, and Ribsy had fought their way through the crowd to the policeman, they found he was too busy trying to get boys off the fence to notice them.

Henry didn't know how to speak to an officer.

"Mr. . . . uh . . . Policeman," he said cautiously.

"All right, boys," directed the man. "Down off the fence."

The auctioneer's voice continued. "Sold!" he shouted.

Henry and Beezus exchanged anxious looks. There went another bike. "Mr. Policeman!" This time Henry spoke louder.

Still the officer did not hear.

Then Ramona marched over to him and tugged at the leg of his uniform. "Hey!" she yelled.

Surprised, the officer looked down at her. "Hello there. Something I can do for you?" he asked.

"Yes." Henry spoke up. "Uh . . . this is my dog, Ribsy."

"How do you do, Ribsy," said the puzzled policeman.

Ribsy sat down and held out his paw, the right

one, too. The officer shook it. Henry was glad to see his dog do the correct thing for once.

"He . . . uh . . . well, he got a parking ticket," said Henry.

"He what?" The policeman sounded baffled.

Henry pulled the crumpled ticket out of his pocket. "He got a parking ticket," he repeated. "I can't understand it. He wasn't double parked. There was money in the meter and there wasn't any car by it." Then he explained about Ramona being hungry and Ribsy following him into the market.

The policeman looked at the ticket and began to smile. Then he laughed. A couple of other officers came to see what he was laughing at. They laughed too. Henry felt uncomfortable and wondered if he had said the wrong thing.

"Did you never hear that it is against the law to tie anything to a parking meter?" the first officer finally asked.

So that was it! "No, sir," said Henry politely. "I just tied him with a thin piece of twine. It wasn't a big rope or anything."

Chuckling, the policeman put the ticket in his pocket and patted Ribsy's head. "Well . . . since you didn't know about the law, I'll see what I can do about this. But from now on you'd better find some place else to park your dog."

"Gee, thanks," said Henry gratefully. "Thanks millions." Ribsy held out his paw again.

What a relief! Now Henry could bid four dollars and fourteen cents for a bicycle. No, four dollars and four cents. He had spent a dime on Cheezy Chips. "Come on, Beezus," Henry said. "Let's get in there and start bidding!"

CHAPTER FIVE

Beezus
Makes a Bid

HENRY, Ribsy, and the two girls struggled into
the mob on the driveway. Sometimes they moved
ahead a foot, sometimes an inch, but most of the
time they stood still. It seemed to Henry that a
lot of awfully big people stepped on his toes. The
children could barely hear the auctioneer above
the noise of the crowd. "What am I bid for bicycle
Number Seven?" the man was shouting.

Henry jumped as high as he could to see the
bicycle.

"Quit jumping on my toes," said the boy behind
him.

Ribsy yelped. "You keep off my dog's tail,"
Henry said to another boy. He wondered how
much he dared bid. Should he start with fifty
cents or should he bid four dollars and four cents
all at once and hope no one else had that much
money?

"I'm hungry," yelled Ramona.

Beezus rummaged in the box of animal crackers. "Here's an elephant," she offered. "You've
eaten all the lions and camels."

"No!" screamed Ramona. "I don't like elephants."

Henry was disgusted. "Don't be dumb," he said,
wondering if Ramona would ever give him a

chance to bid. "All animal crackers taste alike."

"I don't *like* elephants," Ramona screamed again, looking as if she were going to cry.

"Oh, all right." Beezus pawed through the box again. "Here's a monkey." To Henry's relief, Ramona ate the monkey.

It seemed as if everyone were waving his hand and shouting a number at the auctioneer.

"Two dollars!" yelled the boy behind Henry.

"Ten cents!" shouted someone in front of him.

"A penny," screamed a little girl.

"A million dollars," sang out Scooter, who was still on the fence.

"Two million," bid another.

"Quiet, everybody!" roared the auctioneer, mopping his face with his handkerchief. "I've been in this business twenty years, and I've never seen anything like this. We have fifty items to sell and we don't want to take all day. We don't have time for any funny business. Now, how much am

I bid for this bicycle? One dollar from the boy on the fence . . . a dollar and a quarter, a dollar and a half, two dollars from the boy in the red sweater . . . five dollars. Five dollars once, five dollars twice . . . six dollars."

Only fifty items, when the paper had said a hundred! It seemed to Henry that his chance of getting a bicycle was growing smaller by the minute.

"A million dollars," yelled Scooter again.

The auctioneer glared at him and continued. "Six dollars once . . . six dollars twice . . . bicycle Number Seven sold to the boy in the green sweater for six dollars!"

"Aw, it wasn't any good, anyway," Henry heard someone say. "It had only one wheel."

Six dollars for a bike with one wheel! "I wonder how much a bike with two wheels is going to cost," Henry said to Beezus.

"Maybe the people with the most money will

get bicycles and go home, and then the kids who haven't much will have a chance," suggested Beezus.

"I guess I'll stick around and see," said Henry. The next item the auctioneer held up was a Taylor-tot. Henry was disgusted. The paper hadn't said anything about Taylor-tots.

"Stop fussing, Ramona," said Beezus. "I know you can't see anything, but pretty soon Henry will get a bike and we can go home."

Ramona began to pound Ribsy's back with her fist. The dog looked around for a way to escape, but there were too many people.

"Cut it out, Ramona," ordered Henry.

Then a strange woman standing behind Henry spoke. "No, no, little girl. Mustn't hit the doggie. *Love* the doggie."

Ramona stared at the woman. Then she threw both arms around Ribsy's neck and squeezed as hard as she could. Ribsy struggled.

"Hey, you're choking him," objected Henry, as Beezus pried her little sister loose from the dog.

"I want to go home," said Ramona.

"After while," answered Beezus crossly.

Henry saw that he had better start bidding on a bike. If Ramona wanted to go home, they would probably have to go home. Next a bicycle was sold to a boy who bellowed, "Seven dollars and sixty-four cents!" A battered tricycle went for a dollar. Another bicycle sold for five dollars to a boy who got his friends to yell with him, so he could be heard above the crowd. The boy behind Beezus had bid seven dollars, but the auctioneer didn't hear.

Henry saw that, with so many people shouting and waving their hands and the auctioneer trying to sell the bicycles as fast as he could, it was more important for a boy to make himself heard above the crowd than to have a lot of money to spend.

If only there were some way he could make the
auctioneer hear him! Henry jumped as high as he
could for a glimpse of the next bicycle. The handle
bars were missing, but he was sure that if he got
it, he could find a pair of old handle bars somewhere. "One dollar!" he yelled at the top of his
voice. His words were lost in a chorus of bids.

"I'll help you yell," said Beezus.

"Two dollars!" they shouted together. The auctioneer did not hear them.

Just then there was a lull in the noise of the
crowd and Ramona's voice rang out. "I'm going
to throw up," she announced.

Instantly everyone standing near her managed
to move a few inches away. Ribsy used the extra
space to sit down and scratch.

"Beezus, don't just stand there. Do something."
Henry was thoroughly alarmed. Leave it to Ramona to get sick just when he had figured out the
way the auction worked.

Beezus calmly handed Ramona another animal cracker. "Oh, don't pay any attention to her," she said.

The lady behind Henry tapped Beezus on the shoulder and asked, "Don't you think you had better take your little sister home?"

"She's all right. She just says that when she wants her own way," Beezus explained. "Come on, Henry, I'll help you yell again."

"I'm going to throw up," screamed Ramona.

Henry was relieved that Ramona was really all right, even if he had missed another chance to bid. The lady was not so sure. Again she tapped Beezus on the shoulder. "I think you'd better take your sister home. Maybe she isn't feeling well."

Ramona beamed. Beezus and Henry exchanged unhappy looks. It looked as if Ramona was going to get her own way. She usually did.

"Come with me," said the lady firmly. "I'll help you through the crowd."

"Honestly, she's all right," protested Beezus. "She's just saying that."

"She's O.K.," agreed Henry. "Beezus knows." There must be some way to keep Ramona from getting her own way.

The lady did not seem to hear. "Take my hand, little girl," she said, as if she meant to be obeyed. "Come on, children." The people who were standing near them were still eying Ramona uneasily and were glad to make a path to let them through.

Why couldn't the lady leave them alone? Henry didn't see how he could bear to move away from the auctioneer, when it had been such hard work to get through the crowd. For a minute he thought he wouldn't leave. If he let Beezus and Ramona go alone, maybe he would get a chance to bid. Still, his mother said he had to take Beezus with him, so maybe they'd better stay together. He didn't want to catch it when he got home.

"Will you let us through, please? This little girl isn't feeling well," the lady repeated. The crowd, pleased to see that someone was leaving, let them through. Henry begrudged every step that took them away from the auctioneer.

At last they reached the sidewalk. "There you are," said the lady cheerfully. "Run along now and tell your mother she had better put your little sister to bed." Then she turned and made her way back into the crowd.

There they were, all right. Disgusted, Henry turned on Ramona. "Now see what you've done. How am I going to bid on a bike when we can't even hear the auctioneer way out here?"

"I want to go home," said Ramona.

"Don't you want Henry to get a bicycle?" asked Beezus.

"No," said Ramona.

Beezus grabbed her little sister by the hand.

"Ramona Geraldine Quimby," she snapped, "you're coming with us and you're going to behave yourself!"

"Yes," agreed Henry. "I'm pretty tired of being pushed around by a little kid like you."

Beezus glared at her sister. "And if you don't behave I'll . . . I'll tell Mother about the time you waited until she went to the store and then tried to give the cat a bath in the Bendix. Then you'll be sorry!"

Ramona sulked but she didn't say anything. Wearily the children struggled into the crowd. Ribsy's tail drooped. Henry was so hot and tired he felt it was pretty useless to go back at all. Ramona would probably think of something else, anyway. By staying on the edge of the driveway and squeezing along the edge of the police station, they moved slowly ahead.

At last they were able to hear the auctioneer again. Henry was afraid there were so many tall people in front of them that they couldn't be seen even if they could make themselves heard. Beezus and Henry yelled experimentally a couple of times, but they really didn't expect to be heard.

"I wish Robert and Scooter were here," said Henry. "Maybe if we all yelled together he would hear us."

"They're on the other side of the driveway," said Beezus. "We could never get through." Then, looking frantically around, she gasped, "Ramona! Where's Ramona? I can't find her."

"Maybe she went home." Henry looked around, but it was impossible to see more than a few feet in any direction.

"She was down here with Ribsy a minute ago." Beezus looked frightened. "Henry, what will Mother say if I've lost her for keeps?"

"She must be around some place. She couldn't go far in this crowd." Henry was disgusted. First it was a parking ticket on a dog, because Ramona was hungry. Then because of her they were taken out of the crowd. And now she had to wander off when he was trying to bid on a bike. That's what happened when he tried to go some place with a couple of girls. Nevertheless, he looked around for Beezus' little sister while the bidding continued.

"Where can she be?" Beezus was frantic. "Maybe she's kidnaped."

Jeepers, thought Henry. I hope she isn't going to cry. He had enough troubles without Beezus crying all over the place. He knew Ramona couldn't be far away, and he was sure no one would ever kidnap her. Especially not if they knew her. Now all he had to do was find her before the auction ended.

"If we went up in front, we could ask the auctioneer to ask about her," suggested Henry. He didn't mention that his chances of bidding would also be better.

"Have you seen my little sister?" Beezus asked the people around her.

Henry inquired if anyone had seen a little girl in a blue dress, but no one had noticed her.

"What are we going to do, Henry?" asked Beezus, blinking her eyes to keep back the tears. "I can't go home without her. I've got to find her. I've got to."

Then the auctioneer pounded his gavel and roared, "Quiet, everybody!" The crowd was almost silent. "Has someone lost a little girl?" He held Ramona up for everyone to see. Her face was streaked with tears and she clutched her slug in one hand.

"One dollar!" yelled Scooter.

"Quiet!" shouted the auctioneer.

"It's Ramona!" Beezus cried out. "It's my little sister."

"Will you come up and get your sister?" asked the auctioneer. "Make way for the little lady to come for her sister."

Hey, thought Henry, here's my chance. I'll go with her and get up in front where the auctioneer can see me and then maybe he can hear me bid. The people in front moved aside to let Beezus through. Henry started after her.

"Where do you think you're going?" the big boy in front of Henry demanded.

"With her," said Henry.

"You're not going to get ahead of me," said another boy.

By that time the path the crowd had made for Beezus closed up again. Henry couldn't let his one chance at a bicycle get away from him. "Beezus," he called desperately, "if you see a good bike, bid for me. Four dollars and four cents."

"O.K.," Beezus answered through the crowd.

The auction continued. In spite of other people's toes, Henry jumped as high as he could each time a bicycle was held up. If Beezus could make the auctioneer hear, it might be his. Two bicycles went by. Henry grew more and more uneasy, waiting to hear a shout of "Four dollars and four cents!" Beezus must be in the very front row. Why didn't she bid? What had gone wrong?

Then the auctioneer's voice rang out. "Sold for four dollars and four cents! Bicycle Number Thirty-two sold to the little lady who lost her sister."

Beezus had bid!

Joyfully Henry sprang into the air to see his bike. He couldn't see a thing, but that was all right. There was a bicycle waiting for him. A bike of his very own.

After that Henry lost interest in the auction. He was busy wondering what his bicycle looked like. He hoped it was red and had a horn and a light. Gradually the crowd began to leave, and Henry and his dog were able to work their way up to the front where Beezus and Ramona were waiting.

Beezus, who was holding a place in the line of people paying for bicycles, looked pleased and excited. "Henry, I got you a real good one with wheels and handle bars and everything. It's in that pile. I had the man write your name on the tag."

Henry took his place in line, and was trying to guess which bicycle in the heap was his when Robert and Scooter joined him.

"Did you find out about the ticket?" asked Robert.

"Sure, and I got a bike, too," boasted Henry.

"Yeah?" Scooter plainly did not believe him.

"Yes. And I'm not going to jail or anything, either." Then Henry explained about the policeman and the ticket.

"I bet the bike isn't any good," remarked Scooter.

"It is too a good bike," Beezus contradicted. "It has two wheels and everything. Of course it isn't exactly new, but it's a good bike just the same. You wait and see."

"Sure, it's a good bike if Beezus says so," Henry bragged. "You just wait until I ride it in the Rose Festival parade."

Gradually the line moved forward. "Number Thirty-two," said Henry, when his turn came. At last he nearly had his hands on his very own bike. He had had to run along the sidewalk beside

Scooter on the way to the auction, but he was going to ride his own bike home. He counted out the four dollars and four cents.

"There'll be something wrong with it. You just wait and see," said Scooter.

"There will not," said Beezus. "At least not anything important."

The officer finally untangled Henry's bicycle from the rest of the pile.

Scooter and Robert began to howl with laughter. Henry groaned. What could you expect when you went to an auction with a girl? The bicycle had two wheels and handle bars all right, but there was something else wrong with it. It was a girl's bicycle.

CHAPTER SIX

Henry's
Bargain Bike

HENRY was so disappointed he could hardly bear it. He could never ride a girl's bike in the Rose Festival parade.

Beezus was right. The bicycle did have two wheels and handle bars. It did not, however, have a lot of other things. There was no air in the tires and very little paint on the frame. Spokes were missing, and because there was no graphite on the chain, the pedals made a groaning noise when they were pushed around. But most important of all, the bicycle did not have a bar from the seat to the handle bars. If only there were some way

to turn it into a boy's bike, the rest would be easy.
With a few repairs, a coat of paint, and some
paper trimming, it would be good enough to ride
in the parade.

Henry sighed and started to push his bicycle
home.

"I'm sorry, Henry," said Beezus. "After some of
the other bikes it looked pretty good, and I didn't
think about it being a girl's bike."

"Aw, that's all right," muttered Henry. He supposed it wasn't really her fault. He couldn't expect a girl to know anything about bicycles.

"Maybe you could find a girl who has a boy's
bike and make a trade," suggested Beezus.

Henry thought this over. "The trouble is, girls
ride boys' bikes, but boys won't ride girls' bikes.
If I found a girl who had a boy's bike, she'd probably want to keep it." He pushed his bicycle in
silence for a while and then said, "I'll just have to
fix it someway, that's all."

After lunch Henry made a quick trip to the Rose City Bike and Trike Shop. His mother had given him the money for the twenty-two new spokes he needed. The man in the shop explained to Henry how to put new spokes into the wheels.

As Henry left the shop, he could not help noticing a shiny new bike with a racy red frame and a built-in headlight. If only his bicycle looked like that!

Back home, Henry went to work on his bicycle in his back yard. First he slipped off the tires and removed the broken spokes with his father's pliers. Then he poked one end of each new spoke into its hole in the hub and the other end into the rim.

Henry was tightening the nuts that held the spokes in place when Beezus and Ramona came up the driveway. Beezus was carrying her baton and Ramona was riding her shiny new tricycle. The spokes in her wheels glistened in the sunshine as she pedaled along beside Beezus. When she got off the tricycle, she leaned it on two wheels against the house as if it were a bicycle.

"Your bike looks better already," said Beezus, who was anxious to have Henry's bicycle turn out right after her mistake that morning.

Henry tugged the tires back over the rims. "Yes, but not much," he said. "Now I've got to find a way to turn it into a boy's bike."

At least, it does have a parking stand, thought Henry, as he propped the bike up.

He and Beezus studied it. "If I had a pipe and some welding stuff and knew how to weld, I could weld a pipe across to make it into a boy's bike," observed Henry.

"It would be easier to tie a piece of broom handle across," said Beezus.

Henry frowned. Girls always thought of the dumbest things. Still, it might work—at least until he could think of a better idea. "O.K., I'll give it a try," he said.

Henry found an old broom handle in the basement, measured it carefully, and sawed it off on the mark he had made. Then, with a piece of twine he happened to have in his pocket, he tied one end of the handle under the seat. The other he fastened below the handle bars.

Henry stood back to look at his work. Well, it could be better. Maybe if he painted the bike and the broom handle the same color and rode fast, nobody would notice. And, for the parade, he could cover the broom handle with roses or crepe paper or something.

"That looks keen," said Beezus, twirling her baton around her fingers. "It's good enough to ride in the Rose Festival parade."

"Well . . . maybe." Henry thought he'd better make sure he could fix his bicycle before he said anything more about the parade. Last year he had been a snake charmer with a bath-towel turban on his head and a snake made out of a stuffed

nylon stocking around his neck, but this year he
was getting pretty old to wear a costume and walk.
He was determined to get his bike fixed in time.

Henry was examining the tires for holes when
Robert came up the driveway.

"What have you got that piece of broom handle
tied to the bike for?" demanded Robert.

Henry didn't answer. Robert knew very well
why the handle was tied to the bike.

"You just wait," said Beezus, flipping her baton.
"Henry's bike is going to look all right when he
gets it painted. He's going to ride it in the parade."

"I didn't say for sure," protested Henry, relieved that at least there were no visible holes in
the tires.

"I bet you do." Beezus twirled the baton over
her head. This time she dropped it.

"Boi-i-ing!" shouted Robert. Henry was too busy
with his bike to notice what was going on.

"Oh, be quiet!" snapped Beezus, as she picked

up the baton. "You just wait until I twirl my baton in the parade. Mother is going to make me a drum-majorette costume."

"The parade is only two weeks away." Robert twanged a spoke with his finger. "You'll have to be a whole lot better than that. And anyway, where will you get a band to lead?"

"You don't have to have a band." Beezus tried to flip her baton behind her back but dropped it in the grass. "I'm just going to march and twirl. Mary Jane is going to wear her rosebud costume and make a wreath of roses for Patsy to wear around her neck." Patsy was Mary Jane's cocker spaniel.

"I'm going to be the hind legs of a giraffe," said Robert. "A fellow I know on Thirty-third Street is going to be the front half."

"Bet you come apart in the middle," said Beezus, who had once been the front end of a horse in a park circus.

Robert examined the bicycle carefully while Henry plucked at each spoke to see if it were tight enough. Some were tight, but many were loose. "Wish I had a real spoke wrench," muttered Henry. "Now I'll have to take the tires off again."

"Scooter has a wrench in that little kit he carries on his bike," said Robert. "I've seen him use it. It's a thing that fits around the end of the spoke that goes through the rim."

"You watch Ramona. I'll go ask Scooter if you can borrow it," said Beezus, anxious to help. She ran down the driveway before Henry could object. He didn't want to borrow Scooter's wrench, because Scooter might decide to come over and see what he was doing.

"Hey, Ramona, stop pulling Ribsy's ears," ordered Henry. "Why don't you play you're waiting for a bus?"

"O.K.," was Ramona's surprising answer, as she sat down on the back steps.

When Beezus returned with the wrench, Henry went to work on the spokes. He went around both wheels and tightened each spoke. Then he went over them again and gave them an extra twist just to make sure. He wasn't going to have any loose spokes on his bike.

"Come on, Robert, give me a hand," Henry said, after he had found a tire pump in the garage. He was beginning to feel excited. In a few minutes he could try his bike. The boys fitted the rubber tube over the valve on the rim and were taking turns pumping, when Scooter came up the driveway.

"Hi!" said Henry. He wondered what Scooter, who knew a lot about bicycles, would say.

Scooter laughed. "What have you got that old broom handle tied to the frame for?"

Henry, who was beginning to be sensitive about that broom handle, went on pumping.

Scooter walked around the bike and studied it

carefully. He tried the bell, which *pinged* feebly. He wiggled the seat and examined the chain. There was no doubt about it. Scooter was an expert on bicycles.

Henry waited anxiously for the expert's opinion. Except for that broom handle, he secretly thought his bike was pretty good now that the spokes were in. He paused in his pumping to ask, "Not bad for four dollars and four cents, is it?"

Scooter jiggled the handle bars. He ran his finger over the tires.

Henry began to feel uneasy. "Of course," he added, "I still have a lot of things to do to it. Paint it and stuff."

Scooter examined the fork that held the front wheel. He examined the fork that held the back wheel.

Old show-off, thought Henry. Why doesn't he say something?

"Well . . ." said Scooter at last, "I suppose it

will do for a kid your age. Of course, it needs a lot
of work before it'll be safe to use. You'll need a
light and a reflector and a good bell. The handle
bars are loose and you need another handle grip.
You'll have to get a chain guard, and have both
forks straightened, and tighten the seat, and mend
the right pedal, and let's see . . . Those tires are
pretty smooth, and I don't like the looks of that
brake."

Discouraged, Henry stared at his bike. Except
for the missing handle grip and the bell, he hadn't
noticed any of the things Scooter mentioned.
Leave it to Scooter to find a lot of things wrong.
And the worst of it was, Scooter was probably
right.

Henry went on pumping. "Well, one thing at a
time," he said, because he couldn't think of anything else to say.

"Say, Huggins," said Scooter. "I've got an idea
how we could win a blue ribbon in the bicycle

section of the parade after you do some more work on your bike."

"How?" asked Henry.

"Let's take the front wheel off that old bike and fasten the front fork to the back wheel of my bike and make a tandem. You know, a bicycle built for two, only ours will have three wheels."

"Will it really work?" Robert was impressed with the suggestion.

"Sure it'll work," said Scooter. "How about it, Huggins?"

Henry was impressed with the idea too, but he didn't want to ride in the parade on an old piece of a bike fastened to Scooter's good bike. Not after the way Scooter had acted. "Nope. I'm going to do something else," he announced.

"Aw, come on," said Scooter. "Don't you think it's a good idea?"

"Sure, it's a good idea," Henry had to admit. "I'm just going to do something else, is all."

"What?" demanded Robert.

"I bet you think you're going to ride that bike," said Scooter.

"What if I am?" asked Henry. "You just wait. I'll get it all fixed up and trimmed with flowers and things, and nobody'll know it's an old bike I got at an auction."

"Let's see you ride it," said Scooter, when at last the tires were hard.

"O.K. I suppose you think I can't." Just for good measure, Henry gave several spokes an extra hard twist with the wrench.

His mouth was dry as he kicked the parking stand into place. He knew the bicycle would wobble at first, and he didn't want to take a spill in front of everyone. He wheeled the bicycle to the driveway, stepped on the pedal, and threw his leg over the seat. When his foot found the other pedal, he discovered that something was terribly wrong. There was no pull to the pedals. His feet

spun around helplessly. Because the driveway sloped, he was able to coast, wobbling from side to side. Barking furiously, Ribsy ran along beside him.

Henry's ears burned when he heard his audience shriek with laughter. Suddenly the pedals caught, and he was able to use them. Then he realized there was something else wrong with his bicycle. It moved with a peculiar twisting motion that made Henry go up and down as if he were on a rocking horse. The chain, which still had no graphite on it, groaned. Up and down he bobbed as he struggled to keep his balance. Then, in the midst of his confusion, he saw that the front wheel was so bent that it was no longer round. The back wheel must be bent, too, because he could hear it scraping against the fender every time it went around.

The two boys and Beezus, screaming with laughter, ran along behind Henry. Suddenly the groaning of the chain stopped, and he found his feet spinning helplessly on the pedals.

"Ride 'em, cowboy!" shouted Scooter, as Henry coasted on the twisting bicycle and pumped the spinning pedals furiously in his effort to make them work again.

The bicycle was wobbling out of control. Henry frantically tried to apply the coaster brake. Instead of stopping, the pedals began to spin backwards. Henry tried to stop by dragging his foot, but the leg of his jeans caught in the chain. The bicycle spilled him onto the sidewalk and toppled over on top of him.

The others laughed even harder.

Henry worked his jeans out of the chain, untangled himself from the bike, and stood up, scowling and rubbing himself. "All right, cut it out. You're not funny!" he said to Robert and Scooter, who were pounding each other on the back and whooping with laughter.

"That coaster brake . . ." Scooter was laughing so hard he couldn't go on.

"And those wheels!" howled Robert.

Scooter doubled up with laughter. "It's the spokes," he whooped. "Who tightened them for you? Whoever it was sure bent the wheels doing it."

"I did it myself," said Henry with dignity, wondering if he hadn't broken a few bones. As he started to wheel the bicycle up the driveway, he was glad to see that Beezus was no longer laughing at him.

"Are you still going to ride it in the parade?" asked Scooter.

"No," said Henry coldly. He wheeled his bike into the garage, came out, and closed the doors. "I hope you're satisfied, Scooter McCarthy," he said crossly.

Scooter stopped laughing. "Say, Huggins, if I help you straighten out that back wheel, how about riding in the parade like I said?"

"No thanks," said Henry, patting Ribsy's head. Good old Ribsy. At least he had one friend left.

"Aw, come on," coaxed Scooter.

"Nope," said Henry flatly.

"O.K., if that's the way you feel," said Scooter, shrugging his shoulders. "Come on, Robert. Help me roll my *Journals*."

As the two boys left, Henry threw himself down on the back steps.

Beezus sat beside him. "I've got an idea," she said. "Why don't you wear a clown suit and ride the bike in the parade, and everybody will think you meant to be funny."

Henry plucked a blade of grass. "No, I guess not. I'll think of something." He blew on the grass, which made a sputtering noise. Well, anyway, Beezus wasn't laughing at him, and he probably would think of something. Maybe his mother would help him with a costume. It wouldn't be the same as riding a bike, though.

Beezus, seeing that Henry wanted to be alone, decided it was time to go home. Henry was silent as he watched Ramona mount her shiny tricycle and ride off, her spokes twinkling in the sunshine.

He continued to sit and make sputtering noises on the blade of grass.

Mrs. Huggins came out and sat on the steps beside Henry. "I was watching through the window," she said.

Henry didn't say anything. Probably everyone on Klickitat Street was watching.

"I'm sorry we can't get you a new bicycle, Henry," said his mother, "but I think we could manage twenty dollars for a second-hand bicycle. If we watched the classified ads in the paper, we might find a good one that someone wanted to sell."

Henry sighed. "Gee, thanks a lot, Mom, but I guess not. If I can't have a brand-new bike without a single thing wrong with it, I guess I can get along without one."

Mrs. Huggins smiled. "I understand. When I was your age I wanted some brand-new ice skates attached to white shoes. But I had to use my brother's old hockey skates, so I know just how you feel." She patted Henry lightly on the shoulder and went back into the house.

Somehow, Henry found he felt more cheerful. He blew on the blade of grass and produced an ear-splitting whistle. He sat on the steps blowing and whistling and thinking about the shiny red bicycle in the Rose City Bike and Trike Shop.

CHAPTER SEVEN

The Boy
Who Ate Dog Food

THE next Friday afternoon Henry and Ribsy were walking home from school. They were going the long way past the Rose City Bike and Trike Shop so Henry could look at what he had come to think of as his bicycle—the one with the racy red frame and the built-in headlight. The only thing wrong with it was the price—fifty-nine dollars and ninety-five cents. It was exactly what Henry wanted, and he looked at it every time he had a chance.

After making sure his bike was still in the shop, Henry moved on. He was still trying to think of

something he could do in the Rose Festival parade. Across the street from the Supermarket he
stopped to look at the new Colossal Market building that had just been finished. It covered a whole
city block, and Henry had heard that the market
would sell not only meats, groceries, and drugs,
but would also have a filling station, a soda fountain, a florist's stand, a beauty shop, a hardware
store, and almost anything else you could think
of.

Today there was a huge sign across the front
of the building. Henry stopped to read it. The
sign said:

TONITE

GRAND OPENING

MODERN ONE-STOP SHOPPING

DE LUXE NEW COLOSSAL MARKET

NOW READY TO SERVE YOU

25 FREE DOOR PRIZES 25

FREE SAMPLES

FREE GARDENIAS FOR LADIES

FREE BALLOONS FOR KIDDIES

ENTERTAINMENT!

Jeepers, thought Henry. That's a lot of free stuff. He decided to ask his mother and father to go. It was fun to collect free samples, and his mother might like a gardenia.

Henry was still trying to think of a good idea for the parade, when he and his mother and father joined the crowd of people visiting the new market that evening. Beezus was with them, because her mother had to stay at home to put Ramona to bed. Henry had given Ribsy a big bone for dinner so he would stay in his yard. If dogs had to stay out of the Supermarket, they would certainly have to stay out of the Colossal Market.

In front of the Colossal Market six searchlights sent giant fingers of light into the sky. Henry saw Robert and Scooter talking to the men who ran the gasoline generators. As Henry and his father and mother and Beezus entered the market, someone handed each of them a ticket for the door prize. After they had written their names on the tickets and dropped them into a barrel, a girl in a fluffy blue skirt gave Mr. Huggins a package of razor blades. Another girl in a fluffy red skirt gave Mrs. Huggins a gardenia, while a clown offered Henry and Beezus balloons.

Beezus asked if she couldn't count as a lady and have a gardenia instead of a balloon. When the girl handed her the flower, she took it, closed her eyes, and breathed deeply.

"Smell it, Henry," she said. "Did you ever smell anything so beautiful in your whole life?"

Henry gave it a quick sniff. "It's all right," he said, tying the string of his balloon to the button on his beanie. When he put the beanie back on his head, he hung onto it with one hand until he was sure the balloon wouldn't carry it away.

After agreeing to meet his mother and father by the front door at eight-thirty, Henry said, "Come on, Beezus, let's find some free samples."

Sniffing her gardenia, Beezus followed Henry, who had to stop before long and untangle his balloon string from the buttons of a lady's coat. Then they sampled doughnuts, hot from a doughnut machine, and looked over the largest selection of comic books they had ever seen. They tasted frozen orange juice and decided to pass up a free sample of dehydrated Vitaveg soup in order to watch a man demonstrate a gadget for making roses out of beets and turnips. Then they paused at the Colossal Beauty Shoppe to watch a lady have a free facial. Henry thought she looked funny with her hair wrapped in a towel and greasy stuff smeared on her face. As he caught a glimpse of himself in a mirror, he decided he might wear a balloon on his beanie in the parade.

"Look!" Beezus grabbed Henry's arm and pointed to the platform where three girls from a dancing school had been tap-dancing. "The drawing for the door prizes is starting. There's the Rose Festival queen and her princesses."

As the crowd pressed toward the platform, the master of ceremonies announced that the owner of the first ticket the queen pulled from the barrel would receive, absolutely free of charge, one white side-wall tire from the Colossal Filling Station.

"Maybe you'll win it," said Beezus.

Henry wasn't sure his father needed one white side-wall tire, since all his other tires were black, so he wasn't disappointed when his name was not called. He soon lost interest in door prizes, because there were so many grownups in front of him that he couldn't see what was happening.

"Come on, Beezus," he said. "I bet this is a good time to get free samples."

They found Robert and Scooter in front of the doughnut machine. "This is my third free sample," said Scooter. "Come on, let's see what else we can find."

They tasted catsup, potato chips, jam, and cheese. Soon the pockets of Henry's jeans bulged with sample boxes and bottles of Oatsies, Glit, and 3-Minit Whisk-it. Then they came to a display of Woofies Dog Food. The man standing behind the table handed the children pamphlets that explained how Woofies made dogs woof with joy, because it was made of lean red meat fortified with vitamins.

"Aren't you giving away samples?" asked Henry, thinking of Ribsy.

"No, I'm not," answered the man, and then

added jokingly, "but I'll give you a can if you'll taste it."

"No thanks," said Henry.

"Go on, taste it," said Robert.

"I bet you're scared to," scoffed Scooter.

"I'm not either," said Henry. "I just don't feel hungry."

"Ha." Scooter was scornful. "I dare you to eat it."

"Dares go first," said Henry.

"Only scaredy cats say that," answered Scooter.

Other boys and girls who were also collecting free samples gathered to listen to the argument.

"Go on, eat it," someone said. "I bet it isn't so bad."

"Hey, gang!" a boy yelled. "He's going to eat dog food!"

"I am not," said Henry, but no one paid any attention. The Woofies man borrowed a can opener from another booth. Jeepers, thought Henry, how did I get into this mess?

The man clamped the opener onto the can. Henry looked around for a way out, but so many boys and girls were crowded around that he didn't see how he could escape. He wondered how Woofies tasted. Maybe it wasn't so bad. Ribsy ate it. If Henry really did eat it, he would be pointed out at school as the boy who ate dog food. Then he would be pretty important.

"Henry," whispered Beezus, "don't eat it."

Henry watched the can opener chew its way around the can. Ugh, he thought. He didn't want to be the boy who ate dog food, no matter how much it impressed the kids. The man lifted the lid from the can, and Henry looked at the food made from lean red meat fortified with vitamins. At least it isn't raw, he thought, and wished something would happen.

Something did happen.

The voice of the master of ceremonies blared out over the loud-speaker. "Henry Huggins!" The people around the platform laughed.

"Hey, that's me!" exclaimed Henry, bewildered. Why were all the people laughing?

"Will Mr. Huggins come to the platform to claim his prize?" asked the master of ceremonies.

Oh, thought Henry. The man meant his father. His father was Mr. Huggins, but it must be a mistake, because his father's first name wasn't Henry.

"Is Henry Huggins present?" asked the master of ceremonies.

"Henry, wake up," said Beezus. "You won a prize."

Henry looked at the can of dog food. "Here!" he yelled as loud as he could, and the crowd made way for him. Whew, that was close, he thought. He was so glad to get away from the Woofies, he didn't care what his prize was. Probably a basket of groceries.

As Henry climbed the steps to the platform, the audience howled with laughter. Henry looked around to see what was so funny, but he couldn't see anything to laugh at. Then he remembered the balloon tied to his beanie. Maybe that was it.

"So you are Henry Huggins!" boomed the master of ceremonies.

"Yes, sir," answered Henry, starting at the sound of his own voice over the loud-speaker. Why didn't people stop laughing? A balloon on a beanie wasn't that funny.

The master of ceremonies had an envelope in his hand. Henry, who was puzzled, looked inquiringly at him. What kind of a prize was it anyway? He had been so busy at the dog-food booth that he hadn't been listening.

"Henry Huggins, it gives me great pleasure to present you with fifty dollars' worth of work at the Colossal Market's own Beauty Shoppe!"

Henry's mouth dropped open and he felt his

ears turn red. The crowd was a blur of pink faces in front of him, and laughter roared in his ears.

The master of ceremonies opened the envelope and took out some coupons. "Here are all the things this young man is entitled to. Two permanent waves, six special glamour haircuts, six Vita-fluff shampoos, six waves, three facials, six manicures, and last but not least, one set of false eyelashes!"

Henry looked at the floor while the audience shrieked. Jeepers, he thought. Now he really was in trouble. The kids would never let him hear the last of this. Why couldn't he win a basket of groceries or a white side-wall tire like other people? He wished he had stayed and eaten the dog food.

"Well, young man," said the master of ceremonies, "don't you have anything to say?"

"Uh, thanks . . . I guess," said Henry, horrified at the way his voice roared over the loud-speaker.

The master of ceremonies pressed the envelope into Henry's hand, slapped him on the back, and boomed, "Good luck with your prize, young man!"

As Henry stumbled off the stage, Scooter got to him first. "When are you going to get your glamour haircut?" he demanded. "When are you getting false eyelashes?"

"I bet . . ." Robert stopped to howl with laughter. "I bet you're going to be the prettiest boy at Glenwood School."

"Yoo-hoo, Henry!" yelled a couple of strange boys.

Scooter leaned against a shelf of canned goods and guffawed. "How are you going to wear your hair, Beautiful?"

Henry was sure his ears would burst into flames if they got any hotter. "You're not funny," he snapped.

"I know it," snorted Scooter. "I'm not half as

funny as you're going to look with a glamour haircut and false eyelashes."

"I get it. Joke," said Henry coldly.

"Hi, Beautiful," called a strange boy. "How's
the Vita-fluff shampoo?"

"You're not so funny," said Henry.

"I bet you'll look real cute with a permanent
wave," said another boy.

Henry glared and tried to move away, but there
were too many people crowded around him. Jeepers, how was he ever going to get out of this?

"Say, it's the same boy who was going to eat
Woofies," Henry heard someone say.

That gave Henry an idea. "Come on," he said.
"Where's the Woofies man?"

"Are you really going to taste it?" Robert asked,
as Henry passed him.

"Sure, I'm going to taste it," said Henry bravely.
Anything to make people forget that prize, he
thought, as the boys and girls crowded after him.

"I didn't expect to see you again," said the Woofies man, holding out the can and a wooden spoon.

Henry dug the spoon into the dog food. Holding his breath, he popped a bite into his mouth and swallowed quickly. Why, it wasn't so bad. He hardly tasted it. He was pleased to see that all the boys and girls looked impressed.

"He really ate it," said Beezus, squirming through the crowd surrounding Henry. She still clutched her gardenia, which had turned brown from being sniffed so much.

Henry calmly took another bite, held his breath, and got it down. "M-m-m," he said. "It's lots better than K-9 Ration." And it was, too, because Ribsy preferred it.

There, thought Henry, that ought to make them forget the prize. Now if he could just get out of here before anyone mentioned it again.

"Here's your free sample." The man handed Henry a can of Woofies. "You earned it."

"Hey, Beautiful, how did it taste?" asked Scooter.

Leave it to old Scooter, thought Henry. Now he had probably eaten the dog food for nothing.

"Scooter McCarthy, you stop teasing Henry," said Beezus. "You're just jealous, because you didn't win something like Henry did."

"Sure, you're jealous," said Henry, but he didn't sound as if he meant it.

"Joke," said Scooter.

"Henry, aren't you thrilled?" Beezus' eyes were shining.

Henry looked at her. Was she crazy or something?

"I wish I'd won fifty dollars' worth of work at the Colossal Beauty Shoppe," she said enviously.

Well, what do you know! She really means it, thought Henry. These things were different with girls. Why couldn't Beezus' ticket have been pulled out of the barrel instead of his?

"Henry, I have a dollar and five cents at home," said Beezus. "Will you sell me a wave coupon? I know waves cost more, but that's all I have."

Until then Henry had not really thought what he was going to do with the coupons. He supposed he would have thrown them away if there had been a trash can handy. Maybe he should just give Beezus the wave coupon. Still, she was a sensible girl, and she had offered to buy it. A dollar and five cents would certainly come in handy, since he had spent all his money at the bicycle auction.

"Sure, I'll sell it to you," said Henry, delighted with her offer.

"Thank you, Henry," said Beezus gratefully. "Now I can have my hair waved for the parade. I'm sure Mother won't mind just once for something special."

Then Henry saw his parents and Scooter's

mother looking over the heads of the children.

"Come along, Henry and Beezus. We're leaving now," said Mr. Huggins. "Henry, you and your mother will have to get together about those coupons."

"Yes, Henry," said Mrs. Huggins, "I need a permanent. I'll give you the ten dollars and get it at the Colossal Beauty Shoppe. That would help your bike fund, wouldn't it?"

"Gee, Mom, would you?" Henry suddenly felt cheerful. Things weren't so bad after all.

Then Mrs. McCarthy said, "I don't need a permanent right now, but I will in a month or so. I'll give you ten dollars for the other permanent coupon." She opened her purse and took out a bill.

"Jeepers. . . ." Henry was so pleased he couldn't think of anything to say.

"Hey, Mom," protested Scooter.

"What's the matter, Scooter?" asked his mother. "Don't you want me to help Henry?"

"Well . . . uh," said Scooter, "sure I do."

Hey, this is all right, thought Henry. Twenty-one dollars and five cents, just like that. And grown-ups didn't even think about teasing him. If only he could think of a way to sell the rest of the coupons.

Just then his mother said, "As soon as we get home, I'll phone your grandmother. I'm sure she'll be glad to buy some of your coupons."

"And what about his Aunt Doris?" suggested Mr. Huggins.

"Yes, and I can phone some of the girls in my bridge club," added Mrs. Huggins. She always called the ladies in her bridge club girls.

Henry could scarcely believe his luck. He didn't even have to think of a way to sell his coupons. And only a few minutes ago he had been wishing he hadn't won them. Why, he might have thrown his riches away if Beezus hadn't offered to buy a wave coupon.

"I wish I'd won those coupons," said Robert. "You're sure lucky."

"I sure am," agreed Henry. Funny, nobody thought about teasing him now.

"Come on," said Mr. Huggins. "We don't want Beezus' mother to think we've lost her."

"There goes the boy who ate dog food," Henry heard someone whisper as he left the market.

On the way home Mr. Huggins said to Henry, "Your bike fund is growing faster than you expected, isn't it, Beautiful?"

"Aw, Dad, cut it out." Henry pounded his father with his fist.

Everyone Mrs. Huggins spoke to agreed to buy some of Henry's beauty-shop coupons. By Saturday afternoon all the items were spoken for except one. No one wanted false eyelashes.

"Jeepers, Mom," said Henry, "that's almost fifty dollars in my bike fund, and my bike costs fifty-nine dollars and ninety-five cents. I'm almost there!"

"Have you picked out a bicycle already?" asked Mr. Huggins.

"I sure have, Dad. It's a beaut."

Mr. Huggins smiled. "In that case I think we can manage the ten dollars."

"Boy, oh boy! Mom, how soon do you think we can collect the money for the coupons?" Henry didn't see how he could wait another day. He was so close to that bicycle he could almost feel the handle grips in his hands and see the shiny new spokes twinkle as the wheels turned.

His father said, "How would you like me to lend you the money until next week?"

"Would you, Dad?" asked Henry eagerly. "It's a lot of money."

Mr. Huggins rumpled Henry's hair. "Come on. Get your Daniel Boone hat and I'll take you down to the shop in the car. You can ride home on your new bike."

All Henry could say was, "Boy, oh boy!" as he ran into his room and snatched his genuine coon-skin cap. Then he and his father and Ribsy drove to the Rose City Bike and Trike Shop.

Henry went straight to the bicycle with the racy red frame and the built-in headlight. "I'll take this one," he said.

"You're sure that's the right one?" asked his father.

"Yes, that's the one." Of course Henry was sure. Hadn't he gone out of his way to look at the bike at every possible chance for the last two weeks? Henry kept his hand on the bike until his father had written a check and the man had given him a receipt and a guarantee.

"It's all yours now," said his father.

"Gee. . . ." Henry shoved up the parking stand and wheeled his bike out of the shop. His very

own bicycle! He ran his fingers over the shiny
frame and felt the leather on the seat. He turned
on the built-in headlight and sounded the horn.
Then he unsnapped his snap-on raccoon tail and
fastened it to the handle bars. It was perfect.

Henry beamed at his father. "So long, Dad. See
you at home." He threw his leg over the bike and

rode off without wobbling once. Ribsy loped along beside him, and his father smiled and waved.

Henry turned down Klickitat Street so he could pass Scooter's house. When he saw Scooter sitting on his front steps folding *Journals,* he sounded his horn. He had waited a long time for this moment. "Hi, Scoot," he said casually, as he pedaled by with his spokes twinkling in the sunshine and his raccoon tail fluttering in the breeze.

Flambé in Armagnac

A Winemaker Detective Mystery

Jean-Pierre Alaux
and
Noël Balen

Translated by Sally Pane

LE FRENCH BOOK ∎

First published in France as
Question d'eaux-de-vie...ou de mort
by Jean-Pierre Alaux and Noël Balen

First published in English in 2015
By Le French Book, Inc., New York

www.lefrenchbook.com

Translator: Sally Pane
Translation editor: Amy Richard
Proofreader: Chris Gage
Cover designer: Jeroen ten Berge

ISBN:
Trade paperback: 9781939474414
E-book: 9781939474421
Hardback: 9781939474438

Inhale the scent of split oak trees our barrels are made of. They smell of damp earth and marauding herds, a sort of musky odor, from which the eau-de-vie, after four or five years in the cask, forever retains a wild perfume.

—Joseph de Pesquidoux

1

A hot-air balloon was slipping into the clouds above a herd of wild horses. A village of rustic chalets hewn from rough logs stood silently on a ridge against a blue sky. Naiads in Brazilian bikinis frolicked beneath a blue waterfall. Swans in a Japanese-style pond navigated around pastel water lilies and gleaming orange koi.

"Which calendar would you like, Mr. Cooker?" Angèle was standing on the doorstep, stamping her feet and wrapped in a blue and yellow coat bearing the postal service insignia. Benjamin Cooker studied the images, where eternal peace reigned on earth and life was so simple and innocent. He pretended to hesitate between one filled with sandy beaches and rolling surf and another featuring nostalgic side streets in Caribbean locales. He finally chose the dog calendar, with an Irish setter that looked like a younger version of his canine companion Bacchus.

Once a year, Angèle rang the doorbells on her delivery route, not for the mail, but to sell calendars. It was a holiday ritual postal service

workers in France shared with street cleaners and firefighters. Benjamin always bought one from each group, occasionally wondering what the money went for. Perhaps it was for an end-of-year bonus or for widows and orphans. Of course he never asked. That wouldn't do, not with a tradition nearly as old as the postal service itself.

Benjamin offered the woman a cup of tea, but quickly added, "Or a cup of coffee?"

"Frankly, I'd prefer that!"

"One sugar?"

"Two, if you please. And how is Mrs. Cooker?"

"Well. Very well, indeed! She's preparing for our daughter Margaux's impending arrival—out shopping in Bordeaux. This visit is a real treat for us. It's not often that Margaux tears herself away from New York these days. At any rate, I do hope Mrs. Cooker doesn't go overboard, or I may not want to open our next credit-card statement!"

"How you do go on, Mr. Cooker. You of all people know that wine is made to be drunk. It's the same with money; it's made to be spent. Don't you agree?"

The renowned wine consultant and author of the bestselling *Cooker Guide* wasn't sure he wanted to engage in a discussion that he knew he couldn't win. So he walked over to the mantel to pick up the envelope he had prepared. Angèle was all smiles.

"Happy New Year, Mr. Cooker!" Angèle said, leaning in for good-bye cheek kisses. Two pecks, one on each side, was standard in the Bordeaux region. It was three in southeastern France and four farther north.

The winemaker was hardly a fan of such effusion. Angèle's kisses, however, were something no healthy man could refuse. The young woman's cheeks were pink from a morning spent in the cold, and her chestnut hair smelled of coffee.

Benjamin watched from the warmth of Grangebelle as the mail carrier's van disappeared down the drive. The weather was cold enough to chill Champagne, and some of the elderly residents of Saint-Julien were fearfully recalling the winter of 1954, although, on average, temperatures this winter had been warmer than usual. Benjamin had decided against going to his office on the Allées de Tourny. It felt good to be at Grangebelle, quietly watching the flames in the fireplace. The scent of the burning wood mingled with the slightly bitter smell of cigar.

The winemaker poured himself another cup of tea before perusing his mail a bit wearily. Bacchus was dozing on the old Persian rug in front of the fire. This was the dog's favorite pastime in the winter. When the temperature dropped, Benjamin had a hard time rousing him for the long walks they usually loved to take. The old dog would not budge.

3

In the bundle of mail, one envelope caught his attention. In black and red letters, it bore the name Protection Insurance. Cooker & Co. occasionally did work for this company, and Benjamin always wound up chastising himself for not charging more, considering the time the cases took. Judging from the impersonal form letters they always sent, they clearly didn't know him from Adam. In all of southwest France, he was the sole wine expert whose testimony was accepted without question by the courts in Toulouse and Bordeaux. He drew deeply on his Havana and put on his reading glasses.

Protection Insurance
Building Pierre-Paul-de-Riquet, C3
Quartier Compans-Caffarelli
31026 Toulouse Cedex

Dear Sir,

Pursuant to claim No. 455/JV/40, we are pleased to appoint you to estimate the damages suffered by our client, Mr. Jean-Charles de Castayrac, as a result of an accidental fire that destroyed the wine cellar on his property, Château Blanzac in Labastide-d'Armagnac, on December 24.

Your assignment is to provide a precise determination of the Armagnac reserves stored in the claimant's cellar preceding the fire, to assess the quality of his eau-de-vie products up until that

time, to estimate Mr. Castayrac's loss, based on the market value of the Armagnac, and to examine Mr. Castayrac's records.

Your expert report must be sent to our company headquarters within thirty days. It is your responsibility to investigate this matter with the diligence and skill you have always exercised and for which our company is grateful.

Sincerely,
Étienne Valéry
Manager, Claims Investigation

Benjamin considered turning down the assignment. But then he realized that the job would be an excellent excuse to pay a visit to his old friend Philippe de Bouglon. The fact that they had not been in touch for months did not diminish their friendship. And besides, his reserves of Armagnac were running low, and it was high time to replenish the liquor cabinet at Grangebelle.

Just a month earlier, in fact, Elisabeth and he had taken a drive through Labastide, hoping to visit the Bouglons and buy some Armagnac. Unfortunately, Philippe and his wife, Beatrice, had been away on vacation, but in town they had come across Francisco, the cellar master at Château Blanzac. He apologized for not being able to accommodate them immediately, but had promised to personally deliver some of the highly

regarded eau-de-vie that he planned to distill before the holidays. Elisabeth had assured Francisco that they could wait.

"I didn't know the Blanzac cellar master was so charming," Elisabeth had remarked, a smile on her face as she watched the man hurry off.

"Oh yes, as appealing as his Armagnac," Benjamin had said with a bit of a grumble.

Had any of Château Blanzac's fine Armagnac survived the fire? He'd find out. At any rate, Benjamin would catch the Bouglons at home. He decided not to call ahead. He would simply show up unannounced. After all, the Bouglons were two of the most hospitable people he knew. So the New Year was getting off to a good start. The winemaker threw another log on the fire. Bacchus just yawned and closed his eyes again. Benjamin savored another puff of his morning cigar. It was beginning to taste exquisite. What a pity the teapot was empty.

Benjamin opened the door to feel the chill on his face. The outdoor thermometer read six degrees below zero. The Gironde River and the fields of the Médoc, all speckled in white, seemed to be reaching toward the patches of pale sunshine from heaven. He did prefer the cold to the rain, but driving on ice was not his favorite sport. At any rate, Virgile, his assistant, would take the wheel.

Benjamin closed the door and headed to the phone.

"Hello, Virgile? Cooker here. Happy New Year, my boy! Let's celebrate with a glass of Armagnac. What do you say? Meet me at Grangebelle. And bring along some warm clothes and your toothbrush."

Benjamin quickly scribbled a note for Elisabeth telling her where he'd be and went into his bedroom to fetch his own toothbrush and an overnight bag.

2

The heavy wrought-iron gate was open at Château Prada. Virgile drove Benjamin's convertible into the huge courtyard, and the winemaker spotted someone pushing aside the lace curtain at one of the small windows in the kitchen. He thought he recognized the profile of his friend, with his inimitable heavy moustache.

Benjamin watched as his assistant who had never been here, took in the enormous complex. The château's elegant grandeur and perfect symmetry spoke volumes for the Bouglons' past fortune. The outbuildings on either side of the central building attested to the agricultural enterprise of the property. Even in the midst of a glacial winter, Prada symbolized the steadfast provincial aristocracy that had never failed the king of France.

"Look at the chimney, Virgile. Our timing is impeccable!"

"How can you say that, boss, when you didn't even have the courtesy to tell your friends we were coming?"

Benjamin hastily pulled on his Loden, as he assessed his assistant's fatigue after two hours of driving on winding roads covered with ice. The young man looked his usual handsome, athletic self.

"It's an old trick of country priests, Virgile. Back in the day, when clergy called on the nobles of a parish, the priest would look up at the chimneys of the best châteaus. If smoke was rising straight to the sky, he would continue on his way. But if plumes of smoke were escaping in little puffs, he didn't hesitate to knock. He was sure to share in some perfectly prepared feast."

"And why was that?" Virgile asked.

"Think, Virgile! Because then he knew that a simmering pot was hanging from the rack."

"Whatever you say, boss."

Before Benjamin could give Virgile a disapproving look, Philippe de Bouglon was on the doorstep, hands on his hips and a grin on his ruddy face, true Gascon that he was.

"Benjamin! What polar wind has brought you to us? Your reserves of Armagnac must really be running dry for you to come to Labastide in weather like this! Or did Elisabeth kick you out? Don't tell me you've already had lunch, or I'll be offended."

Beatrice appeared behind her husband, radiant in a sky-blue turtleneck and cream-colored velvet slacks. Her eyes were bright, and her voice was deep and warm. They wished one another a

happy New Year. Benjamin introduced Virgile, telling the Bouglons that he was talented in the art of blending but something of a novice when it came to Armagnac.

"You've come at just the right time, Benjamin," Beatrice said.

The winemaker watched as she exchanged a look of complicity with her husband.

"Guess what's on today's menu," she continued.

"Don't tell me you've cooked the farmyard ducks," Benjamin ventured.

"No, even better!"

The winemaker lifted his nose to sniff the aromas coming from the kitchen.

"Pan-seared foie gras, perhaps?"

"If you ask me, I'd say squab, in a stew, perhaps a traditional salmis," Virgile said.

"I would be worried if I were you, Benjamin. He has a keen nose. Your charming assistant is right. He might just steal your reputation one day."

"That will be a proud day for me," Benjamin said.

"You did get the foie gras right, though," Beatrice said. "I roasted the bird and reduced the drippings with Armagnac, before adding some foie gras. Now the bird's cut up and reheating in the sauce. You're right on time."

"Knowing you, it's wood pigeon. Someone's been out hunting again. Wonderful. You know how fond I am of game birds. We haven't had

any at home since I gave up hunting and sent Bacchus into early retirement."

Château Prada's owner related his story of hunting the previous day in the Mézin forest bordering the Gers and Lot-et-Garonne. Philippe and his companions had spent the entire morning in their lookouts, shivering to the bone, gobbling snacks, and overindulging in Armagnac and coffee. For two years now, the migratory birds had proved to be as capricious as they were rare. It was said that their flight corridors had moved to the west for some unknown reason. Ringdoves coming from eastern countries were following the coastline along the Bay of Biscay. Other less adventurous birds were spreading out over the cornfields between Adour and Garonne. The wood pigeons Philippe had bagged belonged to the hungry breed that preferred to hold out rather than take a chance. The hunter from Labastide was quite proud of his booty: four specimens with blue-gray plumage and bloodred beaks.

"It was freezing."

"But you were rewarded for your patience, which—you'd admit—isn't your strongest virtue."

"That's a low blow, Benjamin. But I will be a gentleman and extend a heartfelt invitation to this feast, prepared by the best chef in Gascony. I should know. I married her, and I thank God for every day that I spend with her."

"Let's not go overboard," Beatrice said, pushing back a lock of blond hair from her high forehead.

Philippe de Bouglon smoothed his moustache. "What about a Folle d'Armagnac as an aperitif? How does that sound? I just need to add two place settings to the table and run to the cellar so that we can honor the presence of the most famous winemaker in France. Excuse me—in Europe. I mean the world! I will be right with you, gentlemen."

Checking the grandfather clock, Beatrice excused herself. The chef could not abandon the stew. Benjamin and Virgile took the opportunity to study the Bouglon portrait gallery. Some of Philippe's forebears had distinguished themselves in far-off battles, and others had planted the vineyard at a time when Armagnac was shipped along the Baïse and Garonne rivers to Bordeaux. From there it was sent all over Europe.

A grand piano took up a large portion of the living room. Benjamin watched as Virgile started to slide his fingers across the ivory keys but thought better of it and stopped. Instead, he gazed out at the garden, where a few Lebanon cedars broke the monotony of the frost-covered lawn. The small living room was damp. The marble floor and fixtures, which dominated the room, reinforced the sense of cold. Virgile was visibly chilled—most likely hungry too. He had pulled up his collar. Benjamin felt the same urge,

13

but he didn't want to embarrass his gracious hosts. If only Philippe would hurry back with his Armagnac.

Seconds later, Philippe de Bouglon walked through the doorway, bottle in hand. The transparent Folle d'Armagnac resembled the purest vodka. A mischievous glint shone in the bright eyes of the master of the house. Benjamin, noticing his assistant rubbing his chin in bewilderment, came to his rescue.

"Virgile, did your professors at wine school skip over Folle d'Armagnac? If so, they should be hanged!"

"I have a vague memory of something. They did talk to us about Blanche d'Armagnac, I think."

"It's the same thing, Virgile. It's not to be confused with folle-blanche, the grape variety."

"Yes, now I remember. It was a fatal mistake on my part, made on a written exam. My professor treated me like an idiot. 'You are about as qualified to work in wine as I am to give sermons at Notre Dame,' he said."

"Well he misread you, didn't he?" Benjamin said, extending his glass to the flask proffered by his friend Philippe.

Philippe was grinning. Even before they sipped this Blanche d'Armagnac of his, it had the power to prompt discussion and curiosity. Wasn't that the very characteristic of wine? The French politician

and diplomat Tallyrand had said this—more pompously—some two hundred years earlier.

"It's barely out of the still, clear, white, untouched by wood, never aged, so never sipped by angels," Philippe explained. "If you would allow me a comparison, Benjamin, this eau-de-vie is our virgin of sorts. It's all pureness—and finesse. Taste it! You perceive floral notes of... How shall I put it?"

"You can already smell the fruit," Virgile began to say.

"Philippe, please don't use the word 'virgin' around this skirt-chaser I have for an assistant. He's likely to find qualities in your Armagnac that don't exist."

"Well, this young man must be Gascon. Are you?"

"Actually, I am, on my maternal grandmother's side. She was from Lectoure."

"I knew it," Bouglon said.

By the time they were ready to eat, Benjamin was no longer chilled. The Blanche d'Armagnac had produced the desired effect, warming the mind and the body.

They dined in the kitchen, which was warmer than the dining room. Old grapevine stocks fueled the kitchen fireplace, and the thick glowing embers promised a perfectly cooked stew. The room was filled with wonderful aromas. Enchanting frost crystals had formed around the leaded

windows overlooking the estate's pollarded plane trees. The water pipes had frozen, and the faucet was no longer working, but who cared? At Prada, one was hardly inclined to drink water.

Beatrice brought out one of her vintage jars of duck foie gras, appropriately truffled. A 1989 Suduiraut Cuvée Madame, exquisitely amber in color, accompanied the feast.

Benjamin was relishing his visit with Philippe. The two happily recalled the old days when they were still bachelors. The sauterne had served to re-kindle their ribald memories. Virgile, meanwhile, responded politely to the stream of questions from the mistress of Prada.

"Beatrice, I'm afraid you're going to embarrass our friend with your interrogation," Philippe said, turning to his wife and putting down his fork.

There was no hint of reproach in his tone. Indeed, Benjamin thought he detected a loving intimacy in his smile.

"Oh Philippe, Virgile and I have already become friends. I've found out a lot of things, beginning with the reason for our dear friend Benjamin's visit to Labastide. They're here about the fire at Château Blanzac. It's all anybody is talking about around here."

"Yes, it's horrible," Philippe responded. "You wouldn't wish that on anyone, not even your worst enemy."

Benjamin pierced a piece of bread with his fork and dipped it in the enticing sauce on his plate. "Would you count this Jean-Claude de Castayrac among your friends, Philippe?" he asked before bringing the fork to his mouth.

"He's neither a friend nor an enemy, Benjamin. We know each other well. I even have a certain respect for him. But to be frank, I prefer his Armagnac to his company."

"Can you be more specific?"

Philippe de Bouglon's reddish moustache was beginning to glisten with the stew juices. The Château Pavie he had brought to room temperature by the fireplace had put a gleam in his gray eyes. Before Philippe could satisfy Benjamin's curiosity, Beatrice answered for him.

"You know, everyone here looks out for himself. The producers respect each other, and sometimes we exchange samples. But basically, we see one another at the Armagnac Promotion Committee meetings and competitions at Eauze and Aire-sur-l'Adour. That's about it. As far as the fire goes, the one to feel sorry for isn't Castayrac. He'll always make out okay. It's poor Vasquez! Dying like that in the fire. It's terrible. They say the still exploded. I hope he didn't suffer."

"You mean Francisco, the cellar master? That's terrible. There was no mention of a death in the letter from the insurance company." Benjamin was shocked. How had he missed this piece of news?

Philippe wiped his mouth with his sauce-stained napkin. He picked up the bottle of Saint-Émilion and filled his guests' empty glasses. "One thing is certain: Francisco was the only one who made the baron's Armagnacs. His sons had no say in the matter. Castayrac trusted his cellar master, and he did a good job. Francisco's brandies are among the best in Bas-Armagnac."

"Better than yours?" Virgile ventured.

Philippe was unequivocal. "To you, I can admit the truth. Yes, I am—that is, I *was*—envious of Château Blanzac's Armagnacs. They have an elegance, a finesse. You understand, don't you, Benjamin?"

Benjamin was distracted. He was still thinking about Francisco's tragic death. He pulled himself together and listened to his friend. He was touched by Philippe's candor and admiration. In truth, Benjamin had never tasted Blanzac's brandies, although he had been looking forward to it after his unexpected encounter with Francisco a month earlier. And to think he would have to evaluate the exact worth of the château's reserves.

"I've heard that his paradise was full to the roof," Benjamin confided, referring to the warehouse where he stored his vintages. "At least that's what he told the insurance company."

"Old Castayrac definitely had reserves," Philippe said, offering Benjamin the cheese platter. "These days, everyone has reserves. Unfortunately,

Armagnac isn't selling as well as we'd like. It doesn't matter whether the Armagnac's good or bad. We're all stuck with barrels up to the ceiling and no one to drink what's in them, except the angels. I just wish the angels could pay my bills."

"Yes, but I've been under the impression that your Armagnac is doing well. I see it everywhere. I was in London two weeks ago, on Saint James Street, and I shared one of your brandies with an old friend."

"Don't kid yourself, Benjamin. I have enough in my cellar to supply the French Senate for a century. In both Cognac and Armagnac, we've all got problems, and our government isn't helping."

Beatrice had left the table and returned with a sumptuous-looking pumpkin cake that was giving off the subtle scent of cinnamon. Benjamin and Virgile clapped in unison.

"Beatrice, once again you've outdone yourself," Philippe said, giving his wife a wink.

The master of the house rose to fan the hearth. He threw a worm-eaten black-oak log on the embers, and flames immediately rose from the wood.

"A good Armagnac can only be appreciated around a hearth," Philippe said. "How about a 1983 Prada?"

Virgile nodded in agreement, but Benjamin quickly put his hand on his arm.

"No offense, Philippe, but I'd like to taste a brandy from Château Blanzac. I'm sure you have that on hand. Just to help me form an opinion."

Benjamin detected the hint of a frown on his affable friend's face. "I'm afraid I'm all out. I would gladly have…"

Then his wife betrayed him with her typical spontaneity. "Philippe, go look in Grandmother's display cabinet. I think there's a bottle that Francisco brought us. Remember it, dear? For your fiftieth birthday."

"What would I do without you?" Philippe sighed. His ruse had fooled no one.

Benjamin was taking two cigars in silky wrappers from his leather case when Philippe disappeared behind the double doors to the office. He knew his friend was a big fan of Havanas. The Cubans guaranteed an hour of sheer pleasure. No doubt Jean-Charles de Castayrac's Armagnac would make the occasion even more memorable.

He was about to imagine them raising a glass to the deceased cellar master when an ear-piercing crack pulled him out of his musings. Beatrice, Virgile, and Benjamin ran to the window. A peach tree had snapped under the weight of the ice. The winemaker glanced at Beatrice and saw that she was shivering.

No sooner had they absorbed the sight of the felled peach tree than the sound of breaking glass rang out behind the door. "Damn it all!"

"Oh, that doesn't sound good," Beatrice said, pushing back the lock of blond hair that seemed to have a mind of its own.

When Philippe opened the door, the exquisite fragrances of honey, pear, and orange preserves wafted into the kitchen. A long silence ensued.

In a cloud of smoke, Benjamin finally looked Philippe de Bouglon in the eye. "Now I know why you were envious of Lord de Castayrac's Armagnacs. And if you weren't my friend, I'd almost suspect you of having broken the bottle to avoid comparison."

"Benjamin, I think my subconscious got the better of me."

"That's exactly what I was thinking, you old scoundrel!"

3

Château Blanzac was low and squat. No pointed towers, no mullioned windows, much less tall chimneys. The building's elegance lay in its symmetry and simplicity, along with the lovely tiling that ran beneath the vertigris roof.

A pair of two-hundred-year-old oak trees and three tall cedars dominated the grounds. Their branches caressed the sleepy country manor and its lichen-covered stones. Calling it a "château" was clearly deceptive. As for the titles of nobility claimed by its proprietor, there was no trace, aside from a wrought-iron coat of arms on the front-step railings, whose rust offset any hint of pretention. In the way of assets, the Castayracs owned only this home, with its few acres of vines and one-story outbuilding, along with the family title, which the baron liked to flaunt at the Biarritz casino on special occasions.

Benjamin pushed the doorbell. Its shrill ring set loose three large dogs, whose muzzles appeared at the windows. Benjamin scanned the surroundings. The vines hadn't been pruned. An

antique Citroën DS 19 Pallas was parked in a garage, and on the right, a short distance from the
outbuilding, four immense blackened walls stood
silent. Burned beams, barrel hoops, and staves littered the frozen ground. Shards of glass, vestiges
of the demijohns that had been turned into large
Molotov cocktails, were everywhere. Benjamin
could almost make out wisps of smoke amid the
ruins. It had been less than two weeks since the
catastrophe. Could the fire still be smoldering
under this rubble? Its acrid vapors were stinging
his throat.

The door remained hopelessly closed. Benjamin
rang the bell again, more insistently this time. An
imposing figure, despite the cane, finally appeared.
Jean-Charles de Castayrac fit the image of a
country squire that Benjamin had formed on his
way from breakfast at the Bouglons. Minor provincial nobility, apparently bankrupt but intent on
maintaining his status, even if it meant deluding
people with window dressing, such as an old but
shiny car, a tweed jacket missing a few buttons,
a green felt hat, and a fine shirt frayed just a bit
at the collar. Baron Castayrac stepped toward his
visitors, shooing away the three Labradors.

"Don't worry, gentlemen. They don't bite. Athos,
Porthos, Aramis: get lost! Go lie down! Down, I
say!" The dogs ignored him and bounded out the
door to greet the visitors. "Whom do I have the
pleasure of speaking to?"

Benjamin introduced himself and his assistant. Right away, the baron's tone and expression became more gracious. A smile crossed his face.

"Please come in," he said. The cold was already turning his cheeks and hairy earlobes pink. "These dogs don't have enough sense to stay inside."

"No, it seems that they don't," Benjamin said, petting Porthos's black rump.

Virgile attempted to give the two other dogs a friendly pat, but they scooted past him and ran toward a building where a young man in a fur hat was watching from behind a Massey Ferguson tractor. He looked like a Russian peasant.

Without warning, the timid January sun seemed to dissipate entirely in the freezing weather. A thick cloud of condensation escaped from the baron's thin lips as he pointed his cane at the ruined wine cellar and lamented, "The work of a lifetime up in smoke. A damn shame."

Was it the cold or a surge of emotion that brought the tears to his eyes? Once in the shelter of the entryway, the baron removed his broad-rimmed hat and hung it on a hook next to a long dark coat. He did the same with his cane. He invited Benjamin and Virgile into his library without offering to take their coats. Two dueling embers were struggling in a tiny fireplace. Benjamin noticed that the bronze clock hopelessly showed twelve-thirty. Its pendulum was motionless. Had the baron deliberately left it unrepaired

in the hope of banishing all notion of time from his home?

"Can I offer you anything?"

Benjamin picked up a begrudging tone in his voice. He sounded like a stingy host who had no more than a drop of port or cherry to share. There was no mention of Armagnac. Benjamin declined. Their meeting today was a formality, an initial contact. They would begin their review tomorrow, and Benjamin wanted to give Jean-Charles de Castayrac a heads-up. No doubt, he was still reeling from the nasty business of the fire and the loss of his salt-of-the-earth cellar master, Francisco.

"What a sad end, Mr. Cooker. Can you imagine? Perishing under such circumstances. It's all my fault."

"You have no reason to blame yourself, Mr. Castayrac," Benjamin said.

"And to think that I asked him to distill on Christmas Eve." The proprietor of Blanzac angrily grabbed the fireplace tongs to poke the few embers dying in the ashes.

Benjamin couldn't help thinking of his dear friend Eve, a television producer and classical music expert who had bought a magnificent château in Gers. The château had once belonged to the marquise of Montespan, and it had only one flaw. It was impossible to heat on the coldest days of winter.

"My dear Benjamin, all the forests of Gascony would not have enough lumber to keep my home warm with those high French ceilings," she joked. Benjamin had affectionately nicknamed her the Marquise de Shivering. That gave them both a good laugh, but at the time, it was summer, and they were sitting on the pleasantly warm terrace of Château de Beaumont.

It was just as bad in the baron's chilly library, which Benjamin figured was bearable only in the warmest months of the year. The *toile de jouy* wallpaper, with its repeated pastoral scene on a beige background, was slipping off the moldy plaster walls. The books and encyclopedias lining the shelves offered their musty edges to the notarial décor. Benjamin, who took pride in being something of a bibliophile, cast a wry look at an original edition of *Dictionary of Daily Life in the City and the Countryside*. Virgile had turned up the collar of his leather jacket.

"It's freezing in here," he whispered in his boss's ear.

If Jean-Charles de Castayrac heard Virgile, he didn't let on. "Please excuse the mess, but Blanzac is sorely lacking in women," he said. "Since the death of my wife, Elise, I have no interest in anything."

"Not even in bridge?" Benjamin asked, pointing to a card table where the baron had evidently enjoyed winning a game.

"Very rarely," he sighed. Benjamin thought he detected a hint of evasiveness in the old man's answer.

"You've never thought of remarrying, Mr. Castayrac?" Virgile asked.

Benjamin couldn't believe how socially clumsy Virgile could be sometimes. He couldn't tell the difference between a business client and a friend.

The baron had sunk into a decrepit Voltaire armchair. After blowing his nose on a muslin handkerchief, he stared long and hard at the cheeky assistant.

"I don't think either of my boys would have forgiven me. But my private life is my own business, and no one has the right to make judgments about what I've done or should have done."

"Please be patient with my assistant, Mr. Castayrac. Virgile Lanssien has all the candor of youth. Tact and diplomacy are sometimes optional, as far as he's concerned, and on this occasion, he dispensed with both," Benjamin quipped.

"That's regrettable," the petty noble responded.

Before Benjamin could say anything else, the man stood up and excused himself. He left the room and came back a few moments later with a bundle of vine shoots, which he tossed into the fireplace. The flames had no effect on the room's temperature. The baron turned on a lamp. Its shade smelled moldy. A cup of tea would not have been unwelcome, but the baron was

clearly refraining from any superfluous hospitality. Benjamin and Virgile would have to make do with the quickly waning sparks.

On a white marble pedestal table, the face of a plain woman was encased in a garnet-colored velour frame. Lady Castayrac looked smug in her three-strand pearl choker. Her large forehead and slightly flat nose bespoke peasant origins. Blanzac owed its prosperity to her. The Armagnac cellar, the central heating—when the boiler was still functioning—the Citroën DS 19, the tractor, and much more had all been purchased with her family's money. That very noon, Beatrice and Philippe de Bouglon had given Benjamin and Virgile a detailed account of how this family had enriched itself.

In the seventeenth century, the Riquets de Lauze had made a fortune in water. A gift from God had sprung up from their land. On the wild fields of the Quercy, a region north of Gascony covered with dense forests and dark rocks where goats and sheep roamed in the junipers, a diviner had come upon waters whose curative powers were said to be astonishing. After drinking just one cup, the diviner managed to completely detoxify his system and relieve his chronic constipation. This place, called Alvignac— more specifically Salmière—quickly became a destination for pilgrims from the nearby regions of Corrèze, Aveyron, and even Cantal, all of

whom arrived with bottles and flasks to hold this body-cleansing nectar.

The family began offering their water with miraculous laxative powers the same way they did their aromatic truffles: for cold, hard cash. To promote the spring, they invited the exquisitely elegant Marquise de Pompadour, King Louis XV's chief mistress, to Alvignac. Immediately, Versailles and Paris were abuzz with talk of this water, which was fortified with calcium, sodium, and magnesium, according to the scientists from the Sorbonne.

Louis de Rouvroy, the duke of Saint-Simon, wrote in his memoirs that if there were one boring place on earth that he would gladly visit, it was Alvignac, because he could overeat and not get fat, thanks to the water. Three centuries later, the French writer Pierre Benoit wrote the same thing in his colorful *Lunch at Sousceyrac*. The reputation of the waters of Salmière never waned, and it continued to draw famous writers and even quite a few politicians. Like gas in a stomach, the Riquets' fortune swelled. They wouldn't have been able to stuff all the cash under their mattresses or into their wool stockings even if they had wanted to. It went into the bank and finally fell into the hands of Elise Riquet de Lauze.

As cupid's game of love would have it, she married a Castayrac, whose specialty was trading in eau-de-vie. The dowry was much more beautiful

than the bride, and the groom was more talented in manners than business. The couple experienced a few years of happiness and had two sons, Alban and Valmont, three or four good vintages, and then a rash of disappointments, serious breaches in the marriage contract, and finally the agonies of illness. Breast cancer claimed the miraculous springs heiress. She died on a Good Friday at the age of forty-four without having embraced her two children one last time. The whole town of Labastide-d'Armagnac accompanied her hearse to the Castayrac family vault on a dismal spring day.

"Mr. Castayrac, how much eau-de-vie would you say you lost in the fire?" Benjamin ventured, barely looking at the baron.

"That is difficult to judge, sir. Only Francisco would have been able to tell you to the exact liter," Castayrac said, rubbing his fingers along the moth-eaten armrests. "He kept the books."

"Nevertheless, you're the one who takes care of the accounting, taxes, and the administrative details, aren't you?"

"Or maybe it's your sons?" suggested Virgile.

"Mr. Lanssien, I'd prefer to answer your superior. It's a matter of principle. In this house, only the elders have the right to speak."

"So it's Alban we'd need to—"

"That's enough, Virgile," Benjamin interrupted.

The baron smirked, apparently pleased to have established his authority.

"Francisco was—how can I put it—part of the family," the baron said, looking only at Benjamin. "My father, Jean-Sébastien de Castayrac, thought the boy had an honest face and hired him. Francisco wasn't even sixteen when he walked through the gate. He came from the foothills of the Pyrenees, from Jurançon, where he had been a farm boy. His parents had fled Franco's Spain."

Benjamin nodded. "Do you know anything else about his background?"

"Francisco Vasquez was a private man. He rarely confided in anyone. He had a saying: 'All I know, I put in a bottle!' Even now I can hear him speaking those words with his Aragonese accent."

"He became your cellar master, and no offense intended, I believe he crafted your best eau-de-vie."

"I am indebted to him for many things," Jean-Charles de Castayrac said and sighed. "And one of them is the quality of my Armagnacs."

"Did he live in the château?"

"A few months after he arrived in Blanzac, my father gave him a shack near the old stables that the day workers had used for their breaks during haymaking season and the grape harvest. He never paid any rent. That's how it was. Francisco was family. He often ate lunch with us. That is, when my wife was still alive, because after... After, we made other arrangements."

"He never married?" Benjamin asked, reading his silenced assistant's mind.

"No," the baron said. "But he was never short on girls. They all flocked around him. He was good-looking. Well, that's history now."

"I heard he sowed his seed all over Labastide," Benjamin said with a touch of mischief.

"That's what they say, all right. But people exaggerate. If you believe everything that's said in town... I'm sure some people are whispering that I started the fire in my own wine cellar to collect the insurance."

Virgile spoke up again. "And what were you doing on December 24th?"

The baron crossed his legs, revealing mismatched socks and hairy white calves. He stared at Benjamin without blinking.

Benjamin broke the silence. "As far as the insurance is concerned, the fire was an accident. I'm here to get things moving, Mr. Castayrac. I am counting on your cooperation."

"You'll have it, Mr. Cooker."

"I don't doubt it. I suggest that we meet tomorrow morning to draw up an initial assessment of the reserves that were burned."

"Don't come at the crack of dawn. I like to stay under the covers when it's this cold outside."

"I understand. How about ten o'clock? Will that do?"

"I'd prefer eleven," the baron responded. He then sprang nimbly from his chair and headed toward the vestibule.

The winemaker wondered what use the cane could possibly served, other than that of pompous accessory. Evidently, the proprietor of Blanzac was a better actor than vintner. Was it possible that the fire was not an accident?

The parting was cool and barely polite.

4

Benjamin needed no persuasion to accept Philippe de Bouglon's offer to stay a few nights at Prada, just enough time to assess the loss sustained by the Castayrac estate. With his friend's Gascon gift of gab, the quality of their Armagnacs, Beatrice's undeniable culinary talents, and the magnificence of his old friend's humidor, how could he resist? Naturally, Benjamin didn't intend to hurry his assessment. He'd take his time to dig just a little deeper. But there was still the matter of Virgile.

"Young man, you are welcome to stay in the tower. We have a small room there," Philippe said.

"Honey, that won't work, the pipes have frozen. He wouldn't have any water," Beatrice said.

"Besides, isn't that bedroom the one that's haunted?" Benjamin added with a wink.

"I'm fine staying somewhere in town, boss."

"There's a family in Labastide-d'Armagnac, the Cantarels, who have guest rooms," Philippe said. "You'll be happy as a clam there. The rooms are very simple but comfortable. The owner

is friendly and, to be honest, a bit chatty. She has a son about your age. He's the striker for the Cazaubon team, a champion rugby player. He was named the best player in Gascony. But Virgile, maybe you're not a fan?"

"As a matter of fact, I played two seasons for the Bergerac club."

"What position?" Philippe asked.

"Wing," Virgile responded, thrusting out his chest a bit.

Benjamin was amused. "Philippe, how far away is it?"

"Less than five minutes from here."

With a wink, Beatrice assured Virgile that he could have his meals at Prada. She was already talking to him as though he were a dear member of the clan.

"And Evelyne Cantarel will tell you more about Blanzac," she said. "She worked for the Castayracs for many years. Evelyne's a nice woman who hasn't had an easy life. She and her son live with her father, who's still hale and hearty. I think he's even the local agent for the Protection Insurance, isn't he, Philippe?"

Benjamin smiled politely and fiddled with his glass. Why hadn't the insurance company mentioned the local agent?

"I'm not sure, Beatrice. I think he quit a short time ago," Philippe said. "Benjamin, most of us around here are covered by the Social Agricultural

Insurance. At any rate, when it comes to insurance, we are always at their mercy."

Beatrice called Evelyne Cantarel to make Virgile's lodging arrangements. Evelyne was delighted to have a new guest, especially in low season. No, he did not drink tea in the morning. He drank coffee. How long would he be staying? Hard to say. Three days, maybe four or five...

Before Virgile departed, Benjamin and he had dinner with the Bouglons. On the menu: shirred eggs and cheese from the Pyrenees, which went especially well with the Baron de Bachen white they served, a good representative of wines from Tursan.

"Virgile, my boy, what do you know about this wine?" Benjamin asked.

"Hmm," Virgile said, swirling the straw-colored liquid in his glass and bringing it to his nose. "Fruit... Mango, I'd say, with some citrus notes, floral aromas, and a slight hint of honey." He sipped and swished before adding, "Round, but refreshing. I'd say baroque grapes, sauvignon, and... I'm not sure, another variety, but what?"

"Very good," Philippe interjected. "Petit and gros manseng."

Benjamin nodded. "The property in the Landes region dates back to the thirteenth century," he said. "In 1983, the famous restaurateur Michel Guérard bought the estate. He replanted the vineyards in 1985, for a first harvest in 1988. He's helped to revive the appellation."

"Benjamin, I'm quite impressed by Virgile," Philippe said. "He must be quite an asset."

"I'm not so sure you'd say that if you knew the extent of his ignorance when it comes to Armagnac," Benjamin said.

"Boss! What about 'All for one and one for all'? You're supposed to be on my side, especially now that we're in Gascony, the land of *The Three Musketeers*."

"My boy, you may also remember this from the same book: 'Never fear quarrels, but seek adventure.' I believe we have an adventure set for us tomorrow. Isn't that right, Philippe?"

"Yes, the mobile distiller is coming at the crack of dawn."

Virgile glanced from Philippe at Benjamin and then at Beatrice. "The mobile distiller?"

"That's right. In Armagnac, many distillers don't actually have their own stills. Roving distillers take their alembic from farm to farm and distill according to each cellar master's specifications. Here we always distill in early January," Beatrice explained.

The simple feast wound down, and Benjamin, Virgile, and the Bouglons called it a night shortly after dinner.

Benjamin handed over his keys to the Mercedes convertible, and Philippe gave the directions to the guest house. "When you leave Prada, just go to Place Royale, and take the Rue du Café-Chantant.

The first right is the Rue des Taillandiers. Take it. The Cantarels live in a half-timber house. You can't miss it."

Benjamin retired to his room, where he called Elisabeth to tell her that he would probably be staying longer than he had expected.

§ § §

The sound of a tractor maneuvering in the courtyard woke Benjamin, who had never been a heavy sleeper. He peered out the window at a dawn sky that was purple and rooftops that were painted with frost. Benjamin's room was frigid, and even though he was wide awake, he wasn't looking forward to the prospect of crawling out from under the covers. Fortunately, the aroma of coffee was beginning to creep under the door, and his excitement over the event unfolding outside soon overpowered his desire for comfort. His shower could wait. He wouldn't miss this for anything.

Philippe, gesturing dramatically and yelling "whoa," was guiding the still into the wine cellar. It was a strange-looking contraption, all copper and bedecked with pipes, coils, and odd gauges.

When Benjamin joined them, Philippe introduced the distiller, a cross-eyed bearded man named René Dardolive. He would be the master

of ceremonies. Benjamin couldn't guess his age, but he looked prematurely bald, something he was trying to hide under a shapeless black felt hat. René was speechless when Philippe announced the celebrated winemaker's presence.

In the half-light of the wine cellar, Beatrice and Philippe bustled about, carrying blocks of oak for the boiler. Soon, esoteric permutations would be under way, supervised by the alchemist in a khaki hunting jacket. René had learned his craft from his father. The Dardolive men had been distillers for many generations, and *aygue vive*, or living water, was no mystery to this quiet man. He had been weaned on the vapors of a zealously polished still.

Dardolive was set to begin his rite of offering the wine from the Bouglons' harvest to distillation. But first Beatrice called everyone to the table: ham, duck cracklings, rabbit and boar pâté, scrambled eggs, red wine, and hot coffee. Virgile showed up, looking groggy at this unlikely hour, when night hadn't yet buried its last demons. Evelyne Cantarel had prepared a copious breakfast for him, but Benjamin knew his assistant wouldn't be able to resist Beatrice's terrines.

Benjamin could see the anticipation in Virgile's eyes. Distillation was something Virgile had studied but never seen. Now he was about to witness this miracle for himself. A pure and crystalline

eau-de-vie would soon be flowing through the murmuring copper still.

Despite his rough manners and silences, René managed to exchange a few words with Virgile.

"Did you ever distill for the Château Blanzac?" Virgile asked.

René took a gulp of coffee and wiped his mouth on his sleeve. "Nope. They got their own still. Francisco did good work."

"Yes, what a terrible accident."

"It ain't no accident, I'm telling you. That family's as twisted as an alembic."

Without any further explanation, René rose from the table to get to work. He filled the boiler with water, just enough to start the process. Then he connected the loader vat to a pot topped with a still-head fitted with a long swan's-neck pipe. He lit the fire, feeding it vine shoots first and then old stumps. When the blaze was finally roaring, he threw in large pieces of dry oak. The distillation could begin. Philippe leaned toward Virgile and began a running commentary.

"This is a continuous still. It's made of pure copper and distills only once," he said.

"Cognac gets distilled twice, that I know," Virgile said. "Is it copper because of its superior heat conduction?"

"That's right. This continuous distillation is actually quite simple," Philippe continued. "René here feeds the wine from the loader vat into the

still, where it goes through the bottom of the cooling apparatus. It fills the preheater, then descends through the heating column, flowing over a number of plates and ending up in the boiler. This is when René removes the wine residue. The intense heat causes the wine to boil, and the vapor rises up through the incoming wine to the top of the still. In the process it becomes richer in alcohol and picks up the wine's aromatic substances. Then it flows through the condensing coils, where it's cooled. The resulting eau-de-vie is deliciously fruit-scented, with some floral notes. It's fiery with youth and needs some time to develop its complexity and mildness. A bit like us, in the end."

Philippe's cheeks were flushed from the heat. Standing back a bit, Benjamin was listening to the lesson. Just when he was about to say something, Philippe started talking again.

"Once the alcohol level is stabilized, the still can function continuously. It can change wine into Armagnac day and night without stopping."

"So the distiller's work is pretty much done?" Virgile asked.

Benjamin could see that his assistant was feigning naiveté to encourage his host to continue talking. Virgile knew more than he was letting on.

"Not at all," Philippe responded. "This is precisely where his craftsmanship comes in. He understands everything about the vapors and the

heat exchange happening in the coils. He sees nothing but knows everything."

Philippe continued in a hushed tone. "He's a magician, I tell you. Now and then he consults the alcoholmeter, which allows him to verify the alcohol content, but for the most part he uses his intuition and his senses. He listens. He feels the heater to gauge the heat. He uses his nose, too, and he tastes the product from time to time. He is constantly on the alert."

Benjamin took over. "His main concern is keeping the flow of wine just right. Despite all the heat, distillation is a gentle process. It must not be disturbed."

For an hour, the still murmured and bubbled. Those watching fell silent from time to time. Finally, Philippe led Virgile to a copper faucet, which was emitting a thin, aromatic steam of eau-de-vie.

"Smell this, young man!"

Virgile sniffed it. "I pick up plum jam and white flowers," he said.

"Those aromas, plus fragrances of grape and pear, are characteristic of the folle-blanche grape," Philippe said, with pride evident in his blue-gray eyes.

"What is the alcohol content?" Benjamin asked.

"Fifty-five percent," Philippe responded.

René Dardolive had removed his hunting jacket and was working in his shirtsleeves. He

looked like an organist adjusting the pedals and bellows of his instrument. His movements were precise and impressive as he tended the still, controlling all aspects of the gurgling, hissing, and murmuring machine.

Philippe told Benjamin that it had been a good year for Prada, and René would need at least two days to get through the estate's seven casks, each with four hundred liters of wine. The winemaker and his friend decided to step outside for a few minutes to catch a breath of fresh air, leaving Virgile behind, captivated by the scene.

§ § §

Virgile turned to say something to Benjamin and realized that his boss was nowhere to be found. He left the wine cellar to search for him, heading first to the Prada kitchen, where Beatrice was busy preparing the noon meal. He had no idea what was simmering over low heat in the Dutch oven, but the aroma was tantalizing.

"I think they're in Philippe's office. They're setting the world right. But first, run to the Cantarels. Evelyne called. You need your key to the house in case nobody's around to let you in."

Virgile opened the kitchen door. "Shit. It's cold!" Virgile cursed, pulling his wool hat over his

ears and buttoning up his sheepskin coat. He'd heard the news on Beatrice's kitchen radio. It confirmed what he had already suspected. The thermometer had dipped to a bone-chilling minus ten degrees the previous night, and school busing had been suspended. He rushed to the car and drove through the village, which seemed deserted. Everyone in their right mind was inside.

When Virgile arrived at Evelyne Cantarel's house, he found her in a floral apron, polishing the cherrywood buffet in the dining room with beeswax.

"When you don't have a head, you have to have…"

"Legs, I know," Virgile replied with a smile.

The woman put down her rag, which smelled slightly of rancid honey, and offered her guest a cup of coffee.

"I don't know if I have time."

"Why would you want to rush back outside in this cold?" the Gascon woman asked.

Virgile decided to tell her why he was in Labastide: the business at Blanzac, the damage suffered, the visit to the château… Evelyne Cantarel pulled a porcelain cup from the buffet and poured Virgile some coffee. She waved to a chair, wordlessly telling him to have a seat. Continuing to sip her own coffee from an old mustard jar, she plopped down in a nearby chair.

"Tell me, how is it at the château, Mr. Virgile?"

"What do you mean? The atmosphere?"

"No, the housekeeping."

"Well, it's a bit neglected. The place doesn't appear to be dusted regularly." Virgile didn't know what else to say. He had never given housekeeping much attention.

"When the missus was alive, everything was impeccable. We had to polish the copper every week, and we waxed the floors on the fifteenth of every month."

"It's changed a lot, then," Virgile replied, giving the woman who had once taken care of Château Blanzac a nod meant to show his respect for her work.

"And the baron? Still just as…"

Virgile saw no harm in confiding more. A second cup of coffee might even take the chill off. His boss could wait.

"Spry? Yes, he doesn't seem as old as his years."

"Oh, widowhood is not his problem! When La Riquette died, he got over it pretty quickly."

"La Riquette?"

"Yes, Mrs. Riquet…de Lauze. Forgive the nickname. At the Castayracs, we called them La Riquette and the Robber Baron, if you understand what I mean."

"I see," Virgile said, all smiles.

"But you're going to think I'm a gossip."

"It's only gossip if it's speculation and rumor. As far as I'm concerned, you're giving me the facts."

"That's what my father thinks. Maybe you'll meet him tonight. He spends most of his time hunting these days."

"Wood pigeons?"

"No, woodcocks. They're more challenging, but he's still limber for his age."

Evelyne got up to make another pot of coffee and stoke the wood-burning stove, whose flames were dying down.

"Did you see the sons?"

"One of them, I think. A young man, kind of shy with pale eyes. He didn't come to meet us."

"That had to be Valmont. He still lives there."

"What's the other one like?"

"Alban? He's a Castayrac through and through. A bit standoffish, a loudmouth, ambitious, thinks he's hot stuff. He's really his father's son. He married well to the only daughter of the Nadaillac family. They claim they're descendants of D'Artagnan, the fourth musketeer. It's been five years now, and there's still no bun in the oven. Folks say the bride won't have anything to do with her husband."

"Maybe they just need a little time. Children don't always happen right away." Virgile felt a little self-conscious saying this. What did he know about marriage?

"I doubt that it has anything to do with timing, Mr. Virgile. The Castayracs behave in bed the same way they do at a banquet. As soon as

they're served, they're looking at their neighbor's plate, if you know what I mean. That would be enough to make any bride turn her back to her husband at night."

"I know exactly what you mean," Virgile said, discreetly glancing at his watch. His coffee was getting cold, and he was losing interest in the conversation.

"I've taken up too much of your time with all my stories," Evelyne said. Still, it was clear that she wanted him to stay. She took another tack, changing the conversation to the baron's business. "Do you think, after all that's happened, that he'll end up being chairman?"

"Chairman of what?"

"Chairman of the committee, of course!"

"You mean the Armagnac Promotion Committee?"

"He's been wanting that plum for so long. Imagine—the baron heading an organization that has such an influential say in producing and regulating all our eau-de-vie. And to think that his main rival is Aymeric de Nadaillac, his own son's father-in-law."

"Correct me if I'm wrong, but you don't seem to be very fond of the Castayracs."

"It's ancient history, Mr. Virgile. The day isn't long enough to tell you all that I know."

The woman in the floral apron rose from her chair. Virgile thought her eyes looked misty. Not

wanting to embarrass her by staring, he looked away. On a side table, he spotted a badly framed photograph: two rows of proud-looking and powerfully built young men.

"That's the Cazaubon rugby team, and that one there, on the left, is my son, my little Joachim!"

"Little! He looks quite athletic to me. I used to play too."

"Really, what team?"

"Bergerac."

"So you and Joachim have something in common. I can't wait for you to meet him. Joachim just loves the sport and his teammates." Evelyne's eyes were shining with pride. "They threw him a big birthday party last August."

"You don't say. My birthday's in August too."

"No kidding. What day?"

"August 31."

"I can't believe it. Joachim's birthday is August 31. This is unbelievable. The same sport, the same birthday…"

"Yes, it is quite a coincidence, isn't it? You could call us brothers in spirit." Virgile hoped she wouldn't try to find something else that he shared with her son. He really needed to leave. He stood, thanked her for the coffee, grabbed his coat, and headed to the door.

"You forgot your key again, Mr. Virgile!"

Virgile slapped his cheek. "I'm such a nitwit. You'd think I'd remember this time. Thank you."

49

Evelyne Cantarel took his arm and pulled him toward her. "Your being here is a sign from heaven," she said. "May I give you a hug?"

5

At Château Blanzac, the baron's welcome was even cooler than it was the day before. Castayrac was dressed for business in a well-cut three-piece suit made from fine dark wool, and although Benjamin told him that Virgile and he needed to interview him at length and go through the rubble of the destroyed wine cellar, the baron made it clear that he had more important things to do.

Jean-Charles de Castayrac intended to reduce this meeting to a simple formality. The man was pressed for time, and he left no doubt that his attire was not for the benefit of his honored guest, even if Benjamin was the most famous winemaker in France. The board of directors of the Armagnac Promotion Committee was convening at Eauze that very afternoon, and the election of its new chairman was on the agenda. The matter would be decided during a lunch preceding the meeting at a fine restaurant named Pépita's. Benjamin Cooker would not make him late.

Benjamin sent Virgile to the wine cellar and proceeded with his questions. "How many casks, Mr. Castayrac, would you estimate that you lost?"

Castayrac paced the room, hands behind his back, chafing at each of Benjamin's inquiries regarding his exact losses. "I already told you, Mr. Cooker. We lost thirty-six."

"Are you quite sure?"

"Absolutely. And I lost all those demijohns, most of which I inherited from my ancestors. They were famous eau-de-vies, highly prized by collectors. Their alcohol content was between forty and fifty percent. Some dated back to 1869. Napoleon III loved them. Do you realize how valuable they were?"

"A real treasure," the winemaker agreed.

"You can say that again, Mr. Cooker!"

"How many of those demijohns did you have in your reserves?"

"I could not say precisely, but more than sixty at the very least."

"Had they all been duly declared?"

"Francisco took care of those details."

"That's putting a lot of trust in him," Benjamin said. He wrote some numbers in his spiral notebook.

"As I said, Mr. Vasquez was considered a member of the family. I never doubted his word."

"Yes, but unfortunately the only thing we have to go on is your word, since your books were

destroyed. Moreover, I've been doing this work for quite a while, and this is the first time I've heard of a vineyard owner leaving all his records in his wine cellar."

"How could I have known that my wine cellar—and my office, along with it—would go up in smoke? What are you insinuating, Mr. Cooker?"

"I'm not insinuating anything. I'm just trying to gather information and understand what happened. Failing your cooperation, I shall be forced to proceed with the investigation as I see fit."

Benjamin put down his notebook and scanned the library shelves. Castayrac struck him as a man who liked to collect books and show them off but didn't read very much. He felt the baron's eyes on him. The man was standing in front of the fireplace, which was filled with gray ashes. He hadn't even bothered to light a fire for the winemaker and his assistant.

"If we take a safe and pragmatic approach, sir, we can say that you lost 14,400 liters of Armagnac in casks and six hundred in ten-liter demijohns. In all, then, that gives us fifteen thousand liters, a good round number."

"That must be pretty close," the baron said brusquely.

The Labradors were barking in the courtyard. But there was nothing but silence in the dark and bitterly cold library, where the two men were

challenging each other without making eye contact. Finally, Benjamin said, "At this stage of the assessment, we need to allow for evaporation, the amount taken by the angels." He raised his eyes.

"Of course," Castayrac responded, a half-smile on his dry lips.

"I will have to apply the formula devised by the Directorate-General of Customs and Indirect Taxes: six percent per year."

"Do you want to ruin me?" the baron said, raising his voice.

"If you had been able to give me a precise accounting of the different reserves and which vintages they came from, we might have come up with a better estimate. But as it stands, Mr. Castayrac, it's a guessing game, and we'll have to agree on a figure based more or less on what we believe you lost in this terrible fire."

"Good God!" Castayrac responded.

Before he could say anything else, a man with a thin face, short hair, and steel-blue eyes walked into the library, a cigarillo between his fingers. The baron frowned, but went ahead with an introduction. "Allow me, Mr. Cooker, to introduce my older son, Alban."

"It's a pleasure," the baron's son said, extending his hand.

Castayrac hadn't bothered to shake his hand the day before, when he arrived at Blanzac. Benjamin wondered if this warmer greeting

meant that the son didn't resent his presence as much as the father. But then again, maybe it only meant that his mother had taught him his manners.

"Father, you'll come down with pneumonia sooner or later if you don't start heating this château."

"Must I remind you, Alban, that the boiler is broken, and I don't have the finances to get a new one?"

"That doesn't mean you can't make a fire in the fireplace." Alban started filling the firebox with old vine stocks.

"That's enough! I've seen enough flames lately."

"As you wish, but you can't allow yourself to get sick if you ever want to lead that committee."

Alban de Castayrac turned to Benjamin. "I believe my father-in-law is going to run, too, and he has a good chance of winning."

"Get out!" the baron shouted.

The older Castayrac son gave Benjamin a sly look before leaving the room. "So long, Mr. Cooker. I'm sure we'll meet again."

The winemaker had hardly expected such animosity between the father and his son. He didn't have much sympathy for either of them. Caught forever in the framed photograph on the pedestal table, Castayrac's deceased wife, wearing her self-righteous expression, seemed to be chastising her husband.

The widower had enshrouded himself in an obstinate silence. Benjamin cleared his throat, played with the cap of his pen, and finally picked up his notebook to scribble some words, which he underlined twice.

Then the taciturn baron peered at his watch.

"I'm already late for my lunch," he said, suggesting that Benjamin return later in the afternoon.

"At cocktail hour," he said unctuously.

Summarily dismissed, Benjamin pulled up the collar of his Loden. Cocktail hour at this château would no doubt be as cold as the baron's library. He headed for the burned-out wine cellar, where Virgile was still looking for clues in the ashes. His clothes were smudged from searching through the oak staves that the fire had not completely incinerated.

"I counted exactly nineteen demijohns, boss. I found the necks and have something to show for it." With a grimace, he opened his right hand. A bloody gash ran along his palm.

"Holy smoke, you have to disinfect that right away. Are you vaccinated against tetanus?"

"Yes, I think so."

"You think so, or you're sure?" Benjamin asked.

A figure stepped out from behind the garage housing the old DS. Benjamin recognized the young man from the day before. He had a flask of Armagnac in one hand, and in the other he had a white handkerchief. He went to Virgile and

without waiting for consent doused the wound with eau-de-vie. Virgile let out a howl. His caregiver smiled as he held him firmly by the wrist.

"Don't be a sissy, Virgile," Benjamin said. He turned to the country medic. "You're Valmont, aren't you?"

The young man nodded while pouring more antiseptic on the wound. He carefully folded the handkerchief to make a compress and applied it to Virgile's hand. Virgile grimaced again. His eyes were brimming with tears.

"It's nothing. Don't make such a fuss!" Valmont de Castayrac ordered in a coarse tone.

His features were rough, his eyes pale, and his lips thick. The second son of the estate completely ignored Benjamin's questions and answered only Virgile's. Even then he was noncommittal. "I don't know anything," he said. "The day of the fire, I was hunting for woodcock in the Fatsillières Forest. When I got back, the cellar was blazing."

"You were hunting on Christmas Eve?" Virgile asked.

"Yes, people around here think nothing of hunting the day before Christmas. If we bag something, it winds up on the table the next day. Now let me go look for some gauze and adhesive tape. I'll be right back."

Valmont hurried toward the house. Benjamin, meanwhile, figured this was an opportunity to get a closer look at the DS. He was a car collector

at heart and had quickly identified the model: a 1957 Citroën DS-19 with a gearshift on the steering wheel. The four-cylinder engine had stood the test of time with its inimitable aerodynamics. Benjamin would have gladly offered to buy it from the baron, who could have used the money. He tried to recall the name of the Italian who had designed the body of this astonishingly futuristic jewel, but his memory failed him.

When Benjamin returned from the garage, Virgile's hand was bandaged. He was absorbed in counting the iron hoops from the fire-ravaged casks. Valmont was at his side, helping him with the metal scraps and heaps of wood.

"Tell me, Valmont, is the DS in the garage one of the first models?" Benjamin asked, trying to sound naïve.

"Exactly! A 1957. It's a collector's piece. The most beautiful car Flaminio Bertoni ever designed."

"I see you are a connoisseur," the winemaker said.

"Well, let's say it's a hobby."

At that moment, Benjamin Cooker realized that he would never own the Castayracs' navy-blue DS. "Drop it, Dad!" his daughter Margaux would have told him. "Not even in your dreams!"

Oddly, the disappointment whetted his appetite. He asked Virgile to take a break and join

him for a Gascon lunch at Pépita's, whose foie gras ravioli was said to be excellent.

"Your 280 SL isn't bad, either," said Valmont, who had walked out with them to Benjamin's Mercedes.

Surprised by the remark, the winemaker was quick to respond. "I assure you, young man, it's not for sale!"

Valmont de Castayrac was just as quick to reply. "And neither is the DS-19." Having already given Virgile his handkerchief, Valmont pulled a wadded tissue from his pocket and wiped his dripping nose.

Put in his place and feeling glum, Benjamin felt for his keys and handed them to his assistant, who declined the offer.

"If it's okay with you, boss, with my hand and all, I'd prefer that you take the wheel."

"Oh, of course, Virgile."

As they passed through the estate's rusty gate, Benjamin glimpsed the silhouette in the rearview mirror of the true and only caretaker of Château Blanzac. The younger and crafty Castayrac could read minds. It would be wise to be careful around him.

6

"I am very sorry, but we're full," the restaurant owner said, looking exhausted but acting gracious nevertheless.

The dining room was filled with boisterous voices and the clatter of knives and forks. The conversation at the long table dominating the room was free-flowing. The faces of the diners were flushed from all the alcohol, and they had unbuttoned their shirt collars—the better to enjoy this midday feast. Busy servers filled their glasses as quickly as the men emptied them.

Benjamin Cooker instantly recognized Jean-Charles de Castayrac, who ignored him. At the head of the table, a distinguished-looking man with a white mane and aquiline nose appeared to be orchestrating the proceedings. He had a medal of honor pin in his lapel. Probably the agricultural merit award, Benjamin surmised. With his salt-and-pepper goatee, he resembled a musketeer, a highly regarded figure in these parts. Benjamin guessed that he was Aymeric de Nadaillac, father-in-law of Alban de Castayrac.

The description Philippe would give him that same night would confirm his hunch.

"Try your luck at Au Trou Gascon. It's a mile from here," the woman suggested. By the looks of her apron, Benjamin imagined that she officiated in the kitchen, as well as the dining room.

Leaving the inn, Virgile teased Benjamin. "I guess we won't be enjoying any foie gras ravioli today."

"Maybe that's not such a bad thing," Benjamin muttered. "We are here to work, after all."

"We won't be getting the inside scoop on the Armagnac committee either. You know, boss, my mom taught me not to eavesdrop."

Benjamin didn't deign to respond. Virgile turned away and started peeling off the bandage Valmont had wrapped around his hand. Patience had never been one of Virgile's virtues.

"Just let it alone for now, Virgile," Benjamin said. "We haven't finished our work at the château, and I don't want you getting that hand infected."

Fortunately, Au Trou Gascon more than satisfied their appetites. The waitress was plump and eager to please. "How is it?" she asked time and again. "Do you need anything else?" This finally exasperated the winemaker, who just wanted to enjoy his meal.

Virgile grinned, hardly looking up from his guinea fowl with wild mushrooms. After a few

minutes of silence, he gave Benjamin his assessment of the Castayrac cellar. In his eyes, the only tangible elements were the barrel hoops. With four to a cask, it was easy to estimate the number the baron's paradise had housed, assuming they were all full. As for the demijohns, he had managed to locate nineteen bottle necks. At best, twenty demijohns, swaddled in their wicker casings, had been tucked away in storage.

The assistant took a paper napkin and scribbled a series of numbers. When he was done, Benjamin put on his reading glasses to take a look. Satisfied with the final figures, he copied the calculations into his notebook.

"Good work, Virgile. It seems that we're far from the figures Castayrac gave us. His numbers are significantly higher—three times higher as far as the demijohns are concerned. It's a classic ploy: pad the reserves to bring the business back to an even keel and enjoy the serendipitous flow of cash from the insurance company. And then he can plead ignorance under the pretext that Francisco was the one in charge of the books."

"Yes, but to take us for idiots! I don't care if he's a baron. I'm going to let him know that we're onto his game."

"You're not going to say anything, Virgile."

"Why shouldn't I?"

"It's better not to rush things. We still need to gather evidence."

"But, boss, we have the proof."

"Of insurance fraud, perhaps. But I want to know more. Just to make sure we're not missing something."

Benjamin fell quiet. He had opted for coffee and was now staring at the bottom of his cup. The winemaker's habit of silently musing sometimes irritated his assistant, who always wanted to know what he was thinking. But Benjamin continued to peer into his cup, as if the solution to his investigation lay there.

"I must tell you, I'm not very good at reading coffee grounds," Virgile said.

"I suggest a few drops of Armagnac in the bottom of our cups, Virgile. Perhaps a fresh idea will wind up staring us in the face."

The winemaker called the waitress and ordered a Laberdolive. Benjamin had only to request the vintage from Virgile's year of birth to make his protégé's face light up. Benjamin poured a few drops of the very amber Armagnac into each coffee cup, ignoring the two balloon glasses brought by the young woman.

"I have a hunch," Virgile murmured, "that some liquor might just loosen the baron's tongue."

"I think the same thing, Virgile. But for now, tell me what this eau-de-vie brings to your nose."

"Quince, definitely," Virgile said.

"Exactly!" Benjamin responded. "I will add: quince paste, and little by little, it tends toward prune, doesn't it?"

"I'm staying with quince. Perhaps with a hint of lime?"

"Do you know, Virgile, how the Latin poet who shares your name described the quince?"

"No idea."

"He described it as 'pale with tender down.' Lovely, isn't it? He was referring to the fuzzy skin, of course."

"Since we're displaying our knowledge, do you know where people used to plant quince trees?" Virgile asked, mischief written on his lips.

Benjamin shook his head, feeling a bit embarrassed because he didn't know the answer.

Virgile was quick to fill him in. "Quince trees were often planted in the corners of a vegetable garden to officially mark where the plot ended."

Benjamin smiled at the play on words in French, the word for quince, *coign*, sounding the same as the one for corner, *coin*.

Finishing his Armagnac, Benjamin glanced out the window. The sky looked as ashen as the rubble in the Blanzac cellar. Farmers in the area were predicting that a change in temperature would accompany the new moon. On this point, their waitress happily concurred.

"The weather's going to get milder," she said as Benjamin paid the bill and buttoned up his Loden.

It had become obvious that this gracious and well-endowed waitress was none other than the owner. The food and the Armagnac had restored the winemaker's spirits, and he was sure that he would be seeing this woman and her restaurant again. The marinated duck had been a real treat, the duck breast cooked to perfection.

"So, Virgile, how was that?" Benjamin asked, grinning as Virgile and he slipped into the beige leather seats of the Mercedes. Benjamin started the car and turned on the radio. The local news was on.

> In a surprise upset this afternoon, Aymeric de Nadaillac was elected chairman of the Armagnac Promotion Committee by an overwhelming majority of those voting. Albert Pesquidoux, outgoing president of the APC, had backed his rival, Jean-Charles de Castayrac, owner of Château Blanzac. Nadaillac is the father-in-law of Alban de Castayrac, the baron's elder son. Château Blanzac's cellars were burned to the ground in December, and cellar master Francisco Vasquez died in that fire. An investigation conducted by the Saint-Justin Police Department concluded that an explosion in the still caused the fire.

"The baron may not be in the mood to see us," Benjamin said.

"I won't argue with that. Boss, can you drop me off at the Cantarels? I need a shower after

spending the morning in all that rubble. And frankly, I don't think I'm needed at your meeting with the losing candidate for chairman of the Armagnac Promotion Committee. Unless you object, of course."

Without saying a word, Benjamin turned left at the first fork in the road and headed toward Labastide-d'Armagnac. He let his assistant out at the front entry to the half-timber house. He imagined a cozy room fragrant with a wood fire and goose fat. In his mind, he saw copper pans shining on a wall and a hanging lamp casting a golden circle of light on the table. A figure at one of the windows caught the winemaker's eye. It had to be Evelyne Cantarel. No doubt, she was pleased to see the return of her houseguest.

§ § §

"What happened to you, Mr. Virgile?" Evelyne Cantarel cried when she saw the young man's bandaged hand.

"It's nothing, Mrs. Cantarel, just a little work accident. Nothing serious."

"Let me have a look."

Just as she was peeling away the bandage, a man came into the room. He was wearing brown corduroy pants and a heavy jacquard sweater.

Under his hoary eyebrows were two mouse eyes, and under them were puffy bags that gave away his age. Virgile looked at the man's hands, speckled with liver spots, and saw that he was holding *La Terre*, the weekly farmer's communist-party newspaper. The old man nodded politely and headed toward the worn armchair that was close to the stove. He grimaced as he sank into the cushion. Evelyne had told Virgile that the cold exacerbated her father's arthritis, but he refused to let it slow him down.

"Did you know that our new boarder and Joachim share the same birthday? And Mr. Virgile played rugby, too. Isn't that a coincidence?"

Mr. Cantarel barely acknowledged her remark and opened up his paper.

"My father isn't very talkative," Evelyne said.

The next moment, a young man came running down the stairs. He was in a navy-blue sweat suit, a baseball cap on his head.

"So, there you are!" Evelyne exclaimed. "Let me introduce Virgile, our houseguest. You two have a lot in common."

Evelyne's effusion made Virgile feel uncomfortable. He put out a strong and sincere hand to this Joachim. Although he was not very chatty, the Cantarel son soon warmed up. Before long they were talking about rugby, the Bayonne festivals, Pamplona, the Armagnac that was no longer selling very well, Joachim's recent job as a

volunteer firefighter in Saint-Justin, and then, of course, girls. Joachim apparently was in love, but he didn't have much to say about this, as it wasn't a subject that was discussed under the family roof.

Evelyne went to the kitchen and returned with four dishes, which she set on the oilcloth-covered table. Of course Virgile would stay for the meal. "I was sure you two would become thick as thieves," Evelyne said happily as she filled two shot glasses with a dark and murky but deliciously scented liquid.

"It's walnut liqueur, homemade!" Evelyne said, loosening the cap of the relic-like vial.

The menu that followed confirmed the culinary talents of the former Château Blanzac servant. Pan-fried duck liver, stuffed goose neck, arugula salad, and flakey apple pastries made up this "simple" meal, so called by the creator of the feast. She claimed that she had thrown it together. Virgile, who had just finished eating at Au Trou Gascon, didn't know how he could eat any more, but the food on this table was too tempting. He dug in.

Then they lingered over eau-de-vies from Bas Armagnac: Domaine Boignières, Domaine Roger Luquet, Domaine d'Espérance, and, naturally, Château de Briat.

The elder Cantarel went upstairs, and after clearing up, Evelyne retired to her own room. With the help of the brandy, the two young men

discovered that they had even more in common. Joachim had been drawn to oenology himself. He didn't have the money to study in Bordeaux or Montpellier, though, so he had accepted a job as warehouseman in the nearby township of Le Houga. It didn't pay well, but at least he could stay in the area. At any rate, his mother wouldn't hear of his moving away. He dreaded the day he would have to tell her that he was in love and wanted to marry. He was eager to have a home and life of his own.

"And what about your father?" Virgile asked hesitantly.

"What, my father?" Joachim said. "He took off the day he found out my mother was pregnant. A son-of-a-bitch, that guy! The closest thing I've ever had to a dad is my grandfather."

"But your mother never told you anything about your dad?"

"Never."

"Why?"

"I don't know. All I can say is that as soon as my mother got pregnant, her troubles began. The Castayracs fired her that year, and my grandmother died. She's been single her whole life."

"She never wanted to marry or have a serious relationship with any other man?" Virgile asked, realizing that he was venturing close to the line.

"No, she always said that two men in the house—my grandfather and me—were enough.

At least I don't think she ever loved anyone else. Well, yes, maybe…"

Joachim wrapped his oversized hands around the nearly empty glass of Armagnac. He was holding it too tight. Virgile looked up and saw that his new friend's eyes had taken on a steely hue.

"You have suspicions?"

"I think, when she was very young, she had a crush on Francisco, the Castayracs' cellar master. Anyway, we have those bastards to thank for our problems."

"And what if Francisco was your father?"

"Stop talking bullshit! Why do you say that?"

"Simple hypothesis."

The glass broke, and blood gushed over Joachim's fingers. But instead of letting go, he began to squeeze the glass shards, driving them into his hand. He stared at Virgile, the veins in his neck bulging. Then, to Virgile's horror, he rammed his head into the glass. Witnessing Joachim's self-mutilation, Virgile sprang into action and put him in a judo hold, preventing him from harming himself any further. Now on the floor, Joachim could not overpower Virgile. He surrendered. His breathing became more regular. Color returned to his cheeks. His eyes lost their deathly fixedness, and his mouth began to tremble. Virgile let go and grabbed a kitchen towel, which he soaked in Armagnac and dabbed on the cuts. Despite all the blood, they looked

relatively minor. Virgile heaved a sigh of relief. No stitches needed. He had repeated the first aid that Valmont had administered to him that very morning. Decidedly, in Armagnac country, the truth cut like a knife!

Joachim gave his rescuer a weak smile. When, little by little, he recovered his senses and he stammered a few awkward words of excuse.

"Francisco used to take me in his arms when I was little, on Sundays, when we picnicked with Mom by the Douze River. But he never was man enough to admit it and take his responsibilities. Mom won't talk about it. But you don't even know me. What made you say that?"

"I'm a Virgo, like you," Virgile said, patting him on the shoulder. "We know how to put two and two together."

7

The Labradors announced his arrival as Benjamin approached the door. The sporting dogs quickly quieted, and Benjamin hadn't even touched the bronze knocker on the Blanzac door when Lord Castayrac pulled it open and greeted him with a cold and mocking laugh.

"I was convinced, Mr. Wine Expert, that you wouldn't come tonight."

"To be honest, I thought the same thing after your friends elected Aymeric de Nadaillac chairman of the committee."

"No one can betray us like family!"

"You must admit, the events of the past month didn't help you."

"You don't know me very well. I'll make a comeback. Mark my words!"

"Mr. Castayrac, you're talking like a casino gambler, which you are, I believe." Benjamin said this with a dash of provocation.

"On occasion. Life is a perpetual gamble, isn't it, Mr. Cooker?"

"Yes, indeed it is, but you still have to have the means to bet!" Benjamin rubbed it in. Castayrac hadn't offered to hang up Benjamin's Loden, but he took it off anyway and slipped it onto a hook. The winemaker intended to let the man know that civility and stonewalling would no longer set the tone for their visits.

As he had predicted, the aristocrat was intoxicated. The man smelled of whiskey and Virginia tobacco. With an unsteady hand, he pointed the way to the library. Benjamin already knew the way, as well as the contents of this room. Leather-bound books on natural history on the left, close to the door. Books on agronomy on the upper-right shelves. Toward the back, the Carrara marble fireplace and the two thin andirons. On the mantel, the gilt bronze clock, forever silenced.

The room was even colder than usual. Benjamin took a seat on the faded gold sofa with threadbare fringe. Facing him on the pedestal table was the photograph of Elise de Castayrac, maiden name Riquet de Lauze. Even with that smug look on her face, the photo gave the fusty surroundings a touch of humanity.

"Mr. Castayrac, the initial findings my assistant and I have gathered are significantly different from the figures you suggested this morning."

"So you're calling me a liar," the baron said as he pulled the stopper off a large decanter of whiskey.

The flask, sitting on a nested table whose marquetry had suffered a few poorly extinguished cigars, was largely depleted.

Castayrac continued. "Bourbon?"

"No, thank you."

"Gin, then?"

"Just Armagnac," the winemaker said, close to becoming exasperated.

Castayrac walked to the other end of the room and disappeared down the steps leading to his private reserve. Benjamin figured he had quite a few vintage Armagnacs down there.

"Nineteen eighty-six? Will that do?"

"Perfect! That's the year Simone de Beauvoir died," Benjamin said.

"I don't go in much for trivia."

"Is that so? Or women's rights, either. That's also the year you dispensed with Miss Cantarel's services. But perhaps that was not your decision, but rather your wife's?" Philippe and Beatrice had already told Benjamin the story, and he planned to use the information to his advantage.

"I don't see the connection to the matter at hand," Castayrac said, giving Benjamin his glass of Armagnac.

"There isn't any, I assure you," Benjamin replied, warming the glass with his hands. "Unless..."

"Unless what?" Castayrac grumbled. "I don't like your insinuations, Mr. Cooker. Come right out and say what you're thinking!"

"In Labastide, it was common knowledge that your cellar master had a relationship that was rather...passionate, shall we say, with..."

"With?" the baron exclaimed, emptying his glass in one gulp. Then, looking away from Benjamin, he answered the question himself. "With my wife!"

Benjamin hoped this admission would be the first of many. The Armagnac—plus the alcohol consumed before Benjamin's arrival—was loosening the baron's tongue. Castayrac, clumsy in the darkness, started pacing the room and mumbling half-sentences.

The winemaker refrained from taking notes. Now and then, he clicked his tongue, enjoying the candied-orange flavors of the eau-de-vie and lingering aromas from the time spent in oak barrels. Francisco's blendings were truly fine. The fellow must have been terribly in love that year.

"All that is ancient history. I forgave my wife before she took her last breath," the baron said, looking furious.

"That was the least you could do. You yourself were not above reproach."

"I will not allow you to talk that way."

"You're right. It's not for me to pass judgment on your private life. And yet I do believe that in the past you have often mixed business with pleasure."

"What's your point?"

"You gave me your word this morning that there were sixty demijohns in the cellar. However, we found evidence of only nineteen. So it seems that you weren't being honest with me. Perhaps you disposed of some of your liquid assets before the fire, without declaring the proceeds."

"Why would I do that?"

"To pay off gambling debts, I would think. It seems that Lady Luck abandoned you long ago, Mr. Castayrac."

The man collapsed in his Voltaire chair and poured himself another glass of the 1986 eau-de-vie.

"So I guess you consider me a terrible crook."

"It's a working hypothesis. Nothing more, nothing less."

Jean-Charles de Castayrac took two gulps of his old Armagnac and threw the rest into the fire. Instantly, the hearth lit up. Shadows played on the library shelves, and a delicious scent of grilled orange peel rose in the air.

The man's stooped shoulders and dangling arms cut a pitiful profile. It had been a rough day, and the baron's reputation had come out besmirched. The oldest member of the Castayrac family seemed to be on the road to ruin. The fleurs-de-lis and blue blood mattered little. Now, whatever the cost, he needed to wrest a few pennies from the insurance company and save what he could.

Castayrac pulled himself together and rummaged in the wood basket for a log substantial enough to keep some flames going, and then he tried a smokescreen.

"I haven't led the life you imagine, Mr. Cooker."

"I don't imagine anything, dear sir! I observe. I listen. I keep records if I can gather sufficient information, and then I send my report to the Protection Insurance. I must say you're not helping me get to the bottom of this."

"What do you want me to say? Yes, I sold some demijohns under the table. It was to pay for maintenance on the château and certainly not to..."

He stopped talking and looked at Benjamin, who had picked up his notebook again. Was Castayrac about to try a new tack? Sure enough, the baron began talking about his unfaithful wife and unhappy marriage.

"All my problems began when my wife became unfaithful to me. To think that she was cheating on me with that Spaniard Francisco!"

"I thought you trusted him implicitly."

"Yes, of course, up until the day I found out. Francisco had gotten involved with the Cantarel girl. When my wife discovered that he had cheated on her—with someone younger and prettier, no less—she immediately fired the good woman, who, of course, had no idea why."

"So the father of Evelyne Cantarel's son was none other than your cellar master?"

"It's hardly a secret. All of Labastide knows, except the boy himself. His mother is as silent as the grave. She's the perfect daughter-mother figure that you see so often in the countryside. When my wife died, I thought about rehiring her, but I couldn't bring myself to do it."

"Why not?"

"I don't know. Maybe because of my own sons. I wanted to show a modicum of respect for their mother. I had put all that behind us, and I wanted to keep it there."

"Did she have other lovers?" Benjamin asked, pouring himself a bit more of this 1986 spirit, which more than twenty-five years of aging had mellowed perfectly.

"The Cantarel girl?"

"No, your wife."

"Mr. Cooker, I am familiar with your expertise in the area of wine. I did not know you were so knowledgeable about affairs of the heart."

"Heartbreak, sir, is your best defense."

The Blanzac nobleman poked at his fire. He added another thick block of wood. This generosity was a far cry from the cold hearth he offered earlier. Perhaps he was trying to arouse some sympathy. Castayrac leaned against the mantel, his eyes riveted on the black-and-white picture of the descendant of the famed Alvignac waters. Her fleshy lips—the lips that had known so well how to kiss—seemed painted in bold brushstrokes.

"You were witness this morning to the contentious relationship that I have with my older son, Alban. He's a schemer, and he's arrogant. Thank goodness he married rather well, even though I'm still waiting for a grandchild. You know, sir, he's not a Castayrac."

The confession was both terse and pompous. It wasn't tinged with any remorse, just a hint of fatalism that gave the man a sort of nobility. His wife had sinned, but in the Castayrac family, reputation trumped conventional morality.

Some embers landed on the rug and began to burn the worn wool fibers. Castayrac crushed them under his heel. After a long sigh, he continued in a lower voice.

"Alban's father was a Bordeaux wine trader for Martinique. He saw to it that our Armagnacs crossed the Atlantic safely. He had become a sort of family friend, almost like a relative. I don't need to draw you a picture. He died of pancreatic cancer a few years after my wife."

"Does your son suspect anything?" Benjamin asked, shifting in his weight on the sofa and feeling a bit uncomfortable with these disclosures.

"Not in the least! And allow me to ask, my dear friend, for your complete discretion."

Benjamin nodded to show the request had been granted.

The baron cleared his throat and looked more humble now. No longer churlish and haughty, he started talking again.

"I raised him as my own son, and I am very disappointed that he is pouring his invaluable talents into Aymeric de Nadaillac's eau-de-vie. But can I blame him? Maybe I wasn't a good father. Do you have children, Mr. Cooker?"

"Yes, a daughter."

"I would have loved to have a daughter..."

Jean-Charles de Castayrac's eyes were brimming with tears. Benjamin found this display of emotion both pathetic and distasteful. He got up and started walking toward the shelves of old dictionaries in brown leather bindings.

His cell phone stopped him.

"Excuse me," Benjamin said, pulling out the phone. It was Philippe. "Hello, Philippe. Yes, please expect me for dinner, as planned."

From the corner of his eye Benjamin could see that the baron was paying close attention.

"Of course, Benjamin, we're looking forward to seeing you this evening," Philippe said. "But I'm also calling with some news. Aymeric de Nadaillac has just died in a car accident. He was driving from Gabarret. Black ice, they think."

Stunned, Benjamin ended the call and looked at the baron. "Mr. Castayrac, you've just lost a rival: Aymeric de Nadaillac. He's dead."

8

During the night, the wind from Spain had chased away the blanket of frost that had cloaked the vines and woods of Armagnac for three days. "We're in for some rain," Philippe de Bouglon had announced. His weather predictions were never challenged. He could read the sky the same way he could read the color of his Armagnacs. "When you come down to it, the weather is simply a matter of blending: hot and cold uncontrollably subjected to air pressure," he had joked, smoothing the russet-colored moustache that sometimes gave him the look of an Irish whiskey merchant.

It was just past seven now, and Benjamin was on his way to the Cantarel house to rouse Virgile. Surely Mrs. Cantarel would offer him tea, or at least a steaming cup of coffee. The very thought of it inspired him to quicken his pace.

Two black cats were vying for turf in Labastide-d'Armagnac's deserted Place Royale, where Benjamin parked the car. A figure shrouded in a scarf slipped out of view as the winemaker passed by. Benjamin heard a lock click, ending

any chance of conversation. Then the winemaker, a lover of old stones, stood in the middle of the square and studied the vaulted arcades, which were perfectly aligned along three sides of a quadrangle protected by a church tower. The village had changed very little since the sixteenth century. He thought of what his friend Philippe had told him: Henry the Fourth, who had visited Labastide-d'Armagnac several times, had used this square as his inspiration when he ordered the layout of the Place des Vosges in Paris. Perhaps it was just a legend or a bit of regional boasting, but Benjamin found the idea entirely believable. He was fond of these little encounters with French history, which, in the land of Aquitaine, had merged with that of Old England.

A yellow postal truck interrupted the peace and quiet. Bundled in a dark parka, the driver assessed Benjamin with suspicion and then gave him a nod. The medieval town was stirring.

Taking the Rue du Café-Chantant, the wine-maker imagined the private lives of the residents. Behind a few of the windows, the lace curtains were already pulled back. On the cobblestone street, a balding spaniel was searching for suste-nance in a ripped-open garbage bag. He trotted over to Benjamin and sniffed the winemaker's Loden. Benjamin gave the spaniel a pat on the head and continued on, glad that his own dog, Bacchus, didn't have to forage for food. Finally,

he turned onto the Rue des Taillandiers, where he spotted the half-timber house. He walked up to it and knocked on the door.

"Already here, boss?" Virgile said, sitting at the table with a cup of steaming coffee. Sitting next to him was a young man with a scratched face but lively, almost reckless expression.

With warmth that seemed natural, Evelyne Cantarel invited Benjamin to share their breakfast of plum jam, quince jelly, honey, fresh orange juice, and bread toasted to perfection. Benjamin did not need to be cajoled.

The conversation soon turned to Aymeric de Nadaillac's death. Edmond Cantarel, emerging from his silence, was both suspicious and stubborn. "It was no accident. You'd have a hard time convincing me otherwise."

"Papa, stop that nonsense!" his daughter reproached, pouring a stream of strong black coffee into Benjamin's white porcelain cup with gold trim. "Car accidents happen all the time. Maybe he was worried or tired. I don't know. In any case, things will work out for the Castayracs."

"You'll see. Those bastard wine producers will make Castayrac their chairman, even though he doesn't have a drop of Armagnac in his blood. Don't you think so?" Grumbling, the patriarch took a seat at the end of the table.

Benjamin, put on the spot, nodded as he smeared quince jelly on his toast.

"Indeed, I'm afraid your prediction is probably correct."

"You see, Evelyne, even the gentleman here thinks the way I do!" said Cantarel. He raised his glass of red wine to toast them.

"Here's to your health! Nothing in the morning like a glass of good wine, a slice of Bayonne ham, duck rillettes, and country bread. Real bread, not some Parisian baguette for weaklings! No, a real round loaf with a crust that sticks to your ribs. Because, sir, woodcock hunting ends today. There's no time to waste, and lying in wait all day long makes you hungry," the old man said, slipping the blade of his Laguiole knife into the bread and cutting himself another slice.

Ignoring his grandfather, as well as Benjamin, Joachim gave Virgile a mischievous look. "I think you're on the wrong track, my friends. It's not the baron who'll be elected. It's the Nadaillac son-in-law. Just wait. The election will end up being between the Castayrac father and son. There will be blood."

"Why do you say that?" Virgile asked.

"You'll see. I have a hunch."

"That's a clever notion, sonny!" said old Cantarel.

Benjamin observed this exchange with interest. He was feeling so cozy in the warmth of this household, he could almost make coffee his exclusive morning drink.

"I see all the coffee's gone," Evelyne said. "I'll make some more."

"That's very nice of you, but please don't go to the trouble," Virgile said. He had already left the table with Joachim, who was checking his watch.

"I'm outta here," Joachim said. "Will I see you later, Virgile?"

Virgile agreed to accompany his new friend to rugby practice later in the day, as long as his employer didn't object.

"On one condition," Benjamin said. "That you don't spend the whole match on the bench, and no celebrating afterward. You know what I mean!"

A wink between the two young men and a smile from the winemaker sealed the deal.

The winemaker would have gladly prolonged the breakfast conversation, but Joachim was gone, and Cantarel was busy getting ready for the hunt. The woodcocks would not wait. Cantarel put on his winter coat, took down his Browning rifle from the gun rack, clipped on his cartridge belt, and headed to the door.

"Anyway, when it comes to those two, one is as bad as the other," the old man concluded. He whistled to his hunting dog, who turned out to be none other than the spaniel Benjamin had seen foraging in the village street.

When the winemaker and his assistant left the Cantarel house for Château Blanzac, the weathervane on the church was spinning. The wind

was blowing from Landes, and the dark sky in the west was confirming Philippe de Bouglon's prediction.

§ § §

The rest of the day brought little new information. Virgile sifted through the debris of the charred wine cellar, counting and recounting the cask hoops, as well as the necks of the broken demijohns, but his conclusions were unchanged. The estimates and calculations were significantly lower than what the baron had submitted on his insurance claim.

After a heavy lunch at an inn in Mauvezin-d'Armagnac, Benjamin slipped into his room at Château Prada, determined to work on his report. This could only be accomplished, of course, if his friend didn't try to distract him with an on-the-spot tasting of the robust and fiery eau-de-vie straight from the still. He would never be able to resist temptation if Philippe appeared at his door with vials wafting fragrances of pear, plum, and lime.

In fact, Benjamin Cooker didn't write more than two lines of his report that afternoon, as the call of the mouthwatering Blanche d'Armagnac, with its finesse and irresistible aromas, was too powerful. It got the better of both Benjamin and

Philippe. The two ended the evening slouched in their armchairs. Feeling bawdy, they took turns recalling the women they had romanced in their youth. On occasion, they had even gone after the same girl.

"Those were the days," Philippe said, his eyes glassy.

"Yes, but these days are better, my friend," Benjamin responded. He smiled and closed his eyes. "Who would have thought we'd end up with such fine wives? 'There is only one happiness in life, to love and be loved.'"

"George Sand."

"Correct you are," Benjamin said. Then the look of bliss left his face and he sat up. "But the goings on in Labastide bring to mind Jean-Paul Sartre: 'Commitment is an act, not a word.' That is a lesson lost on some."

§ § §

The strong smell of camphor floated through the Cazaubon stadium locker room. Several players had suffered bumps and bruises, and the trainer, a puny loud-mouthed guy with agile fingers, was busy massaging calves and shoulders that ached from the blows. Joachim and Virgile had emerged unscathed from the practice match against the

Villeneuve-de-Marsan team. Despite the minor injuries, the Cazaubon players were said to be invincible.

"Shit, you guys play like animals!" the former wing of the Bergerac rugby team teased his friend as he came out of the shower.

"Friendly game or championship match, it makes no difference. Show no mercy! But you play awfully well for someone who hasn't touched a ball in a few years," Joachim replied.

Virgile grinned.

The Cazaubon coach appraised Virgile with the eye of a horse trader. "Is your pal from around here?" he said, looking at Joachim. "Think he'd like to play for us?"

"Ask him yourself, but I don't think we could afford him," the striker said, sounding mysterious.

Virgile, with a towel around his waist, pretended not to hear. The man in the sweat suit put a hand on his shoulder and made the offer in a tone meant to be polite.

"Too bad, but I just signed with Toulouse," Virgile answered without blinking.

"Oh, really?" the coach said, taken aback. "And what's your name?"

"Galthié. Virgile Galthié. The cousin of the one you've heard of. Yes, that one, the former captain of the national rugby team."

The Cazaubon coach looked stunned and turned to Joachim. "When you have friends like

that, let me know," he said in a hushed voice. "And don't waste any time."

As soon as the coach had turned his back, the two accomplices grinned at each other, trying hard to suppress their laughter.

In keeping with his agreement, Virgile didn't engage in any post-game celebrating. He settled for a bock beer at the Café de la Poste. This gave Joachim the opportunity to introduce his teammate for a day to his heartthrob, a slender brunet beauty. Her name was Constance.

As soon as he saw her green eyes and graceful figure, Virgile knew he was in trouble. Obviously, he couldn't compromise his new friendship. So he decided to call it a night and go back to Labastide. He was tired from the match, anyway. But he had a hard time banishing the vision of Joachim's girlfriend from his brain, and he slept fitfully.

9

The Estang church was too small to accommodate the crowd at Aymeric de Nadaillac's funeral service. But Father Péchaudoux, addressing the confined assembly in coats reeking of mothballs and dried lavender, was clearly in his element, and the Mass went on and on. The priest's voice rose to the rafters as he swept from one part of the liturgy to the next.

"Receive, oh Lord, into your kingdom your servant Aymeric, who, during his life on earth, never ceased working with determination, devotion, and selflessness for the good of the vineyards."

Behind a dark veil, the Nadaillac widow stared at the coffin through the entire service. Looking dignified in black, her daughter and son-in-law worshipped at her right.

When the pipe organ started playing the majestic recessional hymn, the pallbearers picked up the oak coffin and began walking down the center aisle. The family followed. As the casket passed each pew, the men lifted their berets and

bowed before the remains of the last of the great figures of the farmers trade union.

Once the mourners were outside the church, though, the gossip started. Everyone was speculating on Nadaillac's successor as head of the Armagnac Promotion Committee, and there was hardly any agreement.

"The son-in-law will definitely make a run for it," some said.

"Don't be stupid. Old Castayrac has the election wrapped up," others predicted.

From a distance, Benjamin watched Jean-Charles de Castayrac. He was wearing an appropriately solemn expression. But privately, Castayrac had to be gloating. With Nadaillac out of the way, his election as committee chairman was in the bag.

Benjamin stood beside Philippe and Beatrice de Bouglon at the cemetery. As was the tradition in Gascony, everyone threw a handful of earth on the coffin before making the sign of the cross. The winemaker followed suit and extended his condolences to the family at the cemetery gate. He was taken aback to see Alban de Castayrac refuse his father's embrace. An awkward moment followed, causing a stir in the crowd. Likewise, the widow and her daughter refused to shake the baron's hand.

Seeing this scene play out, Benjamin wondered if Castayrac realized at that exact moment

that his oppositional son was, indeed, dead serious about challenging him for the chairmanship of the committee. If so, the owner of Château Blanzac didn't show it. "My thoughts are with you," he told the widow before moving along.

Just then, a gust of wind lifted Mrs. de Nadaillac's veil. Benjamin wasn't surprised to see that her eyes were clear, and no mascara was running down her cheeks.

§ § §

The next day, when Benjamin slid the large manila envelope into the mailbox outside the post office, he knew his report would send shock waves through Protection Insurance. Benjamin's reservations were numerous, explicitly formulated, and thoroughly substantiated. Once again the winemaker from Bordeaux had demonstrated his expertise. In his detailed account, he had gone to great lengths to prove that the baron's claim differed significantly from the Cooker & Co. inventory. Even with a five to ten percent margin of error, the damage estimate was far less than what the injured party had claimed. Benjamin wrote in his conclusions:

Jean-Charles de Castayrac has admitted that a portion of the reserves stored in his Château Blanzac wine cellar was secretly disposed of before the December 24 fire. Given that admission, I would recommend consulting the Directorate-General of Customs and Indirect Taxes. Of course, the decision to initiate such action remains with your company. It would certainly have serious consequences for your client, who now heads the Armagnac Promotion Committee.

In reference to the appraisal performed at the site, it is highly likely that the maximum loss incurred by the claimant, Mr. Castayrac, is on the order of seventy-five hundred liters, of which barely ten percent could be considered centenarian. Based on the rate approved by the joint-trade association of Armagnac, the compensation should be approximately...

Benjamin had to literally stuff the envelope into the already-full mailbox. This was just a formality, though, as he had sent it by e-mail the day before. The insurance agents were probably already reading it.

Just as he was about to walk away, the baron's DS made a swift U-turn on the Promenade des Embarrats. Jean-Charles de Castayrac waved to the winemaker as he emerged from the car. The Blanzac owner wasn't a humble victor. He was swaggering. The board of directors of the Armagnac Promotion Committee had wasted no

time electing him chairman that very morning—
by a very large majority.

Before returning to Château Prada, Benjamin
decided to lose himself one more time in the
walled town of proud half-timber houses and
gleaming cobblestones. He was tempted to light
up a Lusitania but decided against it. His mind
was troubled. He didn't acknowledge Beatrice
and Philippe de Bouglon's kids as they passed
him, squabbling, on their way home from school.

Lost in thought, the winemaker quickened his
pace toward what looked, in the distance, like an
ancient washhouse. When he got there, he saw
that it was nothing more than a concrete basin
holding stagnant water. Beautiful washerwomen
and their hearty peals of laughter were just a
memory of times long gone. Nostalgic and per-
turbed, Benjamin stared at the duckweed floating
gently on a thick layer of sludge.

The following day, he would leave behind the
Bouglons' hospitality and this fortified town as old
as the Armagnac in its moldy wine cellars. In the
end, he hadn't been able to crack the secret of this
land, where vineyards vied with oak trees for supremacy. Listless and without any appetite, he was
heading toward the château by way of the Rue
des Pas-Perdus and the Rue des Fossés when he
spotted Virgile and Joachim hurrying toward him.

"Boss, I was taking one last look around the wine cellar at Blanzac, and I found something that looked suspicious."

Joachim, who hadn't even said hello, seemed to be breathing heavily. And his face looked tense.

"Too late, my boy. My report is already in the mail. Virgile, you know what I think of the baron. I don't believe I have anything more to say about the man's integrity."

"I know, boss. He's a small-time crook in your eyes. But what if he were a serious criminal?"

Benjamin was skeptical, but he would hear his assistant out. He reached for the double Corona in his coat pocket. Using his teeth, he severed the head of the cigar and lit the Havana. The nutty-smelling twenty centimeters seemed to disturb Joachim, who was wordlessly observing the scene. Virgile said nothing for a few seconds. He was familiar with this lighting ritual. The winemaker always insisted on a second puff to fully experience his cigar before he was ready to listen.

"Near the still that exploded, I found this in the ashes."

Benjamin put on his reading glasses and studied the piece of metal that Virgile had pulled from his pocket. It was barely two inches long and looked like a tube with a melted rod on top. It bore the stamp SGDG.

"So? This is your discovery?" Benjamin said, handing the object back to his assistant. "It's one

of the valves that connect the still's coils to the manometer. It's used to check the vapors."

"That's what you think!" Virgile responded, an excited look in his eyes. "You agree, boss, that it's made of brass?"

Benjamin looked at the object again and nodded.

"But we both know that all the components of an Armagnac still are made of copper."

"That's true," Benjamin said. He wanted to hear more.

"This is actually a butane lighter—a nickel-plated brass lighter."

"Look, sir," Joachim said, grabbing the piece of metal. "It has a tax seal."

"Yes, boss," Virgile said. "From 1911 to 1945, the '*Ministere Finances*' seal was required on practically all lighters. And every lighter manufacturer had to pay for the seal."

"How do you know this?" Benjamin asked.

"My grandfather Armand," Virgile said, clearly eager to continue his explanation. "Anyway, the government has always made money off smokers. When you buy your cigars, how much of the price do you think the Treasury Department gets?"

"Too much," Benjamin replied tersely.

"Three quarters, boss!"

"Virgile, you seem to know a lot about this subject."

"The drawers at my grandfather's house in Montravel were full of lighters. When I was a kid, Grandpa would sometimes let me light up the undergrowth. We were doing slash and burn, and we didn't even know it."

With a twist of the wrist, Joachim unscrewed the base of the lighter. The fuel reservoir was no larger than a thimble.

"Okay," Benjamin said. "We've got an old lighter here. It's quite a leap, however, to say that this proves Castayrac is a criminal. I admire your enterprise, Virgile, but you'll have to do more to persuade me."

Virgile fell silent and looked at his friend, whose face still looked full of tension. Benjamin's cigar was glowing brightly now, the wind from the west having picked up considerably.

"Well, go ahead. Tell him," Virgile insisted.

"It's odd," Joachim stammered. "But I'm certain that Francisco—I mean my father—never smoked."

"Are you sure?"

"I swear to God!" Joachim said. He was getting more agitated.

"That complicates matters," Benjamin said, sensing the young man's anger. He instinctively reached out and put a fatherly hand on Joachim's shoulder.

"That bastard wanted to burn down his cellars, and he killed my dad in the process! First he fires

my mom, then he kills my dad. I'll make that son of a bitch Castayrac pay. I'll kill him, just like he killed my father!"

Night had already fallen, and Joachim let out a howl for all the world to hear. It was the pain of a wounded and humiliated child. Alarmed dogs all around began barking, and Benjamin heard nearby shutters slam shut. Moaning, Joachim started running away. Virgile tried to catch him, but the nimble athlete disappeared under the arches of the Place Royale and slipped into the darkness.

Virgile gave Benjamin a helpless look.

"How dangerous is he, boy?"

"He's hurt, a bit emotional, but honestly, I don't think he'd hurt a fly."

"Go back to the Cantarels and wait for Joachim to return. I'll drive around and see if I can spot him."

After an hour of searching, in vain, Benjamin took out his cell phone and called the local police to tell them about the brass lighter and the hot-headed kid. When he mentioned the name Castayrac, the desk officer informed him that a team was already at Château Blanzac.

Crossing the Place des Ormeaux, Benjamin Cooker called home to tell Elisabeth that he would have to stay even longer. He heard her sigh, and he apologized. He would make it up to her. Right now he had to be where he was. Blanzac was far from revealing all its secrets, and he was

sure now that the findings in his report were null and void.

§ § §

As Benjamin drove up to Château Blanzac, he noted someone standing in a round attic window. Stiff and impassive, Valmont, the second son, was looking down on the courtyard. Indeed, it was a very odd spectacle. A procession of unmarked police cars, along with a van, was spread out on the château grounds. He parked and got out of his Mercedes.

Men in midnight-blue sweaters were quick to order Lord Castayrac to lower his voice. Certainly, this was his home, and he could boast the grandiose title of chairman of the Armagnac Promotion Committee, cry out in protest, and single-handedly represent the entire lot of regional producers, but that did not change the fact that the public prosecutor of Mont-de-Marson had issued a search warrant on behalf of the Directorate-General of Customs and Indirect Taxes.

The orchestrator of this lightning intervention, sturdy and hopelessly bald, was an educated man, and he intended to let the suspect know it.

"Lord Castayrac—since this is how you prefer to be addressed—your nobility does not put you

above the law. I believe your assistance could be interpreted as a form of voluntary cooperation in our search for the truth. That's in our mutual interest, is it not?"

The owner of Blanzac stopped resisting the inevitable. "Then go ahead, gentlemen. Search the whole place. But what exactly am I accused of?"

Meanwhile, the officers were calling to each other. "Hey, Chief!" "This too, Chief?" "Look, Captain!"

In the bustle, Benjamin had walked into the library, where he was met with gaping closet doors and heaps of ripped-open files. Bank statements and paperwork of every kind were strewn all over the floor.

Benjamin took a deep breath. This was his doing. Protection Insurance was living up to its name. The company had evidently agreed with his conclusions and suspected insurance fraud, as well as tax fraud stemming from the baron's covert sale of his Armagnac. The lighter would add another charge with consequences that were much more serious for the ruined aristocrat: destruction of property leading to unintentional death.

Castayrac's bathrobe, made of fine wool from the Pyrenees, was thrown over the back of the sofa. Benjamin just stood there, until he heard gravel crunching in the courtyard, car doors slamming, and engines starting. Then nothing. As he turned to leave, he saw Valmont in the doorway, silent,

with tears running down his face. He wouldn't be seeing his father again anytime soon.

Even the Bouglons' warmth and Beatrice's truffle omelet would not be enough to hearten Benjamin that evening.

§ § §

The next day the Saint-Justin Police Department received a second missing person's report. Alban de Castayrac, after his crushing defeat in the race for chairman of the committee, had not been seen since the election. His wife was worried sick, and his mother-in-law was praying to Saint Rita. It was said that both of them were inconsolable. Some residents spoke of suicide; others, in greater numbers, suspected he had run off because of a love affair gone sour.

But it was Joachim Cantarel's disappearance that worried Benjamin and Virgile. Both of them were aware of the fragile mental state of this great big fellow who fired up the crowds in the stadiums of Gascony.

Evelyne Cantarel was overcome with worry. Trying to be useful, her father started organizing a search in the surrounding woods. Joachim's teammates were distressed, too. Cazaubon was scheduled to play the team from Hagetmau later

in the week, and Joachim needed to show up. The first place in the Aquitaine league was at stake.

That night, a noise in the attic awakened Virgile. He held his breath. Had birds gotten in through a hole in the chimney? Then he heard other noises. Footsteps, muffled conversation, someone carefully shutting the attic door. Between the rumpled sheets, Virgile sensed heavy breathing in the hallway, near the stairs. He slipped out of his bed and quietly cracked his door. He watched as two shadows slipped down the stairs. The front door opened.

Now Virgile sprang into action—but not to shoo the pair out of the house. He wanted to make sure the second figure didn't get away. It was Joachim. Even in the dark, Virgile could see his emotional exhaustion. Virgile grabbed Joachim before he could take another step and dragged him to his bedroom. He ordered his friend to be quiet and lie down. No talking, just sleep.

Virgile wrapped himself in a quilt and collapsed in a tattered armchair, trying to wedge himself between the least uncomfortable springs. He was not reassured until he heard the rugby player fall into a deep slumber. Virgile thought of Constance. Nothing shy about her! He had wondered if birds were nesting in the attic. And they were, all right. Lovebirds!

The aroma of Arabica coffee soon wrested him from his restless dozing.

Evelyne Cantarel burst into tears when she learned that her son was home. She hugged Virgile as if he were a godsend and told her story. Yes, she had loved Francisco. And yes, she had lured him away from La Riquette. She had no regrets. Francisco was a free spirit and they had never married, but he was the only man she had ever loved.

"Tell me, Mrs. Cantarel," Virgile asked when she had finished her disclosures. "Do you believe the baron started the fire in his wine cellar?"

"I don't know," she responded, staring at her cup of café au lait.

"Do you hold him responsible for Francisco's death?"

"Who knows? The baron could have been responsible. But maybe he wasn't. I believe in fate, Mr. Virgile. This might sound horrible, but maybe Francisco's death was just meant to be. Do you really think it was a criminal act?"

"I'm not the only one to think so, Mrs. Cantarel. Joachim is convinced, too."

"Castayrac is certainly a swindler, and he sold his Armagnac under the table, but I don't think he would burn down his own cellar to collect the insurance, even if he was broke. People around here also say that he had to take out a mortgage on the house. Do you believe that, Mr. Virgile?"

"Who might have wanted to start the fire, if not him?" Virgile pressed.

"Who knows? Maybe it was Alban," the woman ventured in a conspiratorial tone. "That father and son hate each other so much."

They heard footsteps on the stairs. It was Evelyne's father, rosy-cheeked and clear-eyed. He had dreamed that his grandson had come home.

"You're right, Papa! Joachim is sleeping like a baby in Mr. Virgile's room."

"What an idiot! And here I rounded up all the hunters in town to comb the woods."

"Stop carrying on like that. You'll make your blood pressure go up."

"But good God, where was he hiding?"

Virgile put on his most innocent face to absolve his friend. "In a deep thicket perfect for emptying a cartridge belt!"

Old Cantarel showed his missing teeth in a peal of laughter that rang through the house. On this morning, no one drinking the smooth Arabica coffee in the Cantarel kitchen would be reproaching Joachim.

10

After breakfast, Virgile showed up at Château Prada, looking for Benjamin. Beatrice Bouglon told Virgile that the news of the baron's arrest had spread through Labastide like wildfire. People all over town were expressing mixed feelings about the whole sad affair. Few were shedding tears for the baron, but some were feeling sad for Evelyne Cantarel. She had never married Francisco, but she had certainly lost the love of her life, and everyone knew it.

"Benjamin's off at the market," she concluded.

"If you see him, tell him I'm with Joachim," Virgile said before leaving with a little skip in his step.

§ § §

An even row of corpses, most of them covered in white, lined the shelves. Shopping bags at the ready, women in berets and woolen shawls lifted

the cloth coverings to inspect the fowl, making sure there were no cuts or bruises. Plumpness was a priority, as well as an ample liver. Destined to be dismembered and cooked, the limp-necked ducks and geese practically implored the prospective buyers to put an end to their humiliating ordeal.

Despite the bitter cold, the Eauze market was teeming with noisy wildlife of the human kind. The morning meat market brought together people from all over the region. Benjamin was fond of this atmosphere of mysterious transactions, knowing smiles, euros quickly tucked into pockets, and handshake deals. It reminded him of the truffle markets in Lalbenque and Richerenches, gourmet pilgrimage sites. He loved to go to Lalbenque with Elisabeth. He wouldn't miss this tasty spectacle for anything in the world. It was more like horse trading than shopping.

In this bustling milieu, Benjamin came upon Alban de Castayrac, accompanied by his wife. So he had turned up. The Nadaillac son-in-law was strutting as if nothing had happened. His father was behind bars, and the APC had convened again that very morning to elect him chairman of the organization. There he was, shaking hands like a politician, plotting in a hushed tone with some of them, and gesturing dramatically with others. Alban de Castayrac knew how to work a crowd. Benjamin overhead snippets of his conversation, which ranged from the market value of

Armagnac to promised assistance from Brussels, which would curb the endemic crisis in the eau-de-vie trade. Jean-Charles de Castayrac's arrest and the resignation he was forced to submit a few hours thereafter had been quite convenient for Alban. Seeing him hold forth in this market, where he even slipped in some words in the local dialect, one couldn't help but wonder if the son had dealt his father's deathblow.

Alban de Castayrac walked toward the wine-maker. Benjamin knew it was more for the sake of courtesy than honest conversation.

"Still with us, Mr. Cooker? You must be very fond of Gascony!"

"You are fortunate, young man, to live in a part of the country that does not readily reveal itself. A person has to travel through it, sniff it, and tame it, in fact, to unlock all its mysteries. And heaven knows, everything is mysterious here. Don't you agree? Oh, by the way, congratulations on your election."

Alban took his wife by the elbow and melted into the crowd. Benjamin Cooker felt a little mischievous as he ambled toward a vendor selling hot chestnuts. Benjamin imagined that the man's face was just a bit anxious now and his handshake a tad weak.

The winemaker moved along, a warm paper cone in his hands. Seeing the ducks, he poked two or three with firm skin before settling on a fat

specimen. The vendor, an old wizened woman, assured him that the liver weighed at least two pounds. Benjamin was trusting enough to take her word for it.

He decided to return to Médoc that morning. Virgile would stay on, but he missed Elisabeth, who had graciously put up with his prolonged absence. When he got there, he would light up the fireplace and slow-cook the duck in one of the large copper pots hanging above the sideboard in the kitchen. He'd do the work, and Elisabeth could just enjoy the warmth of the fire. The ensuing meal would be devilishly caloric, and a little heavy on the salt, but what could be more flavorful than confit? At the Cookers, a Crozes-Hermitage, a Madiran, a Cahors, or an excellent Gaillac would transform this gluttonous meal into a feast fit for a king.

§ § §

That very evening, Joachim, quicker and more agile than ever, attended rugby practice. He made two conversions and scored a fantastic goal. Virgile, however, was not permitted on the field. The Cazaubon coach had not appreciated his outrageous lie and intended to make him pay for it.

The people of Gascony weren't the type to forget. Virgile would have to make note of that, but he thought the coach was overdoing it and grumbled over not being able to play. His friend tried to console him at the Café de la Poste with a Maison Gélas vintage Armagnac. A few words from Constance would have lifted his spirits, but she only had eyes for her hero of the night. The first place in the Aquitaine championship was within reach. The Hagetmau players would be weak in the knees and shaking with fear. As proud as an Andalusian and as obstinate as a Castilian, Joachim was ready to take all bets. But his apparent enthusiasm could not conceal all the unanswered questions coming to light with the sudden fall of Castayrac Armagnac.

Francisco: so meticulous. There was no way in the world that he could have caused that fire. He had distilled at Blanzac year after year for more than a half-century. What about the lighter that no investigator had taken the trouble to examine, somehow assuming it was an archaic part of the Armagnac still? And how could this wise cellar master have been in the dark about his employer's multiple and repeated crimes of deception? All that eau-de-vie spirited away in order to pay off the carefree baron's gambling debts. Surely Francisco knew about it. His silence was as valuable as his blendings!

"Castayrac figured he could reduce the place to ashes and start all over again, like that bird that rises from the ashes," Joachim said.

"The phoenix," Virgile replied as they drove along the road from Cazaubon to Labastide. "The baron had to be desperate to do something so extreme." No sooner had he said this than a figure sprang up from the side of the road and leaped in front of the car. Joachim swerved just in time to miss him.

"Who was that nut?" Virgile shouted.

"Was he trying to get himself killed? Shit, the rush of adrenalin! Are you sure we didn't hit him?"

"Stop, Joachim. We'd better check."

The car came to a stop in the middle of no-where. The beams from the headlights illuminated a stand of mossy oak trees and old bracken. The two athletes ran to the spot where they had seen the stranger. A nimble and graceful shadow finally rose up and quickly vanished into the fog-suffused woods.

"Forget about it, Joachim. He's a poacher. Look, he's running away like a rabbit."

"No, no," Joachim answered. "It's the Castayrac son Valmont. I'm sure of it. I'd bet my life on it."

"Come on, Joachim, you're seeing Castayracs all over the place!"

"No, Virgile. He has the eyes of a wolf. I'd recognize him anywhere."

"What's he doing around here at this hour?"

"I'm telling you, the whole family is crazy."

Once again, Virgile had trouble sleeping. To get at the truth, he had to figure out how to be as shrewd as his boss. Everything in Labastide, it seemed, was disturbing.

11

Virgile came through the gate at Château Prada just as the first glimmers of dawn were spilling over the countryside. Philippe de Bouglon, the only one awake at this hour, asked Virgile why he was up and about. Yes, he was a diligent and hard worker, but everyone needed a little sleep. Philippe had the bonhomie of people of the land who knew there was no need to rush in the winter. But he was unable to persuade the young assistant to go back to the Cantarels and get in another hour of sleep. So he offered Virgile some coffee. If he was going to be awake, he might as well be fully awake.

"I'm going to Blanzac," Virgile said after quickly downing the coffee. "I'll be back in an hour or two."

Virgile needed to satisfy his curiosity once and for all. Benjamin had often called him stubborn, and on that point the winemaker was entirely correct. Virgile didn't intend to let anything get in his way. He took off for Blanzac territory.

Only Athos and Aramis came to lick his hand. Porthos simply urinated copiously on the rear tire of the car he had borrowed from Joachim. He had an air of distrust punctuated by a licking of the chops. Virgile figured it was best to keep the dog at arm's length.

Virgile rapped on the door, but no human came to interrupt the dead silence of the place. Blanzac seemed abandoned. The winter cold reinforced this impression of rust, seeping humidity, and snuffed-out nature. In the courtyard strewn with dead leaves, ceramic pots had broken in the icy weather. The lingering odor of wet ashes irritated Virgile's throat, as if the fire were still smoldering within the collapsed walls, where the charred staves and beams lay tangled in a heap of ghostlike blackness. Completing this macabre impression, an ashen mist shrouded the copper of the disembodied still. In Virgile's eyes, the property had never looked so sinister.

"Valmont? Valmont?" Virgile called out.

No answer. The countryside was without a sound.

Failing to get a response from the mansion, Virgile decided to have another look at the cellar. He had explored every square inch. He knew each bit of rubble, having exhumed, examined, evaluated, and quantified all of it. The explosion and resulting fire had spared nothing. Each strip

of alcohol-soaked wood had been licked by the flames, roasted, and destroyed.

But once again he wandered into the rubble, kicking the muddy scraps of iron and wood as he poked through it. A thick lock was all that remained of the cellar door. He glanced at it— and looked again. Why on earth was the bolt engaged? Then it struck him. The cellar had been locked—from the outside! Francisco had never had a chance to escape. Joachim was right. His father had been murdered.

Virgile called his employer.

"Boss, sorry to disturb you, but you've got to hightail it back here. My apologies to Mrs. Cooker."

"What is it, son?"

"You'll see when you get here. And you'd better call the cops. I'm going to warm up at Prada. Call me when you get near. I'll meet you at Château Blanzac."

§ § §

As Benjamin got ready to leave Grangebelle, Elisabeth handed him cracklings for the Bouglons. She had carefully packaged the greasy treat in a small terrine covered with aluminum foil. Philippe and Beatrice were aware that Elisabeth's

maiden name was Darrozière, a name redolent of the Gascony countryside and slow-cooked food. They would certainly appreciate this gift, even if it was as common as Armagnac in their region.

The winemaker had to return to Labastide-d'Armagnac anyway to collect Virgile, who had stayed behind. He was just leaving a little earlier than planned. The investigation for Protection Insurance was wrapped up, and Benjamin's conclusions had evidently unleashed the wrath of the law and the tax authorities. Nevertheless, Castayrac's precipitous fall troubled him, and he couldn't dismiss his doubts. Virgile, on the other hand, had no misgivings about the baron's culpability. Especially in light of his new friendship with Joachim, nothing would change his mind. Even that opportunist Alban found favor in his eyes.

§ § §

An hour and twenty-eight minutes later, the winemaker arrived at Château Blanzac with two reluctant-looking officers.

Benjamin turned to Virgile. "Well, what do you have to show us, Virgile?"

The assistant handed over his evidence. Benjamin examined it for a few moments and then

gave it to the police officers. "It appears, gentlemen, that the cellar was locked from the outside."

From the beginning, the police—and just about everyone else in the region—had theorized that Francisco Vasquez's death was accidental.

"Considering Mr. Castayrac's reputation..." one of the officers stammered.

His fellow officer looked at Virgile and then at Benjamin.

"Mr. Cooker, will you authorize us to take credit for this crucial discovery by your invaluable colleague?"

"You need to ask him yourself. It isn't my decision to make," Benjamin grumbled.

Virgile shrugged. Although he felt like saying more, "yeah" was his only response.

The two officers walked over to their van, carefully took off their shoes, and pulled on khaki waders, which made them look ridiculous. They started searching for new clues in the charred debris.

With little to do, Benjamin tugged at Virgile's coat sleeve. "Come with me, Virgile. I can't resist stealing another look at the black Citroën DS hibernating at the back of the garage. I know you appreciate vintage cars too. After all, you have one yourself."

The Citroën was covered in canvas. Only the shiny hubcaps were visible. Virgile could tell that the winemaker's desire to slip into this sleek 1957

car—aerodynamic before its time—was irresistible. Benjamin started to lift the cover. Not one
second later, a beady-eyed Valmont de Castayrac
emerged from the shadows.

"I believe I already told you, Mr. Cooker. This
car is absolutely not for sale!"

Instantly, Virgile recognized the supple and robust figure, which the night before had appeared
ready to throw himself under the car.

§ § §

Benjamin slipped into the back of the public hearing room, hoping not to be noticed. Jean-Charles
de Castayrac kept proclaiming his innocence
and denouncing the plot against him. Brought
before the prosecutor, he cited his entire family
tree, the war records of his ancestors, and his
tireless battle to promote Armagnac throughout
the world as evidence of his good character. But
the Landes public prosecutor remained implaca-
ble. The baron's forebears and efforts on behalf
of Armagnac—which weren't selfless, because he
benefitted from them—did not make him a man
of virtue. Indeed, Castayrac had admitted his
bankruptcy, his chronic inability to manage his
property, and his weakness for gambling, society
life, and beautiful women. He also admitted to

the staggering amount of money he had taken from his in-laws before his wife's death to cover his abysmal losses from a deal gone bad.

"They were already so rich, sir, with their Alvignac spring water!" Castayrac had shouted.

To which the prosecutor responded, "You were just as rich from your own waters: eau-de vie!"

But the cavalier and frivolous behavior of the cynical baron wasn't what mattered most to the public servant. The baron had cheated the tax authorities, carried out insurance fraud, and, even more important, committed arson. His own cellar master had died in that fire.

"Does it take courage or heartlessness to set fire to one's own property?" the infuriated prosecutor had asked.

"But I am utterly incapable of that, sir."

"Incapable of love, yes. That I believe. You knowingly locked Francisco Valdez, the unfortunate man who had been faithful to your family for almost a half century, in your wine cellar before reducing it to ashes."

"I did nothing of the sort."

"Everyone knows that you had defaulted on your mortgage, and Crédit Agricole was planning to sell your estate at auction. Only the insurance payout could save you from disgrace."

"I admit I was in a bad situation, but good heavens, I never could have committed such an act!"

"Can you provide the slightest alibi to suggest that on December 24th you were not at Blanzac?"

The baron was quiet for a long time, as if he had run out of arguments.

"None," he finally said, running a weary hand through his hair. "Forgive me, sir, I don't feel very well."

"And for the very good and sole reason that I have put my finger where it hurts. Blanzac was going to be sold, and you were angry with your older son, the only one who could have helped you."

"Alban? You must be kidding! Him, help me? He never stopped humiliating me or prowling like a vulture around Blanzac to the point of trying to dispossess me. As recently as last week, he was my fiercest rival for the chairmanship of the APC! No, if you have to point the finger at someone, sir, you should be looking at him."

"I knew you were capable of many things," the prosecutor insisted, adjusting his glasses. "But with you, the worst is always yet to come. Incriminating your own son to clear your name! No one's buying it. You're providing enough rope to hang yourself. What interest would your offspring have had, no matter how ungrateful he was, to set your wine cellar ablaze? He's not the one who stood to collect the fat check from the insurance company. And why would he have done away with Francisco, as well? I believe

the relationship between your cellar master and Alban was quite friendly."

"I cannot answer that question, sir. For all I know, his father-in-law was conspiring with the bank to buy the estate, and he planned to hand it over to Alban. Nadaillac would have gained control of one of his biggest competitors, and Alban would have been his own boss. My son never had many scruples."

"And neither do you, it appears."

With his head in his hands, Jean-Charles de Castayrac seemed to be trying to drown out the relentless accusations of the prosecutor. The light from the man's desk lamp illuminated the baron's signet ring. One could make out perfectly the Castayrac coat of arms: two unicorns and two matching trefoils.

"I believe we'll leave it at that for today," the prosecutor said, placing his pen in the white porcelain inkwell from another era.

The guards posted behind the suspect put their caps back on and got ready to leave. The hearing was over.

"When you feel the pangs of remorse, Mr. Castayrac, let me know. We'll save time that way. As uncomfortable as Château Blanzac may be, it's still warmer than our jails."

"Actually, I find your cell sufficiently comfortable, sir," the aristocrat answered, throwing his shoulders back.

"Lock him up until further notice," the prosecutor grumbled.

"Very well, sir," the first guard responded, taking the baron by the arm and leading him away. Benjamin noted that the prosecutor looked like an anachronism. His silk pinstriped suit looked like it was made by an eighty-year-old tailor. His bearing was pompous, and his voice was high-pitched.

§ § §

Back in his office, the prosecutor rose from his chair, walked over to the old cast-iron radiator, and warmed his hands while watching the van haul the fallen baron off to the old jail. Then he walked back to his Empire-style desk, picked up his telephone, and called the chief of police in Saint-Justin.

"Magistrate Canteloube here. I need you to do something for me. Pick up Alban Castayrac and bring him in. Right away."

§ § §

"With a father like that, I understand why Alban took off," Virgile told Benjamin during their lunch at Prada. "He would have married anyone to get away from Blanzac. It just happens that he made out rather well by marrying a Nadaillac."

"It seems to be a theme in the Castayrac family," Benjamin said. "The baron himself profited quite handsomely from his marriage."

Philippe and Beatrice de Bouglon were watching this exchange in silence. But after a few sips of a Henri Leroy Romanée-Conti, unearthed from the dark vaults of the Prada cellar, they added their own views. Philippe sided with Benjamin, who was having second thoughts about the whole matter, while Beatrice shared Virgile's opinion.

"There've always been rumors about the old man," Beatrice said. "Remember that underage girl? And the shadowy deals he's made—the people he's cheated. I wouldn't trust him for a minute."

"Beatrice, honey, hardly any of that stuff has ever been proved. It's talk. That's all."

"As far as I'm concerned, where there's smoke, there's fire!"

"In this particular case, my dear Bea, you couldn't be more right!" Benjamin burst into a hearty laugh, followed by Virgile and then Philippe de Bouglon, whose handsome musketeer moustache was glistening with duck-crackling grease.

The lunch was filled with racy stories about the baron and his wife. Tales of the couple's sexual antics—both factual and rumored—kept the four of them entertained to the last bite. La Riquette, the descendant of the famous Alvignac spring waters, wasn't one to forgive and forget. Betrayed by her frivolous husband, she had cheerfully given the baron a taste of his own medicine. Beatrice confirmed what the baron himself had confessed to Benjamin: Alban was the fruit of an adulterous relationship between Elise de Castayrac and a wine trader from Bordeaux, a "great friend of the family."

"And what about Valmont?" asked Virgile.

"As for the second son, they say he's the son of—"

Hearing a car pull into the château courtyard, the diners looked up. When the doorbell rang, Philippe de Bouglon wiped his moustache with the corner of his napkin as he rose from his chair to answer the doorbell. "Could we possibly have lunch in peace someday?"

The winemaker heard an exchange of polite greetings in the Prada entryway. "Benjamin, it's for you!" Philippe called out.

Who would be looking for him? He gave Virgile and Beatrice an inquisitive look. Shrugging, he took another sip of his Romanée-Conti and stood up to find out who had dared to disturb such a fine meal.

"Mr. Cooker? Delighted. Eric Canteloube, Landes public prosecutor. May I have a word with you in private? I'll be very brief. I know your time is valuable."

Although he was polite enough, there was something imperious in his manner that irritated Benjamin. No doubt, this representative of the law in a silk suit was used to intimidating people.

"The parlor is at your disposal," Philippe said as he slipped into the kitchen.

The prosecutor took in the room, examining the paintings and photographs attesting to the lineage of the Bouglon family, and then sat in an armchair that swallowed him. He looked like a pale and sickly wren. Benjamin wondered how a man with such a frail physique could have such an overbearing presence. Indeed, sitting in the oversized chair, a pigskin briefcase propped in his lap, he seemed quite satisfied with the power his position conferred on him.

Philippe de Bouglon popped his head through another door, a bit like a scene from a comedy. "Can I offer you a Prada Armagnac, gentlemen?" Philippe asked.

The prosecutor declined the offer as if it were an indecent proposal. Benjamin, on the other hand, cheerfully told his friend, "Break open your 1983. That's a winner if ever there was one."

The winemaker noticed the reproving look on the prosecutor's face. The man wasted no time

as he launched into the reason for his visit. The Castayrac affair was about to be settled once and for all. He admitted that it had taken him awhile to believe that Jean-Charles de Castayrac was a criminal who had acted with premeditation. He thanked the famed winemaker for his investigation, which had implicated the baron. Benjamin was tempted to point out that it was Virgile who had discovered the evidence that conclusively refuted the accidental-fire theory. But he didn't interrupt the prosecutor. The man was loquacious and confident. Finally, speaking in a hushed tone, the prosecutor divulged what he considered a secret.

"Imagine, Mr. Cooker. Castayrac went so far as to accuse his own son!"

"Which one?" Benjamin asked.

"Alban, of course! The president of the APC."

The old man, according to Canteloube, harbored a profound hatred for his older son. The baron had accused Alban of masterminding the fire in order to hasten his bankruptcy and foreclosure.

As the prosecutor spoke, he became increasingly passionate and finally leaped from his chair.

"A bit of 1983 Prada, Mr. Canteloube? Frankly, you're denying yourself one the best eau-de-vies in Bas-Armagnac. And offending our host!"

"One drop, then," the prosecutor replied, indicating with his thumb and index finger that he wanted only a little bit.

"I agree that the son doesn't seem to be as white as the driven snow," Benjamin said, pouring more Armagnac in his tulip glass after serving the prosecutor.

"He's ambitious, I'll gladly concede. Even an opportunist. I suspect he's more devious than his father. But he wasn't in Gascony on December 24th. He has an alibi, rather shameful but indisputable. We checked."

"Meaning?" Benjamin asked. Now he was curious.

"On December 23rd and 24th, Alban de Castayrac was at Fauchon Paris promoting Nadaillac Armagnac. Accompanying him on this trip was his devoted colleague, who is also his mistress, a woman named Sylvaine Malric. An employee at Fauchon confirmed the presence of both of them and witnessed some very affectionate exchanges between the two."

The prosecutor was smiling for the first time. His coy attitude only added to the humor Benjamin found in his haughty demeanor and affected presentation. It was even more comical than the tales of Lord Castayrac's shenanigans that Philippe and Beatrice had shared just a short time earlier.

"You see, Mr. Cooker, it's all clear now—"

A knock at the double doors interrupted the prosecutor. Before Benjamin could respond, Virgile was in the room. He looked upset. "Excuse

me, boss, but I'm running back to the Cantarels' place," he said. "Joachim's grandfather just had a heart attack. He's hanging on by a thread."

"Go on ahead, my boy. I'll join you momentarily!"

Virgile's announcement put an end to the prosecutor's narrative. The ascetic hadn't even sampled the 1983 Prada. Benjamin concluded definitively that the man wasn't worthy of his esteem. And therefore, his judgments were suspect.

§ § §

When the winemaker arrived at the Cantarel home, Evelyne's eyes were red, and she had her arms around her son. Edmond, her father, was gone. He had died in a matter of minutes—just enough time for the old woodcock hunter to ease his conscience and depart the world in peace.

"No, it's not possible that Castayrac set fire to his wine cellar to collect the insurance money," Edmond had said. "He downgraded his policy a month before the fire, and he knew he was under-insured. I warned him that this was a very risky move. He said, 'My dear Cantarel, my finances will not allow me to pay more. Let's just hope that nothing happens.'"

Already, the priest had appeared, and neighbors were beginning to stream through the door. Following tradition, they covered the mirrors and stopped the grandfather clock's pendulum. They had to start preparing the body for burial right away. Edmond's old spaniel kept scratching at the door. Sensing that the dog was already missing his master, Benjamin let him in and allowed him to settle at his feet.

12

In the countryside of Gascony, far from the big cities where funeral services and burials were efficient and often cookie-cutter, traditions and rites for the departed were immutable. The funeral Mass was always celebrated with incense, prayers, and holy water. Granted, the wake no longer lasted all day and all night, but friends and neighbors paid their respects at the home of the deceased. It was expected, Philippe de Bouglon said as he put his hat back on after leaving the Cantarels' home.

Certainly, Benjamin wasn't at the Cantarels because it was expected. He understood that this was a grievous loss for a warm and simple family. Without Edmond, Evelyne would have had a much harder time raising Joachim. He had been a generous and attentive substitute father to the boy. Now Joachim's teammates were beginning to shuffle in, giving their friend clumsy hugs and pats on the back.

Edmond Cantarel's funeral was scheduled for ten o'clock in the morning. Naturally, the entire town of Labastide would crowd into the church.

Since 1967, he had insured half the residents of this community, and according to everyone, he was a good man who conducted himself with honesty and integrity. It was custom here not to speak ill of the dead. But nobody would have said anything bad about Edmond Cantarel anyway. His only enemies were the woodcocks.

With the Cantarel house full of people, Benjamin took Virgile aside.

"My boy, your friend is in good hands here. What do you say we make another visit to Blanzac?"

"Why's that, boss?"

"Castayrac could not have set fire to his reserves, the old man said. But somebody did. Let's go see what we overlooked."

Château Blanzac was only a mile and a half from the village, and they traversed it quickly, as the weather was windy and wet. Benjamin recognized René Dardolive, the distiller, coming from Domaine de La Coste. He waved to him. René responded with a rather silly smile.

When they arrived at Blanzac, Benjamin and Virgile were soaked. Athos, Porthos, and Aramis undertook to stir the sole occupant of the grounds, but no one came to the door. The courtyard was muddy, and the hood of the DS 19 was raised, making the front of the car look like a gaping mouth ready to swallow anyone who approached.

Benjamin raised the knocker and tapped the door lightly. In vain. Evidently, Blanzac had been given over to the elements. Some of the windows were broken. Others were wide open, and their shutters were banging in the wind. Benjamin and Virgile were looking at each other and wondering what to do when they heard a thud inside the house. Virgile pushed on the door. It didn't resist. They hurried into the vestibule, and Benjamin searched for the light switch to dispel the shadows.

"Shit! No light!" Benjamin cursed.

Virgile motioned to Benjamin to follow him. He clicked on his lighter to see where he was going. But before the winemaker could take even a step, he felt something jabbing his lower back. Was it the barrel of a rifle?

"Don't move, you looters! Don't move, I said, or I'll shoot you like rabbits!"

Benjamin recognized Valmont's voice. He tried to turn around and give an explanation, but a bullet rang out and lodged in the eye of Jean-Sébastien de Castayrac, whose mediocre and charmless portrait adorned the hallway. The painting fell from the wall and broke apart at Benjamin's feet. The winemaker began to pick up the gilded wood frame; immediately a second salvo confirmed the young Castayrac's resolve.

Benjamin looked up from the portrait, and in his peripheral vision he saw a flickering light. Was it a candle? A flashlight? A lighter? A third shot

exploded a demijohn, which immediately sent its eau-de-vie spreading across the floor. Realizing what Valmont planned to do next, Benjamin did an about-face and grabbed the barrel of the gun. Looking him in the eye, Benjamin disarmed the pyromaniac assailant. Virgile wasted no time and threw himself on the young Castayrac. He punched him twice, knocking Valmont unconscious.

"You're going at it a bit too hard, Virgile," Benjamin said, feeling how badly out of shape he was.

"Too hard? I didn't intend to let myself get roasted by a lunatic! And while I'm on the subject, I'm grateful that you managed to get that gun away from him, but you were taking an awfully big chance, wouldn't you say?"

"Yes, I have to agree with you, Virgile," Benjamin said, laboring to catch his breath. "Let's not tell Elisabeth about this. In any case, Valmont de Castayrac has just signed his own indictment."

The unconscious man looked entirely peaceful, despite the trickle of blood running from his nose. His shoulders rose and fell with each breath. After tying him up with wire from the garage, Virgile looked for the bathroom and came back with a wet washcloth. He carefully wiped Valmont's face. Then he carried him to a couch in the library, where he slowly came to.

Benjamin Cooker shut all the open windows and closed the shutters over the broken ones. The wind had not abated, and the rain was causing the gutters to keen. Then he started feeding vine stalks and wood into the fireplace. They needed some warmth. As he did at Grangebelle, he placed two bundles of vine stalks and three blocks of oak on the andirons. Virgile was about to light the vines with Valmont's lighter, a Winchester model from the nineteen forties, when Benjamin stopped him.

"Incriminating evidence, Virgile. You would make a very poor police officer."

"Well, I don't think you'll be recruited by any SWAT team in the near future. You could use a workout or two."

The winemaker smiled. "A word of advice, Virgile: don't ever change. Never take yourself too seriously."

Then, as if he owned the place, he walked to the other end of the library and went down the steps to the private reserve where the baron kept his oldest bottles. He rummaged around and unearthed a vial that was perfectly caramel in color. Written on the label in careful calligraphy:

1964
First blending made by
Francisco Vasquez
Cellar master at Château Blanzac
LABASTIDE-D'ARMAGNAC

The winemaker went into the kitchen and came back with two mismatched glasses. He poured a generous serving in each of the two goblets. Benjamin and Virgile raised their glasses and sipped.

"I don't know, boss," Virgile said, giving Valmont a worried look. "I think I may have hit him too hard."

Benjamin walked over to their bound assailant and held his glass under his nose. A second later, Valmont opened his eyes.

"So, young man, do you have anything to say in your defense?" Benjamin asked, using an ember to light his Cohiba.

The last son of the long line of Gascony aristocrats looked nothing like a dangerous aggressor, but rather like a boy who was unnerved and deeply humiliated by the blood flowing through his veins. Benjamin thought it must have been the years of crying that had taken all the color from his eyes. The winemaker and Virgile fell silent and listened to his monologue, interrupted from time to time by the crackling of the oak log in the fireplace.

"I know, Mr. Cooker, that I will never find favor in the eyes of the law. You'd have to live at Blanzac to understand what can push a person to dire measures. A father who ignores you and spends money that he doesn't have anymore. A brother who hates you as if you were not related.

Ruin, bankruptcy, disrepute. I knew Blanzac was going to be sold. The bank had already talking about repossessing. My father had threatened to commit suicide many times in front of me. So, on Christmas Eve, I decided to burn down the wine cellar. It was the only way to save Blanzac. With the money from the insurance, we could have salvaged the Castayrac honor. It was a matter of life and death, Mr. Cooker. Do you understand?"

Benjamin remained silent. He had put down Francisco's Armagnac to give Valmont his full attention. Virgile had stretched out on one of the library rugs and was tracing the design with his fingers.

"Only Francisco would have known that I was the one who was setting the cellar on fire. So I closed the door and locked it, and I went into the Fatsillières Forest and threw the key into the pond, near the roadside cross. Then I watched the cellar burn. Not a long time—just until I called the fire department."

The oak logs were nearly consumed, and the fire was no longer warming Virgile's back. He threw the remaining contents of his glass of Armagnac on the embers, and the hearth was momentarily engulfed in flames.

"I didn't hear Francisco scream. And then there was a series of explosions. Yes, I think I did hear a scream. Just one."

Valmont de Castayrac was no longer crying.

Virgile looked at Benjamin, who nodded. Benjamin handed his glass of Armagnac to his assistant. Virgile swallowed it in one gulp and stood up to release his hostage from the wire that was cutting into his wrists.

"Listen, Valmont, you need to know something: the person you killed in that fire wasn't just your cellar master."

Virgile couldn't find the words. His throat was dry, his voice lifeless. Unable to endure it any longer, Benjamin walked over to his assistant and put his hand on his shoulder. "Tell the boy. You're the one who needs to do it."

So, looking straight into Valmont's eyes, Virgile said the unspeakable.

"He was your father."

His face haggard, the younger son of Elise Riquet de Lauze, wife of Lord Castayrac, didn't raise a word of objection.

He stared at them, his eyes blank. "I know."

Nobody spoke for a long while. Then Valmont explained. "Last week, right before the police came to arrest father—I mean Castayrac—Joachim Cantarel showed up with a rifle, yelling that he was going to kill his father's murderer. In a rage, Joachim had spit out his mother's confession: she had been involved in a crazy love affair with Francisco while he was sleeping with my Elise Riquet de Lauze."

Valmont looked out the window. "Want to know his exact words? 'Even though Francisco had already knocked up your whore of a mother! When your mother found out that her valiant cellar master had switched beds for a girl more in keeping with his class, that was too much humiliation. When you were born, she threw my mother out without a penny of compensation! The man you called your father your whole life—a first-class cheater and a cuckold himself a hundred times over—didn't lift a finger. Let's talk about the Castayrac honor!' Those were his words."

If Edmond Cantarel's rifle hadn't jammed, Joachim would have killed his half-brother.

Valmont stared fixedly at Virgile. He seemed to expect neither pity nor forgiveness. The steeliness of his eyes could have been interpreted as a challenge. Actually, it mirrored one of his mother's favorite sayings: "The eyes of a Castayrac, in order to shine, must be dry." He had been too sad for most of his life to follow that advice.

Breaking the silence, which had become untenable, Benjamin picked up the bottle of 1964 Armagnac, pulled off the cork with his teeth, filled his glass to the top, and handed it to Francisco Vasquez's son, who emptied it without wincing. The boy wiped his lips on the back of his sleeve and flashed a proud smile redolent of fresh nuts and candied plum.

"Let's get it over with, Mr. Cooker. Call the police."

EPILOGUE

Virgile remained in Labastide-d'Armagnac. He had promised Joachim that he would be his most fervent supporter in the match against Hagetmau. He would be in the Cazaubon stands, yelling, screaming, and generally cheering on his new friend. "You'll bring me luck," Francisco's son had told him this with so much emotion, Virgile wouldn't have dreamed of letting him down.

At each attempted conversion, the striker with the amazing kick looked into the bleachers for his friend's approval. Virgile would give Joachim a thumbs-up, and his friend would return it. Sitting at Virgile's right, Constance was elated. When the final whistle blew, she hugged Virgile. They remained in a momentary embrace while the architect of the Cazaubon victory was congratulated by his teammates. A reporter from *Midi Olympique* photographed Joachim smiling triumphantly as he threw his jersey into the delirious crowd. The final score: 39 to 12.

Joachim Cantarel's future as an athlete looked promising. Indeed, the presidents of some regional

clubs were waiting for him outside the locker room. Joachim ignored them and rushed into the arms of Constance and Virgile. His happiness was theirs. "*Victorioso! Victorioso!*" he yelled in Spanish, feverishly kissing the medal hanging from his neck—a silver one that Francisco had brought back from a pilgrimage to Lourdes. Joachim was only seven at the time. Looking curiously at the medal, he had asked his mother, "Who's she?" "That's Mary, the mother of God," Evelyne Cantarel had answered. "And me: you are my mother, but who is my father?" the little boy had asked. Francisco had smiled and raced to the river with his lover and son, playfully splashing them when they finally got there.

§ § §

Baron Jean-Charles de Castayrac was sentenced to four years in prison for insurance and tax fraud. After his release, he never returned to Labastide-d'Armaganac. Some said he had gone to Biarritz, where an old lover, recently widowed, had taken him in. Others, however, said the woman wasn't widowed at all. She was merely separated, and her angry husband had shown up one night and shot the baron dead. Whether Castayrac was alive or not, no one seemed to care.

Valmont de Castayrac appeared in Landes criminal court. The nine jurors acknowledged mitigating circumstances but still recommended a sentence of twelve years. He would be eligible for parole after serving seven years.

Shortly after his transfer to the central penitentiary in Seysses, Valmont received a letter from Joachim Cantarel. The Toulouse rugby team's new recruit announced his impending selection for the national team, which would soon compete in the Six Nations Tournament. He promised Valmont a visit in the very near future and told him the DS was safely parked in his garage, covered with a sheet. "It awaits your release," he said before closing his letter with "warm brotherly regards."

Thank you for reading Flambé in Armagnac.

We invite you to share your thoughts and reactions on your favorite social media and retail platforms.

We appreciate your support.

THE WINEMAKER DETECTIVE SERIES

A total epicurean immersion in French countryside and gourmet attitude with two expert winemakers turned amateur sleuths gumshoeing around wine country. The following titles are currently available in English.

Treachery in Bordeaux

Barrels at the prestigious grand cru Moniales Haut-Brion wine estate in Bordeaux have been contaminated. Is it negligence or sabotage? Cooker and his assistant Virgile Lanssien search the city and the vineyards for answers, giving readers and inside view of this famous wine region.

www.treacheryinbordeaux.com

Grand Cru Heist

After Benjamin Cooker's world gets turned upside down one night in Paris, he retreats to the region around Tours to recover. There, he and his assistant Virgile turn PI to solve two murders and very particular heist. Who stole those bottles of grand cru classé?

www.grandcruheist.com

Nightmare in Burgundy

The Winemaker Detective leaves his native Bordeaux for a dream wine tasting trip to Burgundy that turns into a troubling nightmare when he stumbles upon a mystery revolving around messages from another era. What do they mean? What dark secrets from the deep past are haunting the Clos de Vougeot?

www.nightmareinburgundy.com

Deadly Tasting

In a new Winemaker Detective adventure, a serial killer stalks Bordeaux. To understand the wine-related symbolism, the local police call on the famous wine critic Benjamin Cooker. The investigation leads them to the dark hours of France's history, as the mystery thickens among the once-peaceful vineyards of Pomerol.

www.deadlytasting.com

Cognac Conspiracies

The heirs to one of the oldest Cognac estates in France face a hostile takeover by foreign investors. Renowned wine expert Benjamin Cooker is called in to audit the books. In what he thought was a sleepy provincial town, he and his assistant Virgile have their loyalties tested.

www.cognacconspiracies.com

Mayhem in Margaux

Summer brings the Winemaker Detective's daughter to Bordeaux, along with a heatwave. Local vintners are on edge, But Benjamin Cooker is focused on solving a mystery that touches him very personally. Along the way he finds out more than he'd like to know about the makings of a grand cru classé wine.

<u>www.mayheminmargaux.com</u>

About the Authors

Noël Balen (left) and Jean-Pierre Alaux (right).
(©David Nakache)

Jean-Pierre Alaux and **Noël Balen** came up with the Winemaker Detective over a glass of wine, of course. Jean-Pierre Alaux is a magazine, radio, and television journalist when he is not writing novels in southwestern France. He is a genuine wine and food lover, and won the Antonin Carême prize for his cookbook *La Truffe sur le Soufflé*, which he wrote with the chef Alexis Pélissou. He is the grandson of a winemaker and exhibits a real passion for wine and winemaking. For him, there is no greater common denominator than wine. Coauthor of the series Noël Balen lives in Paris, where he shares his time between writing, making records, and lecturing on music. He plays bass, is a music critic, and has authored a number of books about musicians, in addition to his novel and short-story writing.

ABOUT THE TRANSLATOR

Sally Pane studied French at State University of New York Oswego and the Sorbonne before receiving her master's degree in French literature from the University of Colorado, where she wrote *Camus and the Americas: A Thematic Analysis of Three Works Based on His Journaux de Voyage.* Her career includes more than twenty years of translating and teaching French and Italian at Berlitz. She has worked in scientific, legal, and literary translation; her literary translations include several books in the Winemaker Detective series. In addition to her passion for French, she has studied Italian at the University of Colorado in Boulder, in Rome and in Siena. She lives in Boulder, Colorado, with her husband.

"You'll travel to France to taste the complex flavors, the unraveling of a mystery, while relishing the French countryside, the gourmet dishes, and the simple pleasurable delight of this rare series."

—5-star educator review

"A smooth, jubilatory discovery of French wine country. I love these."

—5-star reader review

"A good vintage with tasty dialogue and a solid plot."

—*Tele-loisir*

"A fine vintage."

—Award-winning mystery writer Peter May

PRAISE

"For me, this series is like a gift... It takes you on a journey."
—Actor Pierre Arditi, who stars in the TV series

"Difficult to forget and oddly addictive... deserves a high mark for keeping the answers hidden and the pages turning."
—*ForeWord Reviews*

"Another clever and highly entertaining mystery by an incredibly creative writing duo, never disappointing, always marvelously atypical."
—*Unshelfish*

"It is full of intrigue and deceit, and it kept me turning pages and guessing. A very pleasant and enticing read, with a few epicurean suggestions."
—*Books Chatter*

"This is a fun and informative take on the cozy crime mystery, French style."
—*Eurocrime*

"This is is a quick, pleasant read, a good introduction to the country's culinary charms and regional beauty."
—*Crime Fiction Lover*

HISTORY, ART
AND CULTURE

Provence is the name generally given to the entire southeastern part of France. It includes the area known historically as Provence together with the former papal possessions of Avignon and the Venaissin, which border it, and the cities of Orange in the west and Nice in the east. Over the centuries it remained, more or less, a single regional entity until just after the French Revolution, when Provence and its neighboring regions were divided up into new administrative districts (départements). Today these are Alpes-de-Haute-Provence, Alpes-Maritimes, Bouches-du-Rhône, Var, and Vaucluse.

Lying between the Mediterranean, the Rhône valley, and the Alps, Provence offers a cross section of the classic Mediterranean landscape in all its fascinating variety. To the west, countless marshy lakes and lagoons have formed in the flood plain of the lower Rhône valley and in the Camargue. This part of Provence is a vast area of flat countryside, easily cultivated and irrigated, stretching from the Rhône to the valley of its tributary, the Durance. The rest of Provence is either hilly or mountainous. From the Etang de Berre eastward to the Italian border the coastline is characterized by many steep, rugged cliffs and deep inlets – known as calanques – occasionally giving way to flat beaches of the finest sand.

Inland, the landscape alternates between small, fertile plains used for in-

Preceding pages: An experienced boules player having a rest between games. Lavender fields in bloom on the slopes of the Plateau de Valensole. The Pont du Gard, an impressive masterpiece dating from Roman times. Left: The bridge at Arles, immortalized in one of Van Gogh's most famous paintings.

tensive agriculture, and the garrigues, where centuries of deforestation and consequent erosion have left only a thin layer of soil covering the rocks. This impoverished landscape supports only the typical maquis vegetation, consisting of such hardy species as heather, juniper, myrtle, broom and turpentine trees, although there is the occasional wooded hill.

Further inland, the truly mountainous areas of Provence begin: first the plateaux of Vaucluse and Valensole, and then, further west, the mountain ranges stretching from the Lubéron to Mont Ventoux (1909 m/6263 ft). The mountains of Digne, Castellane and Grasse are steep, extremely rugged and deeply fissured with ravines, so that many of the valleys are only accessible by mountain passes used for centuries as trading routes.

The French word "Provence" is derived from the Latin *provincia,* which, as one might guess, means "province," and it is well named – in the course of its long, eventful history Provence has practically never enjoyed independence. For almost 600 years it was a province of the Roman Empire and later it became part of the Frankish kingdom.

Later still, it changed hands several times among Catalonian and French noble families, and was finally added to the lands of the French Crown in 1481. Avignon alone was the exception: when it was suddenly elevated to the position of Papal Residence in the 14th century, it had already been, for some time, an independent kingdom.

For most of its history Provence was not a rich region. The many wild, almost inaccessible mountainous areas, and comparatively few stretches of flat countryside, combined with the hot, dry climate have been an obstacle to cultivation. Despite this drawback, the geographical position of Provence on the shores of the Mediterranean has made it a corridor for the movement, goods, ideas

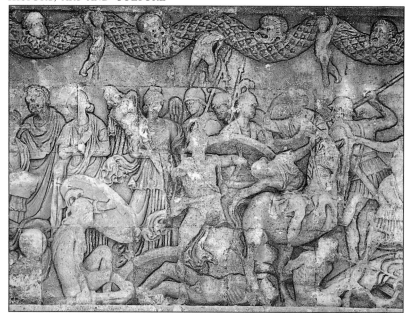

and culture. Over the centuries, Provence was able to develop its own special character by synthesizing the many influences that came from outside. These ranged from a strong Latin influence during the period of the Roman Empire – including the construction of the major Roman roads across the Alps – the period when the popes resided in Avignon, the French influence, which gave the region its language and culture, and, finally, a constant influx of ideas and culture from more distant countries that traded with Marseilles.

THE LEGACY OF ANTIQUITY

Prehistory

Provence is known to have been inhabited since the Mesolithic period (Middle Stone Age). Evidence of early sheep farming, cereal cultivation and pot-

Above: A section of the relief on the Roman Mausoleum near Saint-Rémy.

tery manufacture is used to pinpoint the beginning of the Neolithic or Late Stone Age, when a hunter-gatherer lifestyle was superseded by a pastoral and agricultural society. What is also referred to as the "Neolithic Revolution" came very early to this region, possibly earlier than anywhere else in Western Europe except for Italy. Excavations in Avignon and the lower reaches of the Durance River have yielded stelae (carved stone slabs) in the shape of human figures, which, together with the Provençal megaliths (dolmens), date back to the Middle Neolithic period. Near Tende (Alpes-Maritimes), at the foot of Mount Bégo, unique evidence from the Bronze Age can still be seen in the Vallée des Merveilles (valley of marvels), where the rock faces have been covered with thousands of carvings. This valley is thought to have been a place of pilgrimage during the period from about 1800 to 1000 B.C. Moving forward in time, we find a string of Celtic *oppida* being built all along the Mediterranean coast during the Iron Age. These *oppida* were fortified settlements, protected by massive drystone walls, and containing square or rectangular stone-built houses. Archaeological excavations of the *oppida* have shown that the people who lived here must have had contact with Etruscan traders from the 6th century B.C. onwards. Later on, they also traded with the inhabitants of Marseilles.

Ligurians, Celts and Greeks

The foundation of Marseilles (originally called *Massalia,* later *Massilia*) dates back to around 600 B.C. Greek colonists from the town of Phocaea in Asia Minor (present day Foça in Turkey), established Massalia as a trading settlement. To begin with, relations with the native Celtic tribes seem to have been quite amicable, echoed perhaps in the legend about the Greek sea-captain Protis' love for Gyptis, daughter of a local tribal chieftain. It seems the Greek colony developed quite rapidly. The Massalians soon developed a flourishing trade in olive oil, ceramics, and Greek luxury items. They found an immediate outlet for these goods in the hinterland beyond the city, but also sent them westward to Spain by sea, or northward, up the Rhône valley.

Massalia became even more important when it evolved into a trading center for tin from Brittany and the British Isles, and copper from Languedoc and Spain. Both metals were indispensable raw materials for the smelting of bronze, which was then shipped from Massalia to southern Italy. Starting in the 4th century B.C., the Massalians built a number of fortified settlements along the French Mediterranean coast. All the new settlements were situated on major trading routes, and were often built right beside existing native *oppida*. Some of these Massalian offshoots were *Taureis* (probably present-day Le Brusc near Six-Fours), *Olbia* (present-day Saint-Pierre d'Almanarre near Hyères), Antibes, Nice, and Théliné

(now Arles). Over the centuries Marseilles has been rebuilt so often that the city's ancient foundations are now almost invisible. Only a very small section of its Hellenic town walls can still be seen today. Long term political stability – a rare thing indeed in antiquity – was another special feature of this small, but thriving, Greek trading center. During five centuries of independence, Greek Massalia managed to maintain its oligarchical constitution free of the kind of political unrest and power struggles that were the bane of other Greek city states. This conservative stability was apparently the result of Massalia's geographical isolation in the midst of a sometimes hostile "barbarian" environment. This may well have persuaded the colonists to supress their internal differences.

The Greek Massalians referred to the inhabitants of the surrounding oppida as Ligurians. It is thought that Celts from Central Europe had been settling in southern France since the 8th century B.C. and that they intermarried with the native inhabitants. By the 4th century B.C. these Celto-Ligurian tribes had formed several distinct political groupings: the Vocontians between the Isère River and Mont Ventoux, the Cavari along the lower reaches of the Rhône – hence the place names Vaison and Cavaillon – and another tribe, the Saluvii, whose capital was the oppidum Entremont (near the present-day town of Aix-en-Provence).

Greek culture gradually spread outward from Massalia to the "barbarians" who traded with the city. Coins and ceramics from Massalia were dispersed throughout the hinterland and up the Rhône valley. In the train of this cultural "invasion," the Ligurians developed their own local art-forms, examples of which are the statues found in the oppida of both Entremont (see the Musée Granet in Aix) and Roquepertuse (in the Archaeological Museum of Marseilles). The new tech-

15

niques of modeling and the realism of the figures are clear indicators of Greek cultural influence. On the other hand, it took several more centuries, and the Roman occupation, to suppress the ancient Celto-Ligurian tradition of setting up nail-studded skulls as war trophies.

The Roman Conquest of Provence

Ever since the 4th century the Massalians had maintained good relations with Rome. It was the Romans who aided Massalia in 181 and 154 B.C., when Olbia and Nice were besieged by hostile Ligurians. In 125 B.C. Massalia again sought Rome's help in fighting against the Celto-Ligurian armies, and the Romans duly arrived to pacify the region. On a site below the oppidum of Entremont, the consul Sextius Calvinus founded the town that still bears his name

Above: The portico of the Maison Carrée in Nîmes. Right: A view on the classical theater in Orange.

as well as that of the local thermal springs – Aquae Sextiae, now Aix-en-Provence.

These events were to mark the beginning of the Roman occupation of Gaul, and took place just after the Romans had completed their conquest of Spain. The new *provincia* in southern France, officially established in 120 B.C., was given the name *Gallia Transalpina*. It comprised present day Provence, modern Dauphiné to the north, and the Languedoc, west of the Rhône valley. The town of Narbonne, founded in 118 B.C., became its capital. Right from the start, the Roman occupiers of Provence had two major goals: One was to take over the prosperous markets in which many Italian wine merchants already had a share. The other aim was strategic: to guard the possible invasion routes to Italy.

Very soon, however, invading hordes of Cimbri and Teutons from the north threatened to interfere with these plans. The Roman general Marius finally defeated an army of Teutons near Aix in 102 B.C.

To begin with, *Massilia* (as the Romans now called it) retained its status as an independent republic and an ally of Rome. During the Roman Civil War, however, when Pompey and Julius Caesar became enemies in a struggle for power, Massilia had the misfortune to take Pompey's side. The city was promptly besieged by Caesar's armies and taken in 49 B.C.

Massilia was swallowed up by the Roman Empire, and although it continued to be an important port, it soon had to contend with competition from both Narbonne and Arles. These two towns were not only situated on the coastal route linking Italy with Spain, but were also on the major trading routes to the north. Nevertheless, as a former Greek city, Massilia held a special place in romanized Gaul in the 1st century B.C.

The city's schools had a reputation equal to those of Athens. A famous "old boy" of one of these schools was Gaius Julius Agricola, who became Governor of Britain, and was father-in-law to the famous Roman historian, Tacitus.

The conquest of Provence was not completed until the beginning of the 1st century A.D., when the Alpine areas were finally subjugated. Emperor Augustus established the small province of Alpes-Maritimes, which comprised the valleys of the Verdon and the Var. North of this area lay the tribal lands of a native chieftain called Cottius. After Cottius's death in AD 56, his tribal territory was incorporated in the Roman Empire.

The Legacy of Rome

During the first centuries AD, the *provincia became*, as Pliny put it, more than a province – it became a second Rome. Roman influence was omnipresent; the entire region flourished and under the *pax romana* the network of roads was considerably extended for economic and strategic reasons. Many

more roads were built, in addition to existing roads such as the *Via Domitia* that crossed Mont Genèvre, and effectively formed the vital link between Italy and Spain, and the *Via Aurelia* between Arles and Savona.

Shipping was intensified on the Rhône and this, in turn, made Arles the most important port and trading center in southern Gaul. In rural areas, where pre-Roman *oppida* were still dominant, *villae* were created. A *villa* was an agricultural estate. Traces of the ancient, symmetrical parcels of land can still be found in many fields. A distribution map of the Roman field systems, engraved in marble, can still be seen today at the museum in Orange.

The Romans were also responsible for the foundation of a number of new towns, many of which were built close to the Celto-Ligurian *oppida*. Each of these towns formed an integral geographical and social unit. Remains of buildings in the towns clearly show that Roman-trained architects and artisans were hard

at work in the region. Some of the houses were owned by veterans of the Roman legions who settled in the Roman colonies of Orange, Arles, and Fréjus. The style of building seems to indicate that the Celto-Ligurian elite in the larger towns had become thoroughly romanized, especially after they were admitted to the legal professions during the reign of Emperor Augustus. Certainly many a citizen of the Provincia Narbonensis was able to make a career for himself in Rome!

Despite centuries of gradual but relentless crumbling away, Roman ruins have been preserved in most of the larger Provencal towns. Sometimes this is the result of continual use over hundreds of years, or even renovation. In other cases, the partial destruction gives the ruins a particularly romantic appearance. An example of this are the beautiful twin col-

umns in the theater at Arles, which are fragments of the back wall of the stage. The survival, almost intact, of a few very large buildings is little short of a miracle; for example, the theater at Orange has an almost perfectly preserved stage wall, and the mausoleum of the Julians at Saint-Rémy is remarkably complete.

The Roman towns of Vaison and Glanum (Saint-Rémy-de-Provence) were not extensively rebuilt by later generations and modern excavations have uncovered well preserved Roman monuments and dwellings.

Very often it is the purely utilitarian structures that are of exceptional interest and many of these have a charm all their own, such as Barbegal Mill near Arles, the remains of the ancient harbors of Marseilles and Toulon, the Flavian bridge at Saint-Chamas, or the arsenals and ruins of aqueducts at Fréjus.

The very quality and variety of the impressive Roman legacy in Provence are unique. Since the Middle Ages it has been a source of wonder to travelers, and

Above: The impressive arches of the Pont du Gard span the Gardon valley. Right: The more graceful aspect of the Queen Jeanne Bridge.

18

has supplied endless inspiration for architects and sculptors alike. The fact that Roman law survived and continued in use for so long (and the survival of the *Occitan* language, derived from Latin), is further evidence of the durable legacy of Rome. The hierarchy of the church also dates back to the Roman period: In late antiquity, dioceses were already being established in most large towns of the Provincia Narbonensis.

The towns preserved this Roman order throughout the centuries and it was only replaced with a new system at the time of the French Revolution.

The Beginnings of Christianity

A local legend, that can be traced back to the 11th or 12th century, tells of the beginnings of Christianity in Provence. The most popular saints in the region, Saint Lazarus and two reputed sisters of the Mother of Jesus, Mary Salome and Mary Jacobaea, are said to have departed from Palestine after Jesus's death. They sailed to Provence and landed at Saintes-Maries-de-la-Mer. Here, the two Marys and their servant, Sara, settled down, while Saint Lazarus the Resurrected, so the story goes, became the first bishop of Marseilles. (In reality, he was probably only a 5th century bishop of Aix, whose tomb inscription can be seen in the crypt of the church of Saint-Victor.)

Lazarus's sister, Martha, is said to have vanquished the dreaded Tarasque, a river monster that terrorized the inhabitants of the lower Rhône valley. Her sister, Mary Magdalene, is reputed to have introduced Christian teaching to the people of Marseilles and Aix, after which she went into retreat at the site of the future monastery of Sainte-Baume. When she died, so the story continues, she was buried at the foot of a mountain by the first bishop of Aix, Saint Maximinus, after whom the mountain was later named. Much later, in 1279, his tomb

was established there in an already existing burial chamber dating back to the 4th century.

From a strictly historical point of view, however, nothing definite is known about the beginnings of Christianity in Provence. The earliest known church in Arles dates back to AD 254, and one in Marseille dates back to AD 314. It appears that the aristocracy of Arles very quickly converted to Christianity, a conclusion supported by finds of early Christian sarcophagi in the town of Arles. As Christianity spread throughout the region, new places of worship were built. Many a Provençal town had its own early Christian baptistery, which was a building set apart from the main church building. This was used for adult baptism and was generally designed around a central baptismal font. To this day you can see the foundations of the baptisteries at Aix, Fréjus, and Riez. Archaeological excavations have also uncovered the early Christian basilicas of Riez, Cimiez (Nice) and Digne.

In the early 5th century, the first Provençal monastery was established by Saint Honorat on the Ile de Lérins. It quickly became famous, and produced many bishops. Around this time, Jean Cassien settled in Marseilles after a long pilgrimage through the Middle East, and it was here that he wrote his famous *Conférences*. He is said to have founded two monasteries in Marseilles, one for men and one for women, which may account for the origins of the Abbey of Saint-Victor situated south of the main harbor, and for the Abbey of Saint-Sauveur, opposite, of which, sadly, not a trace remains.

Roman epilogue and Barbarians

At the end of the 3rd century AD, Emperor Diocletian subdivided the Provincia Narbonensis, and formed a new province called Vienne on the left bank of the Rhone. A further division in AD 375 produced the Provincia Narbonensis Secunda, with the capital at Aix. In spite of these changes, Arles's wealth and status grew steadily over the next few hundred years. Far to the north, the town of Trier was subjected to increasingly frequent attacks by Germanic barbarians, and, consequently, in 395, Arles became the new headquarters of the Roman praetor (the head of jurisdiction in Gaul). From 406 to 411, Arles even became the home of Emperor Constantine III, and later shared in the glory of Archbishop Saint Césaire's life and work (470-542).

At about the same time, Marseilles enjoyed a period of renewed prosperity and creativity. Writers and other learned men, like Paulin de Pella and Salvien de Marseille (who originated from Trier), were active in this city.

By the end of the 4th century, most Provençal towns had their own churches and parishes. Then, as the Roman Empire fell into decline and barbarian tribes began their invasions, Christianity spread throughout the countryside too.

During the last third of the 5th century, bands of barbarians from Burgundy penetrated as far as the Durance River. The Visigoths crossed the Rhône and took Arles in 471, and Marseilles in 476. They were supplanted by the Burgundians, and the latter, in turn, were driven out by the Ostrogoths, whose king, Theoderic, an ardent admirer of Rome, temporarily reinstated Arles as the seat of the Roman praetor. After his death, however, during the period from 534-6, the Franks overran the entire region. From then onwards, Provence was demoted to a minor role in history. Charles Martel made no attempt to help the region when Provence was shaken by unrest from 736-9, caused perhaps by Moorish incursions from Spain. Nevertheless, Marseilles remained important as a major trading center between Europe and the Levant. During the last part of the 6th century, a plague spread throughout the whole region and devastated the population; entire parishes were wiped out and the glory of the monasteries faded.

POST-ROMAN AND ROMANESQUE PROVENCE

Beset by Franks and Saracens

The period from the beginning of the 7th century to the turn of the millenium is referred to as the Dark Age. Far removed from the centers of power, Provence did not participate in the Carolingian Renaissance. Gradually, even the old agricultural systems, that had existed since early antiquity, began to fall apart.

Out in the countryside, the population was widely dispersed and not entirely settled. The towns, although protected by their walls and boasting many fine ancient public and ecclesiastical buildings, now faced a long period of stagnation.

Right: The abbey of Montmajour brooding majestically over the plain of Arles.

21

The few architectural remnants of this epoch are a number of crypts, altar screens and other parts of buildings.

The Romance languages were evolving throughout the Dark Age. One of them was the *langue d'oc* (or Occitan): the many variations of Provençal spoken today are dialects of this language. Written documents from the period are extremely rare, and the few we do have are written in Latin. The earliest examples go back no further than the beginning of the 12th century.

When the Carolingian Empire was divided up, following Charlemagne's death in 814, Provence was apportioned to his son, Lothar. When he died in 855, the inheritance went to Lothar's youngest son, Charles. At that time, Provence comprised the Rhône valley and the immediately adjacent regions.

After Charles's death in 863, his two brothers, Lothar II and Louis II, divided up the country between them. However, their uncle, Charles the Bald, laid claim to Provence, and transferred his authority over the region to his brother-in-law, Boso. On 15 October 877, Boso was crowned King of Provence by an assembly of counts and bishops in Mantaille near Vienne. Boso, who reigned from 879-87, was succeeded by his son, Louis the Blind (890-928), and then by his nephew, Hugues de Vienne. Hugues who aspired to a political career on the Italian peninsula, came to a satisfactory agreement with Rudolph of Burgundy in 934, whereby he exchanged Provence for Burgundian possessions in Italy.

Rudolph's son, Conrad of Burgundy, placed his territories under the authority of German Emperor Otto the Great, which made Provence the extreme western part of the Holy Roman Empire. In 1032, Provence was officially added to the Ottonian Empire but presumably the influence of central government did not extend as far west as this. From now on, Provençal rulers themselves owed allegiance to the dukes of Burgundy. The Bosonide rulers of Arles only managed to secure power by seizing a large propor-

tion of public and ecclesiastical real estate, and equipping themselves with extensive powers in matters of jurisdiction and law enforcement. This was deemed necessary, for example, to make it easier to organize resistance against invaders.

The 9th and 10th centuries saw countless attacks on the region, with accompanying pillage and destruction: Marseilles was plundered by the Saracens in 838, and again by Greek pirates in 848. In 842, 850 and 869, respectively, Arles became the repeated victim of similar attacks. Around the end of the 9th century, the Saracens finally managed to secure a strategic bridgehead at La Garde-Freine. From here, they set out on plundering expeditions through France, even penetrating as far as Lake Constance; they sacked monasteries, made the roads unsafe for travel, and slaughtered or drove away the terrified population.

The Dukes and Counts of Provence

The Saracens were not defeated until Count Guillaume of Arles and his troops recaptured the strategically important bridge in 974.

As "liberator" of Provence, Guillaume added to his title of count the additional title of Marquis de Provence. Then, he and his brother together set themselves up as rulers of Provence. They founded the somewhat obscure dynasty of the "Counts of Provence of the First Race", and became virtually independent of the Burgundian overlords and the Emperor. After this victory over the Saracens, a number of other noble families in the region also took the opportunity of dividing up the coastal lands among themselves. They formed their own small armies, and made sure their relatives secured all the important ecclesiastical positions. Among the most powerful of these self-proclaimed ruling families were the counts of Marseilles.

Above: Detail of a capital in the monastery of Saint-Trophime, Arles. Right: A troubadour, depicted in a 13th century book.

22

During the 11th and 12th centuries, a feudal society gradually evolved in Provence: The rural population became more permanently settled, usually close to the castles and monasteries. Clusters of farms and houses tended to develop around a nucleus, then grew into proper villages. Indeed, this restructuring process probably marked the real end of classical antiquity and the beginning of the new order.

The late 10th century saw a great flowering of all the monasteries. One example is the abbey of Montmajour, which was founded at this time.

In 977 the monks of Saint Victor in Marseilles joined the Benedictine order, and by the beginning of the next century were among the staunchest supporters of the church reform introduced by Pope Gregory VII. Later, during the 11th century, monks of Saint Victor founded a succession of priories all over the south of France, in Sardinia and in Catalonia. All of these rural, spiritual centers were in close contact with the mother house; the Abbey Saint Victor thus became the heart of a vast network of priories, and was itself directly subordinate only to the papal court. Under Pope Gregory, the program of church reform spread through the whole of Provence during the 12th century, first in the dioceses, where it was vigorosly supported by the abbots, many of whom were former monks. It was the abbots who put pressure on the great noble families to hand over (or sometimes return) land or estates to the Church, and to acknowledge the authority and rightful claims of the new ruling dynasty of the House of Barcelona.

By the end of the 11th century, the dynasty of the "First Race" was only represented by female descendants, whose portions of inheritance were transferred by marriage to the great noble families of Toulouse, Urgel and Gévaudan. In 1112, one of these ladies, Douce de Gévaudan, married Raimond-Bérenger, Count of Catalonia. After the count had engaged in an armed dispute with the Count of Toulouse, Provence was divided in 1125.

Above: The town walls of Aigues-Mortes, on the edge of the Camargue.

The Catalonian count received all the lands bounded by the Durance, the Rhône, and the Alps, which was named the Comtat de Provence (a *comtat* is the territory belonging to a count).

The Count of Toulouse was given all the territories north of the Durance, which retained the name, Marquisat de Provence. The Comtat de Forcalquier, stretching from the Lubéron to Champsaur in eastern Provence, belonged to the Urgel family. This *comtat* later changed its name, first to Comtat de Vénasque, then later to Comtat Venaissin, named after the small town that became the temporary retreat of the Bishop of Carpentras. At first, the Comtat Venaissin formed a completely independent political unit. After the Pope excommunicated the Count of Toulouse, however, it was joined to the Papal Curia (1215).

In 1229, once the crusades against the heretic Albigensians had come to an end, it was transferred to Alphonse of Poitiers, brother of King Louis of France (Saint Louis). After his death, in 1274, the comtat reverted back to the Church.

Despite the partition of Provence in 1125, Count Raimond-Bérenger I (1125-31) continued his feud with the Count of Toulouse, as did his successors, Raimond-Bérenger (1131-44) and Raimond-Bérenger II, uncle and guardian of Raimond-Bérenger III, who died in 1166. They spent 20 years – from 1142-62 – waging war on the powerful noble family of Baux, whose claims to the Comtat of Orange had been confirmed by Emperor Frederick Barbarossa in 1178. War with the ruling house of Toulouse flared up again under Alphonse I (1166-96) who transferred the *comtat* to his brother, Raimond- Bérenger IV (1178-81), until the peace treaty of Jarnègues (1190) finally restored the old borders of 1125.

A new conflict erupted under Alphonse II (1196-1209) on the occasion of his marriage to a grand-daughter of Guillaume IV, the last Count of Forcalquier.

The latter, who had promised the *comtat* to Alphonse as his wife's dowry, broke his word and war with the Comtat of Provence started up again. After both counts had died in 1209, the southern portion of the Comtat de Forcalquier went to Catalonia, and the regions of Gap and Embrun to Dauphiné. The farsighted Catalonian dynasty steadily built up for itself a veritable army of loyal vassals, and installed them in the castles of Provence. They also reformed the administrative and legal systems in their territories. Many estates passed into the hands of trusted Catalonian lords. Furthermore, Roman law enjoyed a kind of renaissance at this time, and a new system of direct and indirect taxation was introduced. The coronation ceremony of the last Catalonian count, Raimond-Bérenger V (1209-45) did not, as before, take place in Spain, but in the Provençal town of Aix. He made Aix his seat of government and the capital of Provence, not least because of its extremely favorable strategic situation between plains and mountains. From here, he systematically reinforced his position of power all over Provence, even in the more remote areas; in 1229 he subjugated Nice, and in 1232 he founded the town of Barcelonette (little Barcelona) in the Ubaye valley, the easternmost corner of Provence. Only proud Marseilles retained its independence.

An Upsurge of Religious Fervor

During the 12th and 13th centuries, many new churches, monasteries and castles were built, the population gradually increased, villages flourished, and new areas of the country were cleared for cultivation. Some towns whose origins went back to antiquity enjoyed a period of considerable growth, for example, Riez and Vaison. Forcalquier, Manosque, Tarascon and Draguignan are examples of towns founded during this period. Most of the new towns were situated on the major trading routes, which became busy once again. Both Arles and Avignon benefited from the expansion in trade, and the port of Marseilles gained renewed prominence during the crusades. In 1190, Richard the Lionheart, King of England, made this port the starting point for the Third Crusade. This time, merchants accompanied the crusader knights on their voyages to the Holy Land. These resourceful traders set up *fondouks* (trading offices) in various places, for example, on the caravan route to the Caliphate of Baghdad. The trading posts became vital depots for the exchange of goods: Linen cloth from the Languedoc and Flanders, transported down the Rhône to Marseilles, was bartered for spices, sugar, silk, gems, and pearls. Trade spread to North Africa as well, where Tunis, Bougie (present-day Bejaia) and Alexandria became major commercial ports. From here goods were transported via Marseilles and other Provençal ports as far afield as Champagne and other European markets.

The period also witnessed the growing importance of the great Benedictine monasteries of Saint Victor, Lérins, Montmajour, and Saint André in Villeneuve-les-Avignon, all of which accumulated great wealth through gifts of land, and founded many new priories.

Cathedral chapters, made up of the canons who celebrated mass in the great cathedrals, became a standard institution at this time. Some of them even formed brotherhoods similar to those of the monks. The canons also held mass in the collegiate churches scattered around the country. The collegiate church of Saint Ruf near Avignon became very prominent and in turn founded priories in the Rhône valley, in Catalonia, on the Italian peninsula, and even in England.

The 12th century saw the foundation of a number of new orders; among these were the orders of knights that originated during the crusades. Gérard Tenque, the

masterpieces of monastic architecture, were founded by Cistercians who had moved down the Rhône valley and settled in Provence.

Romanesque Art

Secular art experienced a golden age under the Catalonian dynasty.

Two episodes from a famous cycle of songs, called *Le Cycle de Guillaume* (which, however, was written in northern French rather than Provençal) are set in Orange and Arles. The greatest fame was attached to the groups around Raimbauld d'Orange, the troubadour Raimbaud de Vacqueyras and the poet Folquet who was born in Marseilles. The latter became Abbot of Tholonet and later Bishop of Toulouse, and was celebrated by Dante in his famous *Divine Comedy*.

Another cultural highlight of the period was the arrival of the Romanesque style of architecture, which originated in Lombardy but soon blossomed in Provence in the form of majestic Romanesque churches, often with three separate choirs and exteriors richly ornamented with stone-carved friezes.

The design of campaniles, (belltowers decorated with elaborate stone reliefs and other ornamentation), was also imported from northern Italy.

In the plains of Provence stood the decaying walls of many Roman buildings. Here, a style of building evolved that was reminiscent of classical styles and also leaned heavily on ancient Roman building methods. Thus the structure of the monasteries of Montmajour and Saint Victor acquired their various "Corinthian" elements.

Saint Trophime in Arles and Notre Dame des Doms in Avignon were both renovated during this period, and show further examples of the Romanesque style with classical attributes.

The reforms introduced by Pope Gregory VII favored a phase of massive

legendary founder of the Order of the Knights of St. John (later the Order of the Knights of Malta), is said to have come from Provence. In 1314, this order, which already owned vast estates in Provence, "inherited" a large part of the Provençal estates belonging to the Order of the Knights Templar, after the latter had been disbanded. Other orders of monks, who subscribed to the virtues of solitude, religious contemplation and asceticism, settled in the most remote areas. In some cases, they were known to have bought up entire villages, thus forcing the inhabitants out so that they could enjoy complete solitude. The Carthusian order was originally formed in the northern Alps, but later moved to Montrieux and La Verne and settled there. The monasteries of Silvacane, Le Thoronet, and Sénanque, which are considered to be

Above: The Cathars of the Midi region were ruthlessly persecuted as heretics. Right: The Papal Palace at Avignon was built in the 14th century.

building activity during the 12th and 13th centuries. This was the epoch that saw the birth of cathedrals, huge monasteries, and such small country churches as Notre Dame de Salagon. This "secondary Romanesque phase" was characterized by simple, logical ground-plans, a certain harmony and elegance of form, and exterior sculpture of the highest quality.

POPES AND DYNASTIES

The First Dynasty of Anjou

Raimond-Bérenger V died without male issue and new alliances were created through the marriages of his daughters, Margaret, Eleanor, Sancie and Beatrice, often referred to as the "four queens." These alliances moved Provence into the French sphere of influence. Margaret married Louis IX of France (Saint Louis) in 1243. Eleanor became the wife of Henry III of England. Sancie married Richard of Cornwall (who later became a German emperor), and Beatrice

who, at the time of her father's death, had not yet received her portion of inheritance, was finally given Provence, and in 1246 was betrothed to Charles, Count of Anjou.

Like his older brother before him, Charles joined one of the crusades and was captured by Muslims during the battle of Mansurah (Egypt). During his absence, the larger towns, like Arles, Avignon, and Marseilles, lost no time in extending and consolidating their independence. However, in 1250, when Charles returned from his imprisonment, he did his utmost to wrest back power. In 1257, he forced Marseilles to recognize his sovereignty unconditionally. Within a short time, Charles I of Anjou had pacified the Comtat of Provence, tightened up administration and secured his position by means of substantial tax revenues. In particular, he imposed a tax on salt, on which he had secured the monopoly. Supported by a strong Provence, Charles then proceeded to campaign on the Italian peninsula and, in 1263, he conquered

27

the Kingdom of Naples. Unfortunately in 1282, shortly before his death, his successful political career suffered a setback with the "Sicilian Vespers" uprising, actively supported by the ruling house of Aragon. This was to be the start of a long-lasting feud between the house of Anjou and the kingdom of Aragon over who should control southern Italy.

Charles's successors, Charles II (1283-1309) and Robert (1309-43), further extended and secured the borders of the Comtat de Provence, particularly to the east and north and, judging by the lists of tax revenues, Provence was a thriving country in those days. The year 1288 even saw the establishment of a public audit-office. The towns had more freedom again, and, at the turn of the 14th century, were allowed to create town councils and to appoint consuls. This striving towards self-government soon

Above: The Consistoire hall in the Papal Palace at Avignon. Right: A portrait of John XII (pope 1316-34).

spread all over Provence. From the late Middle Ages, even small villages would have their own independent administrative bodies.

By the beginning of the 14th century, the population of Provence probably stood somewhere between 350,000 and 400,000. Some of the inhabitants of the mountainous areas would move down to the valleys during the winter months, but the rest of the population were permanently settled. The towns began to expand beyond the narrow confines of their walls. Marseilles made huge profits from trade with Italy, even though the merchants did not always have an easy time in the face of their financially strong, and well-organized Italian competitors. One drawback was Marseilles's loss of the Middle Eastern trading posts (*fondouks*), after the Muslims recaptured Saint Jean d'Acre (1291), and the crusades came to an end.

The 13th century saw the birth of many new religious orders, both for men and for women, including the orders of mendicant friars. The Carmelites, Augustinians, Dominicans, and Franciscans all had female members too. Then there were the "Brothers of the Holy Trinity," who settled in Marseilles in the early 13th century. This order was later (1609) included among the mendicant orders. It was said to have been founded by a native of Provence, Saint John of Matha, and was dedicated to raising ransom money to buy back Christian slaves from North Africa. The second son of Charles II of Anjou, who began his career as a monk, later became Bishop of Toulouse and died in 1297 at the early age of 27. He was canonized in 1314, and was thereafter referred to as "Saint Louis of Anjou" or "of Provence" to distinguish him from his great-uncle, "Saint Louis," King of France.

Avignon's Golden Age

In the early 14th century, Avignon temporarily became a "Second Rome." From this very city, between 1309 and 1376, a succession of seven popes ruled over all Christendom. They were Clement V (Bertrand de Got, 1305-14), John XXII (Jacques Duèse, 1316-34), Benedict XII (Jacques Fournier, 1334-42), Clement VI (Pierre Roger, 1342-52), Innocente VI (Etienne Aubert, 1352-62), Urban V (Guillaume Grimoard, 1362-70), and Gregory IX (Pierre Roger de Beaufort, 1370-78). They were followed by the two anti-popes, who continued to reside in Avignon during the Great Schism, after the official papal residence had been moved back to Rome. These two, Clement VII (Robert of Geneva, 1378-94), and Benedict VIII (Pedro de Luna, appointed in 1394, deposed 1409, died 1423), no longer appear in the official list of popes.

The magnificent papal residence in Avignon ensured the city's prominence not only in ecclesiastical matters, but also in trade, and Avignon soon managed to

supplant all other Provençal towns. From the turn of the century right through to the Black Death of 1348, the population of Avignon grew from just 5000 to about 30,000. Even the devastation of the plague did little to halt the trend.

Gothic architecture did not appear in Provence until rather late, during the second half of the 13th century. Originally, the style was introduced by the counts of Provence who commissioned a number of projects, among them the basilica and monastery of Saint Maximinus, begun in 1295, over the supposed tomb of Mary Magdalene. Also in this style were the church of Saint-Jean-de-Malte and the family crypt where all the counts of Aix lie buried. The canons of Aix, in the spirit of the times, commissioned the conversion of their ancient cathedral to the new Gothic style. Even the popes at Avignon favored the new style. Most of the halls and the chapel in the New Palace, built under Clement VI, were embellished with typical pointed Gothic arches. The Bishop of Avignon had a splendid new residence built for himself, and other church dignitaries built themselves *livrées*. These were residential buildings, several stories high, that blended easily with the existing architecture of the town (for example, the Livrée Ceccano).

One very beautiful example of southern French Gothic is Saint Didier Church, which was built in only three years (1356-59), and boasted a long, airy, high-vaulted nave, that let in plenty of light, and was flanked on both sides by a row of chapels but had no transept or aisles. This deliberately severe, even abstract, form of art supplanted the figurative and pictorial art of the Romanesque style. Gothic became the predomiant style in southern France from the late 14th to the early 16th century, and Avignon became one of the major centers for the fine arts during the 14th century. The Avignon popes, in particular, commissioned works from a number of famous Italian painters. Among them were Simone Martini of Siena, who worked in Avignon from 1336 until his death in 1344, and Matteo Giovanetti of Viterbo, who designed and executed beautiful frescoes on the interior walls of the New Palace. The poet Petrarch (1304-74) also lived here at this time. He is considered to be one of the chief representatives of Italian humanism. His family had been banished from Florence and had settled in Avignon in 1311. Here the famous meeting took place between the poet and Donna Laura, which was to be the inspiration for Petrarch's famous *Canzonière*. From 1337, he lived in a house by the Fontaine de Vaucluse and r eturned to Italy in 1353.

Avignon's golden era and the dreaded Black Death which afflicted not only Provence, but the whole of Europe, coincided with the regency of Joanna of Naples (1343-82). She was the only countess ever to rule Provence alone, although she spent only six months on Provençal soil. In 1348, she sold Avignon to the Pope. During her regency, She was engaged in constant power struggles with ambitious relatives, who even went so far as to hire local partisans to undermine her position. Unfortunately, none of her four marriages produced an heir.

The plague, which had entered the country through the port of Marseilles in 1347, began to spread through Provence in 1348, and was to wipe out at least a third, possibly even half, of the population. Several further waves of the disease followed in quick succession until 1440. To add to all this misery, bands of robbers terrorized Provence in the years 1357-8, and again in 1365, raiding, pillaging, burning down villages, and driving away the inhabitants.

The Second Dynasty of Anjou

After the death of Countess Joanna in 1382, Louis of Anjou, brother of the French king, took over the suzerainty of Provence but he experienced great difficulty in establishing the authority of this "second dynasty of Anjou." Both Louis, who died soon after in 1384, and his widow, Marie de Blois, who was left to raise their son (Louis II of Anjou), had to put up a bold front against their political opponents, who were known as the Union of Aix, and who demanded an Italian ruler for Provence.

Military support by the French king, and quarrels within the Union of Aix, brought an end to these disputes in 1388. After that, only the eastern part of Provence continued to oppose the rule of the French crown. Barcelonette, Nice and Puget-Théniers placed themselves under the authority of the Count of Savoy. The towns of Annot and Guillaume, on the other hand, joined the side of the French. This state of affairs resulted in the formation of a curiously convoluted border.

Right: The Book of Hours of Louis, Count of Anjou. Far right: The main entrance of Saint Gilles-du-Gard.

The Counts Louis II (1384-1417) and Louis III (1417-34) continued the war against Aragon, which, as it turned out, was to have catastrophic repercussions, especially for Marseilles. Many of the hired Spanish marines promptly formed pirate bands, terrorized the harbor area, and harmed Marseilles's reputation as an international trading center.

On 20 November 1423, a Catalonian fleet dropped anchor offshore, invaded Marseilles, spent three days in pillaging and plundering, and finally burnt the city to the ground. Marseilles took many years – until the second half of the 15th century – to recover completely from the devastation. By then, the overall political climate in Provence had also improved. In the course of the many different crises of the 14th century), at least 177 villages were abandoned, some of which were never again inhabited. Most of them, however, were rebuilt and resettled during the 15th and the first half of the 16th centuries. By 1550, the population figure was back to that of the early 14th century.

From 1470 to 1520 some landowners pursued a policy of deliberate resettlement, in order to revitalize those areas that had suffered particularly heavy population losses. They even settled Italian immigrants in the eastern part of Provence. Even at that time, the population density of the lowland areas was markedly higher than in the mountains, a situation that has hardly changed since.

Economic growth and a consequent population explosion took place during the reign of King René of Anjou (1434-80). He was the last Angevin ruler of Naples, a possession he lost in 1442. Although a 16th-century folktale refers to him as "good King René", this monarch seems to have distinguished himself mainly by his extreme greed for tax revenues. Many of the eminent artists of the period worked at his court, which moved back and forth between his capitals of Angers and Aix. A great admirer and patron of the "second school of Avignon," René commissioned the artist Nicolas Froment to paint his version of

the Old Testament story of the burning bush in the cathedral of Saint-Sauveur in Aix. The Neapolitan sculptor Laurana also worked for the king: Laurana's work combined important elements of the Italian Renaissance with Burgundian realism, which was all the rage in Avignon.

René bequeathed Provence to his nephew, Charles III of Maine, who ruled for only 18 months and died on 11 December 1481, leaving Provence to his distant cousin, Louis XI, King of France.

Union with France

The union of Provence with France had been carefully planned over a long period of time by a member of the ruling elite of Marseilles, called Palamède de Forbin, who had been René's trusted chamberlain. The transfer of Provence to

Above: The castle at Tarascon (15th century). Right: François I and Henri IV, Kings of France (Provence was annexed to the Kingdom of France in 1481).

the French crown was intended to look more like unification than annexation. For this reason, both the municipal and state institutions of Provence were very gradually brought into line with those of France. In Aix, for example, a parliament was established between 1501 and 1503, which was the equivalent of the *Parlement* in Paris. Its position on various matters (for example, the Jews) soon began to match that of France.

There were a large number of Jewish communities in southern France at that time. They had built synagogues, own cemeteries and schools, and employed kosher slaughterhouses. Usually, these institutions were all to be found in the same quarter of the town. The Provençal Jews were especially prominent in the field of medicine and the study of Hebrew. After the union of Provence with France, a number of Jews were murdered, and an anti-Jewish law, first passed in Paris, was soon enforced here too. From 1493 to 1501 Jews were forced to choose between conversion to Chris-

tianity (among those who did were the ancestors of the astrologer-prophet Nostradamus), or emigration. Some found refuge on the papal estates, to which Jews from Languedoc and Dauphiné had already fled; others went to Nice. In Avignon, and in the Comtat Venaissin, "the Pope's Jews" were generally left unmolested, but were allowed to engage only in certain professions, had to live in specially designated streets, and were required to wear yellow headgear.

Just as the counts of Anjou had done, so the kings of France also laid claim to territories in Italy, and once again turned Marseilles into a naval base. However, the city also profited from the friendly relations established between Francis I and the Ottoman Empire. The "capitulations" of 1536 and 1569 once again made it possible for trading posts to be established in the Middle East, but the Italian merchants who had settled in Lyons continued to control all trade in Marseilles, as well as in North Africa where they held the monopoly on coral, and where they bought leather and wheat. Provence quickly began to feel the unpleasant repercussions of the war with Italy: in 1524 the troops of Emperor Charles V (also King Charles I of Spain), led by the Constable of Bourbon, marched into Provence and captured Toulon and Aix but failed to take Marseilles. In 1536 the Emperor himself tried but failed also. This made Provence the southernmost outpost of a powerful kingdom, but one that was still entangled in far too many wars. The French kings continued to strengthen this strategically important border region, even enlisting the help of the Turkish fleet to sack Nice in 1543.

Religious Wars

In Provence, the religious wars of the 16th century took on a sinister character of their own, because of the Waldensians, or "poor of Lyons," descendants of medieval heretics who had settled in the Lubéron region and still lived hidden away in inaccessible valleys.

33

Sometime after 1530, while the Inquisition was busily persecuting Protestants, they stumbled upon this sect, and proceeded to slaughter its followers without pity. In April 1545, the inhabitants of Cabrière d'Avignon, Mérindol, Lourmarin, and a dozen other villages were systematically massacred. In 1532, the surviving members of the sect decided to declare themselves openly as Protestants. This is why, to this day, a Protestant enclave exists in the heart of Catholic Provence. The Protestant faith had a much harder time becoming established in the towns, because Protestants were automatically barred from administrative positions. Orange was the only exception to this ruling. Through inheritance, Orange passed into the possession of the Dutch counts of Nassau, who, shortly afterwards, converted to the Protestant faith. Nevertheless, Protestant communities grew up in a few villages of the Baux and in the Durance valley, only to be wiped out again by the Edict of Fontainebleau a century and a half later (1685). This Protestant minority, supported by other Protestants from Languedoc and Dauphiné, responded to the persecution suffered during the years from 1559 to 1564, with a number of retaliatory attacks of their own. In 1588, however, when it looked as though the Protestant Prince Henri of Bourbon would soon ascend the French throne, the Catholic League managed to gain control of most of lower Provence. In July 1593, Henri of Bourbon, now King Henri IV of France, renounced the Protestant faith, and in January 1594 the parliament at Aix declared themselves for his cause. Thus Henry was soon able to establish his authority over the whole of Provence. There remained only the problem of Marseilles, where the Catholic Leaguer, Charles de Cazaulx, had established his own despotic republic. Henry had him secretly assissinated in 1596.

Above: Louis XIV, shown here traveling around the country with his court, curtailed the ancient rights of Provence.

Cultural Life in the 16th Century

The Renaissance influence came late to the arts in Provence. For a long time, painters had remained true to the Gothic ideals of the "Second School of Avignon." Initially, the new style flourished mainly in the paintings and frescoes of the castles and noble residences around Aix. Fine paintings from this period can also be seen in Lourmarin and Château-Arnoux.

Although the university of Aix was founded in 1409 by Louis II, the town's intellectual life had always lagged behind that of Avignon. The first book was printed in Avignon as early as 1497; in Aix, the first printers were not established until 1575; in Marseilles as late as 1595! The educated elite of Provence were trilingual: They spoke Latin, Provençal and French. The second half of the 16th century saw the flowering of groups of poets who wrote in both, Occitan and French.

The most renowned representative of Occitan poetry is Bellaud de la Bellaudière, while the greatest of the French-speaking poets was Malherbe, who originally hailed from Normandy.

UNDER THE BOURBONS

Ever since the end of the religious wars, Henri IV and his successors had persistently sought to impose absolute rule on distant Provence from Paris and Versailles. From its past as a *comtat,* Provence had retained a representative assembly, known as the *Etats Provinciaux,* which had a voice in matters of administration and taxation. The representatives in this assembly were generally members of the higher clergy or nobles; from 1578 onwards this group had been extended to include representatives of 37 towns, the "assembly of communities." The Etats vigorously opposed the drastic increases in taxation introduced by Louis XIII to finance France's involvement in the Thirty Years War. After 1639, the king summoned only the "assembly of communities," which was considered more docile. In 1664, his successor, Louis XIV, moved its venue from Aix to Lambesc. In these various ways, the absolutist monarchs tried to assimilate the Provençal parliament into the political framework of France. The Provençal parliament was made up of "officers," councillors who had purchased their seats, and who passed them on in their wills to their children, or else sold them to someone else. These "parliamentarians" were deeply attached to the Provençal traditions and way of life, and insisted on keeping their ancient privileges.

During the interregnum, before Louis XIV had come of age, Cardinal Mazarin decided to increase the number of members in the Provençal parliament. A storm of protest from Provence forced Mazarin to scrap the plan. The French kings had hitherto tried to secure their own influence in Provence by installing their relatives, or people they implicitly trusted, in the top positions of relevant local institutions.

In this way, first a certain Richelieu, then someone named Mazarin held the position of Archbishop of Aix. Both men were brothers of the Paris cardinals of the same names. During the reign of Louis XIV, a kind of "Superintendent for Law, Security, and Financial Affairs" was placed at the head of the Provence parliament. Equipped with extensive discretionary powers, he represented the "presence of the King in his province." At least Cardin Lebret (1687-1734), and then the two LaTours, father (1734-71) and son (1775-90), who later held this post tried hard to adapt themselves to Provençal society and its customs. To a certain degree, they even attempted to defend Provençal interests against the central government.

Indeed, Aix enjoyed a relatively favored position within centralist France. No other town in Provence had such important organs of jurisdiction or administration. Aix was the seat of Parliament, the Law Court, the Superintendent's residence, and the only university in Provence. At the height of its power the town boasted splendid buildings and elegant streets. Architects and builders were not the only professions to flourish: printers, lawyers and attorneys prospered, not to mention the many innkeepers and traders who looked after the numerous litigants.

Louis XIV finally managed to break the last vestiges of Marseilles's resistance. Since the beginning of the 17th century, the city had been divided into two hostile factions, led by powerful city fathers vying for supremacy and equally ill-disposed to royal authority.

Above: Mighty Atlas figures support the balcony of the Hôtel Maurel de Pontevis (1647) on the Cours Mirabeau in Aix-en-Provence.

On 2 March 1660, royal troops occupied the city. A new city council, under the control of the king, was formed and the forts of Saint-Jean and Saint-Nicolas which dominated the city were manned by the king's artillery.

Yet at the end of the day, the ports of both Marseilles and Toulon actually benefited economically from French diplomatic, naval and colonial policies. Henry IV had already provided Toulon with a fortified dockyard and naval arsenal. In 1624, Cardinal Richelieu transferred most of the French naval fleet to Toulon, a move which, at least temporarily, weakened Marseilles's position. In 1665, however, Marseilles was again made the principal home-port for the galley fleet. During the 17th century, the naval fleet's antiquated galleys began to be replaced by more modern war-ships. Nevertheless, galleys remained part of the French navy until 1748, partly because the legal use of galley slaves to row the older ships had been written into penal law. This state of affairs continued until 1749, when the last convicts were moved to Toulon, and had to serve their sentences engaged in forced labor at the local arsenals.

In spite of all the efforts made by Colbert (1619-83, French minister of finance) to boost the national economy, Marseilles's trading activity grew only very slowly. An edict of 1669 made Marseilles a free port, and slapped a 20 per cent tax on all goods from the Middle East passing into the country through any other ports. This meant that Marseilles had a virtual monopoly on all goods from the Levant; yet none of these measures appeared to have a positive effect on Marseilles's progress. Despite the setback of several plague epidemics, the rest of Provence enjoyed a certain economic and population growth during the years up to 1689. This was followed, however, by a period of stagnation lasting until about 1740. Continuous wars drained the country's resources. The eastern part of Provence was temporarily occupied by enemies, the devastating outbreak of plague in 1720 resulted in thousands of dead, and in 1746-47 the country was occupied by foreigners yet again during the Wars of Austrian Succession. Military fortifications and citadels from the period can still be seen in Colmars-les-Alpes, Toulon, Antibes, Sisteron, Seyne, and Entrevaux.

Mannerism and Baroque

Countless works of art and examples of architecture from the 16th and 17th centuries are reflections both of comparative prosperity, and of the drastic changes, especially in religion, during this period. The Catholic counter-reformation gained ground during the latter decades of the 16th century and during the 17th century. It went hand in hand with a new flowering of monasteries and religious orders, such as the Carmelites and the Jesuits. These trends were particularly noticeable in the second half of Louis XIV's long reign. New churches, religious communities, and brotherhoods of all kinds were born, and places of pilgrimage, votive statues, and miracle-working saints were kept very busy. The Italian art movement known as Mannerism arrived in Provence, albeit belatedly, at the end of the 16th century. This style formed a gradual transition to the Baroque style. Famous regional examples of Baroque architecture are the "Monnaie" (the Mint) of Avignon designed by the architect Borboni, Marseilles's hospital built by Pierre Puget, and the Theatine Church in Nice, built according to plans by Guarini. The Baroque style quickly caught on in painting and sculpture (Puget, Serre, and Veyrier, to name just a few), also in music and the manufacture of musical instruments (organ workshops). The faïence workshops of Moustiers-Sainte-Marie and Saint-Jean-du-Désert near Marseilles were founded by the Clérissy brothers in 1670. To begin with, pottery was made using a simple method, whereby the unfired vessels were first painted, then given a single firing. The technique of firing was considerably refined by artists like Master Ferrat in Moustiers or Master Robert and the Widow Perrin in Marseilles, during the 18th century. Their methods involved an initial firing of the enamel, followed by painting and a second firing. The technique enjoyed its greatest popularity during the reign of Louis XV.

The increase in population and drastic changes in social structures triggered off a spate of building activity in the towns during the 17th century. In many towns, whole new districts were built, that were based on regular, geometrical ground plans. In many places, large avenues with green parks and fountains were created, where the old and new sections of town joined. This "join" often corresponded to the line of the old town walls. Here, people would stroll, coffee houses were

opened, and town markets were held. Other avenues were created, based on the Italian model of the *corso:* the Cours Mirabeau in Aix (1649), and the Cours Belsunce in Marseilles (1666), and later on, the Cours Gassendi in Digne.

There was a noticeable tendency for Provence – and for the Comtat of Nice – to become the home of poets and philosphers, during the 17th and early 18th centuries. Jean de la Cappède (1550-1622), one of the greatest poets of the late 16th and early 17th centuries, was born and lived here. Honoré d'Urfe (1567-1625), renowned for his widely read pastoral novel *Astrée,* was born in Provence and returned here towards the end of his life. Others, such as Madame de Sévigné, spent much time here. Alongside the French-speaking poets, the Occitan poets also continued to find fame: Brueys and Zerbin from Aix, and, in particular, Ni-

Above: The population oppressed by the aristocracy and the clergy. Right: The storming of the Bastille, 1789.

colas Saboly who still ranks as one of the most popular Provençal authors. Among other great intellectuals were the polymath, Nicolas de Peiresc (1580-1637) of Aix, and the philosopher Pierre Gassendi (1592-1655), who was also a canon of Digne. Natives of Provence also played their part in astronomy and botany (Joseph Pitton de Tournefort).

Economic Upswing

The continued exploration of the world's oceans proved to have a vitalizing influence on the port of Marseilles and the city's growth was hardly affected by the simultaneous decline in the relative importance of the Mediterranean Sea. By the end of the 17th century, ships from Marseilles had opened the way to the Caribbean via Gibraltar. This new impetus benefited Marseilles for over a century. Marseilles also benefited from changes in trade with the Middle East. Now, traders from Marseilles found themselves selling coffee and sugar from

the West Indies to a weakened Ottoman Empire. Many manufacturers of soap, sugar, and cotton goods became prosperous concerns, boasting high export figures. After 1765, there was additional trade with the countries around the Indian Ocean, and, during Louis XVI's reign, trade with the future United States started up. The port's rapid rise to prominence led to Marseilles becoming the third-largest city in France within just one generation. The population figure grew from about 75,000 at the end of the 17th century to about 120,000 by the beginning of the French Revolution. Unfortunately, this growth came to an abrupt halt in 1793, when Britain entered the Napoleonic Wars, and the port was plunged into a critical period lasting a decade. Other towns, however, managed to carry on much as before. Grasse saw the development of a famous perfume industry. Toulon, the second most populous town of Provence, became the chief French Mediterranean naval base. Avignon, though far removed from its medieval heyday,

was able to use its special status to good advantage in trade. Even the small towns in the Provençal plains shared in the social progress of the 18th century. Their population figures increased to several thousand, they enjoyed an active public life, institutions, religious societies and more secular associations, like poetry and writing circles, flourished everywhere, and the building industry was actively supported in the towns (for example, with the creation of the cours). The town diginitaries furnished and decorated their houses in the latest styles and Jewish families (descendants of the "Jews of the Pope," who had found refuge in Avignon during the Inquisition) prospered and built new synagogues. The synagogues of Cavaillon and Carpentras are among the oldest in France. The popularity of the classic Provençal style of furniture, which originates from these towns, was to continue well into the 19th century, even though more and more stucco and ornamentation were gradually added.

39

Literacy spread rapidly, though this happened later in Provence than in northern France. This trend helped to stabilize the French language without completely supplanting Provençal, which now became a minority language. In addition to the Occitan author, Antoine Peirol, Provence produced three other notable writers: the Marquis de Vauvenargues, the Marquis d'Argens, and above all, the notorious author of erotic novels, the Marquis de Sade. Two eminent revolutionary writers also came from Provence: Mirabeau and the Abbé Sieyès.

The Revolution

The French Revolution, like much else in Provence, followed a different course here than in Paris. Violent uprisings were already taking place in the south during the spring of 1789, after an extremely hard winter. For two months the French crown completely lost control of Marseilles, which formed its own citizens' guard. In April 1790, Marseilles's two forts were stormed and in the same year, when the modern French *départements* were established, Provence, as an administrative unit at least, disappeared from the map.

In Spring 1792, the Marseilles-based "Circle of the Friends of the Constitution" sent out " patriotic missionaries" to take the ideals of the Revolution to the very furthest corners of the province. Armed volunteer troops were sent to Aix, Avignon, and Arles, to prevent any counter-revolutionary movements gaining ground. In Marseilles itself, the intellectual framework of the Revolution continued to develop. Marseilles was the first French city to demand the abolition of the monarchy.

Right: This etching depicts Toulon being liberated by Napoleon after its occupation by the army of the Convention.

In the summer of 1792, a battalion from Marseilles marched through France singing the war anthem of the Rhine Army (*"Le chant de Guerre de L'Armée du Rhin"*), composed by Rouget de l'Isle. Later, it became the French national anthem, popularly called the "Marseillaise," in memory of the events of 1792. On 10 August 1792, this battalion played an active part in overthrowing the monarchy in Paris. In the autumn, the revolutionary army crossed the Var and occupied the Comtat of Nice, which, a year later, became the new *département* of Alpes-Maritimes.

THE TURMOIL OF THE 19TH CENTURY

The years from 1792 to 1815, which saw the advent of the First Republic and the Empire of Napoleon, were also marked by political turmoil and great economic difficulties. In 1793, Marseilles, Toulon, and other towns in the Provençal plains raised a rebellion against Robespierre's supporters, who were present in great numbers in Haute-Provence. In the summer of the same year, Avignon and Marseilles had already been recaptured by revolutionary troops, but in Toulon, the royalists proclaimed Louis XVII king and opened their port to the British. The army of the young Napoleon Bonaparte finally put an end to British occupation of Toulon on 18 December 1793.

A number of "revolutionary" measures were adopted in Toulon and Marseilles, such as forcibly abolishing religion, doing away with lengthy court cases (mainly in order to push through death sentences more quickly), and destroying churches and other "reactionary" buildings. The removal of Robespierre on the 9th Thermidor (27 July 1794) put paid to plans for an ambitious project to build a "Temple of Reason" in Marseilles. The artist Réattu had already completed the

decorations for the interior of the building. Today these can be seen in the Réattu Museum in Arles. Even after Robespierre's reign of terror had ended, many more dreadful deads were committed. For example, in Aix, Tarascon and Marseilles, Jacobin prisoners were massacred by royalist veterans, who later ganged together in marauding bands. Napoleon, who had risen to the position of First Consul, managed to re-impose order of a kind in Marseilles, but the Continental Blockade, by which Britain intended to defeat him, paralyzed trade and commerce. Consequently, Napoleon's fall from power in 1814 was met here with little regret. The Comtat of Nice was returned to the Crown of Savoy, and Monaco was given back to the noble family of the Grimaldi. When Napoleon returned, after escaping from exile on the island of Elba, he carefully avoided traveling through Provençal towns or the Rhône valley, and chose instead the more difficult route across the Alps. The Battle of Waterloo triggered off another wave of terror, and Marshal Brune was assassinated in Avignon.

The Restoration period favored all landowners again, but made things worse than ever for the landless population. Provence sent extremist-conservative royalists to sit in the Chamber of Deputies in Paris. During the so-called "July Monarchy" (1830-48), however, more liberal tendencies began to emerge, particularly since electoral reform now enabled the middle classes of the population to go to the ballot. From 1815-48, a relative prosperity gradually developed again, even in Marseilles, which once more attracted foreign merchants, among them Swiss, and Greeks from the island of Chios. France's conquest of Algeria turned one of her traditional trading partners into a colony, naturally to Marseilles's advantage. During the period of the "July Monarchy," Marseilles became the largest port in France and the third-largest in Europe. The city also played an active part in the Industrial Revolution. In particular, several branches of industry

41

experienced an upswing here: the chemical industry (soap manufacture), food processing (semolina and edible oil), brick and tile making , and ship -building. Marseilles's population, which had dropped to less than 100,000 by the end of the Empire, rose to 195,138 by 1851, despite the cholera epidemics of 1834-5 and 1849, and the economic crisis of 1848. Modernization and expansion of the arsenals meant that Toulon became a flourishing industrial city. Development did not really take off in Arles and Avignon until the latter half of the 19th century, when both towns were joined to the rail network. The face of rural Provence changed too. Typically Mediterranean, mixed arable cultivation declined, the mountains of the Haute-Provence, – at the time, more densely populated than ever before – suffered large-scale defore-

Above: An historical etching of Marseille and the islands of Frioul. Right: A photograph of the old harbor of Marseille around the turn of the century.

station and dry-stone terraces were built for cultivation. Towns like Hyères and Nice became fashionable winter resorts, and notable figures chose Cannes as their winter residence.

Architecture was greatly influenced by Neoclassicism during the first half of the century. Penchaud was the architect responsible for many public buildings, churches and hospital buildings. Engineering triumphs were achieved in the construction of railway and road networks: bridges and viaducts, and the famous aqueduct of Rosquefavour, designed by the architect de Montricher. Two noted politicians came from Provence, François Raspail, who proclaimed the Second Republic in Paris on 25 February 1848, and the revolutionary socialist, Louis Blanqui.

Universal suffrage, introduced at the very beginning of the Second Republic (1848), probably reflects a slight shift of political opinion in the Provençal population. As before, most Provençal people were hostile to the Bonapartists, but in

Var and Haute-Provence, a number of progressive Republicans, known as the *montagnards,* were voted into Parliament. When Louis Bonaparte staged a monarchist coup on 2 December 1851 and seized power, one of the main centers of resistance was formed in the alpine region of eastern Provence. Republican troops occupied the town of Digne. They were finally forced to surrender to the Bonapartists at the Battle of Mées on 9 December 1851. The ruthless measures that followed, including executions and deportation to the colonies, left deep scars in Provence. The fact that the region consistently voted "left" for nearly a whole century thereafter, is evidence of the depth of feeling engendered by these measures. Opposition to Napoleon III scarcely diminished in Provence, throughout the Second Empire (1852-70).

Marseilles continued to flourish, in particular after the opening of the Suez Canal, and one way it showed off its prosperity was with its new buildins (especially those by Espérandieu and

Coste). Both trade and industry were modernized and ship owners, entrepreneurs, and bankers moved here (the Société Marseillaise de Crédit was founded here in 1865).

The Provençal economy, which hitherto had been dominated by agriculture and craft-based industries, was radically changed by the expansion of the railway system and large-scale industrialization that gradually spread southward. This resulted in mass emigration of the inhabitants of the mountainous areas to the cities and colonies. But other parts of Provence saw massive inward movements of population. Corsicans came to Marseilles and Italian immigrants settled all over Provence. Gradually, agricultural practices adapted to new demands. In Var, where vegetables and flowers had always been grown in abundance, grapegrowing began, and spread to the lowlands. The produce was shipped northward up the Rhône. In 1860, Napoleon III annexed Nice, and by 1865, the railway network had expanded as far as the

43

Alpes-Maritimes, which meant that the whole region was now accessible to modernization.

During this period of upheaval, Frédéric Mistral (*Mireille*, 1859, and *Le Poème du Rhône* 1897) and Théodore Aubanel (*La Grenade Entr'ouverte,* 1860) wrote works that are supreme examples of the vigorous traditions of Occitan verse and prose. Both poets were founder-members (1854) of the literary and cultural movement, *Félibrige*. Mistral, who received the Nobel Prize for Literature in 1904, was a leading figure of the revival of national consciousness throughout Europe in the 19th century. He was the author of a comprehensive Occitan-French dictionary, called *Trésor du Felibrige,* he founded the *Museon Arlaten* in Arles, which exhibited his collection of art and crafts of pre-industrial Provence, but even he could not stem the relentless incursion of the French language, brought by education and social pressures.

At this time, Marseilles was the only large modern city in Provence. It had spent the entire period of the Second Empire actively opposing the Royalists. Consequently it developed into a stronghold of socialism when the Third Republic (1870-1940) was proclaimed. After Paris, the Marseilles commune was the most significant in the wave of uprisings in 1871. The founding congress of the workers' party, the first socialist party in France, took place in Marseilles in 1879. In 1881, the first socialist representative, Clovis Hugues, elected by voters of a Marseilles constituency, took his seat in the Chamber of Deputies. In 1892, the socialists received a majority vote in the town councils of Marseilles, of the port of Ciotat, and even of Toulon (1893). Towards the end of the century,

Right: A citizen of Marseille deeply engrossed in the sports pages of his daily newspaper.

Marseilles was up against growing national protectionism, and fought for its right to import raw materials from abroad at free-trade prices, process them at home, and then export them again. Marseilles's traders cleverly exploited the backwardness of African and Asian countries by importing their produce and selling it back to them as manufactured goods. By the outbreak of the First World War, Marseilles's economy had reached a new peak. The city had become one of the world's major ports both for freight and passengers. The census of 1901 showed a population of about 500,000, which now made Marseilles the second-largest city in France. By comparison, Aix's population figure had shrunk to 25,000, and it seems to have been in a kind of limbo throughout the 19th century. Nevertheless, it produced one of the century's greatest literary figures: Emile Zola, born and bred in Aix, describes his childhood in the early novel of his "*Rougon-Macquart*" cycle. Painters like Granet and, in particular, Cézanne, were inspired by Aix. The same was true of Arles and Saint-Rémy, where Vincent van Gogh stayed in 1888-9.

The impact of the Provençal landscape on painting was probably one of the major cultural events of the 19th century. During the first half of the century, painters like Constantin or Granet had already captured on canvas the beautiful coastal landscape of Provence. Paul Guigou and Adolphe Monticelli launched Provençal impressionism, which immediately had the kind of enthusiastic audience in Marseilles that Cézanne so bitterly missed in Aix, during his solitary wanderings around the St. Victoire. It can be safely said that modern art began in Marseilles, where Guignon, Cézanne, Braque, Dufy, and others, fascinated by the clarity and brilliance of the light, set up their easels on the hills and around the factories of Estaque. In 1908, Braque painted a picture entitled *Landscape in*

Estaque which is considered the first example of Cubism. Signac, Derain, Braque, Manguin, and Dunoyer de Segonzac all based themselves at Saint-Tropez. Some painters, like Seyssaud, felt themselves drawn to the Provençal hinterland, others stayed in Marseilles, among them, Auguste Chabaud. He started up a late-Impressionist school there, whose major representative was Casile. Early film-making, too, had links with Provence: in 1885 Louis Lumière made the film, *L'entrée d'un train en Gare de la Ciotat*, and later, Marcel Pagnol's film studios in Marseilles and the Studio Victoirine in Nice gained considerable fame.

Authors, too, were inspired by Provence, and they came here to discover the countryside, long considered too arid to be attractive. The people of Provence – friendly and communicative – are the inexhaustible subject of novels by Pagnol, Méry, and Daudet. Authors such as Paul Arène, Edmond Rostand, and Charles Mauras (known in particular for his radi-

cal, right-wing political views), or André Suarès, Germain Nouveau and Antonin Artaud, were born here. Others enjoyed coming to Provence for long periods, among them, Stendhal and Alexandre Dumas, whose famous novel, The Count of Monte Cristo, is set in Marseilles; Arthur Rimbaud died in Marseilles in 1891.

THE 20TH CENTURY

Albert Cohen spent his childhood in Provence. Mallarmé taught at the lycée in Avignon, as did Simone de Beauvoir, a few decades later, in Marseilles. The poet Stephen Liégeard, who came from Dijon and settled in Cannes, wrote a famous description of the "azure coast" of Provence in 1887. The name has remained to this day – la Côte d'Azur. Around the turn of the century, this coastline underwent significant changes: In addition to the winter holiday makers, summer sun-seekers began to arrive. At first, these were mainly painters: Renoir found lodgings in Cagnes, Matisse went to Vence and

Nice, Picasso to Antibes and Vallauris, and Léger to Biot. Many artists were drawn to the interior. André Masson, who had first spent time in Sanary, moved to Aix, De Staël moved from Antibes to the Lubéron, which also attracted André Lhote and Vasarély. Dufy and Soulages settled in Haute-Provence.

The influx of foreign holidaymakers, which soon followed, changed the face of the entire coast for good: With them came the many pensioners who dreamed of settling in the south, and also high-tech industries, based particularly in the scientific-industrial zone of Sophia-Antipolis.

Meanwhile, the Côte d'Azur had also attracted many notable foreign writers, some staying with wealthy patrons, like the Vicomte de Noailles, at Hyères. Nietzsche spent time in Nice, Katherine Mansfield in Bandol, Scott Fitzgerald in Antibes, and Virginia Woolf in Cassis. During the German occupation in the Second World War, Marseilles was a gateway to freedom for many writers and others fleeing from Nazism.

The Second World War came as a severe shock to the whole of Provence. From November 1942 onwards, Provence was occupied first by Italian, then by German troops. The French fleet, at anchor in Toulon, was sabotaged and supplies and reinforcements were cut off. In January 1943, German soldiers destroyed the entire old section of the city of Marseilles, while the Allies engaged in massive bombing of Toulon, Marseilles, Avignon and Tarascon in 1943 and 1944. In the course of the struggle for liberation, the Germans also managed to destroy a large proportion of Marseilles's harbor installations. In the mountains, the partisans (the macquis) were relentlessly persecuted, as were the resistance fighters in the towns. Finally, on 15 August

1944, the Allies landed on the Mediterranean coast and liberated Provence. It was not until after the war that the real tourist boom started up. Beginning on the coast, it rapidly spread into the interior. The writer, Jean Giono, and poet, René Char, worked here during that period. Perhaps it was partly due to them that an ever-growing circle of intellectuals "discovered" Provence. More and more summer festivals take place here each year, among them, the internationally famous theater festival in Avignon, the music festival in Aix, or the Chorégies in Orange. Many new museums of art, history and folk history were opened.

The 20th century, however, brought many problems for Marseilles, despite the record volume of goods handled in the harbors, and an increase in population to 800,000. Marseilles had already weathered one economic crisis between the two world wars, because it had increasingly become a colonial port for French-ruled North Africa. Even so, it did participate in the "Second Industrial Revolution". Huge oil refineries and a petrochemical industry grew up around the Etang de Berre, and in the area of Fos, but, for a long time, the results of the Second World War – extensive destruction of the harbor installations and broken trade links – seemed insurmountable obstacles and many sectors of industry have not recovered to this day.

Eastern Provence, on the other hand, long considered to be the poorest and most backward region, experienced a great upswing. Nice, now with a population figure of around 478,000, has become the second-largest city of the region. Cannes, which was still a sleepy little village during the 19th century, is not far behind with a population of 335,000. Thanks to the arrival of new industries, the Rhône basin too has enjoyed a boom, and Arles, Avignon and Aix are once again considered to be among the most attractive towns in France.

Right: A Provençal woman dressed in the traditional costume of Arles.

BOUCHES-DU-RHONE

MARSEILLES

AIX-EN-PROVENCE

ARLES AND THE CAMARGUE

THE LOWER DURANCE

LES ALPILLES

TARASCON AND

LA MONTAGNETTE

PONT DU GARD / NIMES

The *département* of Bouches-du-Rhône has many faces, and all are different. Whether it is the Durance valley, flanked by ranges of hills, where small villages appear to cling precariously to the steep slopes, or the rugged coast at Cassis, where the sea is steadily eating into the cliffs and forming the famous *calanques,* or the Rhône, whose delta encompasses the wild Camargue – these varied landscapes have nurtured several distinct peoples and cultures, a fact that is aptly illustrated by the great contrast between Marseilles and Arles.

MARSEILLES

Marseilles has been the capital of the region of Provence-Alpes-Côte d'Azur and of the *département* of Bouches-du-Rhône since 1960. It has a scintillating, chaotic vitality, but cannot shake off its reputation for being a dangerous, run-down city – a kind of European Chicago. The people of Marseilles tend to meet such prejudice with a typical Gallic shrug, and will proudly point out that the

Preceding pages: The festival of the cow-herds (Fête des Gardians) in Arles. "The red vineyards" – Provence as seen through the eyes of Van Gogh. Left: The Old Harbor of Marseilles.

city has become France's indispensable outlet to the Mediterranean.

History and Myth

Today, nothing much remains of Greek *Massalia,* the Phocaean colony founded in the 6th century B.C. A few fragments of the eastern section of the town walls, dating from the 3rd century B.C., can still be seen, likewise parts of the Roman harbor installations dating from the 1st century A.D. So it is worth visiting the **Jardins des Vestiges** (an enclosed area full of classical remains) before turning one's attention to the city's major attractions, such as the church, Notre-Dame-de-la-Garde and the Old Harbor (the Vieux Port).

Marseilles has progressed from being a free-trade port, through extensive industrial installations (though periodically affected by strikes), to being France's largest and Europe's second-largest port.

To be a true citizen of Marseilles, you have to be either born there, or adapt yourself to its environment. Without a doubt, Marseilles has been shaped by a culture that has a strongly exotic flavor. For over a century, many Greeks, southern Italians, Sicilians, and Armenians have settled in this city of Mediterranean sun and metropolitan wealth.

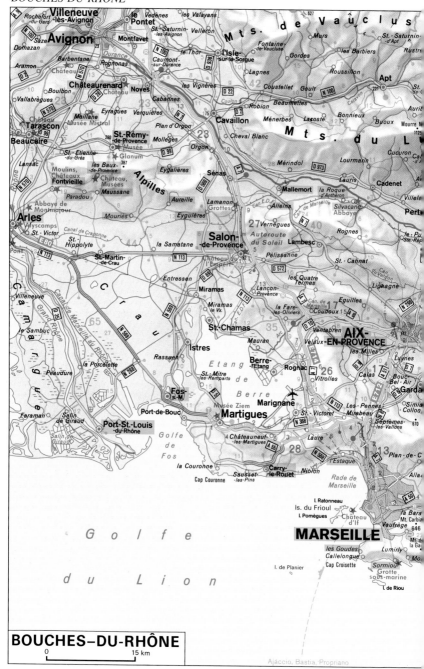

BOUCHES-DU-RHÔNE

0   15 km

This city, which gave its name to the French national anthem, the "Marseillaise," can only be truly appreciated against the background of its long history. Oil refineries and a major sugar processing plant were built here during the 19th century, both of which helped develop a bourgeoisie based on trade and banking alongside a large working class, consisting of mainly black and North African immigrants. These developments secured Marseilles's key position within the French colonial empire.

The negative image of Marseilles as a city of con-men and gangsters was not really created until the 1920s and 1930s (possibly initiated by a massive influx of Italian immigrants). A spate of more recent detective novels and films just tended to reinforce the idea. From *Borsalino* to *Cap Canaille*, this image of a "City of Violence," with its main thoroughfare, the **Canebière**, having become a kind of "Boulevard of Crime," has almost blotted out that other sunny, more endearing image, which Pagnol created in his trilogy of novels about Marseilles and its people.

The Old Harbor

Marseilles's old harbor is dominated by **Notre-Dame-de-la-Garde,** a huge 19th-century neo-Byzantine cathedral. The plans for the church were drawn up by architect Espérandieu, who also created the design for the **New Cathedral of La Major**. The latter is situated right beside the **Old Cathedral of La Major**, one of the most beautiful Romanesque churches of Provence, which, unfortunately, has been closed since 1989. Notre-Dame-de-la-Garde is built on a high, rocky outcrop and towers above the harbor of Marseilles. The church becomes a destination for pilgrims on the feast day of the Ascension of Mary, Queen of Heaven. Seamen and other faithful worshippers still come here to

pray and honor the Mother of God by dedicating votive pictures to her. The town's most famous landmark is also the best vantage point for taking in the whole panorama of Marseilles at a sweep, from the beaches of Prado across to Estaque harbor, and from the offshore islands to the hills of the interior. On windy days, you may enjoy the exhilarating experience of being perched high above the city under an intensely blue sky, matched by an even bluer sea, which form a vivid constrast to the glowing red tiled roofs of the city's old houses, and almost allow you to forget the ugly outlines of modern multi-story buildings. From up here, you will be able to see the **Basilica Saint-Victor,** a church whose pinnacled towers make it appear like a mighty fortress. For many centuries it was one of the most important abbeys in the whole of France.

Above: The Palais de Longchamps in Marseilles. Right: People from all along the coast of Provence mingle in the city's bustling markets.

Hidden away behind massive defensive walls lies a beautiful church dating back to the 13th and 14th centuries, with a veritable labyrinth of chapels, caves, and catacombs. Special features are the statue of the Black Madonna, and the sarcophagi of two Christian martyrs. The worship of these saints dates way back to the 11th century, and the abbots Wilfred and Isarn.

The most important buildings in Marseilles are not, as you might have thought, the Poste d'Aix, dating from the 19th century, nor the obelisk on the Boulevard Michelet, nor even the many beautiful fountains, like the one in the Place Castellane. Nor do the Palais Longchamp, dating back to Napoleon III, or the City Hall, built in the 17th century, with a façade designed by architects, Portal and Puget, qualify for this honor.

Although they all form part of the special ambience of Marseilles, as do the forts of **Saint-Jean** and **Saint-Nicolas** (both were built during Louis XIV's reign), none of these is the most important building in Marseilles.

The true monuments of Marseilles are those that are inextricably linked with myths and legends: First there is the **Vieux Port** which today is only used by yachts and fishing-boats, and which is regularly crossed by ferries connecting the Quai de Rive-Neuve and the Quai du Port. Then, there is the Corniche John F. Kennedy, which is the most popular route to the Prado beaches, and provides visitors with a splendid view of the bay – from the Frioul islands to the famous **Château d'If,** a prison island, and the setting for part of Alexandre Dumas's famous novel, The Count of Monte Cristo. The Château d'If is one of the most familiar features of the Marseilles scene, along with the **Ile Gaby.** This island received its name when the singing star of countless musicals, Gaby Deslys – whom Cocteau once referred to as a "tamed catastrophe" – received it as a gift from a

wealthy admirer. Since then, the well-known jeweler, Morabito, has bought the island, and in 1990, he opened an underwater museum there.

A Shopping Stroll around Marseilles

Any excuse is good enough for the Marseillais to take a ride on the métro (the new pride of the city), or a tram (the old pride of the city) for a shopping expedition to the center. There is plenty to see and do in the elegant streets of the Rue de Rome, the Rue de Saint-Férréol, and on the Canebière, and things have improved even more since Marilyn Vigouroux (wife of the deputy mayor, Robert Vigouroux) opened the **Musée de la Mode** (a fashion museum), and since the multi-story car park, Estienne-d'Orves, a hideous eyesore of a concrete block, was demolished and replaced by an open square with terraced cafés, ice-cream parlors, bistros, book shops, and galleries. **Les Arcenaulx,** another former multi-story car park, has now given way to a

publishing company, Jeanne Laffitte, a restaurant, a gallery, and a book shop – and is a favorite place to see and be seen.

Being true southerners, the Marseillais are never at a loss for words, and their volubility is seasoned with a good sprinkling of common sense. The people of Marseilles like nothing better than a lively but good-natured discussion, whether they are sitting in the sun outside the Café New York, on the Quai du Vieux Port, or while sauntering up and down the Rue Paradis. Among the great passions of this very unconventional city are its much-loved football club, *Olympique Marseille* – currently one of the most successful clubs in France, and the favorite subject of endless verbal sparring matches, and also the two great daily papers, *Le Méridional* and *Le Provençal.* A true Marseillais will devour them with his breakfast!

Other great favorites with Marseilles's inhabitants are the colorful markets all around the city, like the **Marché de la Plaine,** where you can haggle to your

MARSEILLES

- - -○- - - Underground
———○——— Tramway

Rade de Marseille

Iles du Frioul, Ile Gaby, Château d'If

JOLIETTE

Gare Maritime

Bd. R. Schuman

Bd. de Paris

Autoroute Nord A7

▲ Arles 91 km

Faculté des Sciences

Lyc St-Char

PTT Gare St-Charles

Bd. Ca

JULES GUESDE

Rue des Dames

Arc de Triomphe ou Porte d'Aix

COLBERT

Bd. d'Athènes

Cours Belsunce

ST CHARLES

REFORMES
CANEBIERE

Lutétia

Bd. d
Libe

Cathédrale de la Major

Vieille Charité
M. d'Archéologie

Hôtel Dieu

Mont. des Accoules

Musée Vieux Marseille
(Maison Diamantée)

Grand H. Prestiges
de Genève

Jardin des Vestiges

Hôtel de Ville

VIEUX PORT
HOTEL DE VILLE

H. Beauvau

NOAILLES

Bourse

E. des Augustins

Office de Tourisme

Canebière

Théâtre du Gymnas
Grandhôtel Noail
New H. Astoria

La Canebière

Rue Barbaroux

Place

Cours Julien

Jean Jaurè

N-D DU MONT
CRS. JULIEN

Fort St-Jean

Jardin du Pharo

Club Nautique Marseillais

Présid. J. F. Kennedy

Boulevard
CATALANS St-Nicolas

C. Livon

Fort
St-Nicolas

Caserne d'Aurelle

Basilique
St-Victor

Quai du Port

Quai de Rive Neuve

Vieux Port

Théâtre
La Criée

Bd. de la Corderie

Opéra

Rue Breteuil

Rue Paradis

Palais de Justice

ESTRANGIN
PREFECTURE

Banque de France

Musée Gantini
et de la Faïence

Préfecture

Européen

Boulevard Notre Dame

Place
Castellane

CASTELLANE

Rue de Rome

Lieutaud

Boulevard

Castellane

Avenue

Aven.

B

Rue de
H
M

Boulevard

Rue
du Vallon

Auffes

Corniche

Hôtel
Petit Nice

ILES D'ENDOUME

New
H. Bompard

Notre Dame ✝
de la Garde

PERIER

Avenue du

Rue Paradis

Corniche

Président

Rond
du Pr

Prado

John F. Kennedy

H. Palm Beach

Ecole de Voile

Promenade G. Pompidou

Avenue
du

MER   MEDITERRANEE

Stade Olympique

Plage

du

Prado

Avenue
Pierre

*Parc
Borély*

Château
Borély

Clo

Avenue

MARSEILLES

0   500 m

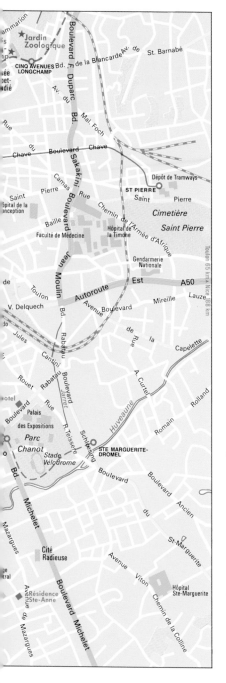

heart's content over almost anything, the **Marché Castellane,** probably the largest market in the city, and the **Marché de Noailles,** which is held along the narrow, winding alleys of the old town quarter, **Quartier des Capucins.** This is where you will get a whiff of the real Marseilles, mixed with the scent of spices, the fragrant aroma of coffee, and the smells of sweet, bottled fruits. This is where you will find local specialties, like *navettes,* biscuits prepared with orange blossom water. Formerly, they were only made for the Catholic feast day of Candlemas but, with a bit of luck, you may find some tucked away in one of the many bakeries.

The Vieille Charité and the Quartier du Panier

After many years of almost explosive expansion, and its concomitant evils, Marseilles (and in particular, the old parts of town with their beautiful old walls) has been rediscovered by its inhabitants. Those parts of town which, not long ago, seemed haunted by a seedy underworld, have now become extremely fashionable. This is what happened to the **Panier,** a very picturesque and miraculously well-preserved quarter. Situated on its fringe is the **City Hall (Hôtel de Ville),** an elegant *palais* which somehow survived destruction by the German occupying forces during the Second World War. The Panier quarter had a bad reputation for a very long time but now it has acquired a certain status as the city's treasure-house of the past. You can enter its maze of alleys via the **Accoules steps.** This quarter, in which the houses are closely packed together, has a very individual, almost Neapolitan charm. Washing lines full of colorful laundry stretch high across the street, from window to window, and stark patterns of sunlight and shadow are formed on the angles of walls and balcony railings in the ravine-like alleys. For generations, Marseilles fishermen, in rough blue linen trousers, with sun-tanned faces and leathery skin, have lived on the hill of Accoules. Their boats, which are moored in the Old Harbor, take them out to Carry-le-Rouet, to the Ile de Planier, or the Ile de Riou. They return at dawn and dock at the **Quai des Belges.** There, you can hear the "fishwives"noisily shouting their wares. The language of the market is a fascinating mixture of Neapolitan dialect and typical Marseillaise slang.

Not far from here is the **Vieille Charité,** the most beautiful building in Marseilles. It was completed in 1706, and first served as a kind of reception center for orphans, the poor, and the sick. Sadly, those who came here tended to end up doing forced labor. The beauty and harmony of the building comes from its three-story galleries of rose-colored limestone. This unusual stone displays a subtle variety of coloring, created by the interplay of sunlight and shadow. After the French Revolution, the Vieille Charité was almost forgotten for about a century and a half, then, during the bombing raids in the Second World War, it became a refuge for those who had lost their homes. Later, a cultural center was installed there in the 1960s. Today, the Vieille Charité is home to the **Museum of Archaeology of the Mediterranean World** where traveling exhibitions can often be visited and the Marseilles Biennale is also held. Its Baroque chapel, built on an unusual elliptical groundplan, is an architectural masterpiece designed by Pierre Puget.

Museums

To discover Marseilles is also to discover its museums. Their cool tranquil rooms are ideal places to relax after a hectic shopping trip.

Right: The vast stairway to the St-Charles railway station in Marseilles.

The **Musée Grobet Labadié,** an enchanting town palais, displays works by famous French artists, for example, paintings by Puget and Monticelli (who influenced Van Gogh and Cézanne), also faïence and wrought-iron work. Close by is the **Palais Longchamp,** a neo-Baroque building by Espérandieu, which houses the natural history museum, the fine arts museum, and coin collections. A small zoo can be found in the park outside. The faïence gallery in the **Musée Cantini** includes some extremely rare and precious items whose beauty is enhanced by being placed in a continuously moving display.

The museum of the history of Marseilles is in the **Maison Diamantée,** an architectural curiosity dating from 1570. Its name is derived from the frontage, consisting of rectangular blocks, that are finished to look like faceted diamonds. In addition to Provençal furniture, you can also admire the products of two typical crafts of this region: nativity scenes and the *santons* (clay nativity figurines).

Great Names in Art and Culture

Marcel Pagnol and Vincent Scotto are not the only people to have celebrated Marseilles and Provence. Many artists, writers and other famous people made Provence their home or even their adoptive country, among them, René Allio, film director and producer, whose aim is to revive the Provençal film industry, the actor Fernandel, whose thick Provençal accent made him famous from Paris to Hollywood, Edmond Rostand, author of *Cyrano de Bergerac,* and Edmonde Charles-Roux, daughter of the chairman of the Compagnie du Canal de Suez. She is the widow of Gaston Defferre, the legendary mayor of Marseilles, who held office for 30 years, and is a successful author and editor-in-chief of *Elle* magazine. The opera-singer Régine Crespin was born in Marseilles and began her career here, as did Marius Petipa who

wrote the choreography for Tchaikovsky's famous ballet music and died in St. Petersburg in 1910. Roland Petit and Zizi Jeanmaire, whose names have always been linked with Marseilles, were not actually born here but always kept their loyal Marseilles fans. Marseilles has fewer theaters and playhouses now than in the past – only about half a dozen establishments. In particular, the **Alcazar**, a famous musical theater, where even the great stars were nervous of appearing before its notoriously critical audiences, has long become a name of the past. A more demanding kind of theater performance can now be seen at **La Criée** (the opera) and **Le Gymnase**.

The **Hotel de Noailles** has a mighty pillared façade, and is one of the gems of the Canebière. Sadly, the future of this delightful building is in doubt, even though the city has precious few of these beautiful old palais left. The **Hôtel Beauvau**, with its view of the Vieux Port and the two forts, Saint-Jean and Saint-Nicolas, has been used as a backdrop for many films. The famous **Petit Nice** was converted by contemporary designer Eric Klein (who also did the interior design for some of the trendy new shops in the inner city). You may decide to stay at this hotel, spend a night in an elegant room overlooking the sea, and enjoy its excellent cuisine, but be prepared to pay a hefty price for the pleasure!

The Corniche and the Prado

The Corniche, a wide coastal road, which links the city with the beaches, is an integral part of life in Marseilles. At the crack of dawn, some people set off to go fishing, others go jogging along the road. Many just dream of owning a house beside the tiny fishing harbor in neighboring **Vallon des Auffes,** but for most inhabitants of this little gem of a place with its waterfront cafes and dance halls, all the money in the world would not induce them to leave. At the end of the day, tourists and locals alike will gather here to enjoy a pizza in *Chez François* or

sample a genuine bouillabaisse in the *Chez Fonfon.* These dishes – fish chowder and pizza – imported long ago by Italian immigrants, have become both local specialties and national dishes. No visitor to Marseilles should miss the experience of strolling across the market in the Rue d'Aubagne, and eating a slice of steaming hot pizza, straight from the oven. On Sundays, you can meet your friends on the **Prado**, the beach promenade, and be tempted into one of the many ice-cream parlors or cafés.

Another almost obligatory day trip is a visit to the **Gardens of the Château Borély,** a charming 18th-century château on the southern outskirts of Marseilles. The inhabitants of Marseilles are very fond of strolling in its park, which has one of the most beautiful rose gardens in Europe. Unfortunately, the château itself cannot be visited at present, and the col-

lections of Greek, Roman and Egyptian art which are usually exhibited there are on temporary loan to the Vieille Charité.

The Prado quarter of the city boasts a number of elegant 17th- and 18th-century houses (now nearly all are owned by banks or insurance companies), and the **Parc Chanot,** where colonial exhibitions took place on a regular basis during the early part of the 20th century, until the Marseilles Trade Fair was moved to this venue. The park is one of the very few public green areas in the city.

Until about 50 years ago, wealthy Marseilles citizens would spend the hot summer months in their second homes in the Catalans quarter, a little way out of the city. The most attractive of these houses are always in demand on the real estate market and are usually owned by rich industrialists or business people.

For something completely different, take a look at some examples of post-war architecture: Le Corbusier built a huge new residential block of apartments on the Boulevard Michelet, the road that

Above: Fishermen carefully spreading out their colorful nets to dry. Right: A catch of fresh fish in the Old Harbor of Marseilles.

leaves the city in the direction of Gineste and Cassis. The block is called the *Cité Radieuse* (the Radiant City), although the Marseillais soon dubbed it *la maison du fadà* (the madman's house). Right after the war, this complex (which now has a preservation order on it), was an entirely new and revolutionary concept – a gigantic concrete shell, supported by 36 colossal columns, containing ultra-modern apartments, a shopping arcade, and a swimming pool. Since 1952, however, this innovative building has been joined by many rather ugly high-rise buildings on the hills surrounding the city.

Fun and Leisure

Marseilles has a character as varied and colorful as a patchwork quilt, and will so easily win you with its charm that you will overlook the hectic atmosphere and the other drawbacks. You will begin to understand some of this if you take the road to Goudes for a stopover at **Pointe Rouge,** which is one of Marseilles's fa-

vorite beaches, where swimmers, sailboarders, and sun-worshippers alike give themselves up to enjoyment and relaxation. Even though the people of Marseilles love to spend time in the open air, they also appreciate their own homes, which they call *paradou* (paradise). This may lead foreigners to think that the locals are not particularly friendly towards visitors. Another point worth bearing in mind is this: If a Marseillais strikes up a conversation with you, he is not trying to prove how cosmopolitan or liberal-minded he is. He simply has a great need to talk, to pass on information, and prove that his opinion is the right one. He would never invite you home for a pastis right away, but would prefer to have a chat with you first, preferably in a café, which might be the *New York* (Quai des Belges) or the *Bar de la Marine* (Quai de Rive Neuve). If he takes to you, he will then go out of his way to help make your stay in his city as enjoyable as possible. The Midi-French are very similar to Italians and Spaniards in this respect. Then

the famous southern charm will suddenly start making things happen. *Bouillabaisse,* for example, is an extremely serious subject for discussion. Every Marseillais believes his or her recipe is the best one. This will generally depend on the right blend of red mullet, monkfish, and other ingredients, and on the finer points of *rouille,* the famous orangey-red garlic mayonnaise *(aïoli)* prepared with paprika. Allow yourself to be initiated into the mysteries of *bourride,* of *pieds-paquets* (sheep's foot and offal in white wine), and of *navettes,* biscuits made with orange blossom water. You will learn why almond cakes are called *lampions,* how to eat sea urchins, and what a good quality olive-oil should smell like! Whether the subject is gastronomy or politics, a true native of Marseilles will like nothing better than to share his opinions with you.

Above: Unusual vantage points – the calanques of Cassis and the turquoise-blue sea (near En-Vau).

The Christmas Market

Every year, from November to early January, the entire upper section of the Canebière is covered with wooden huts that look rather like oversized dolls' houses and which sell clay figurines by the thousand: shepherds, drum-majors, little Arlesian women in national costume, and figures of the Christ child.

The thing to do, every year if possible, is to add another figure (or several) to your nativity collection. It is an outing for the whole family, who will enjoy sniffing the dry winter air (with a touch of the mistral wind in it), while choosing and buying one or two new *santons.* On 4 December, the feast of Saint Barbara, they are traditionally placed on a layer of cotton wool containing germinated wheat grains, between figures of the Three Wise Men. This is also a time to visit friends and relatives, and to admire their new santons. Together, you will go and look at the many nativity scenes in churches and chapels throughout the city, and attend a Christmas mass, also called "fishermen's mass" in the church of Saint Augustine, down at the Vieux Port.

The Environs of Marseilles

There are several alternative day trips out of Marseilles. You might decide to drive to the sea in the direction of Cassis, or travel inland towards Aix-en-Provence and stop at Aubagne, the town where the santons originated.

Cassis and its Coast

The drive to Cassis is a real pleasure in itself. The Route de la Gineste (D559) winds its way through the delightful Gardiole and Carpiagne Massif and the (D41), which takes you to Cassis from Aix via Aubagne, is another extremely picturesque country road.

Cassis is an old-fashioned beach resort that has hardly changed at all over the years. A good place to start your visit is down at the harbor: At *Monsieur Brun* (rather trendy) or *Chez Nino* (more homely) you may like to sample the sea urchins which are sold here by the dozen. This dish is served raw, in the shell, with just a little white wine dressing, which, by the way, is another specialty of the region. With it you should have a bottle of *vin de Cassis*, a light, friendly wine with an unmistakable bouquet of the sea. Should you prefer something sweeter, try a *castel,* a little cake topped with nuts and whipped cream. Or else just stroll along the waterfront and enjoy the sun at one of the terraced cafés opposite the landing stage.

The church of **Saint Michel**, dating from 1860, is worth a visit, as is the museum of art and commerce; then again, you might prefer to wander round the market or do a bit of wine-tasting.

Cassis does not, however, offer much in the way of nightlife. This is because the inhabitants of Cassis are well aware of the danger of their town degenerating into a kind of "Saint-Tropez of Marseilles," and that investors and speculators from Marseilles are keeping a watchful eye on them, ready to grab any opportunity that may present itself. There is a cheerful, almost homely atmosphere about the night-time activities in the town center. The many *boccia* players under the plane trees, as well as the lively young people from Marseilles, create an atmosphere that is much more welcoming than in some smarter places.

The landing stage in Cassis is the starting point for boat trips along the coast to see the spectacular cliffs and bays, the *calanques,* and also to **Port-Pin, Port-Miou,** and **En-Vau**, where you will be dazzled by the spectacular white rocks washed by a blue-green sea. Further to the west are the *calanques* of **Sormiou** and **Morgiou**, pine-shaded gorges cut into the limestone massif of Marseilleveyre and Puget. The French diver, Henri Cosquer, made a sensational discovery here in 1991: Above the **underwater grotto of Sormiou** he found a prehistoric picture gallery. The entrance to this Stone Age cave is 36 m (118 ft) under the sea. At the end of a 200-m (656-ft) long access tunnel, just above sea level, is a cave (300 sq m / 3222 sq ft) full of stalagtites and stalagmites. About 13,000 years ago people of the Stone Age covered the walls of the cave with paintings of animals, mainly wild horses, in shades of blue and terracotta.

Further to the east is **Cap Canaille** with a fantastic view of the Puget Massif, the Marseilleveyre Mountains and the offshore islands. Just opposite the cape, the corniche road passes a high rock, surmounted by the 14th C. **Château of Les Baux,** From here, there is easy access to various beaches, for example that of **Bestouan,** where the water stays ice-cold even at the hottest time of the year, or the beaches of the peninsula, where you can enjoy sunbathing on flat, white rocks.

If you feel like driving a little further into the hills, you will soon come across a number of splendid villas, set in luxuriant greenery, with wisteria-covered walls, their entrance gates half-hidden by flourishing bougainvillea, and all graced with cool, shady gardens.

Aubagne and its Santons

The little town of Aubagne lies on the Huveaune river (take the N8 from Marseilles, or the N96 from Aix-en-Provence) between Sainte-Baume and the Garlaban. Aubagne is renowned for its traditional pottery and the famous *santons* and is home to a number of well-established pottery studios, for example the *Studio Sylvette Amy* on the Boulevard Emile-Combes, or the workshop *Santons d'Art de Provence* in the Chemin Charel.

Above: Countless cafés and restaurants offering seafood delicacies line the little harbor of Cassis.

Fans of Marcel Pagnol will find a trip to Aubagne well worth their while. Pagnol was born here in 1895, and the characters he created in his novels are depicted as santons in a permanent exhibition. The **Musée de la Légion Etrangère** is a reminder that the Foreign Legion has been based in this town since 1962, after previously being stationed in Algeria.

AIX-EN-PROVENCE

Aix-en-Provence is undeniably the historical and cultural capital of Provence. It is set in a landscape of forests and rocks, where picturesque little villages cling to the steep slopes.

The history of the town can be traced back to 123 B.C., to the Roman consul, Caius Sextius Calvinus, who founded the thermal baths of *Aquae Sextiae* here. By the end of the 7th century A.D., Aix had become the main residence of the counts of Provence. Aix enjoyed a heyday during the reign of King René (1471-80), thanks to its influential parliament and its much respected university. It was not really until the 19th century, that Marseilles took over as the leading city of the region, and beautiful, aristocratic old Aix - also referred to as the "Provençal Florence" – seemed to slip into an enchanted sleep lasting about a century. Today, Aix is again one of the most attractive and important towns of Provence, especially from a cultural standpoint. An internationally renowned music festival has been held here every summer since 1948. The university of Aix enjoys an excellent reputation, especially the faculties of Law, Economics and Literary Studies.

With the advent of horse-drawn coaches in the 17th century, wide, shady avenues (the *cours*) were built and taking a walk down the Cours Mirabeau became an important feature of life in Aix. When you stroll along under the plane trees, you are there to see and be seen. Open-air cafés, such as the *Deux Garçons* (the "2

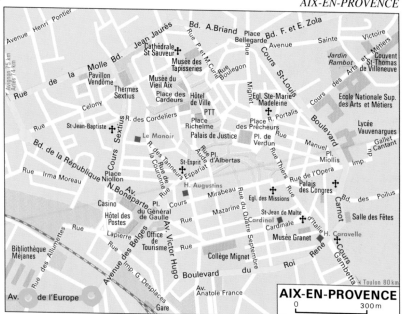

G," as it is called by the locals), or the *Grillon,* invite you to spend entire afternoons or evenings at their tables.

You will gain your first impression of this charming town while strolling along the Cours Mirabeau from the cooling fountain at the Rotonde to the **statue of "good King René,"** created by sculptor, David d'Angers. On the busier, sunny side of this splendid avenue, are rows of shops, cafés and hotels, and on the less populated, shady side are the banks, a cinema and confectioners' shops *(confiseries),* where you will find a specialty of Aix called *calissons.* This delicacy, made of marzipan, is now well known even beyond the boundaries of Aix. Some of the best *calissons* are sold by *Bremond* in the Rue Cardinale, or by *Puyricard* in the Rue Riffle-Raffle, behind the Palais. The south side of the Cours Mirabeau is flanked by imposing former residences of the nobility, whose very names are reminders of their glorious past. Isoard de Vauvenargues, Saint-Marc, Forbin, and Maurel de Pon-

tèves are just a few of the illustrious names of their long departed builders or owners. All were either chairmen of the parliament, counsellors at the *Cours des Comptes* (Audit Office), idle aristocrats or self-made men.

You can find the old part of town by starting on the odd-numbered side of the cours and making your way through the back streets. In the old section of town you will find yourself in a maze of alleys and sleepy little squares (closed to traffic), such as the Place Richelme. Just round the corner is the old Corn House, now the Post Office, and facing it the **Town Hall.** This rather opulent building, a typical example of the style of architecture in Aix, was erected in 1671, although the clock tower is actually about 100 years older. A Provençal "bell cage" was built at the top of the old belfry.

The **Place d'Albertas** forms a perfect ensemble of Baroque architecture, with a bubbling fountain in the center, whose charm typifies the handsome style of the 18th century.

A few meters on is the **Palais de Justice,** built in the early 19th century, to replace the old palace of the counts, the reason being that dispensing justice had become an increasingly important function of the town. The building overlooks the broad "preachers square," **Le Parvis des Prêcheurs**, which today lies on the borders of the old town and the new residential district. A market is held here three times a week. The **Eglise de la Madeleine** can be visited here. If you carry on walking in a northerly direction, you will find the "Holy Saviour" quarter (Bourg du Saint-Sauveur). Here is the magnificent **Cathédrale du Saint-Sauveur,** which features Romanesque cloisters, a unique baptismal font and, above all, the famous triptych called *The Burning Bush* by Nicolas Froment, depicting, among other scenes, King René kneeling before the infant Jesus. Even the Flemish tapestries which decorate the choir and

Above: The splendid Baroque Place d'Albertas with its fountain (Aix-en-Provence).

which were brought from Canterbury Cathedral, in England, are most unusual. The former Bishop's Palace today houses the **Musée des Tapisseries** (the Tapestry Museum). The collection includes a few particularly beautiful examples, such as *Les Grotesques, l'Histoire de Don Quichotte,* and *Les Jeux Russiens.*

Nearby is the museum of the town's history (**Musée du Vieil Aix**), which is housed in the Hôtel d'Estienne de Saint-Jean, and where art and crafts collected by the folklorist Marcel Provence in the years 1931-6 are displayed, examples being a nativity scene with speaking figures, furniture, books, traditional regional costumes, and all kinds of everyday objects and utensils.

The **Musée Granet,** an art museum in the Mazarin quarter, exhibits paintings by Ingres, Puget and Fragonard. Unfortunately, it does not have any important paintings by Cézanne, Aix's most famous son, though the town is trying hard to do him justice. He is constantly mentioned in the museum, and in many places around Aix you will come across trails of brass plaques in the pavement, inscribed with the letter "C," which mark the routes which Cézanne used to take from his home to his studio, to church, or to favorite haunts.

The **Pavillon Vendôme** in the Faubourg des Cordeliers quarter is a typical example of a harmonious blending of several successive architectural styles in a single building. It was built by Pierre Pavillon, altered by Vallon, and another story was added to it in the 18th century. It was owned first by the Duc de Vendôme (the grandson of Henri IV and Gabrielle d'Estrées), whose wife, Laura Mancini (one of Mazarin's nieces) died at an early age. The duke had the palace built so that the merry widower could spend hours unobserved there with his mistress, Lucrèce de Forbin Solliès, also known as the "beauty of Canet." Later, the Pavillon was owned by the painter Jean-Baptiste Van Loo. Now it belongs to the city and is a venue for receptions and exhibitions. If you would like to do a bit of shopping in Aix, try the *Souleiado* at 31, Rue de la Couronne, which offers a large selection of Provençal fabrics.

Wine connoisseurs should make a point of visiting the *Cave du Félibrige* in the Rue du Félibrige-Gaut. And there are several swimming pools, and riding stables to be found in Aix and its surroundings. The *Club Equestre de Trets* is recommended and you can reach the stables from Aix in only 15 minutes by car (on the D6) in the direction of Saint-Maximin.

Vauvenargues and the Sainte-Victoire Massif

Paul Cézanne was the most famous painter of the region. In his paintings, he sought to recreate the outlines and form of the female body which he perceived in the shape of the surrounding hills. Admirers of Cézanne may follow in the footsteps of the great master and spend at least one day roaming the hills of the limestone massif of the **Montagne Sainte-Victoire,** where color, light and shadow create fascinating designs in the landscape. Cézanne made this mountain world famous by painting it dozens of times, in many different lights.

The town of Aix is surrounded by hills, by the Trévaresse chain to the north, by the Etoile mountains to the south, and to the east, by the Montagne Sainte-Victoire, which rises to a symmetrical peak, over 3000 ft (1000m) high. The rugged cliffs of its southern slope are a constant challenge to enthusiastic rock climbers, and form a magnificent backdrop for the town of Aix. Unfortunately, the Sainte-Victoire area suffered a particularly devastating forest fire in 1989. Since then, considerable efforts have been made to reafforest the area and gradually bring it back to its former state.

Aix-en-Provence, Cézanne, and the Sainte-Victoire are inextricably linked with each other. The places and scenes that Cézanne immortalized in his paintings still inspire visitors today, whether it is the house called Jas de Bouffan, which belonged to his family and was sold in 1899, the estate of Montbriant, or the house, Bellevue, which belonged to Cézanne's brother-in-law, and can be found on the road to Tholonet (the D17). On the slopes of Sainte-Victoire, near the Chemin des Lauves, Cézanne built himself a house with a studio, where he painted daily, sometimes starting as early as five o'clock in the morning.

The village of **Vauvenargues** (take the D10) is also worth a detour. Its huge, austere and impregnable castle stands high above the village, commanding the entrance to the valley. It originally belonged to the first consul of Aix, Joseph Clapiers de Vauvenargues, and later passed to the Isoard family, was purchased by Picasso in 1958. When he died, he was buried in its park.

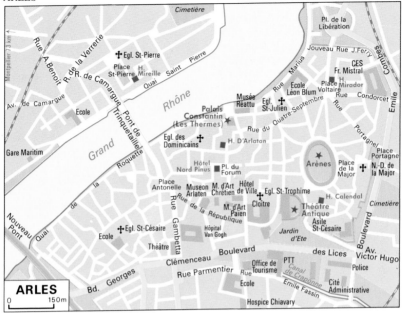

ARLES AND THE CAMARGUE

Arles is an architectural gem among the Provençal towns. It is situated on the edge of the Camargue, a unique landscape of outstanding natural beauty.

Arles

After centuries of fame, first as a Roman capital, then as a major ecclesiastical center, Arles seemed content to look back on past glories, its magnificent ruins and the laurels earned by Frédéric Mistral, Alphonse Daudet and Georges Bizet. For a long time it was known mainly for a few attractive ruins and interesting folk traditions. At last, however, Arles is beginning to stage a comeback, due in part to the *Rencontres Internationales de la Photographie* – an internationally renowned photographic fair – various other cultural events, a new-found French passion for bullfighting, and the influence of fashion designer, Christian Lacroix, whose creations have often been inspired by the colorful Arlesian traditional costumes.

Arles can offer something for everyone: bullfights in the Roman amphitheater (**Arènes**) which can seat an audience of 26,000, the collections at the **Musée Réattu** (Provençal crafts, modern art, and drawings by Picasso), and elegant accommodation in the *Hôtel Nord Pinus*, an old, aristocratic *palais*, renovated in a very unconventional style, and is a favorite haunt for the celebrity crowd who visit the town for the festivals.

The best way to explore the old part of Arles is on foot. The **ancient theater** dates from the reign of Emperor Augustus. Other sites of outstanding interest are the largest existing **thermal baths** in Provence (where extensive excavations are in progress), the early Christian necropolis of **Les Alyscamps**, the Van Gogh Bridge, the painting of which immortalized both the bridge and the artist, and the church of **Saint-Trophime,** where German Emperor Frederick Barbarossa was crowned King of Arles in

1178, and where King René married Jeanne de Laval. The main porch displays a wealth of sculptured detail, and the cloisters are one of the masterpieces of Provençal Romanesque architecture.

You can admire splendid sarcophagi and mosaics in the **Musée d'Art Païen,** the museum of pre-Christian art in the church of Sainte-Anne. Other places worth a visit are the **Musée d'Art Chrétien**, in the old Jesuit chapel, or the museum of folk history, the **Museon Arlaten.** The poet Frédéric Mistral used all of his Nobel Prize money to equip the museum.

Once a year, the cultural center, **Espace Van Gogh,** organizes an event which endeavours to recreate the Arles that Van Gogh and Picasso knew.

Special Arlesian items can be obtained in the following shops: for traditional Provençal clothing, try *l'Arlesienne,* 12 rue du Président Wilson; for fabrics and crafts visit the *Boutique du santon,* 1 rue Jean-Jaurès; genuine Arlesian sausages can be obtained in the *Charcuterie Pierre Milhau,* 11 rue Réattu. The Boulevard des Lices, Arles's promenade, is the setting for a lively nightlife and its terraced cafés are busy until very late.

The **Abbey of Montmajour** is on the D17, about 4 km (2.5 miles) outside Arles. The abbey was founded by Benedictine monks in 949, and is renowned for its Romanesque cloisters and the crypt, hollowed out of the rock beneath.

The Camargue

The Camargue is a broad, marshy flood-plain, bounded by the lesser and greater Rhône, Arles, Saintes-Maries-de-la-Mer and Port-Saint-Louis. The growing threat to its unique fauna and flora caused great concern and it was declared a nature reserve in 1972. Large-scale cultivation of rice in the area was reduced, and the land allowed to revert to its natural state. Since then, many original ani-

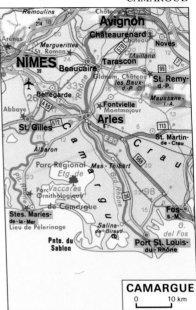

mal and plant species have resettled much of the area. Among the native inhabitants of the Camargue are the famous flamingoes, whose salmon-pink plumage has made them a symbol of this famous delta. They live on an exclusive diet of shellfish and molluscs. Other species, too, have managed to recover. A picture of the Camargue would be incomplete without horses and bulls (considered to be wild), as well as herds of sheep, waterbirds, and migratory birds, such as white sandpipers, herons, bee eaters, and ibises, and also plants which tolerate a salty environment, like blue thistle, tamarind, narcissi, and the *saladelles,* used for decoration in spring, and which are woven into garlands in Maillane on Frédéric Mistral's birthday.

Every year in spring, the Camargue (about 100,000 hectares / 247,000 acres) becomes a riot of color, ranging from the gold of wheatfields to the pristine white of huge salt heaps, from the green of rice paddies to the shining blue of salt water lagoons.

The Camargue has remained much the same for hundreds of years, and retains an aura of unusual tranquility and grandeur. Watching a bull herdsman (*gardian*) on horseback driving his herd of bulls, whose hooves throw up sprays of water that glitter in the sun, is an unforgettable experience. White horses and black bulls are ancient images of the Camargue, and their potent symbolism has always fueled the imagination of the people who live here. *Ferias* and *corridas* (bullfights) are again much in demand, although the locals find the brand-ing of steers almost equally exciting. The horses of the Camargue are bred of very old, robust and highly intelligent stock.

The fame of **Saintes-Maries-de-la-Mer,** on the N570, is based on an old leg-end. Mary Jacobaea, the sister of the Vir-gin Mary, Mary Magdalene, and Mary Salome, her son Lazarus (who had been raised from the dead), and other disciples of Jesus are said to have arrived here around A.D. 40. They were accompanied by their black servant, Sara, who crossed the sea floating on her cloak, which God had turned into a raft. After they had all landed safely, Mary Salome, Mary Jaco-baea and Sara remained here, in the place God had shown them. When they died, a chapel was built over their graves. This little town has been a major place of pil-grimage for centuries, especially for southern French gypsies. Thousands of votive pictures are brought here by the gypsies, to honor Sara, who has tran-scended her original role and become a Black Madonna. In the 9th century, the chapel was replaced by a church, **Notre-Dame-de-la-Mer,** a fortified building, that was incorporated into the town walls, and extended in the 12th century.

Today, the streams of pilgrims who ar-rive here in May and October, are remin-ders of the ardent faith that has hallowed this patch of ground for twenty centuries. It is an extremely impressive and moving

Above: The classical amphitheater, known as the Arena of Arles. Right: Festival at Les Saintes-Maries-de-la-Mer.

72

experience to watch mass being said for the patron saint. A colorful procession of locals – many women still wearing the traditional Arlesian costume – carry statues of the saints all around the town, right down to the beach, and into the sea. Once the saints have been returned to the church, the signal is given for the start of a huge folk festival, with balls, rodeos, horse-races and bullfights.

Although Saintes-Maries-de-la-Mer is a popular beach resort, there are times when tourists may feel a little abashed in the face of the simple dignity of the white-washed houses, the flaming red sunsets, and the untroubled demeanour of the townspeople.

The old town hall is now home to the **Musée Baroncelli,** which displays traditional artifacts from the Camargue. Many of these exhibits were collected by the Marquis Folco de Baroncelli, who dedicated his life to preserving the traditions of his homeland.

Leaving the town on the D202, you will come to the **Château d'Avignon,** a

hunting lodge containing furniture and objets d'art from the 18th century.

The **Bird Sanctuary of Pont de Gau** (on the DN570), which comprises 60 hectares (148 acres) of marshland, is another place worth visiting.

Port-Saint-Louis-du-Rhône (on the D35), a town situated on the estuary of the main branch of the Rhône, is referred to locally as the "town at the end of the world," but is rapidly becoming a favorite port of call for yachtsmen cruising along the coast between Italy and Spain. These days, the magnificent beaches around the town attract sun-worshippers and sand-yacht racers. A course is also laid out for windsurfing championships including those of Belgium and Holland. The most unforgettable image of Saint-Louis is probably the sight of countless fishing huts along the beaches of **Carteau** and **Napoléon,** many of which are only accessible by boat and are blissfully undisturbed.

The **Plain of Crau** lies north-east of Saint-Louis. The northernmost "Petite

Hamlets and Villages

Crau" is notable for its many large orchards, protected from the wind by high "hedges" of cypress trees. The barren south, the "Grande Crau," is a monotonous landscape of gray shingle, also known as "the Provençal desert." For thousands of years, pebbles were carried here from the mountains by the Durance River, before its course shifted. Today, the Durance flows into the Rhône south of Avignon. At the southernmost point of the inhospitable Grande Crau is the former Roman port of **Fos.** An ultra-modern industrial complex has been developed here in recent years.

THE LOWER DURANCE

From Maillane to La Roque-d'Anthéron, a pretty country road will take you through an area of unspoilt villages and fragrant orchards, protected from the Mistral by windbreaks of cypress.

Above: Pink flamingoes and white horses are typical sights in the Camargue.

The poet Frédéric Mistral lived and died in Maillane (between Tarascon and Avignon). His tomb is in the town cemetery, and is an exact replica of the tomb of Queen Jeanne at Les-Baux. Even today, everything about Maillane seems to revolve around the town's most illustrious son, who received the Nobel Prize for Literature in 1904. The house in which he died in 1914, aged 84, now contains the **Musée Mistral.**

In **Châteaurenard** (on the D28) you will find a 10th-century castle built for Count Reynardus. A magnificent view to distant horizons can be enjoyed from the top of the castle's towers, described by Frédéric Mistral.

Other interesting features of this charming village are the flower market in April, a traditional annual market on 14 July, horse races, and the festival of the Horse King (Le Cheval Roi), that includes a procession of 50 decorated floats drawn by horses in Saracen harness.

The castle ruins on the rocks at **Noves** still dominate this little hamlet, which has a history going back to the 5th century B.C. Noves did not become French until the reign of Louis XI. Until then, the popes of Avignon used it as a second residence, then ceded it to France. You can enjoy visiting several Romanesque chapels in Noves and also try the strong local wine, which has a most romantic name - *Cuvée des Amours.*

Cabannes (on the D26) also has several chapels and pretty, shady squares, an interesting market, and offers good angling in the Durance.

A number of attractive villages, as yet undiscovered by tourists, can be found north of Salon-de-Provence, in the hills flanking the Durance valley.

Most visitors traveling along the D73 will only stop at **Lamanon,** which has cave dwellings and a 300-year old plane tree, the "Giant of Provence." The castle ruins, a little Romanesque church, and the folk festivals (in June) are also worth a detour.

Alleins (take the D71 or the D17) has a few pretty, old houses and a ruined castle with a belltower, chapels and a fine passion scene (*calvaire*).

The ruins of a 14th-century castle tower over Mallemort (on the D16). Its tranquil little alleys and squares, along with excellent facilities for horse-riding in the vicinity, make this village a real tourist magnet, despite the presence of a power station nearby.

Drive along the D561, and you will reach **Silvacane.** Its abbey, founded by Raymond des Baux in 1144, derives its name from the marshy terrain that once existed here: in Latin *silva canna* means "thicket of reeds." The abbey belonged to the Cistercians, and in spite of a feud with the Abbey of Montmajour, it enjoyed a long period of prosperity before decay set in due to internal corruption and repeated plundering. After the French Revolution, the abbey became a secular estate, before being bought by the government in 1846. A rather protracted period of restoration followed. Today, you can visit the bell-tower, the monks' hall, the refectory, and the church, all of which possess a dignified, rather severe beauty. Not far from here is **La Roque-d'Anthéron**, which hosts an annual international piano festival. The town dates back to the 16th century and Jean de Forbin, who surrounded his castle, Florans, with a town built in the Renaissance style. He was personally responsible for the design of this charming town, its beautiful town houses, and geometric street plan. Now, the streets are filled in summer with enthusiastic music lovers.

Salon-de-Provence

Salon-de-Provence is the economic center of the region. The town is famous for being the base of a French aerobatic team, *La Patrouille de France.* Everyone cranes their head as the jets streak and loop around the skies. Salon was also the home of Nostradamus, who lived here in exile, and received all the great personages of the kingdom (foremost among them Cathérine de Medicis), who came to seek counsel regarding their future. This is where he wrote his famous *Centuries.* His tomb is in one of the chapels of the church of Saint-Laurent.

Another prominent figure in this town was the 16th-century engineer, Adam de Craponne, who built a canal linking the Durance and the Rhône, which in turn made possible the irrigation and cultivation of 77 sq. miles (200 sq km) of land. Salon is the town where olive oil processing on a large scale began, introduced by Colbert. The soap industry of Marseilles once reached as far as Salon, but the only survivor from its period of prosperity is the *Savonnerie Marius Fabre* (guided tours through the factory are available). The soaps were traditionally made of palm oil and olive oil, enriched with oats,

lavender, and similar natural ingredients. The people of Salon like to recall, with considerable pride, that the town was Provençal long before becoming French, and that it was founded by Celtic salt merchants, *Salyens (Saluvii)*, who settled in this area around the time of the birth of Christ. You will find evidence of Salon's history all around the town. The **Château de l'Emperi,** the Collégiale Saint-Laurent, the remains of the town walls, and the monument to Jean Moulin are all witnesses of Salon's past. The château was built on the Rock of Puech (during the 13th to 15th centuries), and was named *Emperi* as a tribute to the Holy Roman Emperor. Today it contains a museum of art and military history. The **Festival de Juillet** takes place here every year in July, and includes jazz, classical, and *variété* music.

Above: The Château de l'Emperi in Salon-de-Provence. Right: Spectacular ruins and Renaissance town houses in Les Baux-de-Provence.

LES ALPILLES

The Alpilles (meaning "Little Alps") are a range of limestone hills in the heart of Provence, with many charming, little villages and a number of impressive ruins.

Les Baux-de-Provence

A most extraordinary town, called **Les Baux,** (between Arles and Saint-Remy) appears to be perched on an outcrop of the Alpilles. The name Baux is derived from the Provençal word *baou,* meaning "high rock." It is also the site of a grand and imposing castle ruled by generation upon generation of Counts of Les Baux, one of the richest feudal families in southern France, who waged war, composed lyrical poems of courtly love, and indulged in much merrymaking, until Louis XI finally put an end to it all and made them pull down their walls. Later, Louis XIII also had cause to be displeased with these insolent barons, and

Les Baux was taken from them and ceded to the Grimaldi family, counts of Mon-aco. It passed back to France in 1791, but by then its heyday was over, and prob-ably the only important event during the last 200 years was the discovery of the mineral bauxite, the ore of aluminum, named after the town where it was first identified.

Les Baux consists of two parts, the huge castle ruins, which seem to be growing out of the living rock, and the village, which is tended with loving care by its inhabitants.

The **Tour de Brau** houses a museum. The rock chapel of **Saint-Vincent** is a charming architectural mixture of Ro-manesque and Renaissance styles. It is famous for its Christmas service, which includes the traditional shepherds' gifts. The view from the castle's belltower into the precipitous **Val d'Enfer** (the Valley of Hell) way below, is enough to make one's blood run cold. After centuries of decay, Les Baux is still an impressive symbol of medieval splendour.

The Villages of the Alpilles

At the entrance to the valley of Les Baux (on the D17) is **Fontvieille**, one of the most popular tourist towns in the area. The history of the town can be traced back into the dim and distant past, thanks to many prehistoric finds, but its fame is also based on its literary connota-tions: Alphonse Daudet described Font-vieille with its four windmills and thyme and lavender scented slopes in his fa-mous book, *Lettres de mon Moulin* (Let-ters from my windmill).

Today, the town's main source of in-come is tourism and agriculture. It boasts many vineyards and olive groves, and fruit and vegetables are grown in abun-dance, giving a marvellous colour and aroma to the local markets. Sites of inter-est around Fontvieille are the Roman ruins of Caparon, the fort of Paon, the castles of Estoublon, Barbegal, and Mon-tauban, and the Abbey of Montmajour, which belongs to the parish of Arles, but is just a stone's throw away.

Paradou was the home of the famous Occitan poet, Charloun Rieu, who wrote the *Chants du Terroir* and translated Homer's *Odyssey* into Occitan. It is a pretty village nestling among vineyards and olive groves, with the Romanesque **church of Saint-Martin,** and the remains of a castle dating from the 13th century – its towers are especially impressive.

Every year, in the middle of September, the town stages a folk festival in memory of Charloun Rieu.

From here, take the road flanked on one side by cypress trees, with a magnificent view of the Alpilles Massif on the other side, and you will eventually reach **Maussane-les-Alpilles.** Maussane is an attractive little town with beautiful houses and squares and has olive oil presses, a 19th-century wash-house, the **Fontaine des Quatre-Saisons,** and the 18th-century **château of Monblan**. Its inhabitants are proud of their many oratories; foremost among them is the severe, but beautiful **Oratoire de Saint-Marc,** dating to the 14th century. The **church of Saint-Croix** (18th century) is also worth a visit.

The history of **Mouriès**, and of Maussane and Paradou, is almost identical to that of Les Baux up to the French Revolution. Only ruins remain of the **Fort Castellas**, destroyed by the Count of Turenne in 1394, but the **church of Saint-Jacques-le-Majeur,** the chapel of Saint-Symphorien, and the excavations of the *oppidum* of Servanes are all worth visiting. A large number of traditional farmhouses (called *mas*), which all once owned their own windmill, can be found in Mouriès and surroundings: the Mas de Servanes, the Mas de Beauregard, the Mas de Malacercis, and the most eminent one of all, the well-known Mas de Brau,

Right: Daudet's windmill still stands at Fontvielle. Far right: The chapel of Saint-Sixte, near the charming village of Eygalières.

with its beautiful Renaissance façade (a preservation order was put on it back in 1932!). Mouriès, the chief olive-oil producing community in France, owes its agricultural prosperity to the draining of its marshland, and to a system of irrigation canals that channel water from the Durance. On the southern slopes of the Alpilles, where the plain of Crau begins, is **Aureille,** a village which presumably owes its name to the Roman road, *Via Aurelia*. Its many ruins are witness to an immensely long history: Beside the medieval castle ruins, there are remains of an 11th-century church, with a belltower topped by a dome, some very old houses, and Roman ruins. Aureille is also known for its "humane" bullfights where the bull is allowed to live.

In the heart of Les Alpilles is the breathtakingly beautiful village of **Eyguières** (D 24), which is said to have an especially healthy climate. Eyguières also has many architectural treasures: the Romanesque chapels of **Saint-Pierre-de-Vence**, **Saint-Sauveur** and **Saint-Vérédème** (hundreds of votive gifts are presented to the church's patron saint on the second Sunday in August), chapels and passion scenes, Gallo-Roman tombs and other prehistoric sites, as well as houses, such as the **Maison Garcin** (which have preservation orders on them). However, in the height of summer, the greatest attractions are the village's two fountains, the 18th-century **Fontaine Bormes-à-la-Coquille** and the **Fontaine Croix-du-Prêche**, also called *la cocotte,* which is a gem of Renaissance architecture. Bullfights (without bloodshed!) take place here during the summer, and year after year, attract large enthusiastic audiences.

Orgon (on the N569) boasts Roman and medieval ruins, houses with Renaissance frontages, and offers a magnificent view of the Durance valley and the mountains of the Lubéron. This charming village is situated on the left bank of the

Durance, at the foot of a hill, which was once the site of a fortress belonging to the Duc de Guise. Ancient traditions are maintained at the annual fair held at the end of September.

Eygalières is a real picture-book Provençal village. After a turbulent medieval history, followed by a period of near oblivion, it is now in the process of being rediscovered. More and more travelers are drawn here by such pastoral delights as its church, Saint-Sixte, nestling in a grove of cypress trees.

Saint-Rémy-de-Provence

At the foot of the Alpilles (on the D99) is Saint-Rémy-de-Provence. This town owns its fame to the excavations of **Les Antiques** and the nearby ruins of **Glanum**, once a prosperous Gallo- Roman town boasting a triumphal arch and a mausoleum. Glanum was destroyed by barbarians in the 3rd century. The arch dates back to before the birth of Christ. It was built in memory of the town's founda-

tion, unlike later triumphal arches, which were usually erected in honor of a victorious general. The **mausoleum**, probably one of the best preserved Roman buildings anywhere, is actually a cenotaph, thought to have been built in honor of Caius and Lucius, grandsons of Augustus, who died very young.

The entire site of Glanum, which dates back to the 3rd century B.C., is of great interest. The scores of archaeological finds that came to light during excavations – mainly coins and jewelery – can be viewed in the archaeological museum at the **Hôtel de Sade** in Rémy.

Even modern Saint-Rémy has a certain charm, and the old part of the town with its richly ornamented houses, fountains and shady squares, is ideal for gentle strolling. It is intriguing to think that this pleasant way of life was shared bythe prophet Nostradamus (who had a house in the rue des Barri) and Van Gogh (who resided in Saint-Rémy, in 1889-90). A small museum, called *Preserve Van Gogh*, has been set up in the Hôtel des

Pistoye. It provides visitors with a great deal of information about Van Gogh (and even offers a guided tour of Van Gogh's Saint-Rémy), but, unfortunately, it does not have a single painting by the great artist. Exhibitions of contemporary artists' work are held here. The **Hôtel Mistral de Mondragon** contains a museum of folk history, with traditional costumes, furniture, *santons* and a collection of documents connected with Nostradamus.

The Romanesque cloisters and a fine belltower at the former abbey, **Saint-Paul-de-Mausole**, are also worth a visit. The abbey was temporarily used as a nursing home; Van Gogh stayed here, and Albert Schweitzer spent four years of his life (1914-18) in this institution. Popular bullfights, again, of the bloodless variety, are also staged in Saint-Rémy.

TARASCON AND LA MONTAGNETTE

The hills of the Montagnette range stretch from Barbentane in the north to Tarascon in the south along the mighty Rhône river.

Travel along the D35 and you will reach **Barbentane**, which is situated on a hilly outcrop. Its medieval city gates, the **Porte Calendrale** and the **Porte du Séquier** are still partly preserved. The castle is probably the best known feature of the town, but the **Maison des Chevaliers** (the Knights' House) and the **Tour Anglica**, both of which are described in a poem by Mistral, called *Iscles d'Or,* add considerably to the charm of this village. The 17th-century château, still owned by the Marquis de Barbentane, is also called the **Petit Trianon du Soleil,** because of its great beauty and elegant appearance. Its interior decoration was designed by the Marquis Joseph Pierre Balthazar de

Right: The castle at Tarascon, built in the 15th century under "Good King René."

Puget, who was Louis XV's ambassador in Tuscany, and who had the reception rooms decorated and the terraces laid out in the Florentine style.

Nature lovers should not miss a walk to the mill at **Bretoule**. The mill has not been working for over 100 years but the path to it will take you through fragrant pine woods and olive groves, the dreamlike tranquility of which is disturbed by nothing more intrusive than the chirping of countless cicadas.

Tarascon

The town of Tarascon has always been bound up with the well-known legend of the dreaded Tarasque, a terrible, man-eating water monster. It was finally vanquished by Sainte Marthe, who courageously splashed it with holy water from Saintes-Maries-de-la-Mer. Another "trademark" of Tarascon is Tartarin, the colorful hero of a novel by Alphonse Daudet. "Good King René" had a castle built here, where you can see six Gobelin tapestries from the series *The Deeds of Scipio Africanus.*

Even the **Hôpital Saint-Nicolas** with its old apothecary's shop, where hundreds of ceramic bottles and containers are stored in beautiful old wooden cabinets, or just the view across the Rhône and the Montagnette, make Tarascon worth a visit. The list of attractions goes on: the Gothic **church of Sainte-Marthe**, patron saint of the town, where you will find paintings by Van Loo and Mignard, as well as a splendid church organ dating from the late 15th century, the cloisters, **Cloître des Cordeliers,** where, concerts and exhibitions are now held, and finally the **Abbey of Saint-Michel-de-Frigolet,** which is perched on the Montagnette.

The **Maison de Tartarin** is another building to be seen. It is a recreation of a middle-class home of the late 19th century, containing a collection of folk artefacts and traditional costume, as well as documentation about Tartarin, a character firmly established in French theater and cinema. Admirers of Provençal costume and fabrics should definitely visit the **Musée Charles Demery Souleïado,** and the shop called Souleïado at 39, rue Proudhon. If you still have time left for a walk through the old section of town, stroll through the rue des Halles with its arcades, or along the rue Arc-de-Boquy, which is roofed over.

Every year the whole town holds a street-festival to celebrate their beloved hero Tartarin and his victory over the dreaded monster, Tarasque. This takes place on the last Sunday in June.

A Détour to Gard

Even if this trip means temporarily leaving the territory of Provence, a tour to Pont du Gard (D986) via Nîmes (N86), then to Saint-Gilles (D42) and through the Camargue to Aigues-Mortes is strongly recommended.

PONT DU GARD

Almost everyone must have seen at least one picture of the bold span of the Roman aqueduct across the Gard river. The proud dimensions (160 ft/ 49m high) of this monument to Roman engineering skill really have to be seen to be appreciated. The aqueduct was built approximately 2000 years ago, in 19 B.C., by Agrippa, one of the generals of Emperor Augustus, and its perfect construction puts any present-day mains water-supply to shame.

In those days, it provided sufficient water for the whole town of Nîmes (an estimated 20,000 cubic meters or 700,000 cubic ft per day) brought from the hills, a distance of 50 km (30 miles). It is astonishing to realise that the stone blocks used for building the aqueduct each weigh several tonnes and were fitted together without mortar. It was in continuous use for nearly 900 years, and then, after centuries of neglect, was restored in the 19th century.

PONT DU GARD

Today, you can walk across the 900 ft (275m) bridge on three different levels, and there is a road on the lowest level. If you do not mind heights, you can risk walking along the unguarded top level, but should you prefer to see from a distance how well the aqueduct harmonizes with the surrounding landscape, you can step into one of the kayaks that are for hire along the river below.

NIMES

One thing Nîmes and Provence have in common is their Roman past. Nîmes owes its importance to being a major crossroads on the "Road of Hercules," one of the most ancient trading routes. Apart from the many well-preserved Roman buildings and a thriving cultural life, this busy industrial and commercial city has little to attract the tourist.

Above: The Maison Carrée in Nîmes. Right: A group of apostles in the Musée de la Maison Romane in Saint-Gilles.

Many veterans of Emperor Augustus's Egyptian campaigns settled in the *Colonia Augustus Nemausus* at the end of the 1st century B.C., and a crocodile chained to a palm tree, which appears on the town's coat-of-arms, is an emblem of their conquest of the lands along the Nile. The original Celtic settlement beside a spring, was named after Nemausus, god of springs and wells. The famous amphitheater, measuring about 131 m by 100 m (430 ft by 328 ft), which seats 24,000, is better preserved and larger than the one in Arles, and is still used as a bullfighting arena and as a stage for theatrical performances. The **Maison Carrée** is a building of such harmonious proportions, that it is considered to be one of the most beautiful temples in the Greek tradition outside Italy. It contains the **Musée des Antiques**, a collection of classical sculptures and mosaics.

The city gate, **Porte d'Auguste**, was once part of the town wall, and guarded the road to Arles. The Nemausus spring bubbles out of the ground at the foot of

Mont Cavalier in the **Jardin de la Fontaine**. If you climb up the slope above it, you will get to the **Tour Magne**, a Roman tower, which provides a magnificent view of the area. It is worth driving on from Nîmes to Saint-Gilles, in order to see the impressive porch of the Romanesque abbey church.

Saint-Gilles

Saint-Gilles, also known as the gateway to the Camargue, lies in a setting of fertile orchards. This humble little provincial town owes its name to Saint Egidius (French, Saint-Gilles), who founded a monastery here in 1200. It soon became an important station on the pilgrim route to Santiago de Compostela, this important example of the southern French Romanesque style suffered terribly during the religious wars, and again later on, especially during the French Revolution.

Visitors often express surprise when they discover the splendid porch of the west façade is all that is left of the former Romanesque **abbey church,** together with remains of the chancel and the crypt containing the tomb of Saint-Gilles. The west porch is divided into three pictorial stone arches, and above the frieze, majestic stone sculptures gaze down upon the visitor. The scenes of the life and suffering of Christ (such as the Last Supper, the Washing of Feet, the Kiss of Judas, the Flagellation, and the Stations of the Cross) are impressive subjects of religious inspiration. The bestiary frieze is made up of rather fantastic looking creatures. All of these examples of Romanesque symbolism can be traced back to antiquity.

The walls outside the present-day church are all that remains of the former chancel. The fine spiral staircase, Vis de Saint-Gilles, is a good indicator of the size of the belltower, now destroyed, that was built around 1150.

Aigues-Mortes

A drive through the Camargue, along the Rhône, to Aigues-Mortes, now seems the obvious choice. **Aigues-Mortes** is situated at the western edge of this marshland area which was once called "Dead Waters" (*aigues mortes*).

King Louis IX ("Saint Louis") had a naval port built here, mainly as a starting point for ships setting out on two of the crusades. By the 14th century, however, the entrance to the harbor had completely silted up. The town and its surviving medieval buildings are still enclosed by mighty walls, with towers and turrets, and it is worth taking a walk along the top of the wall, over a mile (1700m) in circumference and nearly 40 ft (11m) high. Start at the 13th century **Tour de Constance,** which was a prison for Huguenots after the Revocation of the Edict of Nantes in 1685, and in the ensuing religious wars. From the top you will be able to see right across the salt pans as far as the open sea.

SAINT-GILLES / AIGUES-MORTES

Tourist Information
Information about the region from the **Comité départemental du Tourisme**, rue du Jeune-Anacharsis, 13001 Marseille, Tel: 91-549266.

AIX-EN-PROVENCE
Accommodation
MODERATE: **Hôtel Le Manoir**, rue d'Entrecasteaux, Tel: 42-262720.
BUDGET: **La Bastide**, Les Milles, quartier Robert, Tel: 42-244850.

Restaurants
Abbaye des Cordeliers, rue Lieutaud, Tel: 42-272947. **Le Picotin**, rue de la Paix, Tel: 42-279544, both restaurants are inexpensive.

Museums / Sightseeing / Festival
Musée Granet, place Saint-Jean-de-Malte, Tel: 42-381470. **Musée des Tapisseries**, ancien Archevêché, Tel: 42-230991. **Musée du Vieil Aix**, 17, rue Gaston-de-Saporta, Tel: 42-214355. **Cathédrale Saint-Sauveur**, open daily 10 am-12 noon and 2-6 pm. **Pavillon Vendôme**, 34, rue Célony, Tel: 42-210578.
Festival d'Art lyrique et de Musique, in July.

Tourist Information
Office de Tourisme, place du Général-de-Gaulle, Tel: 42-260293.

ARLES
Accommodation
MODERATE: **Calendal**, 22, place Pomme, Tel: 90-961189. **La Fenière**, Raphèle-les-Arles, Tel: 90-984744.

Restaurants
Le Vaccarès, 9, rue Favorin, Tel: 90-960617, good food at moderate prices. **L'Affenage**, 4, rue Molière, Tel: 90-960767, inexpensive.

Museums / Sightseeing
Musée Réattu, 10, rue du Grand-Prieuré, Tel: 90-963768. **Musée lapidaire d'Art chrétien**, rue Balze, Tel: 90-963768. **Musée lapidaire d'Art païen**, place de la République, Tel: 90-963768. **Museon Arlaten**, 29, rue de la République, Tel: 90-960823. **Espace Van Gogh**, rue du Président-Wilson. **Abbaye de Montmajour**.

Tourist Information / Festivals
Office de Tourisme, esplanade Charles-de-Gaulle, Tel: 90-962935.
Rencontres internationales de la Photographie, from July 4–August 21. *Feria,* festivities at Easter. *Festival,* in July.

BARBENTANE
Accommodation
BUDGET: **Castel Mouisson**, quartier Castel Mouisson, **Tel: 90-955117.**

Tourist Information / Castle
Office de Tourisme, in the town hall, Tel: 90-955039. **Château,**Tel: 90-955107.

BAUX-DE-PROVENCE
Accommodation
LUXURY: **Le Mas d'Aigret**, on route D 27a, Tel: 90-543354.
BUDGET: **La Reine Jeanne**, Grand'rue, Tel: 90-543206.

Museum / Festival
Musée lapidaire, museum of gems, maison de la Tour de Brau, Tel: 90-973417.
Fête du Pastrage, takes place on Christmas Eve in the church Saint-Vincent.

Tourist Information
Office de Tourisme, Hôtel de Manville, rue du Château, Tel: 90-975439.

CASSIS
Accommodation / Restaurant
MODERATE: **Les Jardins des Campanilles**, rue Auguste-Favier, route de Marseille, Tel: 42-018485.
BUDGET: **Cassitel**, place Clémenceau, Tel: 42-018344. **La Presqu'île**, quartier de Port Miou, rte. des Calanques, Tel: 42-013377, elegant restaurant.

Tourist Information
Office de Tourisme, place Baragnon, Tel: 42-017117.

CAMARGUE
Accommodation
BUDGET: **Mas Saint-Germain**, at the road to Vaccarès, Tel: 90-970060.

Sightseeing
Nature Reserve Camargue, pont de Rousty, Tel: 90-971040. **Château d'Avignon**, route d'Arles, Tel: 90-978632. **Parc ornithologique du Pont de Gau**, Tel: 90-478262.

Tourist Information
In the tourist office in Arles or in Saintes-Maries-de-la-Mer.

CHATEAURENARD
Accommodation
BUDGET: **Les Glycines**, avenue Victor-Hugo, Tel: 90-941066.

Tourist Information
Office de tourisme, quartier des Halles, avenue Roger-Salengro, Tel: 90-942327.

EYGALIERES
Accommodation
MODERATE: **Le Mas de la Brune**, on route D 74a, Tel: 90-959077.

FONTVIEILLE
Accommodation
MODERATE: **A la Grace de Dieu**, 90, av. de Tarascon, Tel: 90-547190.

Museum / Sightseeing
Moulin de Daudet et Musée, Tel: 90-976078.

MAILLANE
Museum
Musée Frédéric Mistral, 11, rue Lamartine.

MARSEILLES
Accommodation
LUXURY: **Le Petit Nice**, Corniche Kennedy, Tel: 91-592592.
MODERATE: **Grand Hôtel de Genève**, 3 bis, rue Reine-Elisabeth, Tel: 91-905142.
BUDGET: **Résidence Sainte-Anne**, 50, bd. Verne, Tel: 91-715454.
Restaurants
L'Epuisette, anse du vallon des Auffes, Tel: 91-521782, elegant restaurant. **Chez Fonfon**, 140, vallon des Auffes, Tel: 91-521438, tasty food at moderate prices.
Museums / Sightseeing
Musée des Arts et Traditions populaires, Château Gombert, place des Héros, Tel: 91-681438. **Musée des Beaux-Arts**, Palais Longchamp, Tel: 91-622117. **Musée Cantini**, 19, rue de Grignan, Tel: 91-547775. **Musée Grobet-Labadié**, 140, bd. de Longchamp, Tel: 91-622182. **Maison Diamantée and Musée du Vieux Marseille**, 2, rue de la Prison, Tel: 91-551019. **Le Jardin des Vestiges**, rue Henri-Barbusse. **Vieille-Major**, open 9-11.30 am and 2.30-5 pm, closed Mondays. **La Vieille-Charité,** Tel: 91-562838. **Notre-Dame de la Garde**, in winter 7 am-5.45 pm, in summer 7 am-7 pm. **Basilique Saint-Victor**, 9 am-12 noon and 3-6 pm. **Château et Parc Borely**, av. du Prado, Tel: 91-732160, bus 44 to le Vieux-Port. **Château d'If**, fortification, Tel: 91-555009, regular connections from the Quai des Belges.
Tourist Information
Office de Tourisme, 4, la Canebière, Tel: 91-549111, Métro Vieux-Port.

MAUSSANE-LES-ALPILLES
Accommodation / Restaurant
BUDGET: **L'Oustaloun**, pl. de l'Eglise, Tel: 90-543219. **Ou Ravi Provençau**, av. Vallée-des-Baux, Tel: 90-543111, Restaurant, moderate prices.

NIMES
Accommodation
LUXURY: **Imperator Concorde**, quai de la Fontaine, Tel: 66-219030. *MODERATE:* **Grand Hotel du Midi**, sqare de la Couronne, Tel: 66-210718. *BUDGET:* **Majestic**, 10, rue Pradier, Tel: 66-292414.
Tourist Information
Office de Tourisme, 6, rue Auguste, Tel: 66-362727.

LA ROQUE-D'ANTHERON
Sightseeing / Festival
Abbaye de Silvacane, Tel: 42-504169.
Festival de Piano, in August.
Tourist Information
Office de Tourisme, in the town hall, place des Ecoles, Tel: 42-504040.

SAINTES-MARIES-DE-LA-MER
Accommodation
LUXURY: **Auberge Cavalière**, route d'Arles, Tel: 90-978888. *MODERATE:* **Mas du Clarousset**, roubine du Joly, Tel: 90-978166.
BUDGET: **Bellevue**, 5, rue de l'Étang, Tel: 90-978147.
Museum / Festival
Musée Baroncelli, in the old town hall, rue Victor-Hugo, Tel: 90-478005.
Pèlerinages, Pilgrims' Festival, Mai 24-25 and end of October.
Tourist Information
Office de Tourisme, 5, avenue Van-Gogh, Tel: 90-978255.

SAINT-REMY-DE-PROVENCE
Accommodation
MODERATE: **Castelet des Alpilles**, place Mireille, route des Baux, Tel: 90-920721.
Museums / Sightseeing
Musée archéologique and Hôtel de Sade, Tel: 90-921307. **Musée des Arts et Traditions populaires**, Hôtel Mistral de Montdragon, Tel: 90-920810.
Tourist Information
Office de Tourisme, place Jean-Jaurès, Tel: 90-920522.

SALON-DE-PROVENCE
Accommodation
MODERATE: **Nuit d'Hôtel,** route du Val de Cuech, Tel: 90-560604. *BUDGET:* **Domaine de Roquerousse**, route d'Avignon, Tel: 90-595011.
Museum / Castle / Festival
Château de l'Empéri and Musée, Tel: 90-562236. *Festival de Jazz*, in July.
Tourist Information
Office de Tourisme, 56, cours Gimon, Tel: 90-562760.

TARASCON
Accommodation
MODERATE: **Les Mazets des Roches**, route de Fontvieille, Tel: 90-913489.
BUDGET: **Le Saint Jean**, 24, bd. Victor-Hugo, Tel: 90-911387.
Sightseeing / Festival
Cloître des Cordeliers, pl. Frédéric-Mistral, Tel: 90-910007. **Château**, Tel: 90-910193. **Maison de Tartarin**, 55 bis, bd. Itam, Tel: 90-910508.
Fêtes de la Tarasque, last weekend in June.
Tourist Information
Office de Tourisme, 59, rue des Halles, Tel: 90-910352.

VAUVENARGUES
Accommodation
BUDGET: **Le Moulin de Provence**, route des Maquisards, Tel: 42-660222.

THE VAUCLUSE

MONTAGNE DE VAUCLUSE
AVIGNON
ORANGE
MONT VENTOUX
PAYS DE SAULT
PLATEAU DE VAUCLUSE
PAYS D'APT
LUBERON

MONTAGNE DE VAUCLUSE

The *département* of Vaucluse divides into two distinct parts.

To the north-east are the ranges of chalk hills, the **Monts de Vaucluse** and, south of these, the **Monts de Lubéron,** which are now a nature reserve *(Parc naturel régional du Lubéron)*. To the south and west, bordered by the Rivers Rhône and Durance, is a fertile plain, crisscrossed with irrigation canals. This is the Comtat Venaissin, once an independent "county," lying between the historic cities of Avignon, Orange, Carpentras and Cavaillon.

Monts de Vaucluse

The Monts de Vaucluse is not one of those supposedly undiscovered areas that people like to tip you off about. But even though it is quite close to the beaten track, you can still go there to get away from the tourist hordes in their overcrowded resorts and bask in the sun-drenched solitude of Provence. Not so very long ago it was to these hills that the French themselves came when weary of

Preceding pages: Springtime in Provence. Left: A Provençal beauty in her traditional costume.

civilization, and they often put down permanent roots here. With great flair and initiative they devoted years of their lives to the labor of restoring the ruined houses that had stood empty for generations in mountain villages whose inhabitants had nearly all died or moved away. Most of these villages were built on hilltops for defensive purposes by the persecuted Waldensian heretics.

Still standing at the highest point of these fortress villages there is always a church, sometimes in ruins, which would have provided a last sanctuary for the inhabitants during the bloody battles between the Catholic authorities and followers of Pierre Waldo, a late 12th-century mystic. Rather than surrender to superior force, the heretics in their desperation would set fire to the church and die as martyrs in the flames.

Throughout the ages these uplands have served mainly for rearing sheep and growing lavender. Erosion and a lack of water have always made agriculture on any significant scale virtually impossible. Apart from some thin grass and vast areas of garrigue or scrub, virtually nothing can grow naturally here because the relentless mistral wind, blowing almost continuously between Mont Ventoux and the Alpilles, dries and erodes the chalky soil and uproots young plants.

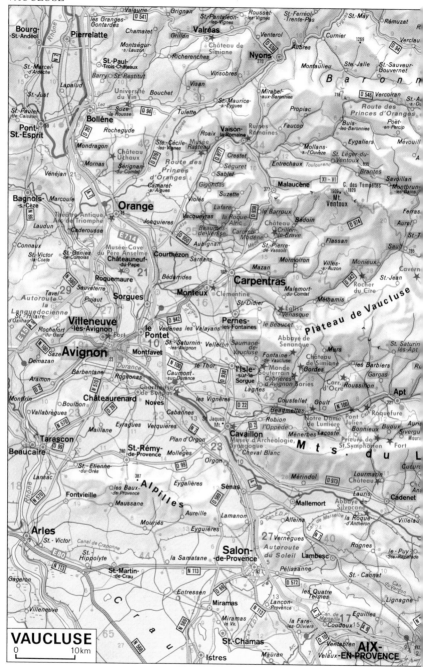

VAUCLUSE

0   10km

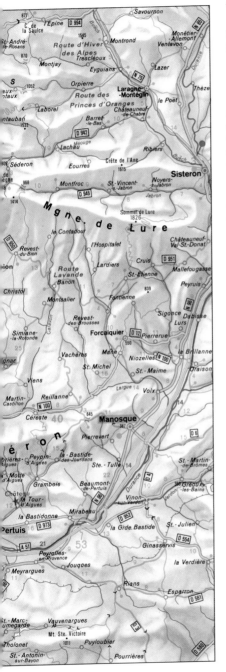

Such rain as there is quickly seeps into the chalk and streams tend to dry up in the heat of the summer.

The Comtat Venaissin

In sharp contrast, the Comtat Venaissin is a broad, well watered and highly cultivated plain flanked by four old cities whose historic patina adds to the picture of tranquil prosperity that so impresses visitors to this region.

The market-gardens, which are the most productive in France, form a mosaic of tiny plots, laced with irrigation canals, ditches and dikes, with here and there a glinting greenhouse. There are shady green copses and windbreaks of tall cypresses. The landscape is almost entirely man-made, but it was not always thus.

Through much of history, people preferred the natural bastions of the mountains for security. Only in times of relative peace – under the Romans, for example – did they venture down into the plain to establish farms and plant olives, wheat and vines. Then, in the 6th or 7th century A.D., monks began to dig the first canals and drain the marshes.

In 1554 the important Carponne Canal was built and with it a more elaborate irrigation system.

At the beginning of the 19th century a new wave of prosperity came with the introduction of silkworms, madder (a plant from which a red dye is obtained) and large-scale wine production. However, this was shortlived as in 1860 a virus wiped out the silkworm population and the vines were attacked by phylloxera. Even the madder became redundant when synthetic dyestuffs were invented.

Fortunately, with the advent of the railways, the region could begin to supply fresh fruit and vegetables to the populous cities of the north. Today, with improved communications to all parts of northern Europe, the growing of fruit and vegetables has become a major industry.

The main crops include melons, tomatoes, strawberries and every imaginable kind of vegetable. Courgettes are one of the most widely grown crops. In spring, the apple, cherry and apricot trees are ablaze with blossom and the terraced slopes are covered with burgeoning grape vines.

The Historic Cities

Leaving behind the broad estates of the plain, the road heads into the hills, through small towns and tiny hamlets, past beautiful churches and the remains of fine mansions. Often nothing is left of the great buildings of the past but ruins - a single tower, a massive portal or a few battlements on a town wall.

In **Monteux** (on the D 942, 4 km or 2.5 miles from Carpentras), nothing remains of the country seat of Pope Clement V but a tower, known as "clémentine," pointing to the sky.

Hidden among the hills in **Courthézon** (on the N 7, 7 km or 4 miles south of Orange), there is a castle with ramparts, a hall and a hospice still standing. **Le Thor** (on the N 100 between Avignon and Cavaillon), which is mainly known for its cultivation of the chasselas grape, has a church with a Romanesque nave surrounded by Gothic vaulting.

La Chartreuse de Bonpas, a Carthusian monastery high above the Durance on the D 973 halfway between Avignon and Cavaillon, was founded by the Knights Templar in the 13th century. The ruined monastery has been restored and converted into a residential building. There is a wonderful view of the distant Monts du Lubéron from its elegant terraced gardens.

The partly fortified village of Venasque (on the D 4, 12 km or 7 miles from Carpentras) was the episcopal seat long before Carpentras, and gave its name to

Right: The Pont St-Bénézet, the Petit Palais and the Papal Palace in Avignon.

the Comtat Venaissin. On a rocky spur of the Piémont Vauclusien stands an impressive 6th-century Merovingian baptistry which is one of the oldest religious buildings in France.

Pernes-les-Fontaines (on the D 938, 6 km / 4 miles from Carpentras) has always enjoyed a favored position thanks to an abundance of water. Its three handsome gates flanked by fortified towers, its ancient corbelled bridge surmounted by a chapel, the keep with its bell-tower belonging to the château of the Counts of Toulouse, the beautiful collegiate church of Notre-Dame-de-Nazareth, and finally the square crenellated tower of Ferrande are all enough to make this one of the most fascinating towns in the region. But what really sets it apart are its many fountains – 37 in all – fed by underground streams and by the River Nesque. Until 1914 each fountain had its own official keeper, but this is an extravagance the modern world cannot afford.

In **L'Isle-sur-la-Sorgue** (on the N 100, 12 km / 7 miles north of Cavaillon) there is more water, but in its natural state. This ancient fishing village built, as the name suggests, among the many branches of the river, has, a little pretentiously, been called "the Venice of the Comtat." This does not lessen the charm of its green waters and shady streets lined with plane trees. Once 70 water-wheels were turned by the Sorgue, driving mills for silk, madder and olive oil. Now only five of these remain and they are mossy and neglected.

The paramount importance of water in this area is illustrated by the legend of Saint Gens and his pilgrimage to **Le Beaucet** (located between Venasque and Pernes). Disapproving of the pagan practises of the local people, Gens deprived them of rain and drought ravaged the land. When the peasants finally repented, the good Saint Gens granted them two springs, one which flowed with water and one which flowed with wine.

Today only the former remains, unfortunately, near the hermitage. (Pilgrimages take place on Easter Monday and Sundays in September.)

AVIGNON

Though historically not part of the Venaissin, **Avignon** is the most important city in this region, having for over a century been the seat of the popes and the center of a religious and political power-struggle. It was a French pope, Clement V, who moved his residence from the traditional papal seat in the Vatican in Rome to Avignon in 1309.

From then on, French popes and cardinals built up a power-base there, much to the annoyance of the rest of Europe. In 1377, under pressure from England and Germany, the papal establishment was transferred back to Rome, but a group of French cardinals, refusing to accept this, elected a series of rival "anti-popes" who continued to exercise authority from Avignon, thus creating what is known as

The Great Schism which lasted until the Council of Constance in 1417.

Today Avignon is the seat of the *préfecture* of Vaucluse and its largest city (population: 180,000). It is a major tourist center with its cheerful, bustling activity, its lively cultural events and the elegance and splendor of its architecture.

July is definitely the best time to visit Avignon, when major drama festivals and other cultural events are held and the city becomes a mecca for internationally renowned performers. At this time of year visitors from around the world crowd onto the terraces of the cafés and in the narrow streets of the old papal city.

Although the festivals have only been in existence since 1947, to some extent they represent the continuation of an ancient tradition. In the Middle Ages the city was well known for the pomp of its processions and its important religious mystery plays. Its streets thronged with emissaries, merchants, scholars and artists who came from every corner of the known world.

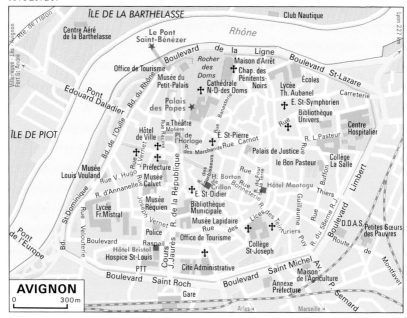

AVIGNON

0   300 m

The best way to approach the city is to enjoy the picture-book panorama from the opposite bank of the River Rhône near the **Pont St-Bénézet.** This bridge has its own claim to fame in the old song *Sur le pont d'Avignon.* The bridge linking Avignon with Villeneuve was originally about 1000 yards (900m) long and was supported on 22 arches. According to legend, in 1177 a shepherd named Bénézet was told to build the bridge by a voice from Heaven, but he had to enlist the help of the brotherhood of bridge-builders *(Frères Pontifes)* to carry out his ambitious plan.

It is also said that when the angel had shown Bénézet the place for the crossing, the shepherd picked up a huge rock which 30 men could not have lifted and swam with it alone to the far bank. The people of Avignon are said to have been so impressed by this feat that they took an

active part in the building of the bridge. As well as giving their labor, they also donated money to pay for its completion. At that time it was the one and only bridge across the Rhône between Avignon and the sea. In ancient times, the Romans had only ever built a wooden foot-bridge over the river.

The bridge was destroyed several times by the fast-flowing Rhône and the ravages of war until in the 17th century it was finally left as we see it today. In the 19th century the four remaining arches were restored and then the tiny chapel of St. Nicolas was also built on the second pier.

This reminds us of the fact that the city has had many patron saints during its history. One of these was St. Martha, who was named patron saint of the city in the 13th century because she had converted the population to Christianity. In fact, it seems she never went near the city at all. Worse still, malicious rumour has it that a number of saints of the city, such as St. Agrico, were merely the product of the

Right: The magnificent fresco by Matteo di Giovanetti in the chapel of the Papal Palace in Avignon.

94

fertile imaginations of a few priests, since no evidence has ever been found that these so-called saints were people who actually lived and breathed. It is probable that some of them really were only pure invention.

The citizens of Avignon have always had a reputation for being broad-minded and tolerant, although this virtue must have temporarily deserted them from time to time during the religious wars that beset the region.

They have tolerated many strange things in the past. From the 13th to the 15th centuries there were the "clubs" of *pénitents* – many orders of mendicant and penitent monks who roamed the streets of the city in their colorful garb. The many chapels to be seen in the city to this day bear witness to their existence.

Then there were the brotherhoods – white, gray, blue, purple, and also a red one which was mainly responsible for the armory and remained in existence until 1700. Most of their members were recruited from among the aristocracy and

the upper classes. As recently as 1950, a Post Office inspector could call himself the "Christ of Monfavet" without becoming an object of general ridicule. His sect claimed some 3000 fanatical followers.

Something not to be missed is the view from Avignon's sister city, **Villeneuve-les-Avignon**. Vicious tongues claimed that the place was built by Cardinal Arnaud de Via at the beginning of the 14th century for the sole purpose of keeping a watchful eye on the papal city opposite. Its magnificent view of Avignon was just a bonus. A recommended lookout point is one of the 40-m (130 ft) high twin towers of **Fort St-André.**

The old part of Avignon lies along a wide bend of the Rhône below the fortress-style papal palace. The circular city wall (around 5 km or 3 miles long) with its bell-towers and watchtowers was built of large, rough-hewn slabs of rock.

Although the massive walls never had to shelter the population from an invading enemy, they have always acted as a flood defense, often to great effect in more recent times. The walls were already obsolete for any military purpose even before they were completed.

Large sections of the walls and the historic heart of the city were destroyed during the French Revolution and the decision to rebuild the ruins of Avignon was not taken until later in the last century. The project was coordinated by the famous architect Viollet-Le-Duc (1814-1879), who clearly brought commitment and expertise to his task.

The people of the city are still proud of its medieval style and fiercely defend it against encroaching development, generally with success, rejecting road-widening schemes, for example, in favor of traffic-calming measures. The people of Provence – particularly the citizens of Avignon – have never been considered the most progressive, preferring to cling to an eternal yesteryear. Despite the fact that the version of Gothic architecture unique to Provence, called the Flamboyant style, was created and practiced by craftsmen in and around Avignon, there was vehement opposition during the transition period to the change from the Romanesque rounded arch to the pointed Gothic arch. What is now generally called the "Gothic of the Popes" has a Romanesque influence brought from Italy. This is seen most clearly in the architecture of the papal palace. Its walls are heavy and solid and its gloomy rooms are of medieval proportions. Even the frescoes look subdued despite their variety of color. The Romanesque influence lasted in this region right through the Renaissance to the Baroque period.

The cathedral of **Notre-Dame-des-Doms** provides a further example of this. It was begun in the 12th century and altered in the 14th and 17th. In the 15th century a further storey was added to the tower, and as late as the 19th C. this was

surmounted by a huge statue of the Virgin. Yet beneath all this the nave consists of thick walls with solid, not flying ,buttresses, narrow unglazed windows and a porch whose design is reminiscent of a Roman temple. Inside there is virtually no statuary, just a few frescoes and pictures providing isolated touches of color. The original paintings hang in the **Musée Petit Palais** (Place du Palais). A large number of secular buildings in Avignon and its immediate environs were still being planned and built in the Romanesque style as late as the 16th and 17th centuries.

Many of the street names in the old city carry echoes of their former occupants. The **rue des Teinturiers** running down to the river was the home and workplace of the dyers. The **rue de la Peyrollerie** was the realm of the kettle makers and tinkers, the **rue de la Banasterie** housed the basket-makers, the **rue de la Bonneterie** recalls the hosiers, the **rue des Marchands** means the street of the merchants, the **rue des Fourbisseurs** the street of the chimney sweeps and the **rue de la Saunerie** the street of the salt-makers. Next to the theater there are streets named after Molière and Racine. Even the great festival theater directors Jean Vilar and Gérard Philippe have had streets named after them.

No matter where you are in Avignon, you can see the **Palais des Papes**. All the streets in the old city lead to it. It is a majestic and defiant building which covers an area of four acres (1.5 hectares). Its massive walls with their embrasures and battlemented watch-towers shelter inner courtyards, vast halls and numberless suites of rooms along endless corridors winding like a labyrinth through the Old Palace (1334-42) and the even more magnificent New Palace (1342-13). The palace can be visited by guided tour only and you should allow a day to see all of it.

One of the main museums in the city is the **Petit Palais** mentioned earlier. This

Right: Musicians and sun-worshippers are found everywhere in Provence.

former residence of the bishops of Avignon has been beautifully restored and now contains important Italian paintings from the medieval to the Renaissance period. Most of the works were commissioned by the popes but some were purchased on their behalf. Also important is the **Musée Calvet** (65, rue Joseph-Vernet). This is the private collection of the physician Dr. Esprit Calvet and includes paintings by French artists from the 16th to the 20th centuries and archaeological finds from the area around Avignon and the city itself.

The **Musée Lapidaire** also deserves a mention. Its main attraction is a statue of the man-eating Tarasque de Noves. In the dim and distant past this mythical beast is said to have guarded the crossing point of the Rhône. Also worth a mention in the lapidarium are the sculptures and reliefs going right back to the Celtic/Ligurian period.

The **Livrée Ceccano** houses the fine city *mediathèque* (film and music archives). The **Musée Requien** is a mu-seum of natural history, the **Musée Théodore Aubanel** is devoted to the craft of printing and the **Musée Félibriges** contains a variety of exhibits on Provençal folklore. The **Musée Louis-Voulard** displays beautiful old furniture and priceless porcelain. Many satisfying hours can be spent wandering round these museums while the mistral blows outside.

The **Place des Carmes** is another place not to missed. While the festival is on, it has open-air theater performances and for the rest of the year a flea-market is held every Sunday, where you can sometimes pick up a bargain or at least an interesting souvenir.

Cavaillon

Helped by the extensive irrigation system already mentioned, the people living in the triangle bounded by Cavaillon in the south, Carpentras in the north and Avignon in the west make their livelihood from market-gardening, carried out on a huge scale.

Almost all the popular varieties of fruit and vegetable are grown here, but the region is particularly well known for the cultivation of melons. Most of the produce is delivered to nearby **Cavaillon,** which has the second largest wholesale market in the country after Rungis in Paris. From here it is transported all over Europe.

Cavaillon, which now lies close to the A7 autoroute, has always been a lowland town. In an age when even the smallest village seems to have been built on some sort of rock or promontory, Cavaillon resolutely turned its back on the hills.

However, you can climb the nearby hill of **St. Jacques,** and from its rocky, pine-scented summit you get a superb view of the River Durance winding round the town, and of the more distant highlands of the **Lubéron, Mont Ventoux** and **the Alpilles**.

Above: Gourmets can buy fresh goat's cheese. Right: The famous honey of Provence comes from many different flowers.

The first inhabitants of this area were Ligurians, then the Gauls established a fortified *oppidum* on the site. Remains of it can still be seen in the shape of stone ramparts, a water-cistern hewn from the rock, the grooves worn by cartwheels and the contents of tombs now on display in the town's **archaeological museum.** Here you can also see Gaulish bread, pastry and grain which were uncannily preserved in the gravel-pits by the road to Avignon. In the **Place François-Tourel** there is a partially restored Roman arch.

Behind, a steep path (15 minutes' walk) climbs through the **St. Baldou** area of the town to the hill of Calvary, which can be reached by car on the north side. The hermitage and the chapel of St. Jacques, set in a cypress grove, are small gems of Romanesque architecture.

The hill of Calvary is a religious symbol with two distinct functions. Firstly, it is a memorial to the thousands of people who died in the great plague of 1629, and its chapel is also dedicated to St. Véran, the patron saint of shepherds. By ancient

custom, a new-born lamb decked out in colored ribbons is blessed at the Christmas Mass.

A well from Roman times was discovered on the northern slopes of the town's ramparts togther with many artefacts from as far away as Egypt. In those days Cavaillon was a busy and important trading center on the *Via Domitia,* linking Italy with Provence, which crossed the River Durance at this point and brought many travelers through the town.

The ferrymen on the river belonged to the guild of *utriculaires.* The name is derived from the Latin word for "udder" and refers to the inflated sacs which provided buoyancy for their rudimentary rafts. This very important ferry link continued long after the land had been abandoned by the Romans and kept the trade route open.

One of the more unusual sights in the town is the **synagogue**, which was built in the 18th century and whose sumptuous Rococo interior is unique in this region. At this point it may be appropriate to

sketch in the history of the Jews in the Comtat Venaissin. The Pope allowed them to settle in this area under his protection and therefore ultimately under his authority. As non-Christian unbelievers, they had to wear yellow hats as an outward symbol of their religion. They lived separately from the rest of the population in a section of the town which formed a ghetto (called the *carrière*) which was sealed off with a chain at night.

There were four of these ghettos in the area, at Avignon, L'Isle-sur-la-Sorgue, Carpentras and Cavaillon. Money-changing, which was a punishable offense for Christians, was in the hands of the Jews. Because many foreigners frequented the papal court at Avignon, money-changing was part of everyday life and the Jews played an essential role in trade, commerce and banking. Originally, 200 Jews settled in Cavaillon, but by the 18th century their numbers had increased to 2000. Since the ghetto area could not grow at the same rate, their houses had to be built taller and taller.

It hardly needs to be stressed that the dealings between the two communities were hedged around with ignorance, distrust and many restrictions. For instance, Carpentras Cathedral had a *port juive* (Jews' gate) on the south side through which converts might enter the building. However, not all those who adopted the Christian faith did so with total conviction. On Good Friday in 1603 some of the more mischievous inhabitants of the ghetto paraded through the streets with a crucified scarecrow. As a punishment they were made to set a cross in the paving in front of the church.

Orthodox Jewish ritual requires the faithful to eat only unleavened bread, which is why there was a bakery on the ground floor of the synagogue. It is now a museum. In the 19th century the ghettos were pronounced a health risk by the authorities and demolished to make way for more modern development.

Above: There is plenty of fresh produce in the markets, even in winter.

Carpentras

Formerly capital of the Comtat, the town of **Carpentras** has now lost its fortifications, but is still the seat of the sub-prefecture. Sited at the intersection of several roads, including what is now the D 938, the town is ringed by a circular boulevard, which encloses the Place Inguimbert and the town's three principal buildings, the **cathedral of St. Siffrein,** the Palais de Justice and the triumphal arch.

The last of these was once the entrance to an earlier cathedral, and then a back-kitchen for the bishops. Though not tremendously imposing, it is the only remaining example of Roman architecture in the town. The elegant, pink stone **Palais de Justice** with its long façade and rows of tall windows was formerly the Bishops' Palace, built in the 17th century on the lines of the Palazzo Farnese in Rome.In stark contrast to it is the sober Provençal Gothic cathedral, only slightly marred by the later addition of a bell-tower. It was built at the order of Benedict XIII, one of the French "anti-popes" whose real name was Pierre de Lune. In the south vestibule of the church is a famous carved globe shown being attacked by rats. It is not known whether this is meant to symbolize "the world gnawed by heresy" or simply a religious attempt to drive away the Black Death which ravaged the population at regular intervals and was carried by rats.

Around the **Place Inguimbert,** which also serves as the venue for an Offenbach Festival every July and August, the town is laid out according to a plan dating from the 18th century. Each district is subdivided into numbered *îles* (islands) and one can still make out the numbers carved on some of the street corners. The *îles* are enclosed by a broad boulevard of plane trees which follows the line of the now demolished fortifications. These boasted 32 watchtowers and four gates, only one of which still stands – the massive and castellated **Porte d'Orange** 80 ft (27m) high.

Opposite this gate you can admire the fine façade of the **Hôtel-Dieu,** a hospital founded by Bishop d'Inguimbert in the 18th century. Inside there is a fascinating the old pharmacy, still fully stocked with pots and jars bearing strange labels.

The same bishop was responsible for the impressive **Bibliothèque Inguimbertine,** a library which has been open to the public since 1746. More than half the 200,000 volumes were confiscated from the Jews.

Like Cavaillon, Carpentras is well known as a distribution center for locally grown fruit and vegetables. Leaving aside the wholesale market – which is only open to traders – the other large and bustling markets are a feature of the town. The most important of the annual fairs is the huge, colorful **Foire Saint-Siffrein** which takes over the whole town on 27 November each year. This is a country fair, a market for horses and truffles and a flea market. The day of the fair traditionally ends with a religious service and a concert of Provençal Baroque music.

The regular weekly market, the **Marché du Vendredi Matin,** is held on Fridays, as its name suggests, under the plane trees on the boulevard and offers a mouthwatering array of agricultural produce and regional specialties. These include *berlingots* (striped sweets) and delicious candied fruits. And, of course, truffles. During the season traders selling this very expensive delicacy take up positions in front of the Hôtel-Dieu carrying their raffia baskets. Even if you don't want to buy, it's worth stopping to watch connoisseurs haggling over the *rabassiers,* the local name for these much-prized fungi.

ORANGE

In the fertile plain of the Rhône in the north-western part of the Plateau de Vaucluse, the Romans built towns such as Orange and Vaison-la-Romaine. In later times these towns were annexed as enclaves of their territory by the exiled popes of Avignon during the time known as The Great Schism.

Even in Gallic times, the settlement of *Arausio* lay at the intersection of busy trade routes and in the year 105 B.C. the Romans suffered a disastrous defeat in this area in a battle against the Cimbri and the Teutons; but this was soon avenged. In 35 B.C. Augustus chose this spot to build a settlement for his veterans stationed in Gaul.

In time this grew into a very important town in the province of *Gallia Narbonnensis.* Commensurate with its status as a "Roman" town, it acquired a circus, a theater, temples and baths.

Orange became an independent principality around A.D.1000 and saw a second era of prosperity between 1530 and 1713 when it fell by inheritance into the con-

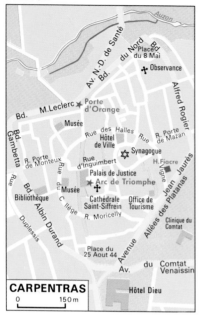

Av. N. D. de Santé
Bd. du Nord
Place du 8 Mai
✝ Observance
Bd. M.Leclerc ✕ Porte d'Orange
Alfred Rogier
Bd.
Bd. Gambetta
Musée
Rue des Halles
Hôtel de Ville
Rue
R. Porte de Mazan
R. Porte de Monteux
Rue
Rue d'Inguimbert
✡ Synagogue
H.Fiacre
Av. Vigne
Palais de Justice
Jean Jaurès
✕ Arc de Triomphe
Allées des Platanes
Bibliothèque
✝ Musée
Collège
Cathédrale Saint-Siffrein
Office de Tourisme
Clinique du Comtat
Bd. Albin Durand
R. Moricelly
Duplessis
Place du 25 Août 44
Avenue
Av. du Comtat Venaissin

CARPENTRAS
0   150 m

Hôtel Dieu

trol of the ruling dynasty of Holland, the Protestant House of Nassau. Most of the population converted to Protestantism but then suffered violent retribution during the bloody Wars of Religion

When Louis XIV, the "Sun King," declared war on the Netherlands he was able to recapture the city in 1672 and it was finally restored to French rule by the Treaty of Nassau in 1713. The first thing the French King did was to order the destruction of the city wall and the citadel. These had been built to protect the city by Maurice of Nassau in the 17th century, having first ordered that the old buildings be dismantled stone by stone to provide the materials.

It is therefore all the more amazing that so many important Roman remains are still to be found in the city, having survived all the ravages of the past, but who knows how much was lost.

Right: Productions at the ancient theater in Orange always have an impressive backdrop.

On the ancient *Via Agrippa* which linked Lyon with Arles (and is now the busy N 7 trunk road running parallel to the Rhône) stands the Roman **Arc de Triomphe**, at the north end of the city. It was the first Roman monument to be built on Gallic soil and was intended to impress the local population as a visible symbol of the power of the Romans. This is one reason why its walls were extravagantly decorated with ornamental reliefs. These portray Roman legionaries victorious over naked Gauls bound in chains. There are also ships, symbolizing Rome's maritime superiority over the whole of the known world of that time.

It is impossible to date the building of this massive triumphal arch with any great accuracy. The latest research appears to favor the year 20 B.C. because a number of celebrations to mark the foundation of the colony took place at that time. Fifty years later the arch was dedicated to the Emperor Tiberius. There is evidence to show that during the Middle Ages the arch was converted into a fortified tower forming part of the city walls which were later destroyed by King Louis XIV. A maze of tiny alleys with many small houses grew up in its shelter.

At the other end of the city, in a park on Saint-Eutrope hill, stands the **ancient amphitheater** which is still complete, unlike the Arc de Triomphe. Its backdrop was described by Louis XIV as the "Finest wall in all my Kingdom." This wall, part of the only Roman theater in the world still remaining intact, is 338 ft (103 m) long and 121 ft (37 m) high. The site is now on UNESCO's world heritage list of buildings needng special protection.

Its entrance, blind arches and rows of columns are quite undamaged and even the stepped seating in the auditorium is in perfect condition. Only the mosaics and some of the ornamentation have been damaged. Most of the statues in the niches have been stolen, but to compensate for this the figure of Augustus with

hand raised in greeting was returned to its original place on the rear wall of the ancient theater earlier this century. The rows of tiered seats can accommodate 10,000 to 15,000 people.

The amphitheater's acoustics are uncannily clear and this is one reason why this ancient setting is put to good use every year in July and August, when drama, opera and ballet performances and concerts take place under the auspices of the *Chorégies d'Orange*. The *Fêtes Romaines,* the oldest festival in Provence, was first held in 1869. A performance here makes for a truly unforgettable occasion.

The Environs of Orange

A few kilometers away from Orange, the ruins of the old castle of **Uchaux** (on the D 11) and the small town of **Caderousse** (on the D 17) are worth a visit. Caderousse lies on a shallow stretch of the Rhône where, in 218 BC, Hannibal is said to have crossed the river with his army and elephants on his way to Rome. The grooves in a rock caused by erosion are often misinterpreted as being the marks made where he secured a floating bridge to enable his soldiers to cross. In **Sérignan-du-Comtat** (on the D 976), a visit can be made to a castle built by Diane de Poitiers which is now in ruins, and a further attraction on the trip is the country house, L'Harmas, where the entomologist and poet Jean-Henri Fabre lived and worked from 1870 onward. For over 40 years Fabre observed caterpillars and ants and recorded his findings in his book *Souvenirs Entomologiques.* His house has been preserved exactly as it was and his garden is designated a Provençal nature reserve.

Back on the Rhône, we come to **Bollène** (on the D94 or A7 north of Orange), a small Provençal town that has been overtaken by progress From its terraces high above the Rhône valley you can see the **Donzère-Mondragon** canal along which a hydroelectric station and the Tricastin nuclear reactor have been built.

Above: The Triumphal Arch in Orange.

Right: Candy-floss seller.

In contrast, **Mornas** (on the N 7 about halfway between Orange and Bollène) still retains much of its medieval charm. It lies under a cliff 450 ft (137m) high, above which tower the ruins of a fortress behind a wall over a mile (2km) long. It formed part of the estate of the Bishops of Arles and was razed to the ground after falling to the enemy during the Wars of Religion. Any unfortunate Huguenots captured were hurled to their deaths from the cliff by the soldiers of the Catholic League.

In **Mondragon** (on the D 26) the Festival of the Dragon is celebrated every year in May, when a monstrous serpent called the *drac* or the *tarasque* is made to climb out of the Rhône and writhe its way through the village, causing much panic and excitement.

At this precise point we cross the border into the department of Drôme with its many miles of terraced vineyards stretch-

North-east of Orange, the former Papal Enclave extends along the fertile valley of the Coronne around the town of Valréas (on the D 976). The exiled popes of Avignon made repeated attempts to annex the fertile land for themselves, against the wishes of the French king.

The Papal Enclave of Valréas

ing along the hillsides on both sides of the river Aigues. Further upstream, on the Plateau de Vinsobres, is Saint-Pantaléon-les-Vignes, where we begin to see lavender fields between the vineyards.

For a number of years the *Université du Vin* and its adjacent research laboratory have been located in **Suze-la-Rousse**, a town with an old castle on the D 94. Guided tours give the interested layman a wealth of information on viticulture. Exhibits and display boards are used to bring the past, the present and even the future of the wine-growing industry to life and of course you can also sample the produce of the area.

In a compromise solution, Philippe the Fair finally allowed the Popes to keep the land that lay immediately around Valréas, on condition that it remain detached from the rest of their territory.

Set amidst vineyards and lavender fields bordered by avenues of cypress and oak trees (under which truffles are found) are numerous castles and old houses; and three fortified villages.

Richerenches was once a seat of the Knights Templar and has a surviving square fortress with towers at each of its four corners. **Grillon** and **Visan** are not far from Valréas. Both have picturesque old town centers with fine houses and chapels surrounded by fortified walls. These villages remain prosperous today, even though the production of silk is now a thing of the past. Wine-growing is now their source of income. The famous *Côtes du Rhône* is produced here. Lavender also grows over wide areas, not to mention the truffle.

Arts and crafts also flourish. These include the production of *santons* (clay figurines) and pottery and the manufacture of furniture. For over 150 years there has also been a large plant producing cardboard and packaging materials, which has its own museum.

Grillon has become well known for the manufacture of plastic products. The village is the headquarters of the *Institut international des Arts et Techniques des Polymères*.

Culture is not forgotten in the region. As in Orange, Avignon, Villeneuve and Vaison-la-Romaine, here too there is a summer festival with *nuits théâtrales* in all four parishes of Valréas. In Grillon the ruins of the old town are used as a backdrop, while in Visan the stage is placed in a glorious natural setting.

Richerenches has no theatricals but drama is provided by a thriving truffle market, rivalling the one in Carpentras, and held weekly on every Saturday in the winter.

The sights of Valréas include a magnificent 16th C. organ in the Romanesque church of **Notre-Dame-de-Nazareth.**

During the summer festivals referred to above, events are held inside the Château de Simiane. Some of the rooms in this large and elegant 17th-century palace are used as a Town Hall (Hôtel de Ville) and others house a **museum.** A permanent exhibition is devoted to the work of the Austro-Provençal painter Scharf and other temporary exhibitions are also held. Every year from the middle of July to the middle of August there is a summer exhibition for Provençal painters.

Each year the summer solstice is also celebrated, and this is when 350 local people from Valréas dress up for the occasion in 16th-century costume. A procession winds its way through the town. When the procession reaches the courtyard of the palace, fanfares ring out and the four-year-old *Petit-Saint-Jean* enters by torchlight. The little boy is the town's mascot for a year, and is proclaimed king for one night.

They certainly know how to celebrate feast days in this corner of France. An enormous, expensively dressed Provençal crib stands in the church of Notre-Dame-de-Nazareth at Valréas every year from Christmas until the end of January.

At the end of August there is a lavender festival called the *Corso de la Lavande*. It lasts for two days and two nights and includes a big procession and much celebration throughout the town.

Finally, at the beginning of September you can join in the colorful pilgrimage of the *Confrérie de Saint-Vincent* at Visan. During the festival the figure of the patron saint of wine-growers is carried out of the small chapel of Notre-Dame-des-Vignes and taken in procession through the vineyards.

Vaison-la-Romaine

Only a few miles south-west of Visan is Vaison-la-Romaine, also known as the Pompeii of France because of its many excavated Roman remains. They may not all be buildings of great historic interest but they are nonetheless impressive in their variety. In Roman times the town had no military or strategic importance, but concentrated on a life of quiet property, with pleasant houses, colonnaded streets, shops, public baths, irrigation canals and gardens.

Vaison is really three towns overlying each other. At the bottom – now called the lower town – was the Gallo-Roman settlement of *Vasio Vocontiorum* which in its day was one of the most important towns in the Roman province of *Gallia Narbonensis*. Large parts of the town were destroyed at the time of the barbarian invasions. Next, the Counts of Toulouse built a castle in the Middle Ages and as time passed a community grew up beneath its walls.

Right: The Dentelles de Montmirail, a range of hills 15 km (9 miles) long.

The modern town was then built, again in the valley, right above the site of the Gallo-Roman settlement. This explains why only the outer sections of historical interest such as the forum and its immediate environs have been excavated - in fact only the fringes of the 32 acre (13ha) site of the Roman town.

There are two separate excavation sites: The larger of the two is the **Puymin quarter** and the smaller the **Villasse quarter**. Excavation has taken place here with only brief interruptions since the turn of the century. In the Puymin quarter, a villa, the colonnaded courtyard of Pompey, a nymphaeum and a Roman theater have been exposed.

This quarter also contains the **museum** where you can see the excavated objects grouped thematically. The main sights of interest in the Villasse quarter are the main street, the baths and a colonnaded street parallel to the main street.

Not far from the excavations is the **cathedral of Notre-Dame** in the Romanesque style of Provence, with a cloister. The bridge which spans the Ouvèze in a single arch is over 2000 years old and is still used by traffic today. It may well stand for another two millennia.

A steeply sloping street leads up to the medieval **Haute-Ville**. Building continued up here on the town wall right up to the 19th century and it is easy to see that many of its blocks of stone were quarried from the ancient Roman houses. For many years this part of town with its steep cobbled streets lay like Sleeping Beauty in a deep slumber, but its charm has now been rediscovered by artists and photographers.

Dentelles de Montmirail and the Route des Vins

West of Mont Ventoux and separated from it only by a narrow cleft is a strange-looking range of mountains, the **Dentelles de Montmirail**, where the last of the Alpine ridges marks the boundary between two geographical areas. This rugged and rocky area extends over a distance of 9 miles (15 km)). Pines and oaks flourish on the chalk range, which is considerably lower than its more substantial neighbour (the highest point being Mont-St-Amand at 2400 ft (734 m) . It is not a comfortable place to be when the rain pours down from the clouds or the mistral whistles round you. At other times, though, the chalk gleams white in the sunlight and the sandstone glows red at sunset.

This area produces outstanding wine and is also the home of an excellent goat's cheese. The landscape, with its eerie quality, has naturally been the inspiration of many legends. Of course, it is also a paradise for climbers, hill walkers and ramblers.

Many narrow tracks and mountain paths lead to villages in hidden valleys, wild almond trees grow on steep slopes, the wind whistles through cracks in the rocks and there are mountain springs everywhere. Even if you're no alpine climber, you can easily manage the **Turc** at 2057 ft (627m) or the 2400 ft (734m) high **Cirque de Saint-Amand**.

Isolated hamlets and farms are dotted around the countryside. Between **Les Beaumes** and **Malaucène** the narrow D 90 passes through the hamlets of **Lafare**, **La Roque-Alric** and **Suzette**. In the north is the charming village of **Crestet** which has the ruins of an impressive château, Renaissance houses and a pretty village square with arbors.

Immediately adjacent, in the Chapelle de Prébayon, is the supposedly miraculous spring of Malézieux, the waters of which are said to heal all sorts of diseases of the eye. The other two villages, **Sablet** (on the D 23) and **Séguret** are similar, with picturesque old houses, narrow streets and ruined castles.

From **Vacqueyras** on the D 8, where they keep alive the memory of the troubadour Raimbaud who died on a crusade, we come to **Montmirail**, which gained fame in more recent times for its spring

DENTELLES DE MONTMIRAIL

containing sulphates and salts, *la fontaine d'eau verte* (spring with green water), in the nearby valley of Vallon de Souïras. In the 19th century the actress Sarah Bernhardt and the poet Frédéric Mistral spoke highly of its therapeutic effects. It became highly fashionable for a time. Today the baths are no more. The resort is deserted and the hotel, the spa and the casino are in ruins.

The wines produced in this region are excellent. At **Beaumes-de-Venise**, muscat grapes flourish on the slopes facing the sun and are pressed in the autumn to make a dessert wine with a strong, sweet flavor. You can taste and buy the wine at the *Cave des Vignerons de Beaumes-de-Venise*, and also at **Rasteau** at the other end of the valley.

Between Beaumes-de-Venise and Rasteau is **Gigondas**, an exquisitely beauti-

*Above: Two attractions of Châteauneuf-du-Pape: Its vines and its 14th-century castle.
Right: A village on the slopes of the Dentelles de Montmirail.*

ful place, where you should visit the *Cave des Vignerons de Gigondas* on the Route de Vaison for its excellent wines. This place bears out the old proverb: "If you want good wine you need good soil, a good climate, a good vine and a hard-working grower."One might add: a good customer.

This region, known as the **Côtes du Rhône**, owes part of its international reputation among connoisseurs of wine to the popes, with their heavy consumption of wine, whether for Communion or other purposes. The best-known of the local wines is actually named after popes in general: *Châteauneuf-du-Pape*. The reason why this unique wine tastes so good is firstly because the red clay, stones and gravel on which the vineyards have been planted, radiate the sun's heat on to the vines like hot bricks and secondly because its bouquet is made up of a combination of no less than thirteen different varieties of grape.

The *Caves du Père Anselme* cellars certainly attract more tourists than the

paintings in the château of Pope John XXII , which survived the unwelcome attention of the Huguenots in 1562 and the German army in 1944.

In this wine-growing region, no less than 23 different grape varieties are cultivated instead of the usual one or two. Grenache, Syrah and Cinsault are the most common. The different types of soil are also important in determining the quality of the wine. The yellow sandy soil and the different proportions of chalk, gravel, clay and loam affect the quality and flavor of the wine just as much as the different characteristics of the grapes. The soil also produces wine of excellent quality in the vineyards between Avignon and Tricastin.

There are four different **Routes des Vins**: The *rousse, dorée, orange* and *lavande*, all of which meander between the **Durance** and the hills of **Châteauneuf-de-Gadagne** as far as the **Coteaux du Tricastin.** Bounded by the **Dentelles** and **Mont Ventoux**, between **d'Aubignan** and **Mazan**, there are many small wine-producing villages which were originally built by the Albigensians as refuges – the so-called *villages perchés.*

Cairanne, on the other hand, is an old Knights Templar fortress. In **Rochegude**, **Lagarde-Paréol** and in particular **Cécile-les-Vignes**, *Appellation Contrôlée* wines are produced. These wines used to be given the nickname *vin de café* because large glasses of them were served in the bars. Now they are sold in supermarkets everywhere.

In this area wine is not just an agricultural product but an integral part of local culture. There is a **wine museum** in Cairanne, and Rasteau and Châteauneuf-du-Pape both have viticulture museums. Even the calendar is ruled by the grape harvest. Nearly every village has its wine festival, vineyard festival, *Légende de la Grappe d'Or* or wine market. Not to mention the great wine market and agricultural show which takes place every year in July and August in the caves next to the amphitheater in Orange. This is the most important show of all.

MONT VENTOUX

North-east of the Monts de Vaucluse the landscape and its coloring change. South-east of Mont Ventoux (6263ft/ 1909m) is the **Pays de Sault**, which is justly famous as an important lavender-growing area.

The peak of **Mont Ventoux** rises majestic and bare above the Plateau of Vaucluse in the shape of a pyramid, visible from a considerable distance. You can drive round part of it on the D 974.

Its forest trees were cut down for charcoal before the beginning of the 19th century. At the end of the last century the entomologist Jean-Henri Fabre described the mountain in the following words: "A great heap of stones like those used for road building ... a huge block of lime-stone with stones that crumble with a dry cracking noise when you walk over them..."

It was not until this century that serious attempts at reafforestation of Mont Ventoux were made. Pines, larches and even cedars, holm oaks, gorse and lavender from Piedmont now thrive up to a height of 5250 ft (1600 m). Above the tree-line the wind howls and the rock shimmers so dazzlingly white in the sunlight that people think that they can see snow on the top even in summer. Not even the hardiest sheep could survive in that desert landscape.

In the winter, though, snow often does lie on the mountain. The temperature falls to minus 27 degrees C. and the wind gusts at hurricane-force around the summit. It is not surprising that only plants like saxifrage, which is native to Spitzbergen, and the Greenland poppy will grow near the summit.

Over the past few years the mountain has developed into a popular skiing area. The *Chalet Reynard* and *Chalet du Mont*

Above: The highest mountain in Provence is Mont Ventoux (1909 m or 6263 ft), a rewarding destination for walkers in summer and skiers in winter and one of the most difficult stages of the Tour de France.

Serein are located on the peak of Mont Ventoux, so you can now enjoy winter sports only 60 miles (100km) from the Mediterranean!

In 1933 the narrow, winding road from Malaucène through Bédoin – which is a nightmare for every Tour-de-France competitor – was extended right to the summit. A new road on the north side climbs more gradually to the top in a series of hairpin bends which offer spectacular views to motorists.

Walkers are advised to tackle the four or five hour climb to the top along the marked paths – *Grandes randonnées* – (GR 9 and GR 4). Every bend in the path opens up new vistas; the northern side is covered with dense scrub, but the path is bare on the southern slopes, surrounded by gorse and olive trees. It is bleak but also beautiful.

On the summit there is a radar station and a transmitter, and also a large car park. If the mountain is not shrouded in cloud, there is a fantastic view from the top as far as the peaks of the Ecrin and Dévoluy. A sea of tiny lights twinkles at night and if you're lucky you will even see the flashing of the lighthouses on the Mediterranean. When not too crowded with parties of walkers it is an awe-inspiring sight.

The Villages on Mont Ventoux

The villages around Mont Ventoux are equally fascinating. In the north the landscape is marked by the course of the Toulourenc in its narrow, rugged gorge. **Entrechaux** is on one of its steep slopes, on the D 13, not far from Saint-Léger-de-Ventoux and **Brantes** on the D 40. In Savoillan there is a center devoted to artificial irrigation and cultivation of aromatic plants like lavender, sage and mint.

Malaucène on the D 938 is an old fortified town where plane trees have long since grown over the old walls, although the fortified church, whose battlements

were once part of the ramparts, is still standing. Its 18th-century organ is famous, as is the nearby Chapelle du Groseau. The spring which rises here, in a deep, shady pool at the foot of a cliff, was venerated as far back as Ligurian times. The Romans, who were skilled engineers and a very practical people, carried its waters over an aqueduct to the baths at Vaison-la-Romaine.

To the south is **Le Barroux** which is surrounded by hills covered with apricot and olive trees. This tiny village of only 500 people lies in the shadow of a restored Renaissance château which now houses the *Centre d'Etudes Historiques et Archéologiques du Comtat* (Comtat Center of Historical and Archaeological Studies).

Continuing along the D 13, we pass through **Caromb** and **Modène**. The village of Bédoin is renowned for its good food. Excellent game is served here in autumn and other interesting local specialties are spit-roasted thrush and wild mushrooms prepared in a variety of ways.

Otherwise it is a very quiet village which appears to have almost accidentally acquired its Jesuit church with its incongruously grand façade. The main attraction for tourists in **Crillon-le-Brave** is the château built by Crillon, a close friend of Henri IV. The village of Flassan is colorful and photogenic. The stone for its ocher and pink colored houses comes from the nearby quarries of **Mormoiron**, where gypsum is also extracted.

The Pays de Ventoux also has its own original and typical local crafts, which will be found on sale at the *Cours Insard* in Malaucène and also at the *Four-à-chaux* in Caromb.

PAYS DE SAULT

In the south-east is the Pays de Sault, the true land of lavender. It might often seem as though you are passing through

You should learn to distinguish between the different types of lavender: the large-leaved *aspic*, or spiked lavender is blue in colour; a mauve tint signifies the wild lavender of the Massif which is grown at an altitude of 2000-4500 ft (600-1400m); and finally the deep purple variety is a prolific hybrid, called *lavandin*, which has a strong but less pleasant perfume.

Swarms of bees buzz constantly over the lavender fields. Connoisseurs maintain that their honey makes the best white nougat, which comes from Sault.

Lavender was once thought to be a universal curative and almost magical powers were once attributed to it. It was thought to prevent inflammation, keep away moths, bestow eternal youth and a great deal more beside. The constituents of its scent can now be separated in the laboratory and reconstituted in a different way, but there is still enough lavender left for honey and nougat and also for lavender water and sweet-smelling sachets and pillows.

Sault, on the D 1, is a mountain village at a height of 2500 ft (765 m) overlooking the valley of the River Nesque. Its humble houses huddle close together along narrow streets which shelter them from wind, sun and winter cold. To the south, a terrace of scented lime trees further enhances the superb view right across the valley to Mont Ventoux. The local Lavender Festival is celebrated here every year on 15 August.

The Sault valley is a plain enclosed by Mont Ventoux and the mountains of Lure, and to the south, those of Vaucluse. There is just room for a handful of hamlets and tiny villages: **Aurel** (on the D950) boasts just 26 souls and the ruins of a fortification, **Montbrun,** perched on a hilltop, also has some ruins, and **Saint-Trinit,** if anything even smaller, nevertheless has a fine 12th century church. Those who champion the gorges of the Nesque, call them the "little Verdon";

the land of lavender in the Haut Comtat, when you see the purple-flowered bushes growing everywhere – among thistles and thyme, in flower pots and gardens – but there you cannot actually smell it. Here in the Pays de Sault the conditions are ideal for lavender. It is a plant that thrives in warm sunshine on chalky sandstone and dry plateaux. When you smell the perfume of the lavender fields east of Mont Ventoux in mid-July, you immediately realize where you are. Between fields of golden wheat, you suddenly glimpse the azure meadows of Haute Provence and the air is full of a delicate, soothing fragrance which will remind you of your great-grandmother's linen cupboards. From the **Plateau de Saint-Christol** to the **Plateau de Valensol,** there is nothing around you but fields of lavender as far as the eye can see.

Above: A village nestles at the foot of Mont Ventoux. Right: The splendid frontage of a bakery in Malaucène.

this is a large claim, but none the worse for that. The narrow defile, about 12 miles (20km) long, makes several curves beyond Mornieux (reached by the D942). This superb medieval vilage looks over the gorge as if from a balcony.

The road follows the gorge like a corniche, while a goat-track winds perilously up the cliff-side, as far as some caves, one of which has been converted into a chapel. The finest sight in the gorges is a rock known as the **Rocher du Cire** (Wax Rock). Since the dawn of time this 600ft (200m) peak has been haunted by bees, which built huge hives on it.

In days gone by, local people used to lower themselves on ropes from the cliff above to gather the honey. Once a year, a mass is still said at Notre-Dame-des-Abeilles (Our Lady of the Bees), a chapel beside the Salt Road, which crosses the plateau among the oak trees, and is itself worth exploring. And on the road from Sault to **Murs** and **Méthamis**, you will find another path which leads almost vertically up the cliff – for experts only...

PLATEAU DE VAUCLUSE

The chalky **Plateau de Vaucluse** is notable for its network of underground rivers. The River Nesque winds through the countryside is a series of loops and then seeps away (east of Carpentras) as do nearly all the rivers in this arid region. These lost underground waterways are usually marked on maps as blue dotted lines. The underground courses of many of these rivers and streams have yet to be clearly identified. Some rivers peter out, flow on underground and reappear on the surface a few miles further on, but others disappear for ever. Where does the water go to in the porous cave-riddled limestone rock?

Henri Bosco, a poet from the Lubéron, wrote of this landscape: *You never know where these springs have come from when they gush out of the ground. Perhaps they are fed by an underground lake or spring. No-one has ever fathomed the secret of the dark, undiscovered caverns down below.*

114

Above left: A field of wheat under the immense blue sky of Provence. Above right: Two elderly men of Provence chatting in the village street. Right: A view of the Sorgue river not far from its source near Fontaine-de-Vaucluse.

In geological terms, this is one huge fold stretching from east to west, but with such steep ridges that it is sometimes described as a fault-line between the Ventoux and Lubéron mountains. At all events the plateau is a wild and mysterious landscape: deep combes carpeted with kermes-oak, myrtle and juniper, from which rise jagged crests of bare rock; and in the desolate valley of the Cavalon, *garrigues*, or semi-desert, where the dry stones form screes, dunes and hollow chambers.

Heading eastward, you pass through **Saint-Christol** on the D 30 and over the **Plateau d'Albion**. In the summer a hot wind blows on these chalk heights and they are often blanketed in snow in winter. Lavender, wheat and many different herbs grow here and now and again you come upon scattered farmhouses surrounded by almond trees to shelter them from the heat of the summer wind and the icy blasts of winter.

The name "Albion" refers to the Albici tribe, whose name is in turn probably

Near **Fontaine-de-Vaucluse** there is an enclosed rocky valley, the **Vallée Close,** from which the Sorgue rushes out of the ground to form a pool nearly 300 m (1000 ft) deep. At this point we are already on the **Plateau de Vaucluse.**

Geographically speaking, there is very little difference between the terms "Plateau" and "Monts" when applied to Vaucluse. The peak of Saint-Pierre is the highest point on the plateau at 4120 ft (1250m), while the mountains of the Lubéron reach almost the same height at the **Mourre Nègre** (3690 ft or 1125m). But the difference in height between the mountains and their valleys is much greater than on the plateau with its relatively shallow valleys.

derived from the Latin *albus* (white), after the color of the limestone. Saint-Christol has a garrison and a military airfield. Underground, the rock is so riddled with caves that it must look like Gruyère cheese. Around 200 caverns have already been discovered, some of them at depths of up to 2000 ft (600m). In the Jean-Nouveau cave to the south of Sault there is a vertical well shaft that is 535 ft (163m) deep.

In the west between Pernes-les-Fontaines and Fontaine-de-Vaucluse, you will notice a number of villages sitting like fortresses high up on hilltops where the cliffs fall steeply into the valley of the Sorgue. Among these are **Saumane-de-Vaucluse, Le Beaucet, Venasque** and **Méthamis,** above the valley of the Nesque.

The walls surrounding Méthamis are still intact and their only entrance is across a working drawbridge, which can still be raised to prevent intruders.

Nearby there is another long stone wall, now overgrown, which was built in 1722 as a protection against the plague. Walls like this, which are found between Cavaillon and Sault, were guarded by soldiers to prevent anyone who might possibly be infected with the disease entering the town – a measure which met with little success.

Fontaine-de-Vaucluse

Where does the water that gushes out of the ground come from? In **Fontaine-de-Vaucluse** the Sorgue emerges from a grotto and becomes a torrential river when in flood. The Gauls, who were certainly not the first to discover this natural wonder, thought the place was the home of a god, while Christians named it the Devil's Hole. In the Middle Ages the pool was thought to be guarded by a dragon. Then came geologists and speleologists (cave explorers) who used dye in the water to trace its course.

Where does the water come from and where does it go to? In an underground labyrinth covering an area of about 800 square miles (2000 sq.km) there is one of the largest springs in the world which supplies the Fontaine-de-Vaucluse with water through an extensive network of underground rivers.

The reason why the flow of water at the source of the Sorgue varies so much has never been satisfactorily explained. In dry periods it produces about 4500 litres (1000 gallons) per second, but in winter and spring this rises to 200,000 litres (44,000 gallons) per second, so it is hardly surprising that the Romans built an aqueduct here. Despite the use of modern technology and exploratory drilling work down to more than 1000 ft (330m), the subterranean depths have not yet yielded their secrets.

You can study the history of exploration in the area in recreated grottoes at the **Monde souterrain de Norbert Casteret** (a museum of the subterranean world). It has certainly been good for the tourist

FONTAINE-DE-VAUCLUSE

trade in the village that so much remains unexplained, because many people love a mystery and so they all come to satisfy their curiosity.

The village has 600 inhabitants, but none of them now make their living from agriculture. And the last paper mill, an impressive reminder of a craft which was once very important here, closed its doors in 1968. Its water wheel 23 ft (7 m) in diameter is still turning, however, evoking memories of the old days when the clatter of the paper mills even drowned out the sound of the rushing waters of the Sorgue.

Every year one million people visit this narrow valley and yet the village cannot prevent the farmers from moving away. Although a big effort has been made to please the tourists, they only come to look at the mysterious pool and just drive on afterwards. All sorts of things have been set up to try to make them stay a bit longer in the village, like *son et lumière* shows, restaurants, craft and souvenir shops and even four museums which are certainly worth a visit. There is a *santon* museum (containing one masterpiece: 39 small figures of saints in a nutshell), a museum on the history of the Resistance from 1870 to 1940 and a small Petrarch museum.

This museum is located in the house where it is generally assumed that the 14th-century Italian poet lived for 16 years and wrote down the story of his unhappy love for Laura. Strangely enough, she was a married woman who died of the plague at the age of 40 leaving eleven children; she was also an ancestor of the Marquis de Sade. Petrarch wrote most of his poetry here in addition to his recollections of Laura. The town erected a column surrounded by plane trees in his honor and his name adorns a number of boutiques and hotels.

Right: Lavender screening the Cistercian abbey of Sénanque.

If you are driving on in the direction of Sénanque, do stop in **Cabrières-d'Avignon** and buy the specialties of the area, which are olive bread and anchovy bread, at the *Boulangerie Dromer.* Other local delicacies such as olive oil with truffles can be bought at the *Epicerie Fine.*

From Sénanque to the Land of the "Bories"

In **Sénanque** on the D 177, about 4 km (2.5 miles) beyond Gordes, the stones used by builders of past days could tell you the story of this land through the ages. In a narrow valley among fields of lavender is the finest of the three Cistercian monasteries in the region. The other two are to be found at **Silvacane** and **Thoronet**.

The abbey is a masterpiece of harmony and symmetry, built according to the rules of St. Bernard to a simple, austere design without exterior or interior decoration. The walls are of finely-cut stone, and the plain glass windows, arches and play of light and shade inside merge into one another to create a rare atmosphere of tranquil beauty that is at peace with itself.

The abbey was founded in the 12th century by an abbot and a dozen monks from the Vivarais – representing Christ and the 12 apostles. The architect Fernand Pouillon has written the story of the building of the Cistercian monastery at Thoronet (on which the abbey of Sénanque was modeled) in his book *Les Pierres Sauvages* (published by Editions du Seuil). It is a compelling and authoritative day-to-day chronicle of how a masterpiece was constructed.

Sadly, Sénanque Abbey began to decline in the 14th century. By the 17th century there were only two monks left. By 1854 it was one of the monasteries belonging to the island of Lérins, and twelve monks from Saint-Honorat lived there from 1927 to 1969. Then a wealthy industrialist, owner of the Berliet truck company, founded the *Association des Amis de Sénanque*, a support group which restored the abbey and is responsible for the two permanent exhibitions in the former dormitory, one on the origins of the monastery and the other on the Tuaregs from the Sahara. Monks have been living here again since October 1989, but the abbey can still be visited by outsiders.

Through the forest of Venasque with its beautiful gorges and beyond the Col de Murs, you come to Murs, where archaeological discoveries have shed light on the early human settlement of Provence. Many flints and other tools are still being found on the slopes of the Combe de Murs and most have been put on display at the museum in Apt. From the tremendous number and variety of examples that have been found, it is clear that stone tools were made in this area in huge numbers.

You are now in the land of the *bories* – huts standing like beehives among the olive trees and hot, dusty scrubland.

The first dwellings of the Ligurians who lived here at the end of the Neolithic period must have looked something like this, although most of these *bories* are only a few hundred years old. The stones for the dwellings can be found everywhere in the area. Their dry-stone walls are built of limestone, hundreds of blocks of which lie in the surrounding fields. Similar dwellings to these can also be found elsewhere in Europe – in France, Corsica, Sardinia, Spain, Apulia and even ancient Mycenae.

There are around 3000 of these stone dwellings in the Vaucluse and the Lubéron, with 350 in and around Gordes alone. They vary greatly in size, the largest of them being about 60ft (20m) long and 30ft (10m) high. The more elaborate ones have an upper storey, a pitched roof, and a fireplace. Most of them were used by the shepherds as corn stores, tool stores or even dwellings. Many of them have now been converted into holiday homes. Their solid walls give excellent protection from both heat and cold.

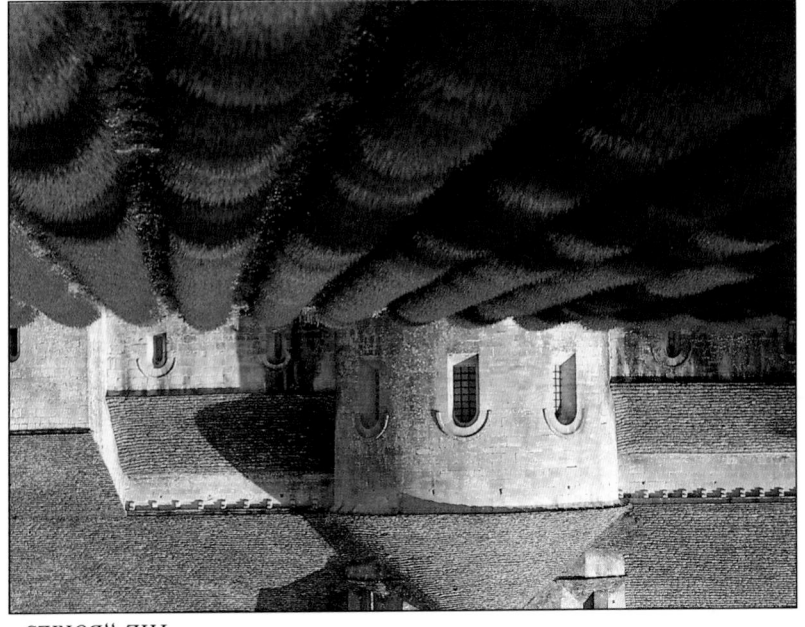

THE "BORIES"

You often come across them grouped together in a little settlement, or as a farm with its outhouses In 1979 a complete restored village between Sénanques and Gordes was opened to the public as an ethnographic museum with twenty bories grouped around a bakehouse.

PAYS D'APT

Wherever you stop in this region, you only have to look upwards to see four or five villages perched on hilltops between 700 and 1000 ft (200-300m) high, sheltering from the wind, their houses made of the same stone as the cliffs. Among these many archetypal villages are Roussillon, Gordes and Oppède.

Gordes

Jean Giono (1895-1970, author of *The Battle of the Mountains and The Hill*) de-

scribed a Provençal village like this: *A village stands on high ground, partly as a defense against the Saracens, but mainly for the good view. From the top they can see the most amazing things passing by: People, rivers, herds of cattle and clouds. The peasants, who know how to enjoy life, take the time to look at things.* Giono was probably thinking of the many mountain villages with brambles growing over the walls and a gate through which to enter the narrow streets, with the wind whistling through it. The village is deserted during the day because the men are in the fields or the café and the children are at school or in the woods. A fountain usually stands in the village square, shaded by bushes.

Gordes, near Sénanque, has always been like this. Even in the high season when tourists crowd the alleyways, it loses none of its charm. Gordes almost died out about fifty years ago, with more and more of the houses around its castle abandoned, but many artists and intellectuals were then attracted to the village for

Above: The old village of Gordes overlooking the plain of Coulon.

that very reason and moved in permanently.

The Hungarian abstract painter Vasarély bought the **Château des Simiane,** completely restored it and donated it to the community. The château now houses the Musée Vasarély, where many of the artist's vivid, optically dazzling pictures are on display. With the opening of the museum, a new lease of life returned to the village. Boutiques and galleries were opened and artists' studios were set up.

Gordes is often described as an acropolis rising from its golden plinth. There is indeed an aura of the ancient world in its symmetrical outlines, crowned by the church and the castle; the former is massive and supported by solid buttresses; the latter is something between a feudal fortress and a Renaissance manor house, with its pedimented doorway and mullioned windows contrasting with the castellations and pepper-pot towers at the corners of its walls.

All around, the village seems to cloak the hill with a multi-colored fabric of tall, grey-roofed houses, wooded terraces, winding staircases, arched passages and gardens. When it comes to giving prizes for the most photographed village, Gordes must be a leading contender.

If you want some souvenirs to remind you of your visit, or gifts to take home to friends, you can buy honey and the local *tapenade* at *Monsieur Peynon's* shop in the market place.

Roussillon and its Ocher Cliffs

In the early 1950s an American university professor spent a whole year in **Roussillon** (on the D 102) and wrote a book about the place which traces its ethnological history but is also of interest to the general reader. (Laurence Wylie, *Un Village du Vaucluse,* published by Gallimard). The book is only available in French. For some unknown reason, he disguised the name of the village and

called it Puyméras; but it is much like the villages that are depicted in the novels of Henri Bosco and Giono.

Neither the people nor the ambiance appeared to have changed much in the intervening years. The professor of sociology delighted in the many priceless village stories that he was told - reminiscent of the *Clochemerle* novels. But what has now become of the idyllic life of the village? So much has changed in the last forty years and television has not just disfigured the roofs with its aerials.

"Here the children draw pictures of houses and hills that would make any psychologist shudder!" wrote Laurence Wylie.

After driving out of Roussillon and negotiating a sharp bend, you might well think you are hallucinating. Precipitous, pine-clad cliffs rise up sheer into the sky, their peaks etched by wind and rain into grotesque shapes. The colors of the cliffs exactly match those of the houses – at least seventeen different shades have been counted, from ocher through carmine to gold and from pink to brown. The fantastically shaped cliffs standing in the **Val des Fées** (Fairy Valley) fall almost vertically, with the dramatic **Falaises de Sang** (Cliffs of Blood) at the center of the scene. Above is the gigantic **Chaussée des Géants** (Giants Road). A large section of one cliff has been broken off and another has a huge black hole that is all that remains of an abandoned mine.

It is sad that so many new holiday homes have ruined the harmony of the old village. Unfortunately the area has become very fashionable with French people from the big cities. But even in 1960 beneath the colorful awnings of the new cafés Wylie felt an atmosphere *as cheerful and contrived as a musical comedy.*

A ramble through the **Parc Naturel Régional de Lubéron** nature reserve is highly recommended as this is one way in which you can learn a lot about the ge-

ology of the area – the structure of the ocher rock, the various types of clay and the iron oxidation.

Visits can be made to the old mines, many of which are now used for mushroom growing. There is much to learn about the quarrying of the ocher rock, the careful extraction by water of the ocher itself and its ultimate use. It is no longer used as a wall coloring material, having been replaced by modern synthetic paints, but it is still in common use in the cosmetics industry and also as a colorant in food.

Further east, there are some mines near **Gargas** where ocher is still extracted. The precipitation-basins are visible from the road. In this region of France about 2000-3000 tonnes of ocher are produced every year.

Between **Rustrel** and **Gignac**, there is a track along which you have to walk

some distance to reach the abandoned, overgrown quarries. Be sure to keep to the signposted paths, because there is much loose rock and also potholes, so it can be dangerous to wander off on your own. At the end of the path a fantastic panorama awaits you, with gorges, cliffs, galleries and natural terraces from which there is a breathtaking view of the vivid range of colors all around. This gorge is sometimes called the **Provençal Colorado**, not without justification.

The man who marked out these paths with little red and white sticks and also signposted the many tracks in the Lubéron is called François Morenas and he lives in **Saint-Saturnin-lès-Apt.** In 1936, when paid holidays for workers were first introduced in France, he founded the Regain youth hostel which he still runs today.

In and around Apt

The town of **Apt** (on the D2) is surrounded by cherry orchards. Their fruits,

Above: A typical village street in Roussillon. Right: The fantastic colors of the ocher quarries and cliffs.

along with many others, are turned into candied fruits and sold at the local market every Saturday. Things might have been very different if the extensive olive groves that once grew around the town had not been devastated by frost in the severe winter of 1953 - Apt might now be the olive and not the candied fruit capital of the area.

Between the Lubéron and the plateau is the valley of the **Pays d'Apt** through which flows the **Coulon,** a tributary of the Durance. Many enjoyable tours can be made around here. Some sections of the great Roman road, the *Via Domitia,* which linked Rome with Spain, still survive, as does an old Roman bridge, the **Pont Julien**, spanning the river supported on three arches.

Taking the N 100, you can visit the church of **Notre-Dame-des-Lumières,** whose Black Madonna has always attracted pilgrims. Legend has it that the statue was found in a bush.

On the road to **Ponty** is the pottery studio run by Anthony Picot where you can buy traditional Provençal ceramics at reasonable prices.

Returning to Apt you will come to the prehistoric settlement of **Rocquefur**. Here there are caves full of snail-shells and a wealth of fossils, the most impressive of which is a fossil of a gigantic tortoise which measures 5ft (1.5m) in diameter.

In the midst of this beautiful scenery, the traditional Provençal town of Apt with its narrow streets of old houses and small romantic squares may look somewhat sad and insignificant, but it hides its light under a bushel. The twin crypts of the church of Sainte-Anne and its treasury containing many valuable relics are well worth seeing. The treasures include an 11th-century Arabian battle banner, once thought to be St. Anne's shroud.

The archaeological museum that has been built above the remains of a Roman amphitheater displays objects from Roman and prehistoric times. Vestiges of the ancient theater itself can be seen in the cellars.

But Apt is mainly a market town for fruit, candied fruit, vegetables and pottery. Every Saturday, especially in the summer, the market attracts large mixed crowds – in which farmers rub shoulders with intellectuals – from the area round about.

LUBERON

Strictly speaking, there are actually three ranges of mountains with this name, not just one. These are the Grand Lubéron with its massifs, the Petit Lubéron where the peaks are not so high but are nonetheless very rugged, and the protected **Parc Naturel Régional**, the Lubéron regional nature park. Overall, it extends from Cavaillon to the banks of the Durance in the east and as far south as Manosque, the Pays d'Apt and the Monts

Above: A wine-grower tasting the fruits of his labor. Right: One of the last surviving shepherds in the Lubéron.

de Vaucluse. In all, over a total of 460 460 sq. miles (1200 sq.km) the landscape, buildings and even the inhabitants are under special protection.

One of the results of this is that farming, and particularly sheep-rearing, have been preserved as the main source of income, but great efforts are also being made to promote "soft" tourism. There is a ban on further interference with nature in the mountains, and rare species of plants and animals are now protected.

The massif is bisected by the gorge of **Lourmarin**. By taking the D 943 from **Apt** towards **Aix**, you can drive through the gorge along an incredibly beautiful winding road. In the north the slopes are covered with dense forests of oak, while in the southern part, which lies in the **Pays d'Aigues**, cypress and low scrub predominate. Between the two, the landscape is almost like a wasteland. You look down from the crest on to cliffs and rocks. In the valleys there are isolated settlements and also a Roman *oppidum.*

Once again, it was Henri Bosco (who was born in Avignon but made his home in Lourmarin) who wrote of the mountains *enormous stone beasts, asleep for so long that the meaning of their names has been entirely forgotten.*

No one can describe better than he the shimmering heat of these highlands and the bitter-sweet scent of gorse, thyme, wild lavender and juniper hanging in the air. The stony fields are hidden away among thickets of oak trees, brambles and holly. The abandoned shepherds' huts have tiled roofs sloping nearly to the ground. You may see the flash of a moving snake as it vanishes from sight or a darting hare or hear a wild boar crashing through the undergrowth.

In this deserted countryside, you can wander all day without seeing a soul, yet the old woman sitting in front of her house pitting cherries knows exactly where you have come from and what you have been doing.

The Villages in the Lubéron

Since the end of the last war, the Lubéron has been invaded by the fashionable crowd, but its villages have retained their melancholy charm – they have seen many worse things and are unmoved by passing trends. One has to read Bosco's book: *L'Habitant de Sivergues*, written in 1933, to appreciate what was there before today's over-restored holiday homes:

It was about five o'clock when I saw Sivergues, a little way below me, on a hillock ... No smoke rose from its chimneys; just a deep silence ... Wooden shutters were hanging from their hinges, and every few yards I saw gaping roofs with large beams poking through; here and there a shred of wallpaper on a crumbling wall, or a cupboard with a few remaining shelves ... and everywhere that smell of soot and plaster that tells of the death and abandonment of what was once a home. Some houses still bore a number, which was perhaps the saddest thing of all.

Those days are long gone now. For years it has been impossible to find even a ruined house for sale or a tumbledown barn for conversion anywhere in the Lubéron, unless you are willing to pay a king's ransom.

The villages of Oppède, Ménerbes, Lacoste and Bonnieux are great rivals, each claiming to be the finest medieval or Renaissance village. In the west tower the ruins of **Oppède-le-Vieux**, the ancient *oppidum* which had almost disappeared under the dense scrub by the time many of the houses were restored and are now occupied by artists.

In the old castle at **Ménerbes** on the D 109, which was restored in the 19th century, over 100 Huguenots led by Scipion de Valavoire were besieged for a whole year by the troops of Henry III. This area acquired an unfortunate reputation during the repression of the Waldensians and later in the Protestant uprisings.

The most brutal episode took place here in 1545: Led by the Seigneur of Oppède, the army of the Parliament of

123

Provence marched into the countryside and razed 22 villages to the ground in only six days. Their inhabitants were massacred. Such things are not forgotten with the passage of time. They remain like a bruise on the soul.

Lacoste is still haunted by the ghost of the Marquis de Sade. His vast château once stood here, although only a few imposing walls now remain.

In the center of the old village, it is worth taking a look at the figures of horses in the naive style made by a local sculptor.

Being a Catholic town, **Bonnieux** was never damaged or even plundered. It seems to stretch over the hillside like a contented cat. The fact that it has a museum of baking is surely significant!

The whole place is full of the scent of the cedars which were planted up here

barely a century ago. The trees are indigenous to North Africa but flourish here just as well as in the Atlas Mountains because the climate is so suitable for them.

Continuing eastwards, you will come to an old abbey, the **Prieuré de Saint-Symphorien,** with its tall Romanesque bell-tower. Next to it is the **Fort de Buoux,** set high on a mound enclosed by tall peaks, its walls now in ruins. Inside it has many staircases, corridors and wells.

Further south you will come to **Mérindol**, reborn from its ashes in the 17th century, and **Cucuron** (on the D 943), where they put up a maypole every year.

Further along the D 943, you finally reach **Lourmarin**, lying at the foot of the mountains. Its Renaissance château is now owned by the Academy of Aix-en-Provence which holds painting courses here during the summer months. The French writer Albert Camus, who won the Nobel Prize for literature in 1957, spent the last years of his life in Lourmarin. His grave is in the small cemetery

Above: The village of Lourmarin has hardly changed over the centuries. Right: The triumphal gate to the Château de la Tour-d'Aigues.

124

under a thick lavender bush. The street in which his house stands now proudly bears his name.

Pays d'Aigues

On the southern slopes of the massif is the **Pays d'Aigues**, protected by what was once almost impregnable mountainous terrain and a virtually impassable river, the Durance. Bridges were not built across the river until the 19th century.

There was always plenty of water here, either from rivers and streams rushing down the mountains or from the marshes which were progressively drained by the first farmers to settle in these parts. They planted orchards and vegetable gardens along the banks of the river and protected them from the strong winds with rows of tall cypress and poplar trees. Vines grew on the terraced slopes. Because it was so rich and fertile, the region and its small capital **Pertuis** (on the D 973) were soon annexed by Aix-en-Provence and treated as its hinterland.

Once a large Gallic *oppidum,* **Cadenet** has since spread downhill, turning its back on the rock from which the ancient fortress has all but disappeared. In **Ansouis** there is a fine Louis XIII château surrounded by terraced gardens of topiary. The Duchess of Sabran has restored the château and gardens and written the history of her family seat and its occupants, going right back to her ancestors Elzéar and Delphine who were canonized in the 13th century.

Sadly, the magnificent château of **La Tour d'Aigues**, built by the Baron de Cental, is not so well preserved. There remains only its portico, freely based on the Arc de Triomphe at Orange, and its many cellars which now house the **Musée de l'Histoire du Pays d'Aigues.** Apparently the Baron de Cental was madly in love with Queen Margot and built the château specially for her, but she never ever set foot in it.

Its wide streets and the elegant façades of its houses give La Tour d'Aigues a magical air of vanished style and substance. In the late afternoon when old and young men play a game of boules together in front of the imposing portico, it's doubtful whether any of them recall the feared Duc d'Oppède and his unsuccessful suit for the hand of the beautiful and wealthy Baroness of Tour d'Aigues, the last inhabitant of the château.

His rejection by her sealed the fate of countless numbers of the Waldensian religious sect. About twenty of their villages belonged to the baroness, whose liberal views led her to grant them her personal protection. But when the bitter and rejected suitor was instructed by the King in person to pursue the "heretics," he made the most of the opportunity to exact ruthless revenge for his humiliation at the hands of the lovely baroness and massacred hundreds of the "heretic" Waldensians, plundering their villages and destroying their homes. The few remaining Waldensians had to emigrate.

Tourist Information
Information about the region from the **Chambre départementale du Tourisme**, place Campana, 84000 Avignon, Tel: 90-864342.

APT
Accommodation
MODERATE: **Auberge du Luberon**, 17, quai Léon-Sagy, Tel: 90-741250.
BUDGET: **Le Ventoux, 67**, av. Victor-Hugo, Tel: 90-740758.
Tourist Information
Office de Tourisme, place Bouquerie, Tel: 90-740318.

AVIGNON
Accommodation
LUXURY: **Mirande**, 4, place de l'Amirande, Tel: 90-859393. *MODERATE:* **Bristol Terminus**, 44, cours Jean-Jaurès, Tel: 90-822121.
BUDGET: **Angleterre**, 29, boulevard Raspail, Tel: 90-863431.
Restaurants
La Vieille Fontaine, 12, pl. Crillon, Tel: 90-826692, elegant. **Le Vernet**, 58, rue Joseph-Vernet, Tel: 90-866453, moderate. **Le Petit Bedon**, 70, rue Joseph-Vernet, Tel: 90-823398, inexpensive.
Museums / Sightseeing / Festival
Palais des Papes, pl. du Palais, Tel: 90-860332. **Musée du Petit Palais**, pl. du Petit-Palais, Tel: 90-864458. **Musée Calvet**, 65, rue Joseph-Vernet, Tel: 90-863384. **Livrée Ceccano**, Tel: 90-851559. **Chapelle des Pénitents Noirs**, Tel: 90-829796. *Festival*, July until beginning August.
Tourist Information
Office de Tourisme, 41, cours Jean-Jaurès, Tel: 90-826511.

BEDOIN
Restaurant
L'Oustau d'Anaïs, route de Carpentras, Tel: 90-656743, moderate prices.

BONNIEUX
Accommodation / Restaurant
MODERATE: **Hostellerie du Prieuré**, rue J.-B.-Aurard, Tel: 90-758078. **Le Fournil**, 5, place Carnot, Tel: 90-758362, restaurant, good food.
Tourist Information
Syndicat d'Initiative intercommunal du Canton, place Carnot, Tel: 90-759190.

BUOUX
Accommodation / Restaurant
MODERATE: **Les Seguins**, Tel: 90-741637.
Auberge de la Loube, Tel: 90-741958, restaurant, moderate prices.

CARPENTRAS
Accommodation
MODERATE: **Le Blason de Provence**, route de Carpentras, Monteux, Tel: 90-663134. **Hôtel Sa-**fari, av. J.-H.-Fabre, Tel: 90-633535. *BUDGET:* **Le Fiacre, 153**, rue Vigne, Tel: 90-636315.
Restaurants
Le Saule Pleureur, le ,,Pont-des-Vaches", quartier Beauregard, Monteux, Tel: 90-620135, elegant.
L'Orangerie, 26, rue Duplessis, Tel: 90-672723, inexpensive.
Sightseeing
Palais de Justice, open Mondays, prior appointment at the caretaker's office is necessary.
Hôtel-Dieu, visits to the old pharmacy Mon, Wed and Thur mornings. **Synagogue**, services Sat, Sun and at Jewish Holy Days.
Tourist Information
Office de Tourisme, 170, allée Jean-Jaurès, Tel: 90-630078.

CAVAILLON
Accommodation / Restaurants
MODERATE: **Christel**, Digue des Grands Jardins, Tel: 90-710779. *BUDGET:* **Le Parc**, pl. du Clos, Tel: 90-715778.
Fin de Siècle, 46, pl. du Clos, Tel: 90-711227, restaurant, moderate prices. **Prévot**, 353, av. de Verdun, Tel: 90-713243, restaurant, moderate prices.
Museum
Synagogue and **Museum,** closed Saturdays and at Jewish Holy Days.
Tourist Information
Office de Tourisme, 79, rue Saunerie, Tel: 90-713201.

CHATEAUNEUF-DU-PAPE
Accommodation
MODERATE: **Logis d'Arnavel**, route de Roquemaure, Tel: 90-837322.
Museum
Musée-Cave du Père Anselme, Tel: 90-837007.
Tourist Information
Office de Tourisme, place du Portail, Tel: 90-837108.

FONTAINE-DE-VAUCLUSE
Accommodation
BUDGET: **Hôtel du Parc**, Tel: 90-203157.
Tourist Information / Abbey
Office de Tourisme, place de l'Église, Tel: 90-203222.
Abbaye de Sénanque, Tel: 90-720205.

GORDES
Accommodation / Restaurant
LUXURY: **Le Moulin Blanc**, route d'Apt, Les Beaumettes, Tel: 90-723450.
MODERATE: **La Mayanelle**, 6, rue de la Combe, Tel: 90-720028.
Mas de Tourteron, chemin Saint-Blaise, Les Imberts, Tel: 90-720016, restaurant, moderate prices.
Castle / Museum
Château and **Musée**, Tel: 90-720289.

Tourist Information
Office de Tourisme, place du Château, Tel: 90-720275.

L'ISLE-SUR-LA-SORGUE
Accommodation
MODERATE: **Araxe**, domaine de la Petite Isle, Les Sorguettes, route d'Apt, Tel: 90-384000.
Tourist Information
Office de Tourisme, place de l'Église, Tel: 90-380478.

LA TOUR D'AIGUES
Castle / Tourist Information
Château, 90-775033. **Tourist Information** in the castle, Tel: 90-775029.

LOURMARIN
Accommodation
LUXURY: **Le Moulin de Lourmarin**, rue du Temple, Tel: 90-680669.
Tourist Information / Castle
Office de Tourisme, 17, av. Philippe-de-Girard, Tel: 90-775029. **Château**, Tel: 90-681523.

NATURE RESERVE LUBERON
Tourist Information / Castle
Information from: **Maison du Parc**, 1, pl. Jean-Jaurès, 84400 Apt, Tel: 90-740855. **Château de la Tour d'Aigues**, Tel: 90-775029.

MALAUCENE
Tourist Information
Office de Tourisme, place de la Mairie, Tel: 90-652259.

ORANGE
Accommodation
MODERATE: **Arène**, place de Langes, Tel: 90-341095.
Sightseeing / Festival
Théâtre antique, open all year, closed on public holidays.
Chorégies, in July and August.
Tourist Information
Office de Tourisme, cours Aristide-Briand, Tel: 90-347088, at the antique theater, open in summer.

PERNES-LES-FONTAINES
Accommodation
BUDGET: **L'Hermitage**, route de Carpentras, Tel: 90-613172.
Tourist Information
Office de Tourisme, pont de la Nesque, Tel: 90-613104.

PERTUIS
Tourist Information
Office de Tourisme, le Donjon, place Mirabeau, 84120 Pertuis, Tel: 90-791556.

RASTEAU
Museum
Musée des Vignerons, museum of wine production, domaine de Beauregard, Tel: 90-461175.

ROUSSILLON
Accommodation
MODERATE: **Mas de Garrigon**, route de Saint-Saturnin, Tel: 90-056322.
BUDGET: **Résidence des Ocres**, route de Gordes, Tel: 90-056050.
Festival
Festival de l'Ocre et de la Couleur, in May (Ascension Day).
Tourist Information
Office de Tourisme, place de la Poste, Tel: 90-056025.

SAULT
Tourist Information
Office de Tourisme, av. de la Promenade, Tel: 90-640121, open in summer only.

SEGURET
Accommodation
MODERATE: **Domaine de Cabasse**, Tel: 90-469112.

SERIGNAN-DU-CONTAT
Park / Museum
Parc botanique et Musée Harmas J.-H.-Fabre, Tel: 90-700044.

VAISON-LA-ROMAINE
Accommodation
MODERATE: **Le Beffroi**, rue de l'Evêché, Tel: 90-360471.
Sightseeing
Admission ticket to the antique theater includes visit to the old town quarters Villasse and Puymin.
Tourist Information
Office de Tourisme, place du Chanoine-Sautel, Tel: 90-360211.

VALREAS
Accommodation
BUDGET: **Le Grand Hôtel**, 28, av. Charles-de-Gaulle, Tel: 90-350026.
Sightseeing / Festivals
Château de Simiane, town hall, closed Sat, Sun and public holidays. *Nuits théâtrales de l'Enclave*, theater festival in July and August.
Tourist Information
Office de Tourisme, place Aristide-Briand, Tel: 90-350471.

VILLENEUVE-LES-AVIGNON
Accommodation
LUXURY: **Hostellerie Prieuré**, 7, pl. du Chapitre, Tel: 90-251820.
MODERATE: **Hostellerie du Vieux Moulin**, rue du Vieux Moulin, Tel: 90-250026.
BUDGET: **L'Atelier**, 5, rue de la Foire, Tel: 90-250184.
Tourist Information
Office de Tourisme, place Charles-David, Tel: 90-256133.

IN THE LAND OF
LAVENDER

HAUTE PROVENCE

DIGNE AND THE FOOTHILLS

OF THE ALPS

GORGES DU VERDON

HAUTE PROVENCE

The département of Alpes-de-Haute-Provence forms a link between the French Alps and the Mediterranean. The Alps of Haute Provence are a popular area for skiing in winter. In summer, when the lavender is in bloom in the fields, the Plateau de Valensole seems almost to float in the air. North of Manosque, little lanes lead to tiny hamlets from where proud Provence stretches away to the horizon.

From Manosque to Forcalquier

The starting point for a tour of Haute-Provence is **Manosque** (on the N 96). This town is an open book to readers of Jean Giono (1895-1970), the most important writer of Provence, whose works, extolling the life of the Provençal peasant, are set in and around Manosque. There are restaurants called *Jean le Bleu,* shops called *Regain,* the inevitable Avenue Jean-Giono and the steep Rue des Vraies-Richesses, on which stands his house, *Le Paraïs.* The writer was born in Manosque and spent his entire life here.

Preceding pages: Lavender field on the Valensole plateau. Left: The chalky sandstone Préalpes de Digne.

Manosque is the commercial center of the region. It is very pleasant to stroll round the old town with its 17th- and 18th-century houses and hotels. Manosque also offers culinary specialties to suit every taste. The cheese shop called *L'Art de la Fromagerie* at 10, boulevard de la Plaine and the *Coopérative Oléicole* supply local products. And Giono sang the praises of the area round his home town where the air *is scented with resin.* Pines, oaks and gorse flourish under a brilliant blue sky.

The route between Manosque and Forcalquier along the D 907 and N 100 passes through many small villages like **Montfuron** with its restored windmill or **Villemus** with its ruined château on an almost inaccessible mountain ridge. A detour along the D 12 leads to the beautiful village of **Reillane** which has a colorful market and handsome bell-tower.

Saint-Michel-l'Observatoire on the D 5 has two places of worship, the upper and the lower church, and some medieval houses. Not far away, the Haute Provence Observatory and the chapel of Saint-Jean can be visited.

Further west, **Simiane-la-Rotonde** is worth a special trip along the D5, which later joins the D18. A fortified castle with a massive 12th-century rotunda towers above the picturesque village, which is

131

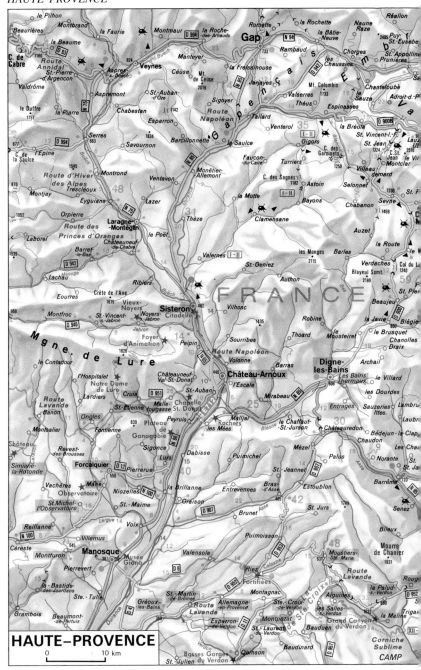

HAUTE-PROVENCE

0   10 km

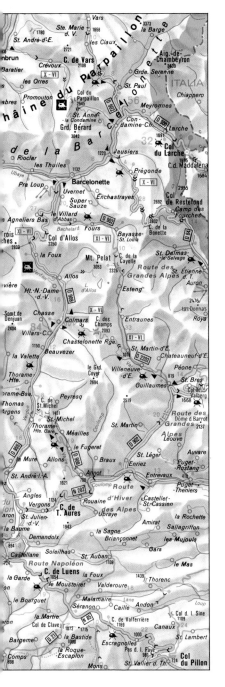

alas virtually uninhabited for ten months of the year. North of Saint-Michel-l'Observatoire is the village of **Mane** which has several fine old houses and the beautiful church of Notre-Dame-de-Salagon.

Forcalquier is a little town set on a sandstone hill on the N 100 with a population of about 3800. In the Middle Ages it was an important place frequented by troubadours, diplomats and traders. In its heyday in the 11th century, the town had four parishes and was a secondary seat of the Bishop of Sisteron. In the 12th century it was the capital of Haute-Provence and the Counts of Forcalquier were a force to be reckoned with. The Couvent des Cordeliers, a Franciscan foundation from the 12th century, and the town's churches and chapels are of architectural interest. Its 12th-century fortified castle is now in ruins.

A market is held in the center every Monday, the best one being on Easter Monday. Honey products can be bought at the *Miel d'Or,* and there is a delicatessen at *La Taste* in Avenue Jean-Giono. Around the town there are some fine farms, where the dovecotes often have higher walls than those of the farmhouse itself, and there are *cabanons* – old huts out in the fields formerly used as shelters by shepherds.

Between Lurs and Les Mées

In the basin 7 km (4 miles) east of Forcalquier is the pilgrimage church of **Notre-Dame-des-Anges** which has a fine 18th-century chancel. The D 12 climbs steeply up to **Lurs**, which is bounded by the bishop's palace in the north and a seminary in the south. From up here you can look over the whole valley of the Durance – a sea of olive groves. Another impressive sight is the 330 yd (300m) long Bishop's Way, where fifteen oratories, built along a narrow rocky spur, mark the path up to the little chapel of Notre-Dame-de-Vie.

High above the Durance is the plateau of **Ganagobie** which can be reached along the N 96. It is littered with caves and old stone refuges and forested with evergreen oak. It contains a very fine example of Romanesque architecture, the **Benedictine monastery.** The west front of the church is particularly impressive with some unusual stone carvings around the entrance. The restored mosaic in the apse of the church is a wonderful work of art laid out between 1135 and 1173.

It covers an area of 86 sq.yd (72 sq m) and is designed in red (sandstone), white (limestone) and black (marble). It looks rather like an Oriental carpet with its complex pattern of mythical subjects borrowed from the world of plants and animals. Its purpose is clearly more than purely decorative since it represents the struggle beween good and evil, symbolised by a knight wrestling with three

Above: In the hot sun, a straw hat is both decorative and practical. Right: The citadel at Sisteron.

monsters. The mosaic in the south transept shows him killing a hideous dragon. Otherwise the interior of the church is quite plain.

The Benedictine monks used to gather seven times a day in the choir stalls and sing Gregorian chant alternating with psalms in French. The cloister is also a model of simplicity, but bathed in light. The Avenue of the Monks, lined with holm-oaks, goes left past the church up to a viewing point on the edge of the plateau. There, over the Durance valley, you can see the plateau of Valensole and the peaks of the Alps of Provence.

The Durance flows at the foot of the plateau of Ganagobie. Above the village of Les Mées, the astounding cliffs of **Les Pénitents des Mées** extend for about 1.5 miles (2.5 km) looking exactly like a procession of gigantic monks. Some of the rocks are more than 300 feet (approximately 100 m) high.

According to legend, these penitent monks cast lascivious looks at some beautiful Moorish girls captured by a knight in a battle against the Saracens. They are supposed to have been turned to stone as a punishment for staring at the girls with such ardor. St. Donat, a priest from Orleans who lived the life of a hermit on the right bank of the Durance, is said to have performed this rather pointless miracle in the 5th century.

Lure Mountains and Jabron Valley

The old pilgrimage **church of Saint-Donat,** right beside the D 101, dates back to the 11th century and is one of the very few remaining examples of the early Romanesque style in Provence. This large and simple building is nothing less than a hymn to the sunlight, which streams in at its windows right through the day. There is a kind of challenge in the unadorned robustness of its white exterior.

The D 951 at the foot of the mountains passes through one village after another:

Mallefougasse, Cruis, Saint-Etienne and Ongles, which has the highest olive grove in the country.

Further west, the road leads to **Banon,** which is known for its excellent goat's cheese. From Saint-Etienne onwards the **Lure Mountains** reach out towards us. A narrow, winding road, the D 113, goes up to their highest peak (1826 m / nearly 6000 ft), with a view of the Lower Alps and the whole of Provence right down to the sea when the mistral is blowing and visibility is good. Not far from the summit is the austere abbey of Lure, which is now a cultural center.

On the opposite side is the **Jabron Valley,** enclosed between the Lure, Ubac and Mare mountains and traversed by the D 946. The road takes you to the fascinating and beautiful ruined village of **Vieux-Noyers** where maple trees surround the Romanesque church (the only building still intact), the château, the inn with its pretty Genoese roof and the ruined ocher sandstone houses, with their crumbling masonry still lying in the village streets.

In and around Sisteron

To the east, on the banks of the Durance, is **Sisteron,** a small town with a population of about 6500, on the borders of Provence and the Dauphiné. Although a quarter of the town was destroyed by a bombardment in 1944, the main part of the old town remained undamaged.

The old cathedral of **Notre-Dame-des-Pommiers** was rebuilt in the 12th century and its style combines Provençal Romanesque with influences from Lombardy. Its main door has a tympanum decorated with mythical creatures.

This attractive town lies at the foot of the steep Sisteron cliffs (where hanggliders launch themselves down into the Durance valley). The old medieval town invites us to explore on foot its narrow, stepped streets, with their overhanging houses and buttressed arcades called locally *andrônes*. Excellent nougat can be obtained at *Canteperdrix* in the Place de la République and should be tasted in any case.

From the citadel, which once guarded the access route to the mountains, you can still see a fine 13th-century castle and the 15th-century chapel of **Notre-Dame**. It was completely redesigned in the 16th century. A festival of music, drama and dance, the *Nuits de la Citadelle*, takes place here in the summer and is popular with natives and tourists alike.

Northeast of suburbian **Faubourg de La Baume**, in the pass of Pierre-Ecrite, there is a Roman inscription. Carved on a rock, it tells of a town and its walls, although no trace of these has been found.

A little further up, in the rocks of Chabert, is the chapel of **Notre-Dame-du-Dromon**. Here the rocks are taking revenge on people for imposing order on nature – the chapel is gradually falling into ruin. Only one of the two crypts can be visited. It has retained some small columns from the 11th century.

Above: The old village of Aiguines near the Gorges du Verdon. Right: Pétanque is played "à pié tanca," with the feet together.

South of Sisteron, the D 4 brings you to **Volonne**, on the banks of the Durance. Its 17th-century château has a beautifully decorated staircase.

At the confluence of the Durance and the Bléone is **Châteaux-Arnoux**. From the pretty chapel of Saint-Jean you can see the great loop of the Durance and the Lac de l'Escale, a popular sailing area.

DIGNE AND THE FOOTHILLS OF THE ALPS

The N 85, known as the **Route Napoléon,** follows the course of the river from the Alps. Napoleon landed at Golfe-Juan in March 1815 after escaping from Elba and marched by this roundabout route to Paris, to reclaim the throne and occupy the Tuileries Palace once more. The road runs for 200 miles (324km) through the mountains to Grenoble and is lined on both sides with reliefs, statues, commemorative plaques and inns recalling the great Emperor of France. At every bend in the road there are fantastic views of the scenery of Provence, and villages display Napoleon's symbol, the imperial eagle and an "N" surmounted by a crown, on their signboards.

It is not surprising that a remarkable woman named Alexandra David-Neel chose the town of Digne to set up a *forteresse de la méditation (*fortress of meditation) at her house, to which she gave the Tibetan name *Samten Dzong.*

This is where she wrote most of her books on Buddhism and eastern philosophy, when she was not actually traveling around Tibet and Central Asia, and it is where she spent the last years of her life. She died in 1969 at the age of 100 and bequeathed to the town both her copyrights and her house, which became a foundation. Researchers and students come here to study the work of this unusual woman. All the works she wrote and the many interesting documents she collected on her long journeys are kept at the house.

On its high hill (600 m / 1970 ft), the town of **Digne** seems to be floating between the lavender fields and the sky. It is the main center for the sweetly scented herb to which all the festivals in the month of August are dedicated.

The spring water of Digne has also been renowned since ancient times for its therapeutic properties. The baths are about 2 miles (3 km) outside the town and are still being extended. The old town is peaceful and attractive. Its medieval walls conceal a vast but airy building, the majestic cathedral of **Notre-Dame-du-Bourg,** which was probably built in the 12th and 13th centuries.

All kinds of local specialties are on sale at the *Provence et Gourmandise* department store in place Général de Gaulle: pottery, sweets, santons, Moustiers faïence and Provençal fabrics.

Digne is also at the center of the important geological reserve of Haute-Provence. Around Digne you can read its fascinating geological history from the

limestone rock itself and study 300 million years of the Earth's past. Guided tours are organized by the **Centre Géologique de Saint-Benoît**, mainly in the summer, visiting the protected sites of special interest, where fossilized ammonites and the claw prints of prehistoric birds can be seen.

7 km (4 miles) south-east of Digne is the village of **Entrages**, in the shadow of the **Cousson**, a steep, almost inaccessible peak crowned by the chapel of **Michel-de-Cousson.**

The N 85 continues through small villages and inhospitable scenery to the next sizeable place, **Saint-André-les-Alpes**, where you can swim in the **Lac de Castillon**. You can also catch the delightful **Train des Pignes** that runs to Nice from Saint-André-les-Alpes. One of its stops is at the mountain village of **Annot** on the N 202.

Annot lies in the valley of the Vaïre surrounded by green alpine pastures and forbidding gray cliffs formed of massive, weirdly shaped rocks which have been

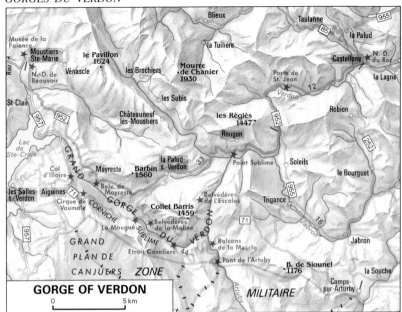

GORGE OF VERDON

0   5 km

honeycombed with caverns since time immemorial. Annot itself is dominated by a Romanesque church with an interesting commemorative plaque showing six people in the costume of the Louis XVI period.

The highest region of Provence begins 25 miles (40 km) north of Annot, at **Colmars-les-Alpes** on the D 908, with its fortified castle. The village is in a high valley almost enclosed by peaks of 6500 - 8000 ft (2000-2500m) Its ramparts are up to 40 ft (12m) high, guarded by towers and bastions and enclosing the interesting old fort of Haut-Verdon. To the south is the artificial lake of Castillon, looking strangely like a Norwegian fjord.

GORGES DU VERDON

At the intersection of the Route Napoléon with the road from Haut-Verdon, on a cliff 560 ft (170 m) high, is the small town of **Castellane**. There is a good view from its chapel of **Notre-Dame-du-Roc**. In the land of lavender and bees you will also find **santons** and faïence - at *Miel Rucher*, the *Boutique Napoléon* and *Douce Provence*. If "white water" rafting attracts you, you can go along to *A.N. Rafting* at the mill of La Salaou (Tel. 92 83 73 83).

Castellane is also the starting point for visits to the famous **Gorges du Verdon**, an area of fantastic rock and ravine scenery. It is an excellent venue for geologists and photographers. Sporty types are also well catered for. There are many paths through the gorges, the water in **Sainte-Croix reservoir** is wonderful for a swim and you can also go rockclimbing on the cliffs from the Verdon, or canoeing in the river itself. And cavers have an incredible amount to explore. Martel, who discovered the Grand Canyon of the Verdon in 1905, called it *a natural wonder unsurpassed in Europe*. Its isolated situation high up in Provence explains why it took so long for this area to be discovered. And because the gorges were so inaccessible, there is still an aura of mystery about them.

The Grand Canyon of Provence

A wonderful circular route runs for 48 miles (77km) along either side, high above the Verdon (D 952, D 957 and D 71). The gorges run from east to west. Beyond Rougon, stops can be made at many marked viewing points on the left bank. There is a narrow footpath to the **Point Sublime**, where you climb to a viewing point at a height of 600 ft (180 m) above the river Verdon at its confluence with the Baou. You can look right down into the Canyon and into the green waters of the Verdon (hence its name). It is a breathtaking experience.

La Palud-sur-Verdon, with a pretty church as you enter the village, is the place for a short pause and a look at the surrounding farms and fields. From here on, there are other spectacular viewpoints on the road beyond the village which again closely follows the contours of the canyon.

At the end of the Grand Canyon is **Moustiers-Sainte-Marie**, where there is a fantastic view of the gorge. The village is divided in two by a huge crevasse in the rock where the Rioul rushes down in a torrent. Both halves are dominated by towering rock faces. The most amazing sight is a gilded chain 745 ft (227 m) long strung between the two peaks, with a gold star in the center, a fabulous votive offering brought here by a nobleman from Blacas. While imprisoned by the Saracens during the crusades, he made a vow that if he was released he would link the two supposedly unassailable cliffs with a chain.

A maze of tiny, narrow streets in Moustiers-Sainte-Marie leads to the **Musée de la Faïence**, where you can discover the secret of making the ceramics which are on sale in many of the village shops. Although pottery has been made in the village since ancient times, it was not until the 17th and 18th centuries that the faïence produced by the Clérissy family brought worldwide fame to the village. At that time there were 700 kilns, 30 workshops, 400 workers and 50 master potters here.

By 1874 the glazed pottery made in the village had gone out of fashion and the last kiln went cold. But work restarted in 1927 when Marcel Provence breathed new life into this traditional craft and it has continued ever since. Visits to the studios of *Faïences Bondil* in place de l'Eglise, *Saint-Michel* in chemin de la Maladrerie and *Faïences Achard* in place Couvert should not be missed and wonderful souvenirs or gifts can be bought here.

East of the village is the church of **Notre-Dame-de-Beauvoir**, also called Notre-Dame-d'Entre-Roches, which perfectly describes its situation: the Virgin Mary hidden away in a great ravine.

The left bank of the Gorges du Verdon begins at the pretty village of **Aiguines**, where there is a beautiful view of the lake of **Sainte-Croix** and the Plateau de Valensole from the picturesque château.

The green waters of the Verdon do not reappear until the **Col d'Illoire**, followed by the Cirque de Vaumale, at the heart of which is the **Signal de Margès** waterfall. This is a good place for refreshment and a rest before tackling the formidable climb up the cliffs of the **Imbut**.

Beyond **Le Maugué** (a pass only 27ft or 8m wide) the Verdon disappears into the **Grotte du Styx**. A few years ago it was decided to build a dam here which would have completely flooded the grand canyon, and tunnels had already been driven when, fortunately, the project was cancelled in time and the tunnels are now used only by walkers, who often come upon half-buried rails and rusty wagons abandoned a few hundred yards from a natural culvert christened "Styx" by the locals.

Beyond the Cirque de Vaumale the road is not quite so spectacular, but the natural beauties are more accessible.

From the **Corniche Sublime** the Verdon looks tiny, more like a stream, but the view is enchanting.

The **Pont de l'Artuby** bridge is the most amazing place of all on the left bank. You cannot help feeling just a little dizzy when you look down into the vertiginous depths spanned by the single 360 ft (110m) arch of the bridge. The River Artuby runs in its rocky bed to join the Verdon and together they unite to form the **Mescla**.

The Lower Gorges

Rather than going direct from Moustiers to Riez on the D 952, it is a good idea to make a detour via the artificial **lake of Sainte-Croix**, along the D 957 and D 49. The dam was built in 1972 at

Above: Moustiers-Sainte-Marie is surrounded by high cliffs. Right: The magnificent Gorges du Verdon. Overleaf: Enjoying the first warm day of spring.

the entrance to a narrow gorge with cliffs 650 - 1000 ft (200-300m) high. The village of Salles-sur-Verdon disappeared and the Sainte-Croix basin was flooded over an area of 10 sq. miles (25 sq.km). There is a splended view from the small villages which were once so high up, especially **Sainte-Croix**, a hamlet which is almost abandoned but revives in the summer when its beach and water sports club are full of visitors.

Between here and **Gréoux-les-Bains** you can enjoy every kind of water sport and after Sainte-Croix swimming is also available in the **Quinson reservoir**, the **lake of Esparron-sur-Verdon** and the **reservoir of Gréoux-les-Bains**.

Baudinard is worth seeing for its château and a church built in the 17th century. Half a mile to the north-east is the chapel of **Notre-Dame-de-Baudinard** which has been converted into a farmhouse, although its attractive apse has been preserved.

Bauduen, which was almost swallowed up by the lake, is set close up

against the mountain and dominated by its interesting Romanesque church.

The former château is now used as the parish offices and the old wash-house has been preserved.

Riez on the D 11 is another interesting place producing leather goods, *santons* and pottery. It is set on a hill 1700 ft (500m) high and is a very popular summer resort. Four granite columns with marble capitals are all that remain of a 1st-century temple and there is very little left of its old 14th-century fortifications, just the clock tower and two town gates, **Saint-Sols** and **Porte Aiguières**.

The fountains are very impressive, one in particular because of the size of its octagonal basin which is 13 ft (4m) in diameter. Onion-shaped fountains like this can also be found in the villages on the Plateau de Valensole.

Though founded in Roman times this town of narrow alleys radiates an atmosphere of the Middle Ages. Take a stroll across the shady square of Quinquonce into the main street with its 16th- to 18th-

century houses or visit the former baptistry and the foundations of the early Christian cathedral.

Above Riez, the **Plateau de Valensole** seems to stretch unendingly towards the peaks of the Lubéron, Sainte-Victoire, the Lure and Ventoux. Ablaze with wheat and lavender fields, the plateau is saturated with the bright light of Provence. It is also the home of the wonderful honey of Provence, generally made by bees that have visited the lavender fields. Riez has its *Maison de l'Abeille* (Tel. 92 74 57 15) and Valensole its *Musée de l'Abeille* on the Route de Valensole, which also sells a range of honey-based products.

To the north, around **Saint-Jurs**, the scenery is wild and rugged. To the west, between the D 6 and the D 11, lie unassuming villages like **Valensole**, in the heart of the plateau, then **Montpezat**, **Allemagne-en-Provence**, **Quinson**, **Esparron** and **Saint-Martin-de-Brômes**. All have beautiful fountains that dance in the sun. It is a marvellous sight, for water has always been scarce here.

Tourist Information

Information about the region from the **Comité départemental du Tourisme**, 42, bd. Victor-Hugo, 04004 Digne, Tel: 09-315729.

ANNOT
Tourist Information

Office de Tourisme, town hall, Tel: 92-832209.

CASTELLANE
Tourist Information

Office de Tourisme, Tel: 92-836114.

CHATEAU-ARNOUX
Accommodation

LUXURY: **La Bonne Etape**, chemin du Lac, Tel: 92-640009.
BUDGET: **Hôtel du Lac**, allée des Erables, Tel: 92-640432.

COLMARS-LES-ALPES
Tourist Information

Office de Tourisme, place Joseph-Girieud, Tel: 92-834192.

DIGNE
Accommodation

MODERATE: **Le Grand Paris**, 19, boulevard Thiers, Tel: 92-311115.
BUDGET: **Hôtel Central**, 26, boulevard Gassendi, Tel: 92-313191.

Museum / Festival

Fondation Alexandra David-Neel, 28, av. du Maréchal-Juin, Tel: 92-313238. **Réserve géologique**, geological treasures, Tel: 92-315131. *Corso de la Lavande*, beginning of August.

Sport

GOLF: 18-hole golf-course in Saint-Pierre-de-Gaubert, Digne, Tel: 92-323838.
WATERSPORTS: **Association départementale d'Eau vive et de Voile**, rue du Docteur-Romieu, Tel: 92-322532.
HIKING: **Centre d'Information Montagne et Sentiers**, 42, bd. Victor-Hugo, Tel: 92-310701.
SKIING / HANG GLIDING: Information from the Tourist Information in Digne.

Tourist Information

Office de Tourisme, place Tampinet, Tel: 92-314273.

ENTREVAUX
Tourist Information

Office de Tourisme, town hall, Tel: 93-054004.

FORCALQUIER
Accommodation

BUDGET: **Hostellerie des Deux Lions**, 11, pl. du Bourguet, Tel: 92-752530, with restaurant.

Tourist Information

Office de Tourisme, in the town hall, place Bourguet, Tel: 92-751002.
Tourist Information for the region Forcalquier, Moulin de Sarret, Tel: 92-753321.

GANAGOBIE
Abbey

Prieuré, open daily 9.30-12 noon and 2.30-5 pm.

MANOSQUE
Accommodation

MODERATE: **La Rose de Provence**, route de Sisteron, Tel: 92-720269.
BUDGET: **Preyrache**, place Hôtel-de-Ville, Tel: 92-720743.

Museums / Festivals

Musée Giono, rue du Mont-d'Or, Tel: 92-875245.
Maison de Giono, treasures from the region, open Fridays only from 3.30-5.30 pm.
Fêtes médiévales, medieval festival in June. *Foire aux jeunes Santonniers*, Christmas market with Nativity play, in December.

Tourist Information

Office de Tourisme, place Dr-Joubert, Tel: 92-721600.

MOUSTIERS-SAINTE-MARIE
Accommodation

BUDGET: **Le Colombier**, route des Gorges du Verdon, Tel: 92-746602.

Museums

Musée de la Faïence, pl. du Presbytère, Tel: 92-746619. **Musée de la Nature**, Tel: 92-778113.

Tourist Information

Office de Tourisme, Tel: 92-746784.

RIEZ
Tourist Information / Museum
Observatory

Office du Tourisme in the **Musée lapidaire**, museum of gems, place des Quinquonces, Tel: 92-745181. **Observatoire de haute Provence**, guided tours Wednesdays 3 pm; from April–Sept on the first Sunday of the month at 9.30 am.

SISTERON
Accommodation

MODERATE: **Grand Hôtel du Cours**, pl. de l'Eglise, Tel: 92-610451.
BUDGET: **Tivoli**, pl. du Tivoli, Tel: 92-611516.

Sightseeing / Museum / Festival

Citadelle, open April–October. **Musée du vieux Sisteron**, av. des Arcades, Tel: 92-611227.
Nuits de la Citadelle, end of July.

Tourist Information

Office de Tourisme, Town Hall, Tel: 92-611203.

VALENSOLE
Special Event

Foire aux Santons de Haute Provence, fair with sale of santons, end July/Aug.

VERDON
Tourist Information / Leisure

Verdon Accueil, Tel: 92-836114. **Verdon Activités Plus**, excursions, watersports, Le Cabanon La Palud-sur-Verdon, Tel: 92-773838.

RED ROCKS AND GREEN FORESTS

PAYS D'AUPS

CENTRE-VAR

TOULON

HYERES AND LES MAURES

SAINT-TROPEZ

EASTERN VAR

CORNICHE D'ESTEREL

The département of Var provides the greatest possible variation of scenery: rural, with villages set mainly amid vineyards, unspoiled, with woods and almost impenetrable forests, highly urbanized on the coast, yet unspoiled again where rocky inlets wind between spectacular red cliffs.

FROM THE PAYS D'AUPS TO LA SAINTE-BAUME

On the western fringes of the department is the area around Aups, where pines, oaks, olives and vines flourish; here is Barjols with its many springs and waterfalls; and the Sainte-Baume massif where you could be in fairyland. Everywhere there are quiet, sleepy villages which are surrounded by green, well-watered meadows.

The Villages of the Pays d'Aups

Between Aups and Barjols lies the pleasant village of **Fox-Amphoux,** built around a Romanesque church. The dancing waters of the waterfall at Sillans 45 m

Preceding pages: Traditional costumes in Roquebrune-sur-Argens. Left: A picturesque corner of the harbor at Saint-Tropez.

(150 ft) high have hollowed out the soft stone. In the village of **Aups**, reached by the D 60, you can hear the gentle splashing of fountains from the shady squares and the esplanade lined with plane trees. The most entertaining time to visit is in mid-May during the three-day festival in honor of St. Pancras.

Taking the D 31, you will come to **Salernes,** where about a dozen factories still survive, making the earthenware for which Provence is renowned. The hexagonal red tiles called *tomettes,* used as floor coverings everywhere in France and one of the oldest forms of ceramic to be made in Provence, were first made here. The best tiles will be found on sale at the *Poterie du Soleil*, 27, rue Victor-Hugo, and the *Poterie du Nai*, 25, avenue Victor-Hugo.

The most surprising of all the villages around Aups is surely **Cotignac**, on the D 22. Built at the foot of a brightly colored cliff, it is dominated by the ruins of a medieval castle.

About half a mile (1km) further on is the chapel of **Notre-Dame-des-Grâces**. Pilgrimages are made every year on 8 September to the chapel, which has been of great religious importance since the earliest times. Louis XIV and his mother left a commemorative plaque of black marble here.

Barjols

All the springs, waterfalls, wash-houses and fountains in the entire world appear to be gathered in **Barjols** and its surroundings. The village itself has about twenty fountains.

There are also a few old tanneries. These were set up by a certain Paul Vaillant around 1600 and for a long time they were the economic backbone of Barjols. A few craftsmen are now trying to renovate and operate the old tanneries again. It is worth visiting the *Atelier Cuir-Cuir* or the *Tannerie Budket*, on the old road to Brignoles.

The village church is also worth a look. Every four years (in 1990, 1994 and so on) on 16 January, which is the Feast of St. Marcel, the ancient *Tripettes* dances are performed.

The Feast of the *Tripettes* begins in the morning with a procession to the accompaniment of pipes and tambourines. In the afternoon an ox bedecked with ribbons is paraded through the streets escorted by butchers and mounted guards, to the sound of drum-rolls.

In front of the church the ox is blessed by the priest and then slaughtered and placed on a cart decorated with flowers. As darkness falls, the musicians gather around the high altar and start to play, which is the signal for the congregation to perform their boisterous, leaping dance. The music and merriment continue into the small hours and the feasting ends next day when the huge roast ox is eaten.

Southwest of Barjols lie fields and vineyards, while in the Font-Taillade valley the countryside is lush and green. In nearby **Brue-Auriac** a very large dovecote can be visited. Further on, a footpath leads to a viewing point with a panoramic vista over Mont Aurélien, the Sainte-Baume and the plain of the Argens and to the source of the Argens, the main river in the department of Var.

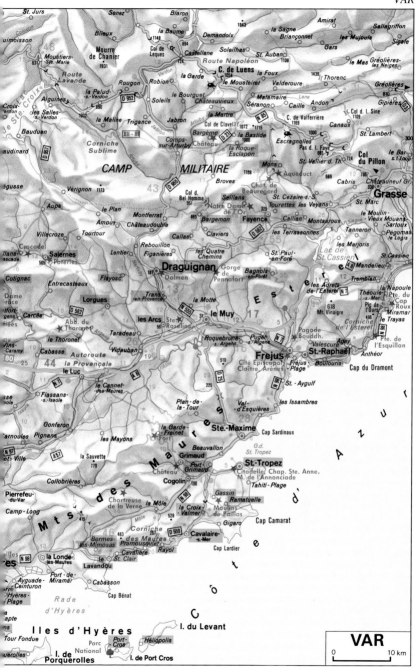

St. Jurs Senez Blaron 1943 Amirat Sallagriffon
uimoisson Blieux la Sagne Briançonnet les Mujouls Sigale
la Baume 894 Demandolx Gars
Moustiers- 1148 Castellane Soleilhas St. Auban 1108 le Mas Gréolières-
Ste.-Marie Col de Route Napoléon les Neiges
631 Mourre Leques 724 Gréolières
de Chanier Verdon la Garde C. de Luens la Foux 1439 Thorenc 810
1931 1054 Valderoure Gipières
Route Rougon Robion le Mousteiret Lane
Lavande le Bourguet Châteauvieux Matamaire Caille Andon Col d. l. Sine
la Palud- Soleils Séranon 1109
Croix- s-Verdon 890 la Martre 1072 1715 C. de Valferrière Canaux St. Lambert
erdon Alguines 1000 1169 1000
la Maline Trigance Jabron Bargème Escragnoles Pas d. l. Faye le Bar
1032 Comps- Château la Bastide St. Vallier d. Th. 724 s. l. Loup
Bauduen XII - III sur-Artuby la Roque- Mons Col
audinard Corniche Esclapon 1198 Aqueduct Cabris Châteauneuf Gr. du Pillon
Sublime 1198 689 330 le Bar
égusse CAMP MILITAIRE Broves Chât. de Beauregard St. Cézaire-s.-S. Grasse
Vérignon 1173 Col d. Seillans Tourettes les Veyans St. Marc
Aups Bel Homme Notre Dame 485 le Moulin- Vieux Mouans-
le Plan 951 de l'O Fayence Callian Montauroux Tanneron Sartoux
Montferrat Bargemon les Terrassonnes Pégomas
Ampus Châteaudouble les Marjoris le Logis
Villecroze Tourtour Claviers St. Cassien
Cascade Rebouillon Callas les Quatre Lac de Mandelieu
llans- Salernes Lentier Figanières Chemins St. Paul- St. Cassien
cascade 505 Poteries en-Forê
Cotignac Entrecasteaux Flayosc 181 Draguignan Gorge Bagnols- les Adrets- Tremblant
Dolmen de en-Forêt de-l'Esterel la Napoule
Dame Trans- Pennafort 618 Théoule- Pte. du
race Lorgues D 562 en-Provence la Motte Mt. Vinaigre s.-Mer Cap
fort- le Muy Roux
gens Carcès Abb. du les Arcs Ste.- Pagode Miramar
ées Thoronet Roseline Roquebrune Puget- Bouddh. de Trayas
Taradeau -s.-Argens s.-Argens Corniche Pte. de
Ins- le Thoronet Vidauban Frejus Valescure de l'Esterel l'Esquillon
Caramy Cabasse Autoroute 510 Agay
80 44 la Provençale Cité Episcopal St-Raphaël Anthéor
le Luc Cloître, Arènes Frejus- Boulouris Cap du Dramont
le Cannet- 225 Plage St. - Aygulf
des-Maures Plan - de - Val- les Issambres A
Flassans- la-Tour d'Esquières
sole s.-Isole
Gonfaron Ste.-Maxime Cap Sardinaux z
arnoules Pignans la Garde- G.d. u
el - Ville les Mayons Freinet Beauvallon St. Tropez
la Sauvette Fort Grimaud St-Tropez r
779 Port- Citadelle/ Chap. Ste. Anne,
Collobrières Château Grimaud M. de l'Annonciade d'
Pierrefeu- Cogolin 100 Tahiti - Plage
du-Var Chartreuse Gassin A
Camp - Long de la Verne la Môle la Croix- Ramatuelle z
528 Valmer Moulins Cap Camarat
415 Corniche de Paillas
la Londe- des Maures Gigaro u
les-Maures Bormes- 483 Cavalaire- r
les-Mimosas Pramousquier s.-Mer
es le St. Clair Rayol Cap Lardier
Lavandou
Port-de- e
Ayguade- Miramar Cabasson
Ceinturon Cap Bénat t
Hyères- Rade
Plage d'Hyères ô
apte
ns Iles d'Hyères I. du Levant
Tour Fondue Parc Port- Héliopolis
uerolles I. de National Cros
Porquerolles I. de Port Cros

VAR

0   10 km

149

Strangely, the Var itself does not flow in the area bearing its name.

La Sainte-Baume

The main attraction in the fairytale scenery of Sainte-Baume is the basilica at **Saint-Maximin-la-Sainte-Baume**, on the D 560. St. Mary Magdalene is perhaps the most impressive Gothic church in Provence. In the late 13th century Charles II of Anjou ordered it to be built by Jean Baudici, the architect of the palace of the Counts of Provence in Aix.

It was built over a tomb which was traditionally venerated as being that of the biblical Mary Magdalene. Innumerable legends surround the place. Angels are said to have brought the body of the saint here when she died after completing thirty years' penance at her grotto in La Sainte-Baume. Her tomb is said to have emitted a wonderful perfume.

Above: Coffee break on the terrace. Right: Stocking up with baguettes.

The construction of the basilica itself lasted until the 16th century, but was never completed because the money ran out. Its simple interior is given a majestic air by the brightness of the sunlight that streams in through huge windows, bathing the choir in light. The monumental organ above the entrance has 2981 pipes which work as well as the day they were installed at the end of the 18th century by a Dominican friar, Jean-Esprit Isnard.

Adjoining the church is the royal monastery, formerly a theological college and now a cultural center hosting conferences, seminars, concerts and exhibitions of modern art.

The **Massif de la Sainte-Baume**, crossed by the N 560 and D 80, offers some beautiful walks. From the Trois Chênes (Three Oaks) crossroads you can walk to the famous **grotto** lying at the foot of an awesome escarpment 886 m (over 2900 ft) high from the top of which there is a superb view. In the 13th century the Dominicans built a monastery at this place of pilgrimage. They were expelled during the Revolution but in the 19th century a new monastery was built a short distance away in the middle of the Plateau du Plan d'Aups. This is now the Hôtellerie, a cultural and religious center that is open to all.

La Sainte-Baume is not just a place of pilgrimage, it is also a botanic marvel. On the Plateau du Plan d'Aups there is a dense forest of 340 acres (138 hectares) which is just like a great, green cathedral where the sunlight rarely penetrates. Many species that are unusual in these latitudes grow here, including maples, gnarled beeches, limes, poplars and others, as do flowers native to both north and south.

The most beautiful walk is to the **Glacières de Fontfrège** from the Saint-Pilon pass – about five hours there and back. From the ridge the view encompasses the Alps, Mont Ventoux, Mont Sainte-Victoire and the Mediterranean.

CENTRE-VAR

Bauxite and marble are quarried around Brignoles, which is also the center of a wine growing area. Between here and Toulon there are many beautiful side roads through picturesque valleys.

Brignoles

Between Saint-Maximin and Brignoles the N 7 crosses the **Caramy valley**. In **Valbelle**, the monolithic columns of the château bear witness to the 18th-century preference for the Greco-Roman classical style. Close by in Tourves, which was founded by the Romans, they make their living by producing wine, as do most of the villages in the region. Its commercial center is **Brignoles**. Until the 16th century "Brignoles plums" were world-famous. Now the famous plums are more likely to come from Digne. Brignoles hosts the great Provence Wine Fair every year in April, attracting some 40,000 visitors. The best wines of this region can

also be bought throughout the year at the *Syndicat des Coteaux Varois*, 15, avenue Foch.

The museum at Brignoles exhibits the oldest known Gallic Christian sarcophagus, **La Gayole**. Carved by a Greek sculptor in the 2nd century AD, it comes from the chapel of La Gayole and depicts St. Peter as a fisherman. In the church of Saint-Sauveur there is a Descent from the Cross and a statue of the Black Madonna.

North of Brignoles, the medieval citadel of **Montfort-sur-Argens** overlooks the valley of the Argens. The town with its strange fortifications has preserved its walls, its feudal castle and its 13th-century portcullis. In 1207 Simon de Montfort was granted to the Knights Templar who made it their main stronghold in Provence.

Close to the citadel is the chapel of Notre-Dame-de-Spéluque. Not far away is the lake of Carcès, popular with anglers and also good for swimming. Another 2 km (just over a mile) further is the village of Vins-sur-Caramy where the château is in the process of restoration at the time of writing.

To the south, near the Loube Mountains, is the abbey of **La Celle,** now a hotel. The convent was built in the 6th century and was originally a priory and then an abbey until 1770. It had acquired a very bad reputation in the 16th century, as very few of the hundred or so nuns, who mainly came from the wealthy families of Provence, seem to have spent much time praying or fasting. According to an old chronicle, they were renowned for their many lovers! Finally, Cardinal Mazarin transferred the sisters to Aix and the convent collapsed.

The village church at La Celle contains a very fine crucifix from Italy.

Camps-la-Source owes its origins to a mineral spring that was much prized by the Romans. The village prospered later from the production of felt hats and by the 19th century there were fifteen factories exporting hats all over the world. Some of these factories are still standing as a reminder of the wealth of the past.

Between Brignoles and Toulon

Forcalqueiret (further south on the D 554) is dominated by the impressive ruins of its castle recalling the days when a military fortress stood here in the 16th century. Several fairs are held each year in the town. There is a goat fair on 1 May, a horse fair in June, a hunting festival on 5 September and last but not least the *Fête de la Blaque* at the beginning of July.

A few miles further is the village of **Garéout,** set among vineyards.

Roquebrussanne (along the D 64), with its delightful name, has a graceful clock-tower. In the village center there are elegant Renaissance style houses. Its Fairy Fountain is so called because it temporarily dries up in summer, the water later returning as if by magic. The spring which supplies its water is at the

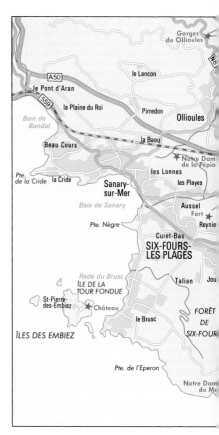

end of the tiny Fortune valley which gets its name from the many Roman coins that have been found there.

In the **Vallée du Gapeau**, be sure to visit the village of **Méounes-les-Montrieux** (via the D 5) to see its fine fountains and Gothic church. Immediately beyond the village is the **Ferme de Grand-Loou,** a former residence of the Knights Templar. It is now an archaeological museum displaying finds from the Neolithic and Roman periods.

More traces of the history of the area can be found in the ruins of **Montrieux-le-Vieux.** Evidence of the earliest years of Christianity lies hidden behind the walls of the Carthusian monastery of **Montrieux-le-Jeune,** but the monks are

152

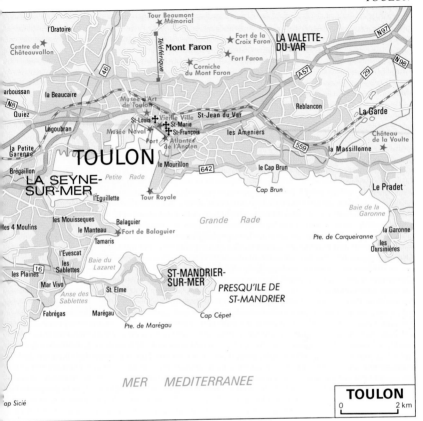

l'Oratoire

Tour Beaumont
Mémorial

Mont Faron

LA VALETTE-
DU-VAR

N97

Centre de
Châteauvallon

Fort de la
Croix Faron

Fort Faron

N98

N29

46

Corniche
du Mont Faron

Téléférique

A57

arboussan

la Beaucaire

Musée d'Art
de Toulon

N8

Reblancon

La Garde

Quiez

St-Louis

Vieille Ville

St-Jean du Var

St-Marie

Lagoubran

Musée Naval

St-François

les Ameniers

Château
de la Voulte

la Petite
Garenne

Port

Atlantée
de l'Ancien

559

la Massillonne

TOULON

le Mourillon

642

le Cap Brun

Brégaillon

**LA SEYNE-
SUR-MER**

Petite   Rade

Cap Brun

Le Pradet

l'Eguillette

Tour Royale

Baie de la
Garonne

les Mouisseques

Balaguier

Grande   Rade

les 4 Moulins

le Manteau

Fort de Balaguier

Pte. de Carqueiranne

la Garonne

Tamaris

les
Oursinières

l'Evescat

Baie du
Lazaret

16

les
Sablettes

ST-MANDRIER-
SUR-MER

*PRESQU'ILE DE
ST-MANDRIER*

les Plaines

Mar Vivo

Anse des
Sablettes

St. Elme

Fabrégas

Marégau

Cap Cépet

Pte. de Marégau

MER   MEDITERRANEE

ap Sicié

TOULON

0 _____ 2 km

anxious to preserve their tranquility and do not allow visitors. Not far away are two lakes, the **Petit and Grand Loou,** which are strange crater-like formations whose water level varies.

South of Méounes are the mountains of the **Massif des Morières**, which looks like an enchanted forest with its impenetrable vegetation. Many legends of fairies and fiery dragons have been woven around its oaks and yews in the past and the dolomitic rocks are weird enough in themselves to evoke thoughts of giants and monsters, even today.

Going westward along the D 2, we soon reach another pretty village. This is **Signes,** which lies among vineyards and has some quite delightful fountains. The

feast-days at Signes in honor of St. Eloi and St. John are celebrated with processions, cavalcades, dancing and feasting which lasts for four days and nights (20-24 June).

TOULON

The city of **Toulon** looks over a beautiful Mediterranean bay. Toulon was one of the main ports in the region in Roman times. In those days the area supplied the famous *murex* snails from which a greatly prized purple dye was extracted. Only the highest Roman dignitaries were permitted to wear purple. Later, in the reign of Louis XIV the port was the main Mediterranean base for the French fleet,

with the largest arsenal of weapons. By the end of the Second World War it was France's principal naval port, stretching for a distance of more than 4 miles (7 km) along the coast. Some of its military importance has now declined, but the dockyard is still an enclosed city within the city. Toulon is now France's leading yachting center and the only big ships which berth here are cruise liners and luxury yachts.

Visitors who knew the old city of Toulon in earlier days, with lines of washing outside the windows, pungent cooking smells, murky streets and many small squares with fountains (place à L'Huile, place de la Poissonnerie etc.) are in for a surprise. Some parts of the city have retained nothing but their names. Since 1985 the old city has become a building site. Whole streets have disappeared and old houses have been gutted or pulled down. The modern pedestrian zone could

Above: A view of Toulon, which is between Mont Faron and the sea.

be in any city you care to name. Its Mediterranean charm has almost vanished, leaving only a small part of the old city to preserve its distinctive atmosphere.

From the busy **Place Puget**, with its Fontaine des Trois Dauphins (Fountain of the Three Dolphins) planted with a host of flowers, you can head towards the port along narrow streets to the **Cours Lafayette,** shaded by plane trees and the venue for one of the best known markets in Provence.

The **cathedral of Sainte-Marie-de-la-Seds** is a strange mixture of styles, the original Romanesque church having been remodeled in the 17th century. The church of Saint-François has a Baroque front with the many curves typical of 18th-century Baroque churches.

In contrast, the port is rather an ugly place. Following heavy bombardment during the Second World War, it was hastily rebuilt with many high-rise blocks. Some figures of Atlas by Pierre Puget were saved from destruction, however, and these are now mounted, somewhat incongruously, on the front of the unprepossessing new City Hall.

The history of Toulon since the 15th century can be studied at the **Naval Museum**, but the dockyard which covers the western half of the port cannot be visited. Beside the docks was once the infamous prison, described by Victor Hugo, which could house 4230 prisoners.

Opposite the main dockyard gates, in place d'Armes, is the **church of Saint-Louis**, an interesting neo-classical building. Around the church the narrow streets of the city's red light district spread out.

The **Musée de Toulon** contains a fine collection of around 300 works of art from Provence. A modern section also displays works that date from the 1960s onward.

The coastal scenery around Toulon is beautiful and in parts very rugged. The bay of La Garonne has fine beaches and rocky inlets. Beyond Le Pradet is Les Oursinières, with its small fishing and yachting harbor.

West of Toulon near Ollioules, a big international dance festival takes place every year at the **Centre de Châteauvallon**, which is set in a beautiful position overlooking the city and the waterfront.

The **Corniche du Mourillon** is the smartest suburb of Toulon, with superb houses and leisure facilities. Tourists like taking a stroll along the Corniche by the *sentier des douaniers* path from the new marina to **Cap Brun**.

The Toulon roadstead is the largest in Europe and among the safest and most beautiful in the Mediterranean. Harbor tours are possible by boat (from Quai Stalingrad) or by car, to Saint-Mandrier via La Seyne-sur-Mer and the **Fort de Balaguier** (17th century). There is a fantastic view from the keep of the fort. The best places for sea bathing are Tamaris and Les Sablettes.

Excavations at the chapel of Notre-Dame-de-la-Pépiole at **Six-Fours-les-Plages** have produced some surprising

discoveries – lots of old pottery shards dating from the 8th to the 17th centuries. One of the fragments has provided evidence of occupation by the Greeks. Other pieces have been found to be of Arabian and Spanish origin.

From **Mont Faron**, which is covered with pine groves and offers some of the finest walks that can be taken in the Toulon area, you will have a view of the whole coastline.

HYERES AND LES MAURES

The slopes of the Massif des Maures are extensively forested. The road from Hyères to Bormes-les-Mimosas is bordered with scented flowers – and we approach the Côte d'Azur along a steep and narrow coast road.

Hyères and its Islands

From the beginning of the 19th century **Hyères** was an important resort for the wealthy, who spent the winter in their imposing houses and subtropical gardens. Palms and orange trees surround these old villas and also line the streets. Beautiful flowers bloom all the year round in the Saint-Bernard park in the heart of the old town. In the upper section of the park is the **Villa de Noailles,** a Cubist-inspired design of 1924 providing a reminder of what was once considered to be the avant-garde in architecture. It was designed by the architect Mallet-Stevens for the Vicomte de Noailles and relies on a wonderful harmony of proportions and simplicity rather than ornamentation and a variety of materials.

Many great names have stayed here, including Man Ray, Giacometti, Buñuel and Poulenc. A feature of the villa is its indoor swimming pool, with huge windows which can be lowered into the floor, opening it to the air. There are about 40 rooms in the house, some of them with furniture designed by the Bau-

haus studio. It stood empty for about ten years, but is now being restored to its former glory by the town of Hyères.

Along the D 97 not far from Hyères-Plage, at **L'Almanarre**, archaeologists have discovered the remains of the Massilian colony of *Olbia*. The square walls of the settlement (600 m or 650 yd round the perimeter) can be seen and have been gradually excavated since the end of the last war.

The Greek settlement of *Olbia* was succeeded by a Roman colony called *Pomponiana*. The Roman baths have been fully excavated and the old harbor, which is now under water, is being explored by divers. The name L'Almanarre is Arabic and recalls the period when this area was occupied by the Saracens.

Another archaeological discovery has been made in the south of the gulf of **Giens**: a cargo vessel from the later years

of the Roman Republic, which is 130 ft (40m) in length and 40ft (12m) wide, with a capacity of 450 tonnes. It was probably carrying about 8000 amphora (large ceramic jars), some 3000 of which have been found. Some of them still had their original corks and contained reddish dregs which were identified as the remains of old red wine.

The Giens peninsula is surrounded by the only salt marshes on the Côte d'Azur. It has many beautiful beaches with good views of the Iles d'Hyères, which can be reached by boat from Hyères-Plage. These islands are true havens of peace. Their mica-rich rocks have given them the nickname Iles d'Or or Golden Isles. The three islands of **Port-Cros, Porquerolles** and the **Ile de Levant** offer the tourist or French holidaymaker unspoiled scenery with luxuriant Mediterranean vegetation and pine forests, steep cliffs and glorious sandy beaches.

Porquerolles is the largest of the three, 4.5 miles (7.5km) long and about a mile (2km) wide. Its north coast has lovely

Above: Fishermen at work. Right: Sailing is a favorite pastime along the Côte d'Azur.

beaches of very fine sand, backed by pine forests - **Notre-Dame beach** is a bathers' paradise and quite safe. The schist cliffs of the south coast fall steeply to the shore. From **Brégançonnet** there is a fabulous view.

The island of **Port-Cros** is rocky and rugged. There is a nature trail above the village of Port-Cros, with an underwater nature trail for divers and snorkelers. There are marked paths all around the island, which is designated a national park. No one is allowed to scuba-fish, camp or pick flowers.

Ile de Levant resembles a fortress with its rugged, inaccessible cliffs. A naturist colony was set up here in 1931 in the village of **Héliopolis**.

Massif des Maures

The **Massif des Maures** begins east of Hyères. The N 98 crosses it through the mountains, while the busy N 559 turns towards the coast and becomes the Corniche des Maures.

The name of the small town of **Bormes-les-Mimosas** evokes the perfume of the mimosa which bursts into flower in February. Flowers and trees grow in profusion around here, especially the eucalyptus, although this was badly decimated in the severe winters of 1984 and 1985.

Beyond Bormes-les-Mimosas, you can drive up into the **Massif des Maures**, a forbidding mountain range extending for 60 km (nearly 40 miles) between Fréjus and the Giens peninsula. Extreme care must be taken in the Maures forest because every summer the area is regularly ravaged by forest fires, despite firebreaks, cleared tracks and innumerable water points.

Because these ecological disasters follow one another relentlessly and because the Mediterranean pine is threatened with extinction due to disease and attack by parasites (also a threat to the sweet chestnuts), the forest of Maures is progressively becoming an area of maquis, with arbutus, broom and heather.

Nevertheless many oak trees do still survive to form fine stretches of woodland and their numbers are now being increased as much as possible to keep back the march of the maquis.

The interior of the massif is largely unpopulated. A road that climbs through chestnut trees brings you to the village of **La Garde-Freinet**, at the summit of a pass.

From **Fort Freinet**, south of the village and accessible only on foot, there is a beautiful view over the valley of the Aille right down to the gulf of Saint-Tropez. The best vantage point for viewing and photographs is in the splendid ruins of the medieval village and its fortifications, which were destroyed at the end of the Wars of Religion in the 16th century. The 13th-century chapel and its belltower still survive, however, and around them are the remaining foundations of about 50 small houses.

Above: Strolling along the many open-air cafés and yachts at Saint-Tropez.

In the heart of the Massif des Maures, hidden in dense chestnut forest, is the **Chartreuse de la Verne**, a monastery resembling a fortified castle – and now trying to defend itself from the invading vegetation. The monastery was founded in the 12th century but little is left of its Romanesque buildings, as it was later rebuilt in the 17th and 18th centuries.

Monks have now returned to the monastery. The charterhouse is a large rectangular building perched on the mountain top and looking down to the sea far below. It has interesting decorative carvings of serpentine rock (a green stone from the Maures) on the doors, faces and windows, set against walls of schist. From the hermitage the view extends as far as the Iles d'Hyères.

The **Route des Crêtes** runs along the ridge for 22 miles (35 km) leading you past the highest peaks and offering fantastic views of the sea and the Alps of Provence.

In contrast, the Corniche des Maures winds its way along the rocky coast.

There are beautiful beaches at Le Lavandou, Saint-Clair with its red cliffs - where there is a nature trail that follows the coast through arbutus, cistus and scented lavender – Cavalière, Pramousquier, Rayol with its superb rugged scenery and Cavalaire-sur-Mer right at the very end of the bay.

SAINT-TROPEZ

The novelist Colette once wrote about **Saint-Tropez**: "Having seen it from above, deep mauve at twilight, then like bright steel in the moonlight, I had to see how the dawn would color the plain fronts of its old houses ... Worries and cares just melt away. The clear blue light is found elsewhere only in dreams but suffuses the reality of life on the coast of Provence."

Long before the arrival of film and showbiz stars, writers such as Colette and painters like Matisse, Bonnard and Signac loved the place. No doubt it was rather more delightful at the beginning of the century, and it was certainly quieter. Nowadays the crowds in summer can be suffocating. But if you avoid the high season it is still enjoyable to wander round the harbor or play *boules* in the Place des Lices, shaded by plane trees that are centuries old. Do not miss the lovely views from the terrace of the citadel or the old cemetery.

The **citadel** houses a maritime museum containing archaeological remains, mainly from wrecked ships. The most recent discovery was made in 1971 - what was probably an Etruscan vessel with its planks held together with rope rather than being nailed or pegged as later vessels were.

The **chapel of Sainte-Anne** high above the town is dedicated to the patron saint of seafarers. It contains so many votive offerings that it is almost like a maritime museum, with replicas of ships and models of the harbor. Also displayed are the chains and iron collar worn by a prisoner in Algiers prison.

The **Musée de l'Annonciade** is a reminder of the role that was played by Saint-Tropez in the lives of many great artists at the turn of the century, and it houses exhibitions of many major paintings by Matisse, Bonnard, Vuillard and Braque as well as sculptures by Maillol.

The most important of the town's many festivals is the **Bravade de Saint-Tropez** which has been celebrated for over 400 years in honor of St. Tropez. It recalls the warlike past of the town, concerned throughout history with defending the gulf against invaders.

The festival begins on 16 May, when the mayor in a solemn ceremony presents a traditional lance to the historic *capitaine de la ville* who is elected from among the townspeople to serve for a year. When a few salvoes have been fired, everyone processes to the church where the lance is blessed by the priest, who is dressed in red. The figure of St. Tropez is then paraded through the streets, which are decorated with red and white bunting. Unusually for a saint, St Tropez had a moustache and is said to have been extremely handsome. Amid a tremedous din of gunshots and shouting, the procession goes past the fish market to the harbour, to pay homage to the sea.

There are many excellent beaches with gorgeously soft sand around Saint-Tropez. You can also walk along the 12-mile (20km) coastal path right round the peninsula to **Cavalaire bay.**

Inland on the peninsula is **Ramatuelle**, a village whose twisting streets, picturesque houses and fig trees lend it an ageless charm.

There are some old windmills, of which Paillas situated at over 1000 ft (325 m) is the highest, offering a magnificent view. Sadly, the village of **La Croix-Valmer** is overrun with housing developments, but the Place des Barry in **Gassin** is still a pleasant spot for a stroll.

Port-Grimaud, in the gulf of Saint-Tropez, is an entirely modern development that has risen from the dunes and marshes since 1966. Its architect, François Spoerry, dreamed of creating a village of lagoons where roads would be replaced by canals and cars by boats. Even though the 2000 or so brightly painted "fishermen's cottages" do make up a waterside community, they are mainly inhabited by summer visitors rather than local people.

The old village of **Grimaud**, only 4 miles (6 km) away, is more authentic, with its attractive small squares, fountains and houses ablaze with flowers. The Romanesque church of Saint-Michel dates from the 11th century, as do the ruins of the castle and the chapel of the Pénitents Blancs (which has been much remodeled over the years).

Above: How about a trip round the bay?
Right: The abbey at Le Thoronet, a master-piece of Cistercian architecture.

EASTERN VAR

From the plain south of Draguignan, criss-crossed by valleys and covered with vineyards and olive groves, the road climbs to the north, through gorges and passes, to the villages of the upper Var.

Around Draguignan

The area south of Draguignan is one of France's most important wine-growing regions. The road goes past large estates with famous names like the *Domaine d'Ott*.

The larger wine villages like **Trans-en-Provence** (on the N 555) and **Les Arcs-sur-Argens** offer a good excuse to stop, as does the Romanesque **chapel of Sainte-Roseline**. The splendors of its interior include a beautiful mosaic by Chagall, *Le Repas Servi par les Anges* (the meal served by the angels), stained-glass windows by Ubac and Bazaine, a lectern in the shape of a tree and a bronze bas-relief by Giacometti.

The chapel is part of an old abbey that was converted into a château in the 18th century. It has a beautiful park landscaped in the French style, watered by a spring situated at the end of an avenue of tall plane trees.

The small town of **Draguignan** seems very quiet compared with the noisy coastal resorts.

Half a mile (1 km) away on the road to Castellane stands an impressive Neolithic dolmen consisting of three standing stones which are over 7 ft (2.25 m) tall, topped by a slab 6 m long, 4.70 m wide and half a metre thick (20ft by 15ft by 1.5 ft). Needless to say, there are many local legends and superstitions associated with it.

If you want to buy the delicious authentic local olive oil, take a detour through **Flayosc** (on the D 557) to where it is sold at the *Moulin Rivera*, in the Foncabrette area, or else try the *Moulin Doleatto* at Le Flayosquet.

The D 562 leads to Lorgues, which is a small country town with fine plane trees shading its square. The **chapel of Notre-Dame des Sablettes**, which is also known as *Notre-Dame de Benva* is beautifully sited on a rocky outcrop. The exterior of the chapel is rather plain but the interior is decorated with fine frescoes throughout.

About 10 km (6 miles) to the west is the **abbey of Le Thoronet**, long considered to be one of the jewels of this region. The architecture of this Cistercian abbey is truly inspired in its unity and simplicity. The austerity required by the rules of St. Benedict finds its most sublime expression here, in the awesome harmony of space and light. The extraordinary acoustics of the church are an indication of the importance of plain chant in the life of the Cistercians.

In the cloisters there is total quiet, broken only by the sound of the fountain, which was used by the monks for water and washing as long ago as the 12th cen-

tury. The monastery has not been used as a religious house since the 18th century, but the beauty and atmosphere of the abbey of Le Thoronet continues to dominate this lonely area.

Close by is the hamlet of **Cabasse**. There are dolmens and a menhir near the **Maison des Fées grotto**, a source of legends from the Gallo-Roman period. A strange necropolis has been excavated near the village: here there are 34 tombs in which the corpses had been incinerated under a thick layer of branches; each one contained a lamp of Roman design to light the way after death. The reason for the many nails, mostly ordinary shoe nails, in the tombs is obscure, but they may have been intended to fix the spirits of the dead in their last resting-place and prevent them from wandering.

The chapel of **Notre-Dame-du-Glaive** in Cabasse is a very plain 17th-century building. It has some ancient votive offerings and a superb gilded wooden altarpiece. From the hill on which it stands there is a fine view stretching away over

glorious scenery to the ridge of Les Maures.

East of Draguignan, on the D 25, the **Gorges de Pennafort** lead to the waterfall of Pennafort. A fifteen-minute walk brings you to this beauty spot where the waters cascade down between the red cliffs.

A short distance away, the River Nartuby plunges into a chasm 115 ft (35m) deep at the **Saut-du-Capelan** and emerges about 100 yards away. Legend has it that a clergyman fell into the river above and survived the fall into the chasm. He was later found safe and well, sitting on a sandbank and reading his prayer-book.

The aptly named village of **Bagnols-en-Forêt** on the D 74 is the starting point for walks to the **Gorges du Blavet**. Its country **church of Notre-Dame-de-**

Selves and the **chapel of Saint-Auxile** with its ruined priory overlooking the village of Callas are all possessed of great charm.

Callas, further along the D 25, is remarkable for its unusually tall, narrow houses. Its **church of Notre-Dame** has a large 17th-century gilded wooden altarpiece.

In **Bargemon**, most of the fortified walls and gates surrounding the old town have survived intact. The village is dominated by the chapel of Notre-Dame de Montaigu, renowned for a statue of the Virgin Mary which is said to have performed many miracles. The road then climbs to the top of the **Bel-Homme pass** where there are lovely views over towards the coast.

Pays de Fayence and the Valley of the Artuby

Above: Rural houses, one with a typical pigeon-loft. Right: Pottery and lavender bags – local souvenirs.

The narrow streets of **Seillans**, on the D 19, are paved with cobblestones worn smooth by the sea and its houses glow ocher and pink in the sunlight. A church, a castle, ramparts – this pretty village has everything, even shaded squares like the Place du Thoron with its tall trees and fountain.

Just outside the village, **Notre-Dame-de-l'Ormeau** is another example of the purity of the Romanesque architecture of the Cistercians. In the 15th century the monks who lived and worshipped here were replaced by religious recluses or hermits, one of whom may have carved the fine wooden altar-piece in the chapel.

Fayence is a small rural town which lives mainly from tourism. Its worth-seeing Romanesque **chapel of Notre-Dame-du-Cyprès** is still surrounded by the cypress trees which gave it its name. This 11th-century building has impressive proportions and an imposing atmosphere, enhanced by the addition, two or three hundred years ago, of a monumental canopy. The chapel has always been venerated by the people of Fayence and, in particular, was a place of special prayer when drought ravaged the area.

Not far away lies **Tourrettes**, mainly famous these days as a center for the exhilarating sport of gliding. Its ideal thermal conditions attract gliding enthusiasts from all over Europe.

At **Callian**, which used to be known for its excellent olive oil that was served at the king's table at Versailles, the climate is so mild that bananas and avocados can flourish here. The village was built in the 12th century and has a pretty Renaissance-style château. Its Romanesque chapel is now used as a cultural center in the summer.

About 6 miles (10km) further on the D 37 is the artificial lake of **Saint-Cassien**, which covers an area of around 1.7 square miles (4.3 sq.km). Footpaths lead along its banks to beaches where the swimming is excellent. There is lots of room for sunbathers and picnickers.

To the north, the D 563 leading to **Mons**, passes some beautiful châteaux –

the **Château de Borigaille**, a 17th century *mas* (manor house), and the magnificent Renaissance-style **Château de Beauregard**, none of which is open to the public.

The road then crosses the Roman aqueduct of **La Roche Taillée**, an amazing structure along the rock extending for more than 3 miles (5 km) down the right bank of the River Siagnole. The Roman engineers cut a gully through the rock, 55 yards long, 28 ft high and 12 ft wide (50m x 10m x 3.6m), and the marks of their iron bars are still visible on a rock overhanging the gully. The aqueduct was used then – as it is today – to tap the mountain springs and carry drinking water to Fréjus.

At the mouth of the Siagnole gorge is the impressive village of **Mons**. It originated in the 11th century, but after its population was greatly reduced in 1348 by the plague it remained abandoned until 1468, when it was resettled by a colony of Italian immigrants from Genoa. These people worked hard to restore the ruined village. The villagers of Mons still speak a unique language called *figoun*, inherited from their Italian forebears. The place Saint-Sébastien overlooks the valleys of the Siagne and Siagnole and in clear weather you can see as far as the Iles de Lérins and the Italian frontier.

Crossing the valley of the Fil, which is dominated by the peaks of Malay (1426 m / 4678 ft) and Lachens and the Clavel pass, we come to the **valley of the Artuby**. This shelters some old villages such as **La Martre, Châteauvieux** (with a 12th-century church) and **La Bastide-d'Esclapon**, where **La Roque-Esclapon**, built by the Knights Templar in the 12th century, is only half a mile (1 km) away. From La Bastide a path leads to the remains of the old village that was abandoned in the 14th century. Its ruined church is very impressive.

The wonderful village of **Bargème** (along the D 21) is the highest in the Var at 3600 ft (1097 m) and has a fine view of the Préalpes de Grasse and Les Maures. **Comps-sur-Artuby** is another mountain village that was finally abandoned by its people in favor of a new settlement lower down.

THE CORNICHE D'ESTEREL

From Fréjus, near the mouth of the River Argens, the coast road, the Corniche de l'Esterel, winds its way past cliffs and sands from one pleasant holiday resort to the next.

Fréjus

The aqueduct which begins 25 miles (40 km) to the north in Mons ends in the center of **Fréjus**, where its arches border the Avenue du XVe-Corps. The town is rich in remains from the Roman period,

when it was an important political and commercial center. Julius Caesar set up the settlement of *Forum Julii* as a staging post on the road round the Mediterranean from Rome to Spain, later known as the *Via Aurelia.* Octavius then converted it into a naval base. Concerts and bullfights are now held in the ancient arena.

The old defenses are still to be seen north of the town. Unfortunately, the only remains of the Roman theater are a few piers which once supported the stage. From the hill of Saint-Antoine it is possible to see the outline of the ancient harbor. This covered an area of 54 acres (22 hectares) and was linked to the sea by a canal about 500 yards long. At one end of rue Jean-Carrara there is a funerary *exedra* – rarely found in France – in which the ashes of an important personage were preserved. A large number of small amphora used for storing wine and oil have also been found in and around Fréjus. The discovery of many kilns indicates that pottery making was commercially important in times gone by.

The old town of Fréjus has preserved much of its medieval history. Particularly fine are the **cloisters**, remarkable for their ceiling of painted wood panelling depicting people and animals. The main entrance to the **cathedral** consists of huge double wooden doors that date from the Renaissance period and are richly decorated with scenes from the life of the Virgin Mary. The pink sandstone cathedral looks solid and impressive with its high walls and pillars.

An interesting rite is celebrated here every year in August when grapes are squeezed on the altar and their juice mixed with the communion wine. After the ceremony comes the *Danse de la Souche* – the priest blesses a fire into which a vine has been thrown, whereupon the congregation dances around it. This grape festival with its somewhat dionysian features is quite unique in the Christian world.

Right: Patterns of tiles – the rooftops of Roquebrune-sur-Argens.

West of the cathedral is the octagonal **baptistry** from the 5th century which still has its ancient capitals. Excavations have uncovered the original marble-paved floor, mosaics in the niches (one of which, bearing a design of a leopard, is in the Archaeological Museum) and baptismal font. The first floor of the baptistry, also octagonal, is beautifully lit by eight windows.

Around Fréjus

West of Fréjus, the N 98 follows the coast while the N 7 crosses the Massif d'Esterel.

Along the valley of the Argens, we reach **Roquebrune-sur-Argens**, overlooking the orchards and fields of cultivated flowers down in the valley. Half a mile (1km) away there is a beautiful view from the **chapel of Notre-Dame-de-Pitié**, charmingly set among pines and eucalyptus trees. The jagged, fissured sandstone cliffs, the Rochers de Roquebrune, are more spectacular still.

Along the aqueduct to the east there is an unexpected building: a **pagoda** with its entrance guarded by two statues of Buddha, one lying and one standing. It was built in 1918 for the Indochinese immigrant community in Fréjus and now belongs to the *Société Bouddhique de France*. Ceremonies are held here every year.

The newly built **Port-Fréjus** is hardly an architectural masterpiece – in fact this whole section of coast is scarred by poor-quality development. **Saint-Raphaël**, adjoining Fréjus, is no better, with the shore-line disfigured by the ugly modern conference center. Happily, a few Belle Epoque villas have escaped destruction. Saint-Raphaël has been settled since prehistoric times, but it remained a sleepy little place until the turn of the century. With the arrival of the railway, it developed within twenty years into a fashionable resort with a casino, some big hotels and more than 200 villas. But as rapidly as the town came into fashion, it soon declined again.

The old town nestles round the attractive Romanesque **church of Saint-Pierre**. This dates from the end of the 12th C, and is the third church to have been built on this site. Stones from the Roman period were re-used by the medieval builders, which explains the presence of a strange winged phallus on the choir vault.

From the **Plateau Notre-Dame** above the town there is a good view over Saint-Raphaël and Fréjus to the Massif des Maures. The hilltop **Quartier de Valescure** used to be the most elegant suburb of the town, with villas and beautiful gardens. The villa owned by the journalist and critic Alphonse Karr was destroyed during the Second World War, but the garden laid out by Carvalho (director of the Paris Opera) still exists. In it he incorporated some important remains from the Tuileries Palace in Paris.

Above: One of the beaches at St-Raphaël.
Right: The untamed Côte d'Azur – the red Cap de l'Esterel.

The Corniche d'Esterel

The road along the coast joins the Corniche d'Esterel, which has been nicknamed the Corniche d'Or. The cliffs with their characteristic red glow rise straight from the blue of the Mediterranean. Similar cliffs are also found across the sea on the island of Corsica.

The wild, unspoilt scenery of this area of porphyry and sandstone cliffs which were eroded by the waves in the cource of time, with many tiny islands and reefs, contrasts strongly with the rather overdeveloped coastline found at Fréjus and Saint-Raphaël. Here the only access to the rocky coves is down narrow footpaths and complete solitude is still to be found by those who seek it (even at the height of summer).

The first small village along the road is **Boulouris,** which has some charming old holiday homes from the turn of the century bordering the road among mimosas and pines. The route frquently passes old blue porphyry quarries which have not

been worked for some twenty years. **Agay** has a beautiful beach sheltered in a bay. Along the road, various paths have been laid out in the inlets for tourists to explore the forest park. There are a number of megaliths in the vicinity. The **menhir of Ayre-Peyronne**, which stands overlooking the bay, has nearly 200 indentations on one side and gets its name from the Provençal word *peiroun* meaning carved rock.

The **menhirs of Veyssière** are composed of granite cut in roughly square blocks. One of them is over 6 ft (2 m) long and shows an oval-shaped human head in relief, towards which a sinuous snake with a broad, flat head seems to be turning.

From the pleasant beach resort of **Théoule-sur-Mer,** there are many tracks leading to magical places like the **Pointe de l'Esquillon,** the **Pic du Cap-Roux** (the aptly named Red Cape) and the **Pic de l'Ours**, all headlands which plunge down and thrust into the sea, creating glorious and dramatic seascapes.

The Corniche d'Or is the beautiful seaward edge of the **Massif de l'Esterel** which extends to the plain of the Siagne. So much of the indigenous forest, which once clad these mountains, has been lost that it is now almost completely covered with *maquis*. Here too, fierce fires have often raged and these continue to threaten the vegetation which still survives.

Access by members of the public to some areas is banned, in order to promote the re-afforestation program which the *Office Nationale des Forêts* has started by planting various species of oak and chestnut.

Mont Vinaigre, the highest point of the Esterel at over 2000 ft (618 m), has many marked trails that were originally intended for surveillance of the area but are now also open to the public, with plenty of car parks and picnic areas.

The paths have magnificent and most photogenic views of the close-by Italian coast, away to the east, and inland to the peaks of Sainte-Baume and Mont Sainte-Victoire.

167

Regional Tourist Information

Information about the region from the **Comité départemental du Tourisme**, 1, bd. Foch, 83007 Draguignan, Tel: 94-685833.

AUPS
Tourist Information

Office de Tourisme, place de la mairie, Tel: 94-700080.

BARJOLS
Tourist Information / Festival

Office de Tourisme, bd. Grisolle, Tel: 94-772001.
Fête des Tripettes, traditional dances at the Holy Day of Saint-Marcel in January.

BORMES-LES-MIMOSAS
Accommodation

MODERATE: **Le Palma**, "Le Pré aux Bœufs" at the D 559, Tel: 94-711786.
BUDGET: **Le Paradis**, "Mont des Roses", quartier du Pin, Tel: 94-710685.

Festivals

Fête du Mimosa, mimosa festival in February.
Festival de Musique, in July and August.

Tourist Information

Office de Tourisme, 1, rue J.-Alcard, Tel: 94-711517.

BRIGNOLES
Accommodation

MODERATE: **Mas La Cascade**, in the direction Toulon-La Celle, Tel: 94-690149.
BUDGET: **Château-Brignoles**, av. de la Libération, quartier Tivoli, Tel: 94-690688.

Museum

Palais des Comtes de Provence et Musée, Tel: 94-694518.

Tourist Information

Office de Tourisme, place Saint-Louis, Tel: 94-690178.

CAVALAIRE
Festivals

Corso du Mimosa, mimosa festival in February.
Festival du Théâtre méditerranéen, theater festival in May and June.

COLLOBRIERES
Sightseeing

Chartreuse de la Verne, Tel: 94-548623.

COGOLIN
Tourist Information

Office de Tourisme, place de la République, Tel: 94-546318.

COTIGNAC
Accommodation

MODERATE: **Hostellerie Lou Calen**, cours Gambetta, Tel: 94-046040.

Tourist Information

Office de Tourisme, cours Gambetta, Tel: 94-046187.

DRAGUIGAN

Office de Tourisme, av. Georges-Clémenceau, Tel: 94-686330.

FAYENCE

Office de Tourisme, place Léon-Roux, Tel: 94-762008.

FREJUS
Accommodation

MODERATE: **Résidences du Colombier**, route de Bagnols, Tel: 94-514592.
BUDGET: **Les Palmiers**, bd. de la Libération, Tel: 94-511872.

Museum / Sightseeing / Festival

Musée archéologique, in the monastery near the cathedral, rue de Fleury, Tel: 94-512630. **Cité épiscopale**, bishopric, Tel: 94-512630. **Pagode bouddhique**, Tel: 94-810377.
Forum de la Musique et des Arts, in July. *Grande Féria,* in August.

Tourist Information

Office de Tourisme, 325, rue Jean-Jaurès, Tel: 94-515414.

GASSIN
Accommodation

MODERATE: **Mas de Chastelas**, quartier Bertaud, Tel: 94-560911.

GRIMAUD
Accommodation

MODERATE: **La Boulangerie**, route de Collobrières, Tel: 94-432316. **Les Arcades**, quartier "Les Vignaux", Tel: 94-432484.

Restaurant ·

La Bretonnière, place des Pénitents, Tel: 94-432526, elegant, high-class restaurant.

Castle / Festivals

Although the castle is undergoing restoration work, it is open to the public free of charge.
Festival de Danse, dance festival in May. *Nuits musicales,* music festival in July and August.

Tourist Information

Office de Tourisme, place des Ecoles, Tel: 94-432698.

HYERES
Accommodation

MODERATE: **Pins d'Argent**, La Plage d'Hyères, Tel: 94-576360.
BUDGET: **Centurion**, 12, bd. Front-de-Mer, Tel: 94-663363.

Sightseeing / Festivals

Departure for the Iles d'Hyères from la Tour Fondue, Giens-Peninsula.
Festival de Jazz, in July. *Festival de la Bande dessinnée,* comics, in September.

Tourist Information

Office de Tourisme, Rotonde Jean-Salusse, Tel: 94-651855.

LA GARDE-FREINET
Tourist Information
Office de Tourisme, chapelle Saint-Eloi, Tel: 94-436741.

LES ISSAMBRES
Accommodation
MODERATE: **Le Provençal,** San Peire, Tel: 94-969049. *BUDGET:* **La Quiétude,** parc des Issambres, Tel: 94-969434.

LE LAVANDOU
Accommodation
LUXURY: **Club de Cavalière,** plage de Cavalière, Tel: 94-058014. *MODERATE:* **Auberge de la Calanque,** 62, av. du Général-de-Gaulle, Tel: 94-710596. *BUDGET:* **L'Escapade,** 1, chemin du Vannier, Tel: 94-711152.

PORQUEROLLES
Restaurant
Le Mas du Langoustier, baie du Langoustier, Tel: 94-583009, high-class restaurant.
Tourist Information
Bureau d'information, Tel: 94-583376.

RAMATUELLE
Accommodation
MODERATE: **Le Baou,** avenue Georges-Clémenceau, Tel: 94-792048.
BUDGET: **Auberge des Vieux Moulins,** quai des Moulins de Pampelonne, Tel: 94-971722.
Tourist Information
Office de Tourisme, 1, av. Clémenceau, Tel: 94-792604.

SAINT-MAXIMIN-LA-STE-BAUME
Sightseeing
Basilique Sainte-Marie-Madeleine, daily 7 am-12 noon and 2-7 pm. **Couvent royal,** April–October daily, Nov–March Sat and Sun only.
Tourist Information
Office de Tourisme, town hall, Tel: 94-780009.

SAINT-RAPHAËL
Accommodation
MODERATE: **San Pedro,** av. Colonel-Brooke, Tel: 94-836569. *BUDGET:* **France,** place Galliéni, Tel: 94-951703.
Tourist Information
Office de tourisme, Le Stanislas, rue Barbier, Tel: 94-951687.

SAINT-TROPEZ
Accommodation
LUXURY: **Mandarine,** route de Tahiti, Tel: 94-972100. *MODERATE:* **Le Provençal,** ch. Saint-Bonaventure, Tel: 94-970083. *BUDGET:* **Les Lauriers,** rue du Temple, Tel: 94-970488.
Restaurants
La Bastide de Saint-Tropez, route des Carles, Tel: 94-975816, elegant. **La Ponche,** place Révelin, Tel: 94-970253, moderate prices.

Museums / Festival
Musée de l'Annonciade, quai Saint-Raphaël, Tel: 94-970401. **Musée naval,** maritime museum, in the citadel, Tel: 94-970653.
Grande Bravade, religious festival, mid May.
Tourist Information
Office de Tourisme, quai Jean-Jaurès, Tel: 94-974521.

SEILLANS
Accommodation
MODERATE: **Hôtel de France,** pl. du Thouron, Tel: 94-769610.
BUDGET: **Les Deux Rocs,** pl. Fort-d'Amont, Tel: 94-768732.
Tourist Information
Office de Tourisme, town hall, Tel: 94-768591.

LE THORONET
Abbey / Restaurant
Abbaye du Thoronet, Tel: 94-738713. **Relais de l'Abbaye,** Domaine des Bruns, Tel: 94-738759, restaurant, moderate prices.

TOULON
Accommodation / Restaurant
MODERATE: **La Corniche,** in Mourillon, coast of Frédéric-Mistral, Tel: 94-413512.
BUDGET: **La Résidence,** 18, rue Gimelli, Tel: 94-929281. **Le Dauphin,** 21 bis, rue Jean-Jaurès, Tel: 94-931207, restaurant, moderate prices.
Museums / Sightseeing
Musée d'Art de Toulon, 113, bd. du Maréchal-Leclerc, Tel: 94-931554.
Musée naval, pl. Monsenergue, Tel: 94-020201. **Mont Faron,** by aerial cableway from bd. Amiral-de-Vence, closed Mon.
Tour de la Rade, harbor round-trip from Quai Stalingrad. Fort de Balaguier, 83504 La Seyne-sur-Mer, Tel: 94-948472.
Festivals
Festival de Musique and *Festival de Danse de Châteauvallon,* in July and August.
Tourist Information
Office de tourisme, 8, avenue Colbert, Tel: 94-220822.

VINS-SUR-CARAMY
Sightseeing / Tourist Information
Castle, Tel: 94-725040. **Abbaye de la Celle,** abbey with Tourist Information, Tel: 94-690844.

SPORTS IN THE REGION
HORSERIDING: **Comité départemental de Randonnée équestre,** Les Aludes, 83310 La Garde-Freinet, Tel: 94-436285.
SAILING / SURFING: **Comité départemental de Voile,** 59, rue Romulus, 83000 Toulon, Tel: 94-928102. **Comité départemental de Planche à voile,** base nautique du Port Saint-Pierre, 83400 Hyères, Tel: 94-386167.

ALPES-MARITIMES

CANNES

VALLAURIS / ANTIBES

FROM CAGNES TO VENCE

ALPES D'AZUR

NICE

MONACO

MENTON

The Alpes-Maritimes, as the name suggests, is a mountainous region with a dramatic coastline. There is an extreme contrast between the coastal area, most of which has been intensively developed, and the mountainous hinterland, which has remained largely unspoilt. The coastline, known as the Côte d'Azur, with its high corniche roads, elegant villas, grand hotels, crowded promendades and harbors full of luxury yachts, has become a byword for glamor and sophistcication. It has a beauty of its own, resulting from a succesful blend of man-made splendor and the natural beauty of cliffs, promontories, beaches and sea. Then, only a short distance inland, you are in a different world, of sleepy villages perched above rocky ravines, of cool, green forests and bare mountain-sides. Wherever you are, the brilliant blue of sky or sea dominates every view.

The Côte d'Azur begins at Mandelieu and **La Napoule** (on the N 98), where a fort stands on a promontory overhanging the sea. Unfortunately, it was converted it into a tasteless Baroque château early this century by the American sculptor Henry Clews. From Cannes the N 85, the Route Napoléon, leads to Grasse.

Preceding pages: The Riviera Corniches.
Left: The Hotel Carlton in Cannes.

CANNES

The first luxurious villas to appear between the concrete apartment blocks indicate that we are coming into **Cannes**. In common with all the other towns along the Côte d'Azur, and the Riviera, further east, much of the old Cannes has been destroyed by modern development.

Unfortunately, the original charm of the resort which was made popular by the 19th-century English nobleman Lord Brougham has now completely vanished, leaving only its magnificent setting against the background of the Massif de l'Esterel.

At the time of its "discovery" in 1834 it was a village of 3944 inhabitants, but by 1896 its population had risen to 20,000. Tourism has been the life-blood of Cannes ever since.

The first visitors were the European aristocracy, the wealthy French middle classes and artists, but they only came to the town during the winter. Then in the 1930s it became the fashion for Americans to visit the Riviera in the summer. At that time a German hotelier named Ruhl opened the first casino in Cannes, the *Palm Beach*, where Harpo Marx and the eccentric and jet-setting Fitzgeralds, Scott and Zelda, used to frequent the gaming-tables.

173

Today Cannes is still the place to spend a holiay on a big budget, with its palatial hotels, expensive boutiques and millionaires' yachts. Cannes is also famous for its International Film Festival. Every year since 1946, famous names and faces from round the world have gathered here for two weeks in May. The festival is held in the new Palais des Festivals on **La Croisette,** the seafront promenade which itself resembles a Hollywood film set, with the inevitable palm trees, the beach of artificial sand and the white, weddingcake architecture of *belle-époque* hotels like the world-famous *Carlton*.

The former Palais des Festivals, with its high picture windows, is now the nostalgic Palais-Croisette. The new festival building will never win praise for its architecture but it is now very much part of the scenery and does at least function efficiently.

Cannes now has four harbors, but three of them are simply marinas for private yachts. Inland, parallel to La Croisette, is **rue d'Antibes**, a succession of ultra-expensive boutiques patronized by the rich and famous.

Further west towards the old port is rue Meynadier, a pedestrianized street popular with window-gazers. The **Marché Forville** is the main market in Cannes and is patronized by chefs from around the region. A flower market is held every day except Saturday in the gardens of the Allées de la Libération. Just beyond here, the narrow streets of the old town known as **Le Suquet** climb steeply to the 16th-century church of **Notre-Dame de l'Espérance**. Opposite are the remains of the ramparts of the old castle. There is a very good view from the Tour du Suquet, the former watch-tower.

The main feature of the **Musée de la Castre** is the archaeological and ethnological collection that was bequeathed to it by Baron Lycklama at the end of the 19th century, but the museum also puts on exhibitions of contemporary art.

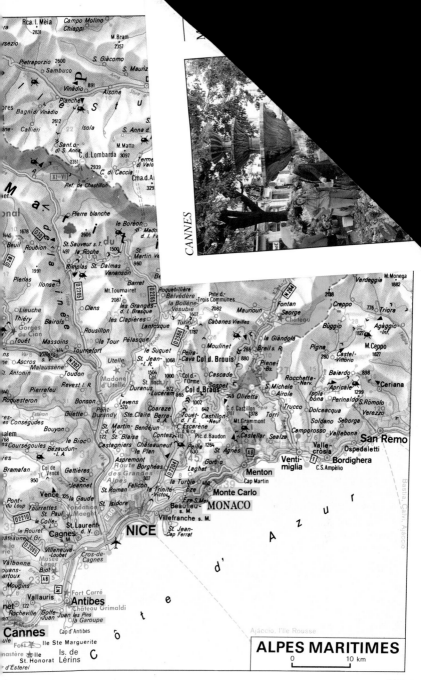

CANNES

ALPES MARITIMES

The architectural fantasies of the *fin de siècle* period are represented by villas that have been built in an incredible mixture of styles. The municipal library is now housed in the former **Villa Rothschild**, an elegant neo-classical building tucked away in a beautiful park in avenue Jean de Noailles.

Above it, the route du parc des Croix de Gardes leads to another magnificent view. The **Super-Cannes** and **La Californie** areas contain the most luxurious villas, but many of these have now been replaced by modern buildings.

An excursion by boat from the old port to the **Iles de Lérins** which lie off the Pointe de la Croisette is an absolute must for all visitors.

The island of **Sainte-Marguerite** is covered with eucalyptus and pine forest. Its fort, restored by Vauban, used to house high-ranking prisoners like the

Above: The flower market in the Place aux Aires in Grasse. Right: Floral essences for perfume.

Man in the Iron Mask, whose identity still remains a mystery, although many have speculated about a royal connection. The island's hotels and restaurants all face towards Cannes.

The long, narrow **island of Saint-Honorat** is more interesting. Its fortified 11th-century monastery looks just like the prow of a ship about to tow the island out into the open sea. Monks have tilled the soil here for 1500 years, but the abbey did not come under the rule of the Cistercian order until the last century. It is now occupied by 38 monks and about a dozen nuns. It is possible to stay at the monastery but bookings should be made two or three months ahead. The monks produce a delicious, heady liqueur called Lérina.

On the way out of Cannes, within a cypress grove on a hill, is the pretty 12th-century **chapel of Notre-Dame-de-Vie,** near where the painter Picasso spent the last years of his life. Not much further on, the village of Mougins is pleasantly peaceful, though it has been colonised by wealthy outsiders.

In and around Grasse

The town of **Grasse**, lying languorously on its hillside, is renowned the whole world over for its perfume, although in more recent times it has actually become much more important for artificial fragrances, with the largest companies in the industry in France, such as Elf-Sanofi, having production facilities in the town.

The perfume industry began here because lavender, jasmine, tuberoses, violets and orange blossom thrived in the exceptionally mild climate. Distillation of the essences of the flowers growing around Grasse began in the 16th century with encouragement from the Medicis.

Then in the 18th century leather became an important second industry. The two complemented each other because perfumed gloves became fashionable.

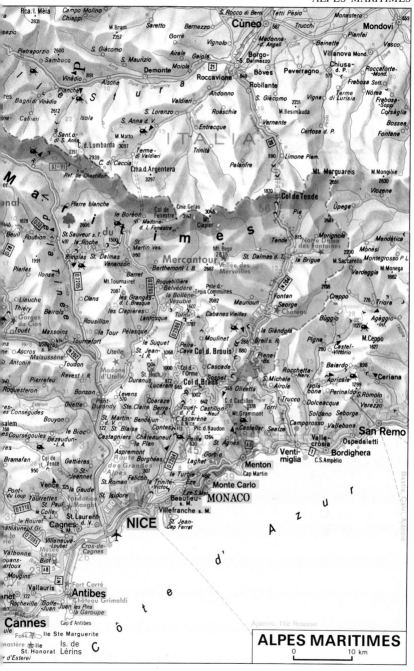

ALPES MARITIMES

0   10 km

The architectural fantasies of the *fin de siècle* period are represented by villas that have been built in an incredible mixture of styles. The municipal library is now housed in the former **Villa Rothschild**, an elegant neo-classical building tucked away in a beautiful park in avenue Jean de Noailles.

Above it, the route du parc des Croix de Gardes leads to another magnificent view. The **Super-Cannes** and **La Californie** areas contain the most luxurious villas, but many of these have now been replaced by modern buildings.

An excursion by boat from the old port to the **Iles de Lérins** which lie off the Pointe de la Croisette is an absolute must for all visitors.

The island of **Sainte-Marguerite** is covered with eucalyptus and pine forest. Its fort, restored by Vauban, used to house high-ranking prisoners like the

Above: The flower market in the Place aux Aires in Grasse. Right: Floral essences for perfume.

Man in the Iron Mask, whose identity still remains a mystery, although many have speculated about a royal connection. The island's hotels and restaurants all face towards Cannes.

The long, narrow **island of Saint-Honorat** is more interesting. Its fortified 11th-century monastery looks just like the prow of a ship about to tow the island out into the open sea. Monks have tilled the soil here for 1500 years, but the abbey did not come under the rule of the Cistercian order until the last century. It is now occupied by 38 monks and about a dozen nuns. It is possible to stay at the monastery but bookings should be made two or three months ahead. The monks produce a delicious, heady liqueur called Lérina.

On the way out of Cannes, within a cypress grove on a hill, is the pretty 12th-century **chapel of Notre-Dame-de-Vie,** near where the painter Picasso spent the last years of his life. Not much further on, the village of Mougins is pleasantly peaceful, though it has been colonised by wealthy outsiders.

In and around Grasse

The town of **Grasse**, lying languorously on its hillside, is renowned the whole world over for its perfume, although in more recent times it has actually become much more important for artificial fragrances, with the largest companies in the industry in France, such as Elf-Sanofi, having production facilities in the town.

The perfume industry began here because lavender, jasmine, tuberoses, violets and orange blossom thrived in the exceptionally mild climate. Distillation of the essences of the flowers growing around Grasse began in the 16th century with encouragement from the Medicis.

Then in the 18th century leather became an important second industry. The two complemented each other because perfumed gloves became fashionable.

In the 19th century Paris became the center for production of the actual perfumes while Grasse produced the essences and natural raw materials for processing. One of these is the famous essence (or extract) of jasmine, but the cost of one kg (2 lb) of this is over £10,000 sterling (nearly $7,500 per lb), so it is obvious why Egyptian essence is now imported as a substitute at only a tenth of the price – or a synthetic product is used instead. Synthetic fragrance production in Grasse is now one of the main industries of the *département* and uses the very latest technology.

The perfumeries of *Galimard* (73, route de Cannes), *Molinard* (60, boulevard Victor-Hugo) and *Fragonard* (20, boulevard Fragonard) can still be visited as reminders of former days. The House of Fragonard also has a "flower factory" at Les Quatre-Chemins, rte. de Cannes.

The **Musée Internationale de la Parfumerie**, housed in the former Second Empire perfumery of Hugues Aîné, provides a fascinating history of perfumery, soaps, cosmetics and toiletries from ancient times to the present day.

Grasse was an important center in the Middle Ages and retains its medieval structure. The **Place aux Aires**, where the flower market is held, dates from the 15th century and is framed by 17th- and 18th-century arcades. Its clock and fountain are 19th century. Number 13, the 18th-century house of Maximin Isnard, has a beautiful wrought-iron balcony.

In Place du Petit-Puy, the local white limestone in which the Romanesque cathedral of **Notre-Dame-du-Puy** is built enhances its plain, stark lines. It contains some fine paintings including the *Crown of Thorns, St. Helen at the Elevation of the Cross* and the *Crucifixion of Christ* by Rubens.

The former Bishop's Palace is now the City Hall and thanks to the Medicis has retained some of its medieval features, the oldest of which is the square tower.

There is a fine view from the place du Cours Honoré-Cresp over the countryside to the sea.

AROUND GRASSE

A turn-off from the D 3 along the D 12 leads up to the bare and rocky **Plateau de Caussols,** where you can tour the CERGA Observatory. Its strange shape gives the plateau the look of a lunar landscape. Hereabouts you can see many buildings with drystone walls, called *bories,* which were used as shelters by peasants and shepherds.

The road to **Coursegoules** (D 3 then D 2) passes through attractive countryside. The village and its streets are built of gray stone. From the Coursegoules pass you can again look down to the sea. Farther down, the **valley of the Loup** is dotted with peaceful villages. The **church of Saint-Jacques** at **Bar-sur-Loup** contains an extraordinary 15th-century painting on wood of a *danse macabre.*

The medieval origins of **Tourrettes-sur-Loup** (on the D 2210) can be seen in the way the houses follow the line of the old ramparts. Two original medieval gates open onto the place de l'Église. This village is France's leading producer of violets, which are grown in beds among the olive trees from October to March.

West of Grasse, **Cabris** (along the D 11) is built on a rocky spur. Not far away are the Grottes de St. Cézaire which go 50 m (160 ft) underground. The caverns were first discovered and explored in the last century and have many strangely shaped stalactites and stalagmites in shimmering colors.

The fine medieval village of **Saint-Cézaire** on the D 13 has a simple white 13th-century funeral chapel which is called **Notre-Dame-de-Sardaigne.**

Northward, on the Route Napoléon, a path leads to **Le Castellar du Thorenc,** where there are the remains of a church and castle from the 12th century. The buildings were destroyed after a gang of brigands had used them as a hide-out. Just before you reach Séranon on the Route Napoléon (N 85), the chapel of

Some of the town's finest houses have been turned into museums, including the **Musée d'Art et d'Histoire de Provence** in the rue Mirabeau, with its Italian-style red walls. It displays rooms in different styles, including a lovely old Provençal kitchen and 17th- and 18th-century bedrooms and has a fine collection of Moustiers faïence. A charming 17th-century house where the Rococo painter Fragonard lived for a few months has been converted into the **Villa-Musée Fragonard.** A number of his paintings on view here beside works by his son and grandson.

In the area around Grasse there are many beautiful villas, often with romantically overgrown gardens.

The road to Châteauneuf (D 2085) passes the **Opio olive-oil mill.** Further on, along the D 3, is the small village of Gourdon, set on a clifftop, which has a fantastic view of the area.

Above: A potter demonstrates her skill in Vallauris. Right: This café's name may say something about its customers.

Notre-Dame-de-Grâtemoine. which was originally Romanesque, stands alone on a bare hill. Of its original three bays, only one remains, but inside it there are seven blind archways with elegant rounded arches.

VALLAURIS AND ANTIBES

World-famous museums, a futuristic science-city, little fishing harbours and long stretches of beach: In just a few miles you have a microcosm of today's Côte d'Azur.

Vallauris

Three miles (5km) west of Antibes, **Vallauris** and **Golfe-Juan** form a single community. Vallauris was revived in 1950 under the influence of Madoura and Picasso and the town is now one of the main centers of ceramic art in France. Unfortunately there is now rather too much second-rate work on sale in the shops, but visitors wishing to buy the best ceramics Vallauris has to offer at the right prices can contact the *Syndicat des Potiers de Vallauris*, Espace Grandjean, Avenue du Stade.

The Romanesque chapel in the place de la Libération now houses the **Picasso Museum.** The artist presented the town with his composition *La Guerre et la Paix* (War and Peace), a painting which measures 1350 sq. ft (125 sq.m) and covers three sides of the crypt.

The château has also been turned into a museum. It contains some fifteen canvasses, many collages and gouaches and a large mural by the Italian painter Magnelli, who spent most of his life in France and died here in 1971. Three rooms are devoted to 20th-century ceramics, including some by Picasso. In front of the church of **Saint-Martin,** with its Romanesque bell-tower and Renaissance front, is place Paul-Isnard, in which stands a bronze by Picasso, *L'Homme au Mouton* (Man with a Sheep).

The sandy beaches of **Juan-les-Pins** are a popular meeting place in summer.

CAP D'ANTIBES

Above: A mural in the Picasso Museum at the Château Grimaldi in Antibes. Right: Detail of a mosaic by Léger.

when the small town teems with life until the small hours, being mainly famous for its exuberant night life. The **Jazz Festival** is held every year among the pine-trees, attracting large and noisily appreciative and crowds.

The promontory of **Cap d'Antibes** along the D 2559 provides a pleasant and quiet contrast. Its luxurious mansions are well hidden among greenery and umbrella pines. The **Jardin Thuret**, a botanical garden, contains some magnificent trees, particularly the various species of eucalyptus and monkey puzzle, but they are now beginning to suffer from their great age and from parasites.

There is a good view from the hill of **La Garoupe** and its lighthouse is one of the most powerful on this coast.

Annually on the first Thursday in July, seamen walk barefoot up the hill to the **chapel of Notre-Dame-du-Bon-Port**.

They carry its wooden statue of Our Lady down to the cathedral in Antibes, where a mass is held in her honor, ending with a traditional sea-shanty. On the Sunday it is carried back in another procession.

If you want to rub shoulders with famous faces such as showbiz stars and politicians, stop and have a drink on the terrace by the sea at one of the most exclusive hotels on the Riviera, the *Eden-Roc*. It is considered extremely chic and its exclusivity is reflected in the prices.

Antibes

Only the massive ramparts of **Antibes** prevent the old town from being flooded by the sea. Its **Château Grimaldi** was Picasso's studio in 1946 and he donated most of the works he produced there to the town. The château became the **Picasso Museum** and contains paintings, drawings, murals and cement sculptures which he donated to the museum in the 1950s, together with 25 ceramic pieces produced at Vallauris.

Twenty contemporary artists, from Adami to Viallat, paid homage to the master with their collection called *Bonjour Monsieur Picasso.*

There are also modern works by Léger, Calder, Picabia, Hartung, Magnelli and Nicolas de Staël.

The terrace leads to a garden overlooking the sea, where stone and bronze sculptures by Germaine Richier, Miró and Bernard Pagès are displayed among flowers and trees.

It is pleasant to take a stroll along the narrow streets of the old town, with their evocative names, like the place de Safranier and the cours Masséna, where the covered market echoes to the cries of the traders every morning. The **Marché des Artisans et Brocanteurs** (craft and flea market) which is always held here on Tuesday and Friday afternoons attracts large crowds.

The **Port Vauban** was converted into a yacht marina in 1970 and can take 1500 boats. On the edge of the town is the old **Fort Carré** which has defended Antibes against its enemies since the 16th century. You can look round it and also attend the sporting and cultural events held there.

A few kilometers from Antibes in **Biot** is the **Musée Fernand Léger**, housing a collection of the works of the famous modern artist who, as Reverdy put it, was able to "*face the reality of his time.*" The museum was built on the site of the villa that had been bought by Léger shortly before his death in 1955. Its 4300 sq.ft (400 sq. m) façade includes a splendid multi-colored mosaic.

From a design by Léger, master glaziers created the glass mosaic in the entrance hall which is 30ft (9m) high and 16ft (5m)wide. The museum contains about 300 works including drawings, original lithographs, almost 300 ceramics and mosaics, bronzes and tapestries.

From the museum, the **Chemin des Combes** leads to the Biot glassworks, which was set up in 1956 by a ceramic designer from the Sèvres school, Eloi Monod, and produces a special kind of

glass called *verre bullé* or bubble glass. A visit to the glassworks is very instructive, showing the various stages of production from glowing molten glass to finished articles in the colorful Provençal style.

Up the hill in Biot itself, the combined gallery and shop called *Le Patrimoine* in Place des Arcades sells traditional arts and crafts. Biot is also well known for pottery (especially earthenware jars), a craft practiced here since the 14th century at least.

The village also has a number of attractive churches and chapels. A typical rustic example is **Saint-Julien** which is set right beside the road. This rather interesting chapel has an unusual open canopy with three openings inserted between wooden pillars.

Driving through maquis-clad hills, we reach the quiet village of **Valbonne** (on the D 4). It is mainly known for the area nearby known as the **Valbonne-Sophia-Antipolis** science park, which extends over an area of 17 sq. miles (43 sq.km). It is a kind of futuristic industrial estate bringing together many small high-tech businesses in one place.

The first company moved in in 1974 and there are now more than 6000 people employed at Sophia-Antipolis in nearly 200 organizations, which are mainly involved in electronics, information technology, pharmaceuticals, bioengineering, energy, education and training.

Landscaped areas account for two-thirds of the park and its buildings are designed to harmonize with the landscape and promote effective communication, the current buzz-word at the park. Symposia and seminars are held regularly during the year, as well as important cultural events, particularly top-class concerts (mostly in July and August).

Leaving Antibes along the road to Cagnes-sur-Mer, after passing the long

shingle beaches it's impossible to miss the rows of ugly concrete blocks (they were begun in 1970 and for some reason are still unfinished) which make up **Marina-Baie des Anges**.

The main attraction in **Villeneuve-Loubet** is the museum of culinary arts that has been established in the house where the famous chef Auguste Escoffier was born. He was the first member of his profession to be awarded the *Légion d'-Honneur*, in 1928, and is best known for inventing the dessert called Peach Melba which he created for the Australian singer Nellie Melba.

FROM CAGNES TO VENCE

The first landmark reached at **Cagnes-sur-Mer** is its racecourse beside the sea. The town is overlooked by its 14th-century castle, where exhibitions and festivals are now held.

By the sea in **Cros-de-Cagnes** there are some excellent fish restaurants. You can still see some of the small local boats called *pointus*, and the few fishermen who are still allowed to fish by night at certain times of the year, using lamps to attract the fish. The new town divides the seaside area of Cros-de-Cagnes from **Haut-de-Cagnes**, which is encircled by 13th-century ramparts and has narrow streets leading up to the **Grimaldi castle**. About 1 km (half a mile) away is the **Domaine des Collettes** with the villa where Renoir spent the last years of his life between 1908 and 1919. It is now a museum where some of his works are on display.

North from Cagnes, the D 36 leads to the most famous of the local villages, **Saint-Paul** and Vence, set in countryside studded with villas and exclusive developments.

Saint-Paul has long been a magnet for painters, writers and actors and it is still the in thing to be seen playing *pétanque* in the square or lunching at the *Colombe*

Right: The medieval tower dominating the small town of Vence.

ALPES D'AZUR

About half a dozen sur...
decorated with mu...
markable feature...
50 or so carvin...
main chapel...
From V...
mous R...
foot o...
Sai...

d'Or restaurant which has paintings by Braque, Matisse, Vlaminck and others.

Enclosed within its medieval walls, it is a pretty village, but its narrow streets have far too many souvenir shops and mediocre art galleries.

A short walk brings you to the main attraction, the **Fondation Maeght.** This is a superbly designed building and a worthy setting for the masterpieces of 20th-century art it contains. Cubism was the main influence on its Spanish architect, José Louis Sert, and its appearance is enhanced by its superb position on a hill opposite Saint-Paul looking down to the gulf of Antibes. Sculptures by Miró and Giacometti adorn the terraces and gardens. An important collection of paintings from Braque and Léger to contemporary artists like Adami and Viallat is on permanent display. Major exhibitions are held in the summer and the foundation also has a cinema and library and organizes meetings and conferences.

The small town of **Vence** is less caught in the past than Saint-Paul. Its climate is reputed to be very healthy, being mild and free from the sweltering heat of the coast, and it is a fashionable resort in both winter and summer. The park is a pleasant place, with olive trees and sculptures. The town has many medieval houses, narrow streets and alleyways and pretty squares, and also some Roman remains which have been incorporated in newer buildings.

Particularly impressive is the **Cathédrale de la Nativité**, the origins of which go back to antiquity. There are also many chapels in and around Vence.

Below the road to St-Jeannet is the **Chapelle du Rosaire**, which was designed by Matisse between 1947 and 1951, with decorative elements from the liturgy, and was considered by the artist to be one of his masterpieces. The glorious windows and murals appear to be bathed in heavenly light.

In the suburb of Ara, the **Chapelles du Calvaire** form an amazing collection. There were originally fourteen of them when they were founded around 1700.

ive, some of them
...als. Their most re-
...of all, however, is the
...gs of painted wood in the

...ence, you can tackle the fa-
...aou (Provençal for rock), at the
...of which lies the pretty village of
...nt-Jeannet. Serious climbers take the
vertical route but more gradual marked paths also lead to the top for those who feel less inclined for strenuous activity.

A few miles to the north on the D 2, the **Col de Vence** is a magical spot. Beyond an abandoned quarry, there is a bare hill. Up here at about 2700 ft (900m), the scenery is wild and rugged, with just a few copses of oak and chestnut trees. Don't spend too long contemplating your surroundings, but continue to the hamlet of Saint-Barnabé along a road that comes to a dead end and follow the path to the *village nègre,* a stone circle whose origins are unknown.

ALPES D'AZUR

The contrast between the heights behind Nice and the coast is quite remarkable. Until the last century the valleys in this area were cut off from the world, connected only by paths across difficult passes. The opulence along the coast makes it easy to forget how poor and isolated the villages in the hinterland used to be, as their strong individual identities show.

From Pont-Durandy, the D 2565 leads into the **valley of the Vésubie**, which has always been more accessible. The way has long been open to the plains of Piedmont across the Col de Fenestre and to the sea via the commercially important road along which precious salt was exported through Piedmont from the salt-

works of Provence. At first the road follows a mountain stream which cuts a narrow gorge through solid rock and it then runs through a high valley with some unusual villages.

The now virtually depopulated village of **Utelle** was once at the crossroads of two mule routes and has some fine 16th- and 17th-century houses with richly carved doors.

A few miles further on stands the chapel of **La Madone d'Utelle**, a well-known place of pilgrimage, as is shown by its many commemorative offerings. There is a fantastic view from the rock shelf on which it stands.

From **Lantosque** onwards, rock gives way to greenery and the valley is gentler and more friendly. The villages of **Bollène-Vésubie, Belvédère, Roquebillère, Saint-Martin-Vésubie** and **Venanson** and the former spa town of **Berthemont-les-Bains** are starting points for wonderful excursions.

The road ends at a height of 6250 ft (1909 m) at the chapel of **La Madone de Fenestre**, another popular place of pilgrimage.

Along the valley of the Var, beautiful *villages perchés* line the road (the N 202), including **Malaussène** with its chapels, **Villars-sur-Var**, at the center of a fine vineyard (the only one in the Alpes-Maritimes which has the *appellation contrôlée* of *Côtes de Provence*) and **Touët-sur-Var**, which has tall houses forming part of the ramparts, fortified gates and covered streets. Beyond Touët are the red cliffs of the **Gorges du Cians,** alongside the D 28.

The next village we come to, **Lieuche,** makes the drive through the gorge worthwhile in itself. Encircled by a wooded, mountainous amphitheater and perched on a promontory 2900 ft (880m) high, it is a tiny village with a population of less than two dozen, but its small 17th-century Baroque church contains a masterpiece dating from 1499 by Louis Bréa,

Right: The fortified town of Entrevaux is still entered through its 17th century gate.

the most important of the Nice altar-piece painters.

Some of the fronts of the old houses in **Rigaud** and **Beuil** have retained their *trompe l'oeil* decoration, which was once very popular in the Nice area. Beuil is also a ski resort, as is **Valberg.**

The road then becomes narrow and twisting before reaching **Péone**, which overlooks the wild torrent of the Tuebi, often dry but capable of carrying down huge quantities of pebbles and rocks when in flood.

Arriving at the old fortified town of **Guillaumes**, which for 400 years was a French-owned enclave within Savoy, the road joins the **Gorges de Daluis**, which are as red as the Gorges du Cians and also have fine views over the waters of the Var.

A short walk from the town is **Notre-Dame-du-Bueyi** which has an unusual painting by Jean Ardisson called *L'Incendie de Guillaumes en 1682* (The Fire of Guillaumes in 1682) which gives a good impression of what the fortified

town must have looked like in days gone by. Outside Guillaumes, the D 2202 plunges into the most remote valley in the Alpes-Maritimes. **The Val d'Entraunes,** with its shingle roofs and forests dominated by the high peaks and alpine pastures, seems to be existing outside space and time. From Entraunes there are magnificent walks in the **Parc National du Mercantour,** which was set up in 1979 for the conservation of local plants, wild life and its habitats and the protection of the mountains which are the source of water for the Côte d'Azur.

If you cross the park over the Col de la Cayolle early in the morning, you will have a good chance of spotting marmots which are quite tame. In the spring you may also see chamois, ibex or wild sheep looking for lush grass under the larches. There are many other more timid species in the park and also rare birds, including the ptarmigan whose plumage turns white in winter. Among the brightly-colored butterflies some very rare species are to be found.

Above: The palatial Hotel Negresco in Nice dates from the turn of the century. Right: The famous Promenade des Anglais along the shore at Nice.

Returning southward along the N 202, we come to **Puget-Théniers,** beside the gorges of the Roudoule and the Var. Its part Romanesque parish church of Notre-Dame-de-l'Assomption has a magnificent 16th-century carved retable, the *Retable de la Passion,* and also a polyptych of Notre-Dame-de-Secours which is in the style of Antoine Bréa, brother of Louis. In the town's park there is a remarkable sculpture carved by Aristide Maillol in 1908, symbolising "Action in Chains."

Only a short distance away but over the departmental border is **Entrevaux,** where the military defenses, unchanged since the 18th century, still defiantly face the encircling mountains. With its ramparts, drawbridges and ramps defended by cannon, the citadel was impossible for

any besieging army to take. In the 17th and 18th centuries Entrevaux was one of the main frontier bastions in the Alps south of Briançon and it retained its strategic military importance until the beginning of this century.

South of the Var, the D 17 crosses the peaceful countryside of the **Vallée de l'Estéron.** Here too, we come upon a number of villages with beautiful small churches in simple Romanesque style. **La Penne** is one of these serene villages with a green valley lying below.

Beyond the Clue du Riolan gorge, the village of **Sigale** is perched high above the valley.

Beside the road, about 2 miles (3km) further on, is the prettily named chapel of **Notre-Dame-d'Entrevignes** (Our Lady among the Vines) which is still a favorite destination for pilgrims. Inside, the frescoes by unknown artists mainly depict scenes from the life of the Virgin Mary in a picturesquely realistic style.

Roquesteron is the largest village in the valley and is made up of two separate parishes, one on each bank of the Esteron – **Roquesteron-Grasse** with its fortified 12th-century church of Sainte-Pétronille, and over the bridge there is **Roqueste-ron-Puget.**

Four miles (6 km) away, east of the pretty village of **Pierrefeu,** **La Cerise** bridge spans the Esteron. This is a good place for a swim in the summer. Beyond the last village, **Gillette,** overlooking the valley, the **Charles-Albert** bridge crosses the Var again.

NICE

Nice has been part of France since 1860, having previously belonged to the Italian kingdom of Piemonte, when it was called Nizza. It still does not feel entirely French, but with its international airport, modern industry and growing population, its is the most important city on the coast, after Marseilles.

First impressions are that Nice is rather chilly and unwelcoming, but the second impression is one of color – the white of its stucco *Belle-Époque* hotels, like the world-famous *Négresco* on the **Promenade des Anglais**, the red of its Turin-inspired squares like the Place Masséna and the Place Ile-de-Beauté near the harbor, and the blue of the Mediterranean.

The city does not earn its living from the sea and yet the sea is very much a part of it. You only have to arrive in Nice and see the famous and yet still startlingly beautiful **Baie des Anges** (Bay of the Angels) to realize how important the sea is in the life of this city.

The architecture of Nice has nothing in common with that of Provence. The sole wealth of the peasants who once lived here was their small houses of simple design which were remarkable only for their colored plaster and *trompe l'oeil* decoration. The cheerful outside disguised the poverty of what lay behind and maintained an illusion of wealth and plenty which was really a sham.

In the rue Droite is a fine 17th-century Genoese palace called the **Palais Lascaris**, which is an unusual saffron color. The city has many Baroque churches, including the **Cathedral of Sainte-Réparate** in the place Rossetti with its fine façade and the **Eglise du Gesù**, the oldest in the area in this style. Its austere interior was later decorated with frescoes and plasterwork. To the left of the choir is a tabernacle from 1535, one of the oldest in the *département*. The Chapelle de la Miséricorde des Pénitents Noirs in the cours Saleya is another Baroque masterpiece, remarkable for its elliptical shape, the beauty of its ornamentation and its 15th-century altar-pieces in the sacristy by Louis Bréa and Jean Miralhet.

A flower and vegetable market is held every morning (except Monday) in the **Cours Saleya**, with a profusion of tulips, roses, carnations, gladioli and fruit and vegetables, their colors challenging the vivid blue of the sea, which can be glimpsed between the old fishermen's cottages on the harbor.

NICE

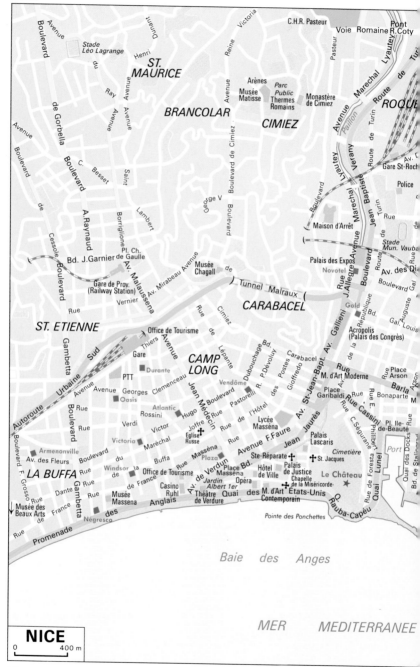

Avenue Boulevard
Stade
Léo Lagrange
Henri
du
Dunant
Victoria
Reine
Victoria
C.H.R. Pasteur
Voie Romaine R. Coty
Pont
Pasteur
Route
de
Turi
ROQUE
Marechal
Lyautey
ST.
MAURICE
Ray
Avenue
Avenue
Avenue
Arènes
Musée
Matisse
*Parc
Public
Thermes
Romains*
Monastère
de Cimiez
Avenue
de
Gorbella
BRANCOLAR
CIMIEZ
Turin
Route
de
Turin
Verany
Paillon
de Cessole
C. Besset
Saint
Avenue
Boulevard
A.Raynaud
Boulevard de Cimiez
George V
Lyautey
Gare St-Roch
Av. C
Police
Boulevard
de
Boulevard
Borriglione
Lambert
Boulevard
Jean Baptiste
Avenue
Marechal
Rue
de
Turin
Maison d'Arrêt
Pl. Ch.
de Gaulle
Bd. J.Garnier
Av. Malaussena
Av. Mirabeau Avenue
Musée
Chagall
de
Stade
Mun. Vauba
Palais des Expos
Novotel
Boulevard
Av. des Di
Route
Gare de Prov.
(Railway Station)
Vernier
Rue
Tunnel Malraux
Cimiez
CARABACEL
Boulevard
Gal.
Rue
Gold
République
Bd.
Gal. Auguste
Gal. Louis
ST. ETIENNE
Thiers
Office de Tourisme
Rue
de
Lépante
Acropolis
(Palais des Congrès)
de
la
Gambetta
Sud
Urbaine
Avenue
Gare
CAMP
LONG
Bd.
P.Devoluy
Dubouchage
des Postes
R.
Carabacel
Av. St-Jean-Bapt.
Av. Gallieni
Rue
Place
Arson
PTT
Durante
Georges Clemenceau
Vendôme
Pastorelli
Gioffredo
M. d'Art Moderne
Barla
Arson
Rue
Avenue
Avenue
Oasis
Boulevard
Jean Médecin
Rue
de
l'Hôtel
Place
Garibaldi
Rue Cassini
Place
Bonaparte
M
Boulevard
Rue
Atlantic
Rossini
Hugo
Lycée
Masséna
Rue
C.Séguran
Rue
Pl. Ile-
de-Beauté
Verdi
Victor
Joffre
Eglise
Russe
Rue
Avenue F.Faure
Jean Jaurès
Palais
Lascaris
Port
Victoria
Marechal
Rue
Ste-Réparate
St. Jacques
Cimetière
Rue de Foresta
Quai des Docks
Bd. de Stalingrad
Av. des Fleurs
Boulevard
Buffa
Masséna
Plaza
Palais
de Justice
Le Château
Lunel
Quai
Armenonville
LA BUFFA
Rue
Windsor
la
Office de Tourisme
de
de France
Place Bd.
Masséna
Hôtel
de Ville
Chapelle
de la Miséricorde
Philbert
Rauba-Capéu
du
Dante
Rue
Gambetta
Casino
Ruhl
Jardin
Albert 1er
Opéra
États-Unis
Rue
de Verdun
Musée des
Beaux Arts
France
Rue
Musée
Masséna
Anglais
Théâtre
de Verdure
Quai
des
M. d'Art
Contemporain
Négresco
Promenade
des
Pointe des Ponchettes

Baie   des   Anges

NICE
0   400 m

MER   MEDITERRANEE

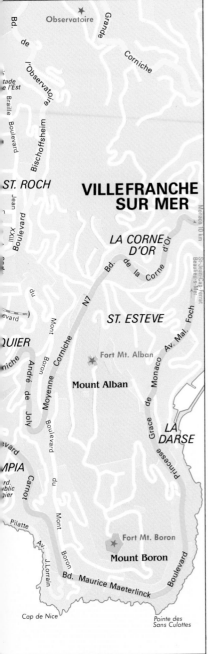

Encouraged by the market traders shouting in their almost incomprehensible local *patois*, you can buy *socca*, a huge pancake made from ground chickpeas, *pissaladière*, a kind of onion tart, and occasionally *poutine*, tiny fish fry which is only caught around Nice.

The **Marché d'Art et d'Antiquités** (art and antique market) is held in rue Ségurane and rue E.-Philibert from 10 a.m. to midday and 3 p.m. to 6.30 p.m. every day except Sunday. Another local attraction is the *Confiserie du Vieux Nice*, a famous baker's shop in Quai Papacino.

Only a few ruins remain of the castle which once dominated this part of town. The building was destroyed by the Sun King, Louis XIV – jealous perhaps of the sun of Nice.

But the view from the **castle hill** over the city and the sea is still unforgettable. The whole of Nice is spread out before you, with the red-tiled roofs and terraces of the old city contrasting with the pristine whiteness of the grand hotels. Also visible from this height are the green and gold cupolas of the Russian Church, one of the most beautiful Orthodox churches outside Russia itself.

Many artists have been attracted to Nice. It first made its reputation with the Nice School, whose main representative was Louis Bréa. Matisse initially found the heat of Nice intolerable but eventually his love for the sea overcame his exhaustion; he settled in the elegant *Régina* hotel in the suburb of Cimiez. At the time there were no other Nice-based artists of note except Alexis Mossa with his frenzied symbolist paintings. He was also the originator of King Carnival, reviving the ancient carnival festivities that had begun in Nice in the 13th century.

It was not until the 1960s that the artists of Nice became more adventurous. The impetus was provided by the "New Realists" Klein, Arman, Raysse and César and from 1961 what became the renowned Nice School grew up around

Ben, Malaval, Venet and others. Later the *Supports/Surfaces* group and painters like Viallat, Dolla, Cane and Saytour tried to deconstruct reality in their paintings while Bernard Pagès and Toni Grand enlarged the scope of sculpture.

The visitor can eavluate these developments at the **Musée Matisse** in Cimiez, the **Musée Chagall** not far away, the **Museum of Modern and Contemporary Art** near the conference center of the Acropolis (a collection of buildings of no great architectural merit with a museum and a hotel, built over the River Paillon), the **Musée Masséna**, the **Musée des Beaux-Arts** and the **Galeries des Ponchettes** devoted to works by Dufy and Mossa.

One of the finest squares in Nice is the 18th-century, circular **Place Garibaldi**, which commemorates the famous freedom-fighter who liberated and united Italy, and was in fact born in Nice. Leading out of it is the rue Catherine-Ségurane. The 15th-century exploits of Joan of Arc in the north were repeated here in Nice by the less-famous Catherine Ségurane during the siege of the city by the Turks in August 1543.

In the hills at **Cimiez** are the elegant old hotels which were very exclusive places to stay a hundred years ago but have now mostly been converted into apartments. They include the *Majestic*, the *Winter Palace,* the *Alhambra* with its minarets and the *Régina*, where Queen Victoria used to spend the winter. Designed by Biasini, the hotel stands opposite the amphitheater of Cimiez where the jazz festival takes place every July.

The adjoining **Roman baths** are very well preserved. The monastery at Cimiez has great charm and there is a beautiful view of the city to be seen from its delightful terraces and rose gardens. The altar-pieces of the Pietá and the Crucifixion inside the church are considered to be among the greatest works of the Nice-born artist Louis Bréa.

On one of the hills of Nice to the west of the city are the vineyards which produce the famous Bellet wine much prized by connoisseurs. The vineyard is said to have been established by the Phoenicians in the 3rd century B.C. and covers about 75 acres (30 hectares). The estate of *Château de Bellet* can be visited by arrangement and wine may be tasted (Tel. 93.37.81.57).

The road up the hill called **Mont Boron** passes some extraordinary buildings dating from the turn of the century, such as the Château de l'Anglais, commonly known as Smith's Folly. It is painted a bright candy pink and was built by a British colonel in order to remind him of his days in India.

Higher up from Mont Boron, the Mont Alban fort is one of the extremely rare examples to be found in France of military architecture dating from the second half of the 16th century.

The Corniches of the Riviera

The real hinterland of Nice is the **valley of the Paillon.** Though not gentrified like the country round Vence, it is attractively rural rather than bleak and abandoned. Along the coast, the corniche roads, at three different levels, connect Nice with Monaco.

The villages in the valley of the Paillon are all delightful. From **Berre-des-Alpes** on the D 2204 there is a beautiful view of the surrounding mountains. **Coaraze** clings to a rocky peak and enjoys long hours of sunshine.

It is an hour's walk from here to the impressive ruined village of Roccasparvière, whose inhabitants abandoned it in the 17th century for lack of water and founded the village of **Duranus**.

The road continues past a desert landscape through the austere village of **L'Engarvin** to the Col Saint-Roch. Beyond the pass the D 2566 climbs to Peïra-Cava and **Turini**, surrounded by one of

CORNICHES DE LA RIVIERA

0   5 km

the most extensive forests in the *département*, consisting mainly of conifers.

Lucéram, high above a bend of the Paillon, has a fine collection of altarpieces within its 15th-century Romanesque/Gothic church. The *Retable de Sainte-Marguerite* in ten sections by Louis Bréa is one of the most remarkable in France.

From the **Col de Braus** there is a good view of the coast and the view is even better from the unsurfaced road leading to the village of **Sainte-Agnès**. Further down are the superb villages perchés of Peille and Peillon.

There is a choice of three roads at different heights to travel the 18 miles (30 km) between Nice and Menton. The three corniches are all equally beautiful and a network of side roads leads from one to the other.

The Lower Corniche (N 98) is the busiest of the three because it passes through all the coastal towns. Immediately beyond **Nissa la Bella,** the road plunges into one of the most beautiful

bays in the whole of the Mediterranean. The bay of **Villefranche-sur-Mer** shelters the old town and its harbor which have hardly changed since the 18th century. The narrow streets slope down to the harbor and the arcaded Rue Obscure which has remained unchanged since the 13th century. The harbor is an inviting place for a walk, extending from the **Chapelle Saint-Pierre**, decorated by Jean Cocteau, and out along the shingle beaches.

Further west is the **citadel of Saint-Elme**. It was built in the 16th century by Provana de Leyni and is in a good state of preservation. Soldiers were stationed here until 1965 but it is now used as an administrative and cultural center. The walk can be extended to the docks where boats are repaired.

Just opposite is the **Cap Ferrat** peninsula where luxurious villas lie hidden. The villa formerly called Ile de France now houses the famous **Musée Ephrussi de Rothschild** with its magnificent art collection.

191

The best way to see Cap Ferrat is on foot. Starting from the Résidence du Lido, a path follows the shore to the **Pointe Saint-Hospice**, with a chapel at the end. Standing nearby is a strange and rather ugly bronze statue of the Virgin about 40 ft (12m) high.

The next town on the **Corniche Inférieure** (Lower Corniche) is **Beaulieu**, where the white marble casino and rotunda make a spectacular contrast against the blue of the sea.

On the **Pointe des Fourmis** is the **Villa Kerylos**, a reproduction of an ancient Greek villa.

At **Eze-sur-Mer** the famous Nietzsche path (also called the Zarathustra path) climbs steeply to the village of **Eze.** When the philosopher decided to visit the Riviera in 1883, he stayed at Villefranche (before going on to Nice which pleased him so much that he spent the next six winters there) and discovered the path from Eze station to the old *village perché*, where he is said to have conceived the idea for *Thus Spake Zarathustra.*

The old medieval fortress village of Eze which is overlooking the sea can also be reached by the **Moyenne Corniche** (Middle Corniche - N 7). Don't miss the view of the village from the ruined castle after taking a walk in the Exotic Garden with its rare plants. This is an experience not to be missed by gardeners.

The **Grande Corniche** (Great Corniche - D 2564) is the highest at between 985 and 1775 ft (300 -540m) above sea-level; and it has some incredible views. It passes the **Nice Observatory**, an important center of astronomical research built by Charles Garnier, the **Plateau Saint-Michel viewpoint**, the **Belvédère d'Eze** and the **Point Capitaine** where it reaches its maximum height, arriving finally at the village of **La Turbie**. Here stands the ancient monument called the **Trophy of the Alps,** 165 ft (50m) high, which was erected by the Senate and people of Rome in the year 7 B.C., according to the

inscription, to remind the local populace of their subjugation to Rome.

The Lower Corniche continues to **Cap d'Ail**, where some luxurious villas and hotels from the turn of the century still survive.

From the recently established Marquet beach, it is possible to walk all the way along the seashore to Mala, a small beach tucked away in a cove. Beyond Cap d'Ail the extravagant architecture of Monaco comes into view.

MONACO

It is hardly possible to imagine greater contrasts in an area of only 470 acres (190 hectares) than can be found within the **Principality of Monaco** (reached by the N 98 or N 7). The independence of this tiny sovereign state is easier to grasp when you see it enclosed within its amphitheater of mountains. A climatic paradise and tax haven combined, Monaco is a land of fantasy come true, with the story of Prince Rainier, married in 1956 to the beautiful film star Grace Kelly who played a starring role beside him until her tragic death in a motor accident.

Although the new developments and concrete blocks are symbols of modernity, the old city on the Rock has remained almost completely unchanged. Surrounded by massive ramparts, it stands high above the sea and glows with the mellow colors of Italy. Within it are the government buildings, the Prince's palace, the city hall and the cathedral.

The **Oceanographic Museum** with its superb aquarium was founded earlier this century by Prince Albert I and is one of the most interesting of its kind. Although its population is a mere 27,000, Monaco is a major business center and continues to grow, both upwards and out into the sea. The **Fontvielle** quarter is an area of 54 acres (22 hectares) reclaimed from the sea. The **Jardin Exotique** is one of the largest and most beautiful of its kind.

Mont des Mules

Turbie
Supérieur
Boulevard
la
Moyenne
Corniche
France
Grace

LARVOTTO

Egl.
St-Joseph

Centre de
la Culture et
d'Expositions

Musée
Nation.

BORDINA

Bd. de la République

Egl.
St-Charles

Marché

Hôtel
Mirabeau

*Jardins
du
Larvotto*

N7

BEAUSOLEIL

Boulevard

Métropole
Palace

Av.

Information

Jardins
du
Casino

**MONTE
CARLO**

Princesse

Boulevard

Théâtre
Princesse
Grace

Casino

LES MONEGHETTI

Radio
Télévision
de

Sporting
d'Hiver

PTT

Suisse

Alice

Hôtel
de Paris

Hôtel
Hermitage

Auditorium
Centre de Congrès

Stade
Couvert

Sacré
Cœur

Egl.
St-Dévote

Avenue de la Costa

H.Balmoral

d'Ostende

Boulevard

Boulevard

Avenue
Av. Présid. J.-F. Kennedy

Jardin

Boulevard de Belgique

Boulevard

Exotique

Grimaldi

Boulevard

Quai

Port de Monaco

Egl.
Réformée

Rue
Suffren Reymond

Stade
Nautique
Rainier III

PTT
Police Maritime
Yacht Club

Théâtre du
Fort Antoine

LA CONDAMINE

du

Parc
Princesse
Antoinette

Egl.
St-Martin

Rue
Princesse Caroline

Albert 1er

Antoine

Quai

Neuve

Gare

Place
d'Armes

Marché

Av. du Port

Porte

Ministère
d'Etat

Lycée
Albert 1er

M. d'Anthropologie
Préhistorique

N 98

Avenue

de la

Saint

Martin

Palais du Prince

Mairie

Musée
Océanographique

*Jardin
Exotique*

Zoo

Centre
d'Acclim.
Zoologique

Place du
Palais

Palais
de Justice

Cathédrale

MONACO

Centre
Hospitalier
Princesse
Grace

Boulevard

Charles III

Quai

Avenue du Prince Héréditaire

des

Port de Fontvieille

*Jardins
St-Martin*

Avenue

N7

Boulevard

Albert

Rainier III

FONTVIEILLE

Sanbarbani

Police
PTT

Egl. St-Nicolas

Stade
Louis II

*Roseraie
Princesse
Grace*

MONACO
FRANCE

Espace de
Fontvieille

Héliport

MER MÉDITERRANÉE

Port de Cap-D'ail

MONACO

0   300m

Within Monaco, the **quartier de Monte Carlo** is the area dedicated to high living. Its center is the place du Casino, nicknamed the *Camembert*. In the square are the world-famous *Hotel de Paris* and *Café de Paris*, built at the end of the last century and frequented by the rich and famous ever since.

The **casino** is probably the most famous in the world and since the days of its first director, François Blanc, has been a glittering meeting-place for those who have made it to the top. In the early days it was the haunt of famous courtesans like La Belle Otero, Liane de Pougy and Cléo de Mérode whose beauty bedazzled the gentlemen in the exclusive gambling rooms and was then immortalized by the artist Gervais in his painting Grâces Florentines.

Its theater, designed by Charles Garnier, is one of the most important of those built in the Belle Epoque style. You may

Above: The harbor at Monaco, with Monte Carlo behind.

be lucky enough to get a ticket for the opera, which is generally excellent. Try to book well ahead.

MENTON

On the last mountain slopes of the Alpes-Maritimes, before reaching the Italian border, lies **Menton**, backed by two magnificent valleys, the Vallée de la Roya and the Vallée des Merveilles. Between Monaco and Menton lies **Roquebrune-Cap-Martin** (it can be reached along the N 98 or N 7), rising from the sea to a height of nearly 1000 ft (300m) The old village nestles around its castle and clings to the cliffs above the sea.

The path around the cape is called Le Corbusier. The famous architect often stayed at Cap Martin and the little house where he lived and worked still exists. He is buried in the cemetery on the cape under an extravagant concrete tombstone designed by himself.

The cape is covered with pine, ilex and mastic trees, which conceal splendid villas like the Villa Cyrnos where the Empress Eugénie, wife of Napoleon III, used to stay.

Menton is a place of nostalgic charm. The cemetery above the old town has a wonderful view over Menton and the sea. The **church of Saint-Michel** is a fine example of Baroque architecture and has a pretty black and white paved square in front. Its great bell-tower is 175 ft (53 m) high with five stories and has a domed roof with glazed tiles and a pinnacle. The main feature of the interior is a 16th-century altar-piece showing St. Michael, St. Peter and St. John the Baptist.

An important chamber music festival, begun in 1950, is held every year in August in the square in front of the church.

It is very pleasant to take a walk in the narrow streets of the old town or past the splendid Edwardian hotels like the *Winter Palace* and the *Riviera Palace*.

But the quintessence of Menton can be found in the scented sweetness of its air. The perfume emanating from its magnificent gardens is intoxicating – a blend of the Mediterranean and tropical flowers which thrive in the superb climate. In 1922 the Spanish author Blasco Ibáñez designed a garden called the **Jardin Fontana Rosa** dedicated to writers, where you can wander between statues of Balzac, Cervantès, Dickens and Dante, amid a riot of colourful flower-beds. This garden of literature remained abandoned and forgotten for a long time, it has now been restored with its busts, columns, pergolas covered with climbing plants, fountains and smart tiled benches.

From here you can look over to the beautiful **Oliveraie du Pian**, not an olive-grove but one of the restful parks of Menton.

On its other side is **Val Rahmeh,** the town's botanic and tropical garden. On the terrace, hibiscus and datura mingle with the ocher background of the house, built in 1925 and ornamented with loggias and arcades.

Still in this area, known as **Garavan**, there is a wonderful garden at **Les Colombières**. It was designed by a caricaturist, painter and inveterate traveler named Ferdinand Bac, who designed many gardens for his friends. Les Colombières is his greatest achievement, incorporating memories of his travels around the Mediterranean while retaining the natural features of the garden – for example he built a bridge and an avenue to show off a carob tree, and a flight of steps for an olive tree.

He continued his journey in the house, which is now a hotel and tea room. The rooms contain paintings by Bac depicting the high points of his odyssey, from the Middle East to Spain. The dining room looks out over the "real" Menton, but on the walls its towers are turned into exotic minarets and campaniles.

There are exotic fruits for sale everywhere in Menton. You can buy them fresh to eat on the spot, or candied to take home as a souvenir, at *Confitures artisanales,* 2 rue du Vieux-Collège.

Foothills of the Alpes-Maritimes

Above Menton there are wonderful villages in the hills with magnificent views over the coast. Four miles (7 km) to the north is **Castellar**, an old fortified village. Its ancient streets, each with its fountain, are connected by curious covered passageways.

The simple chapel of Saint-Sébastien has a pretty arched tower. There is a picturesque old cemetery nearby. To the north there are the remains of the walls, loopholes and towers of the abandoned village.

Sainte-Agnès is the highest village on the coast at 2130 ft (650 m). It has retained its medieval character, with narrow streets, houses built into the rock and doorways with pointed arches. From the belvedere of the Hotel Righi there is a stupendous view eastward into Italy,

The road then follows massive beds of limestone through which the Roya cuts a path. Suddenly, round a bend, the village of **Saorge,** one of the most beautiful in the Alpes-Maritimes, comes into view. This superb medieval village, set on a spur 650 ft (200 m) high, was on the old salt road between the coast and the Tende pass. It was an important strategic staging post on the first main route to Piedmont. In the 18th century Saorge was one of the four largest towns in the region, with Nice, Sospel and Villefranche.

The delightful old center of Saorge, with its winding streets, is well worth a visit. Olive-wood carvings are a traditional craft in both Saorge and Breil and two names are worth noting: *Monsieur Rech* in the old town at Breil-sur-Roya, and *Pierre Franca*, avenue du Docteur-Davéo in Saorge. Saorge has some fine churches like the early Romanesque church of **La Madone-del-Poggio**, a short distance from the village overlooking the Roya gorge.

Saint-Dalmas-de-Tende on the rail line from Nice to Cuneo, was a frontier post from 1929 to 1939 and the old station (now a holiday center) is an enormous building in the Italian style of the period.

Through peach plantations, the road leads to **La Brigue** with its greenish stone houses. About 2.5 miles (4km) from the village, at a height of nearly 3000ft (900 m) is the sanctuary of **Notre-Dame-des-Fontaines**, which is overlooking seven springs said to have miraculous properties, and a famous place of pilgrimage since 1375.

It is situated in an amphitheater of green among high mountains, on an ancient mule route between La Brigue and Triora. The outside of the chapel appears plain and uninteresting, with no bell-tower, but the interior is breathtaking, with its many paintings covering all the walls and the choir (about 220 sq. m / 2400 sq. ft).

west Saint-Jean and in clear weather, south to Corsica. A path leads to the very interesting remains of the 12th/13th-century castle fortifications.

Gorbio is equally impressive. Here, as in many villages in the Comté de Nice, an unusual festival takes place on a night in mid-June. It is called the *Procession aux Escargots* or Procession of the Snails.

Along the N204, 18 miles (30km) to the north, is **Breil-sur-Roya,** on a small artificial lake. This is the beginning of the **Vallée de la Roya**, an untamed valley with scattered *villages perchés*.

Breil is a charming village which has a number of interesting sights including old houses and churches, arcaded squares and *trompe l'oeil* decoration.

In an olive grove a short distance to the west is the early Romanesque chapel of **Notre-Dame-du-Mont**. The chevet dates from the second half of the 11th century and is very well preserved.

Above: A village high above the Entraunes valley. Right: Menton and its harbor.

The frescoes were painted in 1491 and 1492 by the two most celebrated artists of the period, Giovanni Baleison and Giovanni Canavesio. The *Life of the Virgin* and the *Childhood of Christ* were painted by Baleison and the *Passion of Christ* and the *Last Judgement* by Canavesio.

Using an accessible and dramatic style, the frescoes by Canavesio express torment by their sheer movement, violence and expressions. The figure of the *Hanged Judas* is typical of the painter's extravagant style, in contrast to the serenity and calm of Baleison's subjects.

Like La Brigue, **Tende** remained subject to the rule of the House of Savoy in 1860, although the population would have preferred to join France. The area did not become part of France until 1947, when a referendum was held and the people made their preference plain.

The many muleteers who passed through the village along the salt road formed a large guild under the protection of St. Eloi. Every year on the second Sunday in July a celebration of the saint takes place, when mules with splendid harnesses are taken to the church of **Notre-Dame-de-l'Assomption**, the finest building in Tende, built in the Gothic style with Lombard influence. The flight of steps leading to the entrance seems almost to lift the building towards the sky. The door itself is made of green schist and is decorated with figures of Christ and the Apostles.

Tende is the starting point for excursions into the famous **Vallée des Merveilles**, with the 9450 ft (2875 m) Mont Bego at its center. The marks of the last glaciers of the ice age which hollowed it out have remained intact - glacial lakes and slabs of schist polished by the glaciers, on which thousands of rock carvings were discovered in the 19th century. These carvings were probably done by Ligurian peasants and herdsmen during the Bronze Age, around 1500BC. The most frequently drawn symbol is that of the "cornu," a triangle framed by two horns, which is sometimes modified to form a human face.

Tourist Information
Comité régional de Tourisme Riviera-Côte d'Azur, 55, promenade des Anglais, 06000 Nice, Tel: 93-445059. **Bureau de Tourisme Côte d'Azur,** bd. Jean-Jaurès, Nice, Tel: 93-808484.

ANTIBES
Accommodation
LUXURY: **Cap Eden-Roc,** bd. Kennedy, Tel: 93-613901. **Helios,** 3, rue Dautheville, Tel: 93-615525.
MODERATE: **La Gardiole,** Chemin de la Garoupe, Tel: 93-613503.
BUDGET: **Pierre Loti,** 29, rue Pierre-Loti, Tel: 93-615509.

Restaurants
Les Vieux Murs, promenade Amiral-de-Grasse, Tel: 93-340673, moderate prices.

Castle / Museum / Festival
Château Grimaldi and **Musée Picasso,** pl. du Château, Tel: 93- 349191. *Jazz Festival in July.*

Tourist Information
Office de Tourisme, place de Gaulle, Tel: 93-339564.

BEAULIEU-SUR-MER
Accommodation
LUXURY: **Carlton,** av. E.-Cavell, Tel: 93-011470.
MODERATE: **Résidence Carlton,** 9, av. Albert-1er, Tel: 93-010602.
BUDGET: **Havre Bleu,** 29, bd. du Maréchal-Joffre, Tel: 93-010140.

Tourist Information
Office de Tourisme, place de la Gare, Tel: 93-010221.

BIOT
Accommodation
MODERATE: **Hostellerie du Bois Fleuri,** 199, bd. de la Source, Tel: 93-656874.
BUDGET: **Auberge de la Vallée Verte,** route de Valbonne, Tel: 93- 651093.

Museums
Musée Fernand Léger, Tel: 93-656361.
Verrerie, art of glassmaking, Tel: 93-650300.

Tourist Information
Office de Tourisme, place de la Chapelle, Tel: 93-650585.

CAGNES-SUR-MER
Accommodation
MODERATE: **Brasilia,** bd. Maréchal-Juin, Tel: 93-202503. *BUDGET:* **Chantilly,** Rue de la Minoterie, Tel: 93-202550.

Museums / Sightseeing
Château-Musée Hauts-de-Cagnes, Tel: 93-208557. **Villa Renoir,** Les Collettes, Tel: 93-206107.

Tourist Information
Office de Tourisme, 6, bd. Maréchal-Juin, Tel: 93-206164.

CANNES
Accommodation
LUXURY: **Le Grand Hôtel,** 45, bd. de la Croisette, Tel: 93- 381545.
MODERATE: **Hôtel America,** 13, rue Saint-Honoré, Tel: 93- 646928.
BUDGET: **Le Bristol,** 14, rue Hoche, Tel: 93-391066.

Restaurants
Relais des Semailles, 9, rue Saint-Antoine, Tel: 93-392232, elegant. **Le Caveau,** 45, rue Félix-Faure, Tel: 93-390633, moderate prices.

Museum / Maritime Links / Festival
Musée de la Castre, in the Château de la Castre, Le Suquet, Tel: 93-385526.
Ferry connections to the **Lérins-Islands,** information in Cannes harbor, Tel: 93-391182.
International Film Festival, in May.

Tourist Information
Office de Tourisme, palais des Festivals, boulevard de la Croisette, Tel: 93-392453.

EZE
Accommodation
LUXURY: **Château Eza,** rue de la Pise, Tel: 93-411224. *BUDGET:* **Auberge Le Soleil,** av. de la Liberté, Basse-Corniche, Tel: 93- 015146.

Tourist Information
Office de Tourisme, town hall, Tel: 93-410303.

GRASSE
Accommodation
LUXURY: **Le Régent,** route de Nice, Tel: 93-364010. *MODERATE:* **Parfums Best Western,** bd. Eugène-Charabot, Tel: 93-361010. *BUDGET:* **Hôtel du Patti,** place du Patti, Tel: 93-360100.

Museums
Musée international de la Parfumerie, 8, pl. du Cours, Tel: 93- 368020. **Musée d'Art et d'Histoire de Provence,** 2, rue Mirabeau, Tel: 93-360161. **Villa-Musée Fragonard,** 23, bd. Fragonard, Tel: 93-360161.

Tourist Information
Office de Tourisme, place de la Foux, Tel: 93-360356.

JUAN-LES-PINS
Accommodation / Restaurant
MODERATE: **Le Pré Catalan,** 22, avenue des Lauriers, Tel: 93- 610511. **Le Parc,** av. Guy-de-Maupassant, Tel: 93-616100.
Auberge de l'Estérel, 21, chemin des Iles, Tel: 93-618655, restaurant, moderate prices.

MENTON
Accommodation
MODERATE: **Le Napoléon,** 29, pte de France, baie de Garavan, Tel: 93-358950.
BUDGET: **Le Dauphin,** 28, av. du Général-de-Gaulle, Tel: 93-357637.

Gardens / Festival

Jardin exotique de Val Rahmeh, av. Saint-Jacques, Tel: 93-358672. **Jardin des Colombières**, bd. de Garavan, Tel: 93-357190. *Festival of chamber music* in August.

Tourist Information

Office de Tourisme, place de l'Europe, avenue Boyer, Tel: 93- 575700.

MERCANTOUR
National Park

Information: rue d'Italie, Nice, Tel: 93-878610.

MONACO
Accommodation

LUXURY: **Metropole Palace**, 4, av. de la Madone, Tel: 93- 151515. *MODERATE:* **Balmoral**, 12, av. de la Costa, Tel: 93-506237.

BUDGET: **Terminus**, 9, av. Prince-Pierre, Tel: 93-302070.

Museum / Garden / Festival

Musée Océanographique, av. Saint-Martin, Tel: 93-153600. **Jardin exotique**, bd. du Jardin Exotique, Tel: 93-303365. *Circus festival* in January.

Tourist Information

Direction du Tourisme, 2A, bd. des Moulins, Monte-Carlo, Tel: 93- 308701.

MOUGINS
Accommodation

LUXURY: **Muscadins**, bd. Courteline, Tel: 93-900043. *MODERATE:* **Le Mas Candille**, bd. Clément-Rebuffel, Tel: 93-900085. *BUDGET:* **Acanthe**, 95, bd. du Maréchal-Juin, Tel: 93-753537.

NICE
Accommodation

LUXURY: **Beau Rivage**, 24, rue Saint-François-de-Paule, Tel: 93- 808070.

MODERATE: **Le Windsor**, 11, rue Dalpozzo, Tel: 93-885935. *BUDGET:* **Hôtel de Savoie**, 39, rue d'Angleterre, Tel: 93-883573.

Museums / Festivals

Musée des Beaux-Arts, 33, av. des Beaumettes, Tel: 93-445072. **Musée Matisse**, 164, av. des Arènes de Cimiez, Tel: 91-531770. **Musée Marc Chagall**, av. du Dr-Ménard Tel: 93-817575. **Palais Masséna et Musée**, 65, rue de France and 35, promenade des Anglais, Tel: 93-881134. **Palais Lascaris** 15, rue Droite, Tel: 93-620554. *Carnaval*, in February. *Grande Parade du Jazz*, jazz festival in July.

Tourist Information

Office de Tourisme, 5, av. Gustave-V, Tel: 93-876060.

ROQUEBRUNE-CAP-MARTIN
Accommodation

LUXURY: **Vista Palace**, Grande-Corniche, Tel: 93-356545. *MODERATE:* **Alexandra**, 93, av. Winston-Churchill, Tel: 93-356590.

BUDGET: **Westminster**, 14, av. Louis-Laurens, Basse-Corniche, Tel: 93- 350008.

Tourist Information

Office de Tourisme, town hall, Tel: 93-356067.

SAINT-JEAN-CAP-FERRAT
Accommodation

LUXURY: **Cap Ferrat**, bd. Général-de-Gaulle, Tel: 93-760021. *MODERATE:* **L'Oursin**, 1, av. Denis-Séméria, Tel: 93-760465. *BUDGET:* **Bagatelle**, av. Honoré-Sauvan, Tel: 93-013286.

Tourist Information

Office de Tourisme, Tel: 93-013686.

SAINT-PAUL-DE-VENCE
Accommodation

LUXURY: **Saint Paul**, 86, rue Grande, Tel: 93-326525. *MODERATE:* **Les Orangers**, chemin des Fumerates, Tel: 93-328095. *BUDGET:* **Les Remparts**, 72, rue Grande, Tel: 93-328064.

Museum

Fondation Maeght, Tel: 93-328163.

Tourist Information

Office de Tourisme, 2, rue Grande, Tel: 93-328695.

VALLAURIS
Accommodation

MODERATE: **Les Jasmins du Golfe**, Golfe Juan, Tel: 93- 638083.

Museum / Tourist Information

Musée Picasso, place de la Libération, Tel: 93-641805. **Office de Tourisme**, av. de la Liberté, Tel: 93-637312.

VENCE
Accommodation

LUXURY: **Château Saint-Martin**, route de Coursegoules, Tel: 93- 580202.

MODERATE: **Diana**, av. des Poilus, Tel: 93-582856. *BUDGET:* **Parc Hôtel**, 50, av. Foch, Tel: 93-582727.

Tourist Information

Office de Tourisme, place du Grand-Jardin, Tel: 93-580638.

VILLEFRANCHE-SUR-MER
Accommodation

MODERATE: **Les Olivettes**, 17, av. Léopold-II, Tel: 93- 010369. *BUDGET:* **Le Provençal**, 4, av. du Maréchal-Joffre, Tel: 93- 017142.

VILLENEUVE-LOUBET
Accommodation

MODERATE: **Bahia**, Bord de Mer, Tel: 93-202121. *BUDGET:* **Palerme**, av. de la Batterie, Tel: 93-201607.

Museum / Tourist Information

Musée de l'Art culinaire, art of cooking, Fondation Auguste Escoffier, 3, rue Auguste-Escoffier, Tel: 93-208051. **Office de Tourisme,** place de Verdun, Tel: 93-202009.

FESTIVALS

The heat of summer brings forth a profusion of lively festivals in Provence and there is also a wide choice of musical, theatrical and dance events to visit in the evening.

The **Festival of Avignon** is the oldest festival in southern France. In 1947 a major exhibition of contemporary art was organized by Yvonne and Christian Zervos in the Papal Palace and this attracted the attention of the actor and producer, Jean Vilar. The writer René Char then introduced Vilar to the Zervos, who suggested that he might stage T.S.Eliot's play *Murder in the Cathedral,* which he had just directed in Paris, in the main courtyard of the Papal Palace. Vilar did not want to perform a play out of doors that had been designed for an enclosed

space, but suggested instead putting on Shakespeare's *Richard II, Tobias and Sarah* by Paul Claudel and *Terrasse de Midi* by Maurice Clavel. The city agreed to fund the *Semaine d'Art d'Avignon* (Avignon Arts Week), which was the forerunner of the present festival.

The Shakespeare play was performed in the main courtyard of the palace, suitably equipped for the occasion, the Claudel in the Orchard of Pope Urban V and the Clavel in the city's theater. The plays performed the following year were *The Death of Danton* by Georg Büchner and *Scheherazade* by Supervielle. The tone was set for an annual drama festival presenting works which had not previously been performed in France.

In 1951 Gérard Philipe appeared in the title-role of *The Prince of Homburg* and made the reputation of the festival. From then on Jean Vilar' s career was closely linked with the Festival, which he directed until 1965; and the performances in the warm summer evenings of Provence were nearly always sold out.

Preceding pages: Ready for a game of boules. The Fête des Gardians (cowherds) in Arles. Above: Drummers in Roquebrune-sur-Argens. Right: Street musicians.

In 1967 the program was extended to include dance, cinema and concerts and eventually took over the whole city, often making use of historic buildings previously neglected by the public. A fringe festival soon grew up alongside the main program and this still attracts a large number of experimental and avant garde theater groups every year. It is essential to book tickets in advance.

A parallel development to the festival has been the **Rencontres Internationales d'Eté de Villeneuve-lès-Avignon**, held in the beautiful old Charterhouse of Val-de-Bénédiction in July and August, to which artists and creative people from around the world come to share their experiences and exchange views.

Since 1973 a variety of cultural events such as study courses, exhibitions, plays and concerts have been held in the Charterhouse throughout the year.

The exceptional acoustics of the ancient theater in Orange were rediscovered at the end of the 19th century by Félix Ripert and Anthony Réal. They are now used to the full by the world-famous **Chorégies d'Orange.** Ripert and Réal launched the initial concept of what they called the *Fêtes Romaines* on 21 August 1869. The programme included *Joseph* by Mehul, *Les Triomphateurs*, a cantata by Réal in praise of the Romans and *Roméo et Juliet*, an opera by Vacaille, a composer who has been entirely forgotten today.

The name *Chorégies* began to be used around 1902. The classical Greek and Latin repertoire remained predominant, with directors like Frédéric Mistral, Paul Mariéton, Paul Arène and Marcel Provence. In 1920 the *Comédie Française* appeared here for the first time. Drama took center stage until about 1965.

Since 1970, however, the *Chorégies* has found its true vocation with opera, for which it has become an internationally famous venue. Under the direction of Jacques Bourgeois, many celebrated singers now come here to perform, mainly in works by Wagner and Verdi.

It is not far from the Chorégies in Orange to the **Choralies** in **Vaison-la-Romaine**. This ancient town hosts a choral festival every three years (1991, 1994 etc.) at the beginning of August, when choirs arrive from all parts of the world for a gathering of as many as 7,000 singers.

In 1945 the musician César Geoffray realized his dream of celebrating song through young people. He founded a famous choir called *A Coeur Joie* (Joy at Heart) in Lyon, which was then emulated in other parts of France. This movement led to the festival that is now called the *Choralies*. The climate in Vaison-la-Romaine was right for singing in more ways than one and the youth choirs and related groups have flourished.

The **International Festival of Photography** is held in Arles in July. It was founded by Jean-Maurice Rouquette, the curator of the Musée Réattu, where a photographic section was set up in 1965, forming the first phase of the *Centre International de la Photographie et de l'Image*. The festival, which is now one of the region's major summer events, started in 1970 as a result of the efforts of Maurice Rouquette, Lucien Clergue and Michel Tournier.

As Avignon has its Maison Jean Vilar, a permanent home for the dramatic arts, so Arles has the National School of Photography which was set up in 1982 as a direct result of the festival. During the festival the city is transformed into a vast photographic studio and there are exhibitions of photography on every corner.

Since the renovation of the Musée Ziem in **Martigues,** an annual festival has been held there, which aims to combat industrialisation by returning to the sources of popular culture. Every year the place is full of sculptors, theater groups, musicians and performers and visitors from far and wide.

Right: The beach at Nice in spring.

The castle housing the museum at **Lourmarin** is sometimes called the Provençal Villa dei Medici and accommodates young artists, including musicians, painters and sculptors all the year round. At the end of their stay the young artists present their work in a series of exhibitions and concerts.

During the first two weeks of July this fine Renaissance building is home to the **Rencontres Méditerranéennes Albert Camus,** named after the great French novelis and playwright who died in 1960 and is buried in Lourmarin cemetery.

One of the oldest castles in Provence, the Château de l'Empéri, perched high on a cliff at **Salon-de-Provence**, is the venue for a **Jazz and Theater Festival** every year in July.

The **Opera and Music Festival** at **Aix-en-Provence** has now re-emerged after a period in the shadows. It was begun in 1948 by the Countess Pastré. In 1949 the architect Cassandre designed the first theater in the courtyard of the former Archbishop's Palace. With the support of the conductor Hans Rosbaud, the festival became world famous within a few years and was internationally recognized for its excellence.

The operas of Mozart, which were little known in France at the time, were performed by an array of then unknown artistes like Teresa Stich Randall and Teresa Berganza, but the festival also covered the main musical repertoire and works by contemporary composers. Famous artists like Derain, Masson, Clavé and Clayette were responsible for the stage design. This creative collaboration between opera singers, theatre directors and painters and the presence in the audience of eminent figures like Darius Milhaud, Jean Giono, François Mauriac and Francis Poulenc gave the festival a very special cachet.

The theater soon became too small, so a new one was designed by the architect Bernard Guillaumot and built in 1985. It

is equipped with the latest technology and can now seat 1630 people. Its programme has also been extended, with four major opera productions and a series of concerts every year. Mozart still has pride of place, but 20th century composers are also well represented, mainly due to co-productions with the *Centre Acanthes* which invites a major living composer to bring his or her work to the festival every year.

The **Festival International de la Danse** is staged every year in the Centre de Rencontres at **Châteauvallon**. This is an international dance festival held near Toulon in an open-air theater that is set among pines, olive trees, broom and rocks. The idea was born in 1964 at a meeting between the painter and sculptor Henri Komatis and a journalist, Gérard Paquet. Both wanted to make this wonderful spot into a shrine for the arts and so they built an open-air Greek amphitheater in which to stage productions of the great plays of Aeschylus, Racine, Claudel and others.

In the 1970s Châteauvallon became famous for its jazz festival, but this had to move to Antibes when it became too successful. Another indoor theater seating 600 has now been built. In 1980 the place discovered its true vocation in dance, which has had an explosion of popularity in France. Since the arrival of Denis Guenoun as director in 1984, new heights have been reached. A complex of studios and rehearsal-rooms has been built, and internationally renowned choreographers now come to the dance festival in July to stage their latest, often very innovative, works.

For almost twenty years the town of **Hyères** has staged an international festival for young film-makers and brought names like Claude Lelouch, René Allio and Margarethe von Trotta to the attention of the public long before they were featured at the Cannes Festival. Loyal to the visual image, the town now also holds a very popular **Festival of Comic-Strip Art** *(Festival de la Bande Dessinée)* every September.

The famous **Cannes International Film Festival** takes place every year in May. It was held for the first time on 1 September 1939 but was interrupted by the outbreak of the Second World War and was not resumed until 20 September 1946, when it was an immediate success. The films were shown in the Casino and the first acting awards were won by Michèle Morgan and Ray Milland. The Grand Prix winners were René Clément's *La Bataille du Rail* and the English film classic, *Brief Encounter*.

In 1947 the Festival Palace was built at the center of the Croisette and soon became a Mecca for the film industry and its stars for two weeks every May. The architecture of the new palace which was built in 1982, also on the Croisette, has been much criticized, but it is much better equipped inside than the old building. The old festival building was renamed the Palais-Croisette and its famous fa-

Above: High-powered luxury is de rigueur in Monte Carlo.

çade with its high picture windows is a listed monument. Some of the glitter of the Film Festival has faded and there are now fewer starlets hoping to dazzle a producer or director, but it is still considered to be a very important media event.

Other events in Cannes are the **Festival International du Café-Théâtre** in June, which is very popular with amateur groups, and the **Nuits du Suquet** in July, with music-making outside the church of Notre-Dame d'Espérance.

In Antibes, a **festival of bel canto**, with romantic opera productions of Donizetti, Rossini, Bellini and Spontini, was held for the first time in Port Vauban in June 1991.

And every year the beautiful pine groves of Antibes and Juan-les-Pins echo to the sounds of the **International Jazz Festival**. The great names in jazz consider it an honor to be invited to make music here by the sea on hot July nights. The music tends to be the more ebullient, less introspective kind of jazz.

This festival tends to overshadow the **Grande Parade de Jazz** which also takes place in July in the old arena at **Cimiez**. This festival pays more attention to modern and experimental jazz. John MacLaughlin and Keith Jarrett are among the famous names who have played here. The arena at Cimiez is the ideal venue and there is something for every taste. Many people in the audience bring a picnic with them and whole families sit around on the grass relaxing and listening to the music.

The prestigious **Monaco Circus Festival** is held at a less popular time of year when there are fewer tourists – in February. It was inaugurated in 1974 by Prince Rainier of Monaco, who is a circus lover, and it is still the only one of its kind in the world. The big top is put up in Fontvielle and the best circus performers from round the globe take part. The festival is almost like a Circus Olympic Games with top acts from the West and from China and North Korea, both specializing in acrobatics. The **Monaco Spring Festival** focuses on sculpture, opera and ballet.

Other festivals take place in many towns along the coast, including **Menton,** where the **Chamber Music Festival** is held every year in August in front of the Baroque church of Saint-Michel. This magnificent site overlooking the sea has welcomed famous ensembles, conductors and soloists like Karl Münchinger, Arthur Rubinstein, Rostropovich, Jean-Pierre Rampal, Isaac Stern, Yehudi Menuhin, the Bartok Quartet and the Golden Gate Quartet, to name but a few. The festival began in 1949 and it soon gained international recognition, putting Menton on the musical map.

Many other less well-known festivals also take place in Provence.

In **Cogolin** there is an international festival of contemporary poetry. Poets come from all over the world to read their works.

At **Vitrolles**, there are craft displays, plays, concerts and films in the Centre Fontblanche.

There are also festivals and so-called *nuits* in the Haut-Var, such as the **Music Festival** which is directed by Landowski and staged at the Théâtre de Verdure in **Cotignac**.

In **Fréjus**, the **Forum of Arts and Music** takes place around the cathedral in the old town. **Saint-Tropez** also holds **Nuits Musicales** at the Château de la Moutte through the summer until early September.

In **Biot**, the **Music Festival** held every July attracts famous singers from all over the world.

In **Sophia-Antipolis,** seminars and conferences are held throughout the year, but in July and August the scene changes to a less serious note and some excellent productions of drama, ballet and music are put on.

The new **International Dance Festival** at **La Colle-sur-Loup** promises well for the future. It is already attracting much attention from performers and spectators alike.

Important events in motor sport are the famous **Monte Carlo Rally** at the end of January and the **Monaco Grand Prix** which takes place in the streets of the principality.

Many traditional festivals take place in Provence throughout the year, including the traditional lavender, wine and olive festivals dating back far into the past. At the end of April the *gardians*, the mounted herdsmen of the Camargue, celebrate with processions and rodeos. At Easter there is a *feria* with Provençal bullfights in Arles, and one in Nîmes at Whitsun.

On 14 July, Bastille Day, the whole of France is on its feet. On the first Sunday in August the Corso de la Lavande takes place in Digne and Grasse has its jasmine festival. The olive festival is celebrated in Les Baux in September.

THE GREAT MUSEUMS

In the crowded, noisy resorts of today, it is hard to imagine that so many painters were first attracted by the undisturbed landscape, the peacefulness and the unique light of Provence. They came seeking inexpensive spots to live on the coast, where they would create a society of like-minded people dedicated to liberating the human spirit.

Paul Signac was the first to discover Saint-Tropez and capture the beautiful effects of its shimmering light on his canvasses. He lived most of the time on his boat in the bay and spent many hours studying the reflections in the water before attempting to paint them.

Tourists interested in painting and the arts will find plenty to see, with around 120 different collections in museums on the Côte d'Azur: one every 12 miles through the Var and Alpes-Maritimes!

Above: The international exhibition of photography in Arles.

Cities like Marseilles and Arles also have superb museums, many of them founded in the 19th century. A great deal of money has been invested over the last twenty years to make these collections more attractive to the public.

When the popes chose Avignon as the papal city in the 14th century, it developed into one of the main centers of the arts in Europe and attracted important painters, mainly Italian, between 1330 and 1380. An original school of painting called the Avignon School grew up and continued to thrive until the end of the 15th century. One of its main members was the Sienese painter, Simone Martini. Although none of the frescoes in the Papal Palace can be definitely attributed to him, his influence is quite clearly present in their execution. His pupil Matteo Giovanetti worked on the murals in the Robing Room of the palace.

The **Musée du Petit Palais**, the former residence of the bishops and archbishops of Avignon, is a handsome 14th- and 15th-century building which contains an impressive collection of nearly 1000 religious paintings and sculptures from the Middle Ages to the Renaissance. They include the Calvet collection and the 350 Italian paintings from the 13th to the 15th centuries in the Campana collection. It also has an exhibition of interesting local archaeological finds that date from the medieval period when Avignon was already a city of importance. The old masters are displayed in chronological order, with works from painters who lived and worked in Avignon occupying the first two and the last three rooms and the Italian paintings displayed separately in the fourteen other rooms. The standard of presentation is outstanding, using no cheap effects, but letting the works stand on their own merit.

There is a much greater variety of exhibits at the **Musée Calvet**, a delightful 18th century palace, where you can see an Egyptian mummy of a young boy, Gallo-Roman pottery, Renaissance furniture and clocks, and paintings of all periods including some fine works by Géricault, Utrillo, Dufy and Vasarely.

The **Musée Réattu** at Arles is in a former priory belonging to the Knights of Malta. It is one of the cultural jewels in the city's crown. In addition to a small number of old masters, it has a collection of 17th- and 18th-century works by local painters (of whom Raspal is the most important) and almost all the works of the artist Réattu. As far as contemporary art is concerned, this museum was one of the first in France to admit photography and it now has a collection of prints by many of the major French and international photographers like Weston, Brassai, Beaton, Boubat, Cartier-Bresson, Dieuzaide and Sudre.

The museum also focuses attention on works of modern and contemporary art by artists associated in some way with the region – those who were born, lived or found their inspiration here or who are working here still. The collection started with the acquisition of some 57 drawings by Picasso that he produced in the brief period between December 1970 and February 1971. The enthusiasm, power and willingness to experiment which are so characteristic of Picasso are plain to see in these drawings. They are executed in a variety of materials and media – crayon, wash-tint, ink or charcoal.

The Musée Réattu also has works by Toni Grand, Bernard Pagès, Bernard Dejonghe and Jean Degottex. Do not miss the fine *Torso of a Woman* by Zadkine. Major art exhibitions take place every summer, two of the most recent being a memorable retrospective of Van Gogh and a journey through Provence seen through the eyes of Picasso.

The **Musée Ziem** was opened in Martigues in 1908 at the instigation of the landscape painter Félix Ziem. On his death he bequeathed a further 30 paintings to the museum. The collection was reorganized in the 1980s and is now housed in a former customs house built in the last century. In addition to displaying the original paintings, the Ziem is now also a local museum and a showcase for work by local contemporary artists. Objects that were found in recent archaeological digs, including the remains of several Roman ships, and a collection of commemorative panels are on view here, alongside the works of Ziem himself and landscape painters of the late 19th century. There are also contemporary works of sculpture, painting and drawing. It makes for an intriguing comparison of old and new.

The museums in Marseilles have recently been refurbished and given a new sparkle. The **Musée Cantini** is in a fine mansion built in 1694 for the *Compagnie du Cap Nègre* and left to the city by Jules Cantini, who owned a number of marble quarries.The house, with its collections of furniture and antiquities, was opened in 1936. Planned initially as a museum of decorative arts, including a fine collec-

tion of Provençal faïence, it changed direction in 1953 to concentrate on permanent and temporary exhibitions of modern art. The museum has made so many acquisitions of modern art that only a proportion of them are on display at a given time – even less when there is a temporary exhibition running – but you should be able to get an overview of all the movements in 20th century painting and sculpture, from Fauvism to the present day, and see representative works by such artists as Dufy, Léger, Bacon and Vasarely.

The **Musée des Beaux-Arts** in the Palais Longchamp has a large collection of French, Flemish, Dutch and Spanish paintings from the 16th and 17th centuries, as well as works by Honoré Daumier and Pierre Puget.

Above: There is plenty of room for large works at the Musée Vasarely in Aix-en-Provence. Right: In the Fondation Maeght at Saint-Paul-de-Vence and in the Musée Marc Chagall in Nice.

The **Musée Granet** at Aix-en-Provence has a considerable number of oils, drawings, etchings and watercolors by Cézanne. The artist was born in the city and spent his life in the solitude of the family properties and rented cottages outside the city. He loved the broad panoramas and rugged mountain landscapes of the district, particularly Mont Sainte-Victoire which he often painted. In addition, the Musée Granet also contains an excellent collection of paintings by local artists such as François Marius Granet, some archaeological finds and paintings by French, Dutch, Flemish and Italian masters from the 14th up to the 20th centuries.

The focus of the collection in the **Musée Municipal d'Art** in **Toulon** is painting in Provence from the 17th to the 20th centuries. From the 17th century, there are major works by Michel Serre and Meiffren Comte. Alongside works by Fragonard, Revelly and Simon Julien, the 18th century is represented by seascapes of Vernet and his circle. The 19th-

century portraiture is centered around Paulin Guérin. The landscapes of the 1850s by artists of the so-called School of Provence are surprisingly modern in style, while the Oriental influence is represented by Ziem and Jules Laurens. The avant-garde movement of the early 20th century is represented by the *fauvistes* of Provence, leading on to the symbolism of Mossa and Ménard. An interesting collection of contemporary art has been set up since 1978, giving a general picture of the artistic achievement since the 1960s. The collection has concentrated on certain styles such as New Realism, minimalist art, *Supports/Surfaces* and recent painting from the 1980s, giving the museum an experimental feel. Be sure to take in the fine collection of photographs donated to the museum by Jean Dieuzaide in 1977.

The **Musée de l'Annonciade**, housed in a deconsecrated chapel in Seint-Tropez, brings together on of the best collections to be seen anywhere of late Impressionist and Post-Impressionist paint-

ing, with works by Signac, Braque, Dufy, Seurat, Derain, Matisse, Marquet and Camoin and by Bonnard and Vuillard from the Nabis Group. It is incredible to realize that all these artists were brought together here by Signac, who lived on his boat in the bay.

In Fréjus, the **Fondation Daniel Templon** is temporarily housed in warehouses that were provided by the local authority and converted by the architect Didier Guichard. The collection covers the main trends in art over the last 30 years, a rich and complex period of artistic creativity. The post-war work of over 60 French artists can be seen, including Picasso, Matisse and Léger, and special exhibitions are held in the summer, the most recent of which covered French sculpture. The collection is due to be rehoused in the Villa Aurélienne in 1993.

The **Château Grimaldi** in Antibes became a museum of art and archaeology in 1928. The castle is surrounded by ramparts on a magnificent site overlooking the sea and the old town. In 1946 Picasso had his studio in the castle for a few months and when he departed he left behind most of his works from the period, notably the 25 paintings called the Antipolis Series and 44 drawings and sketches which amount to a diary of the artist's inspiration. The fresco The *Les Clés d'Antibes* is one of the few murals painted by Picasso. He also donated to the museum a large mythological composition called *Ulysses and the Sirens* and a fascinating collection of ceramics. Four hundred works by other 20th-century artists including Miró, Modigliani, Picabia and Balthus have been acquired by purchase or donation. Works by Nicolas de Staël painted at Antibes are hung in a separate room. His *Fort Carré* and the *Grand Concert* (his last unfinished work) are displayed, surrounded by Picassos from the 1946 Antibes period that had been discovered in foreign collections. The museum's intention is to collect works and artists associated with the town and to encourage young artists by buying their work. The museum's terrace has a wonderful garden containing sculpture and perfumed flowers and herbs which can also be enjoyed by the visually handicapped. Sculptures by Germaine Richier, Poirier, César and Bernard Pagès can be touched as well as admired.

Lovers of modern art should not fail to make a pilgrimage to the **Musée Fernand Léger**, opened in 1960 at Biot. Built originally by Nadia Léger, it has recently been greatly extended, doubling its area to over 20,000 sq ft (2000 sq.m), so that all the works in the collection can now be exhibited. Just before his death in 1955, Léger completed the designs for a mosaic fresco intended for Hanover Stadium. It was made up and now covers the 1300 ft (400m) long southern front of the museum, this fulfilling Léger's intention to *generate the maximum power and even*

violence on the walls. The new buildings are also decorated with large frescoes from designs by the artist. We can follow Léger's progress from his first drawings in 1904 through to *Birds on a Yellow Background*, a canvas on which the artist was working a few days before his death. The collection includes large paintings like *Woman in Blue* (strongly influenced by analytical Cubism), *Contrasting Forms, Mona Lisa with Keys* (1930) which is a sort of painted manifesto (a human being, a bunch of keys and a tin of sardines casually placed around) and finally a series from the 1940s and 1950s on popular themes – *Cyclists, Leisure,* and *Construction Workers.*

Adrien Maeght's dream of a "living museum of contemporary art" became a reality in 1964 with the building of the **Fondation Maeght** at Saint-Paul-de-Vence. The architecture of the museum (by José-Luis Sert from an idea by Aimé Maeght) is quite plain, with beautiful, simple lines. Concrete and pink Roman brick combine in a harmonious unity of materials, their colors glowing between the umbrella-pines which catch the sunlight and dapple the building with it.The distinction between interior and exterior disappears and the two seem to merge into each other. The works housed within are enhanced by their superb setting. The garden is a unified continuation of the building, with luxuriant vegetation, interior and exterior landscaping, fountains, pools and even a maze decorated with ceramics by Miró. Many artists contributed to the decoration, with mosaics by Chagall, Tal Coat and Ubac as well as Miró, a stained-glass window by Braque and a set of sculptures by Giacometti. The Foundation has a large collection of 20th-century paintings, sculptures, drawings and prints.Nice is a city of museums par excellence and admission to all of them is completely free.

The **Musée des Beaux-Arts** is housed in an old Genoese-style villa and contains

214

works from the 17th century to the Impressionists. Among the most interesting exhibits are works by Jules Chéret, the inventor of the modern poster who died in Nice in 1932, some Orientalist paintings, an important collection of sculptures by Carpeaux and paintings by artists who worked on the Côte d'Azur, from Signac to Vallotton. The bizarre world of the Nice symbolist Gustav-Adolf Mossa is displayed in the Galeries Ponchettes on the sea front.

The **Musée Marc Chagall**, in a park planted with holm oaks, olives and cypress, has many of the artists's large paintings, mosaics, sculptures, tapestries and stained-glass windows, all works on Biblical themes.

In the very heart of the city and totally pretentious and inappropriate in design is the new **Musée d'Art Moderne et d'Art Contemporain**. Virtually all the contemporary French and American artists of the avant-garde movement since the 1960s are represented here, though it must be said that the minor works of some of our leading artists do not perhaps merit inclusion. However, it is interesting to trace all the main influences: New Realists, Fluxus, the *Supports/Surfaces* Group, Group 70 and Free Representation, together with American movements like Pop Art, abstracts from the 1960s, minimalist art and graffiti. Works by Klein, Arman, Ben Raysse, Viallat, Pagès and others are a reminder of the importance of Nice in revolutionary artistic movements. The audiovisual section of the museum plays an important part in detailing the progress of modern art and is of great benefit to students.

The **Musée Matisse**, sited in a superb location among olive groves, Roman ruins and the garden of a Franciscan monastary, is of prime importance for modern art in the city of Nice. It contains sculptures by Matisse, canvasses painted in Nice, gouache cut-outs from the 1950s, sketches, drawings and engravings. The museum has been reopened in 1992 following considerable and much needed refurbishment.

BELL-TOWERS AND FOUNTAINS

Visitors from the north are struck by a number of recurring sensations and images of Provence. First, of course, is the ever-present sun in a sky of azure blue and fierce winds like the mistral and the *tramontana* which blow in summer and winter alike, first sultry and hot, then icy-cold. Then there are the many fountains in small squares lined with plane trees, and lastly the bell-towers rising up to the heavens.

Bell-towers

In days gone by, before modern transport and hi-tech communications shortened the distances between towns and neighboring villages, the communities living in remote villages of Provence were very close-knit and self-sufficient and the fountain, the church and the bell-tower formed the heart of the village.

The bell-tower summoned the faithful to mass and rang for weddings, funerals and festivals. As the church and bell-tower were the spiritual center of the village, so the fountain formed its social heart. These days everything has changed and village life is less isolated. However, in many a Provençal village the bell-tower and the fountain are still maintained with great pride.

Bell-towers are found on most churches in the region. Their architecture is typically Provençal and they all look quite similar whatever might be the style of the church, with spires, sometimes of wrought iron, crowning square towers. Whether plain or highly decorative, they are the simplest solution to a difficult structural problem. The winds in Provence can be so strong (the mistral can blow at speeds of 125 mph/200 kph) that the stone spires of traditional bell-towers

Above: A detail of the truly splendid monumental Fontaine de la Rotonde at Aix-en-Provence.

216

would be blown down. Thus climatic conditions shaped the Provençal church architecture for centuries.

So the artistic glories of Provence are not just at ground level: Wherever you are, just look up and you will see the interlaced tip of a campanile, even in the very poorest village. Although their detail is as varied as man's imagination itself, their geometrical forms all follow a completely uniform and similar pattern.

The photographer Etienne Sved devoted an entire volume to these towers and divided them into various types: He referred to them according to shape as bulbous, campanular, cosmological, pyramidal and spheroid.

Although they can be seen everywhere, the best areas for viewing bell-towers are around Aix (Bouches-du-Rhône), in the villages below Mont Ventoux (Vaucluse), between Manosque and Sisteron (Haute-Provence), between Brignoles and Salernes (Haut-Var) and in the hills behind Nice (Alpes-Maritimes).

Village Fountains

The fountains in the heart of the village were until quite recently a lifegiving source for human and beast alike. It was also the center of the village's social life, to the accompaniment of the continuous sound of splashing water, because the women had to keep coming to fetch water for cooking and drinking. All the local gossip and useful information was exchanged here.

Village fountains are simple with little or no decoration. They are close to the houses and have a basin or drinking-trough into which the water is pumped so that it can never be polluted, as can be seen, for example, at the Bonne Fontaine at Forcalquier.

The water can be drained out by removing a plug, often just an upside-down tile. The overflow from the first basin fills another basin below where the women used to come and wash their clothes.

In some villages, the women still do the washing in the fountain, more for nostalgic reasons than from any necessity. Their wash-day or *bugade* was traditionally once a week. The dirty washing was piled in a wicker or wooden *tinéu* (basket) and covered with wood ash, soap and eggshells. Hot water was then poured on top and the washing was left overnight. The potash in the ash absorbed the dirt and the washing came out beautifully clean. The water was then used to fertilize the garden so that nothing was wasted!

Various types of decoration and roofing then began to be built around the fountain, primarily with the intention of concealing the activities of the washer-women from the curious gaze of visitors and walkers.

There are various types of fountain which can be classified as rustic, including roadside fountains away from villages, used for livestock and for big washes twice a year, "love nest" fountains tucked away in the shade with mossy roofs, and fountains with domed roofs facing south so as to be accessible in winter when the freezing winds blew cold and water sources turned to ice.

Ornamental Fountains

Ornamental fountains in city squares were not built for purely ornamental reasons, but were intended to provide water for city centers and suburbs which had no independent pipe-fed water supply of their own.

Their basins are round, oval or rectangular and their pedestals can be simple or richly decorated with reliefs and statues. As in the villages, the fountain used to be the place to meet in the city for a friendly chat, a gossip to exchange news or, more often than not, an assignation between young lovers.

Over the years its purpose changed, however, with prestige becoming more important than utility and civic pride demanding the building of ever more richly ornamented fountains. The Golden Age of the ornamental fountain lasted from the middle of the last century right through until the end of the First World War in 1918.

Because the superstructure of a fountain is so clearly visible, architects and craftsmen gave their imagination full rein in their designs. The taps were carved to represent the heads of birds, angels, dogs etc. Fountains with deep, wide basins which use vast quantities of water, a concept previously unheard-of in Provence, are unique to areas that were being built at the end of the 19th century, when the newly rich bourgeoisie saw them as a way of leaving their own personal mark on posterity.

Above: Wall fountain at Grasse. Right: The château and park of Le Tholonet near Aix-en-Provence.

With the advent of piped water supplies some of these ceased to fulfill their original function of providing water from the ground and became mere ornamental fountains in parks or squares. Water was no longer a necessity, just an ornamental luxury to improve a square.

The most recent decline in the fortune of the fountains is, happily, still a rarity – some of them have been converted into flower beds. These are fountains in name only and without their silver, splashing torrent they look more like tombstones than lifegiving springs.

Another type of ornamental fountain – quite different from those in the squares – is the wall fountain. These were built against a wall, often facing south, when there was little space available. They are quite simple, with two or three water taps, but they usually look very stylish and add great elegance to street or little square in which they are situated

The wall fountains were originally used to water livestock and horses on their way through the city, but in common with all the other fountains, these days their water is given to the plane trees and the gardens nearby.

In Aix-en-Provence you can see evidence of the crucial role played by water in the development of the city. It has many fountains, particularly in the Cours Mirabeau, which are fed by hot springs. Most of the fountains date back to the 18th century, but two notable exceptions are the **Fontaine des Quatre-Dauphins** in the Mazarin district which dates from 1667 and the fountain in the **Place d'Albertas**, which is a reconstruction built in 1912.

The **Fontaine Nostradamus** in Saint-Rémy-de-Provence is a fine 19th-century wall fountain. In Séguret, near the Dentelles de Montmirail, the charming 17th-century **Fontaine des Mascarons** is one of the sights of the village and it is often the subject of sketches or photography by visitors. At Eyguières near Salon-de-

Provence, the **Fontaine à la Coquille** is the prettiest of the many fountains.

Last of all in this selective list, the village of Pernes-les-Fontaines probably has the largest number of attractive and famous fountains in Provence. They include the Gigot, the Cormoran and the Porte-Neuve fountains, all of which were built or remodeled in the 18th century, and the **Fontaine Reboul,** which built in the 15th century and remodeled in the 17th century

Water Gardens

During the Renaissance period, garden design was influenced by the Italian style. Grottos, pools and fountains were built in the gardens of châteaux. The most famous garden designer of the 17th century was Le Nôtre, whose gardens featured geometric designs that made constructive and artistic use of water courses, ponds and fountains. In the 18th century "romantic" gardens with artificial lakes and islands, and landscaped parkland in the English style were in vogue. Parks of this type are rare in Provence. However, the best examples of them are quite incomparable and are mainly to be found in the Alpes-Maritimes department.

At Menton, the Serre de la Madone features serene waters which are mirroring an orangery, all aspects beautifully in proportion. At Grasse, the swimming pool at the **Villa de Noailles** is surrounded by waterfalls and statues of tritons and dolphins which provide a constant spray of water water around the gardens.

The **Musée Ephrussi Rothschild** in Saint-Jean-Cap-Ferrat has a Spanish garden containing a grotto supported on pink marble pillars and a dolphin fountain, and also a French garden with huge pools on which lotus flowers and water lilies float.

Near Aix-en-Provence, at Les Pinchinats, the **Jardin de la Gaude** is an 18th-century garden in the classical style with ponds and pools bordered by lawns and mazes of box hedging.

RURAL DWELLINGS AND COUNTRY FURNITURE

Every country has a recognizable character that is strictly its own and which has evolved over centuries of human settlement. Just as farmers have created a special "look" through their management of the landscape, so, too, the buildings that have been constructed add to the unique atmosphere of every region.

The towns of Provence have their own special flavor, although in some places this has been much altered by the introduction of new ideas in architecture and fashion. It is mostly in the rural areas that the character of traditional Provence can still be seen. Here you will find the isolated farmhouses and shepherds' huts that bear witness to the age-old human struggle against the elements, and the

Above: A borie, a traditional Provençal shepherd's dwelling with drystone walls. Right: A barn door with a small dovecote above.

profound peacefulness of the timeless villages.

The Bories

Stone rather than wood or brick is the traditional building material of Provence. The region has many ancient cave dwellings and unique and remarkable drystone structures such as retaining-walls of terraces which are called *restanques*, and huts, known as *bories*.

These are scattered about the countryside between the Etang de Berre and the Montagne de Lure, but they occur in very great numbers around Grasse, Mane and Gordes, where a whole village of these strange dwellings has been renamed the *village noir*, or black village, after the dark-colored stone that was used to build them.

The buildings are of various shapes – pyramids, cones, domes or rectangular – and include barns, cookhouses, stores and workshops, as well as dwellings. With their roofs of flat stones arranged like fish-scales, and hardly tall enough for a man to stand under, these buildings look exactly like prehistoric ruins, and indeed some examples dating from the neolithic period have been found further west, in Languedoc.

However, the ones near Gordes were built between the 15th and 19th centuries. They were generally used as shelters by shepherds and farmworkers at harvest time, or as stores for tools.

Mas and Bastides

Throughout its history Provence has been a frontier area that was subjected to many influences from outside, but surprisingly enough these have scarcely affected its architecture. You can forget about the influence of Gothic or Moorish architecture – the Provençal style, which owes more to the power of the mistral and the sun than to any invader, has been by far the most durable influence.

The only heritage left in the region by the Saracens is the many fortified villages built by the local populace as a defense against them! Attempts have been made to discover traces of Italian influences in Provence, either from Florence or elsewhere, but nothing can be plainer and more simple than the Provençal settlements scattered over the plains and hillsides, or huddled round a bell-tower.

The supreme achievement of Provençal domestic architecture are the *mas* and *bastides*, which can be anything from an isolated dwelling to something like a complete village. Their distinctive features are their low, sloping profile, their walls in the colors of earth and vegetation, pantile roofs and windows that are smaller on the first floor than the ground floor. This is the typical rural dwelling of Provence and the basic design is the same for a small peasant's house and a *mas*, which is a large farm incorporating several buildings, almost a hamlet.

In Provence, the term *cabanon* is used as well as *mas*. This term originated in the 11th century, when it meant a house, sheepfold or barn or could even be used to refer to a whole group of buildings. While the basic plan is the same throughout Provence, there are regional differences which are dictated by climate and culture.

In Arles, the *mas* consists of low buildings, one added to another over the years, often built facing outwards over the surrounding fields. To give better protection from the mistral in the Crau and the Camargue, the *mas* is often built in a square, with the master's house flanked by outbuildings and dwellings used to house seasonal workers. In the Alpilles, the *mas* is built high, both for defense and to give a separate floor each for the animals, the living space and the granary, in that order.

The *mas* was always an incomplete building that was intended for further extension and development and thus mirrored the financial fortunes of its occupier. Its main room was the living room, the place for a convivial evening round the fire and for the meals which punctuated the working day. The other essential element was the *pile*, a stone recess and water store. When construction developed horizontally along the site, with the result of totally blurring the distinction between the owner's house and the ordinary agricultural buildings, the *mas* then became a *bastide*. But a *bastide* is just as difficult to define as a *mas*.

The *bastide* first appeared at the end of the 16th century in the areas around Aix and Marseille. A *bastide* meant an estate, with physical separation between the farm and the farmworkers' quarters. A *bastide* was an isolated dwelling designed for self-defense, as shown by the watch-towers that were built on some of them, which Louis XIV did not permit to be higher than the roof.

Among other architectural features, the *bastide* has a hipped roof, which is rare in Provence, a central door facing south, shutters at the windows and interior fittings which are much more sophisticated than those in a rustic *mas*. Quarry or hexagonal tiles on the floor, separate kitchens, bedrooms upstairs and luxuriously decorated drawing-rooms and dining rooms were the original features of these houses. However, their original purpose was soon forgotten and they become second homes in the countryside for wealthy people from Aix and Marseille to spend the summer months.

The Château de Roussan at Saint-Rémy-de-Provence is a classical 18th-century *bastide*, while the Mas de Brau in Mouriès is an elegant 16th-century Renaissance-style *mas* that has been built onto the existing walls of an oil mill. Both of these houses show great originality but they are both firmly based on the typical Provençal style.

Right: In an abandoned farm in Haute-Provence.

Every *mas* of any size has its pigeon loft, which may be anything from a simple pinnacle to an impressive tower up to 25 ft (8 m) high. These are common in Haute-Provence and the Vaucluse, particularly in Forcalquier, Gordes, Lourmarin, Lurs, Mane, Reillane, Saint-Michel-l'Observatoire, Simiane-la-Rotonde and the Pays de Sault.

The incongruous sight of pigeon-lofts built on top of a pigsty or chapel is explained by the fact that the owner of the *mas* had to pay a special tax if the entire building was used only for rearing birds from floor to roof!

All *mas* also have terraces paved with clay tiles and covered with a thick trellis. These used to be open spaces with flat stone paving where the corn was threshed by the shoes of horses and donkeys or with a roller. The space has now been replaced by the low walls and iron frame supporting the trellis. Up till now many *mas* still have their old wells and water-troughs.

All these country houses, both *mas* and *bastides*, meet local needs and preferences, with many original decorative touches to add individuality to their standard design. The doors and windows are intended to protect the inside of the house from sun and wind and the double wooden shutters protect it from the wind chill of the mistral in winter and the scorching heat of summer.

The living room is the center of attraction in winter for its warm fire and in summer for its shady coolness. The tiled roofs are fixed to the walls by a triple row of overlapping tiles (called Genoese), designed to prevent the wind blowing under the edge of the roof and tearing it away.

Country Furniture

Over the years, the *mas* and *bastides* of Provence have lost their original function and become the highly sought-after country residences of wealthy urban

dwellers, carefully restored by their new owners and now frequently displaying both the rustic and the more luxurious design features of bygone days.

This continuity of tradition is seen most clearly in the furnishings of these houses. The local people have always clung to their traditions, whether they lived in a *mas* or a *bastide*, and the Provençal style of traditional furniture grew up from this.

To the craftsman, every piece of furniture made has always been another opportunity to display his talent and imagination, with a typically exuberant result, full of grace and movement.

The most characteristic pieces are those which were intended to be part of the dowry of a Provençal bride. The dowry would also contain things like the famous *boutis* (embroidered bed-covers with floral motifs), sometimes the bed – called a *litoche* – and beautifully patterned Moustiers pottery, together with basic household items like bread bins, flour bins and sieves.

The one essential dowry item or wedding gift was the wardrobe, which would be richly carved with symbols of love like hearts or flowers, symbols of prosperity like fish, pine cones or sheaves of corn and the symbol of longevity, vine leaves.

The two main centers for furniture were Arles, with a florid, lively style, and Forques, with a plainer, more robust style. The two schools flourished side by side because customers in the more urban areas of Provence liked curves and fancy carvings, while the country people preferred simple shapes and geometric designs. Chests of drawers were only owned by the well-to-do and were displayed in their drawing rooms and bedrooms. Lastly, we should not forget a piece of furniture unique to Provence and another indicator of social standing – the *radassié*. This is a straw-bottomed settle seating between two and five people which always stood in the chimney recess ready for anyone who wanted to have a confidential chat or gossip.

HISTORY OF TOURISM ON THE COTE D'AZUR

Geographically speaking, the Côte d'Azur is the Mediterranean coastline between Hyères and Menton, a region which has always been distinguished by the beauty of its scenery and the mildness of its climate.

In the 16th century, Marguerite de Navarre, the intellegent and progressive sister of François I, decided to spend her winters in Nice, because it was *less severe than anywhere else.* More than a century later, the great military architect, Vauban, was to remark: "The sun that shines on Saint-Paul is the most beautiful in Provence and it is the area which grows the best oranges of every kind; in winter and in summer and even in high winds, they can still be found there – something which happens nowhere else." It has always been a place to dream

Above: Sitting in an open-air café in the busy Cours Saleya in Nice.

about, somewhere beyond the realm of everyday reality. Around 1750, the first few aristocratic families began spending the winter months in the delightful surroundings of the coast at Nice, long before it had been given the name of Côte d'Azur. The word spread, and the arrival in 1764 of the Duke of York, brother of King George III of England, confirmed Nice as a fashionable resort for high society. Writers like the Scottish novelist, Tobias Smollett, and Sulze from Switzerland extolled the scenic charms and healthy climate of Nice to readers all over Europe and thereafter international reputation was assured.

In 1787 no fewer than 115 foreign families spent the winter in Nice. At that time the idea of migrating to another country for part of the year was totally new and you could really say that the tourist industry began here. It is often forgotten that up to this time the seaside had only inspired fear, and even revulsion, but now it became a desirable place to go for healthy air, exercise and relaxation.

The arrival of wealthy foreigners certainly changed the landscape. The seafront at Nice was soon lined with a continuous row of luxurious villas with gardens facing the sea along the Promenade des Anglais, named for the English visitors, who were the first to to lay out the beautiful gardens, which were to bring such color to the future Côte d'Azur, the ideal setting for them.

In 1782 Antoine Thomas wrote from Nice: "Nowhere is there a lovelier sky, nor are there walks with more beautiful views ... Everywhere you find olive trees, myrtle and lemon and orange trees; under your feet there is thyme, rosemary, lavender and sage sown by nature among landscapes of desert and rock." What was most striking for travelers to this area, however, was the unusual blend of cultivated fields and untamed nature, giving the countryside the appearance of a vast and fertile garden.

At the end of the 18th century the people of Nice became interested in the cultivation of tropical plants. This was pioneered by Jean-François Bermond, who designed a garden below the hill of Piol in the north of the city when he returned from the West Indies in 1795, concentrating on American species like sugar-cane, banana-palms, cotton plants and indigo plants.

In 1804 the Empress Josephine sent the Director of Gardens in Nice some Australian species to be "naturalized," mainly eucalyptus, and did so again the following year. In 1820 the Nice naturalist Antoine Nisso introduced some subtropical plants to his estate in the Sainte-Hélène district, and at the same time botanical gardens at Hyères and Toulon started collections of palms, eucalyptus and acacias (the genus which includes all kinds of mimosa), which were then propagated the whole way along the coast. From then on there was intense competition between the French landowners and newcomers who bought property on the coast, as to who could achieve the most successful transplants of tropical species.

In 1836 the English liberal politician Lord Brougham settled in Cannes, launched the small town as a resort and attracted a colony of English people who laid out many gardens. By 1850 nearly 200 families were living there in the winter, even though the town had few facilities and was difficult to reach.

Meanwhile, experiments in exotic horticulture continued at Nice. The Chevalier Hilarion de Cessole managed to grow pineapples in a heated greenhouse and later produced edible fruits from a hybrid date-palm. The Comte de Pierlas imported several species of conifer like cedar, sequoia and araucaria, and the Vicomte de Vigier introduced to the park surrounding his Venetian-style palace near the harbor the *phoenix canariensis*, now the commonest species of palm on the Riviera. At Cap d'Antibes the botanist Gustave Thuret planted an arboretum where, since 1856, 18,000 different plants from subtropical areas the world over have been studied, 2500 varieties of which will grow on the Mediterranean coast.

But while the landscape was step by step enhanced and restructured, political troubles loomed large. After the revolution in 1789, Nice, as an Italian frontier city, became a place of refuge for Provençal nobles and churchmen fleeing the Terror. Like Koblenz in the Rhineland, it was soon a center of counter-revolutionary activity. The French government acted quickly to quell the uprising. On 28 September 1792 a French attack was imminent, and undesirables, emigrés, clergy, officials and the Sardinian army all fled the city along the salt road into Piedmont. There was total panic and confusion, with wild scenes of looting in the torrential rain which fell at the time. The authorities who remained were left defenceless and had no choice but to surrender Nice to the French.

In 1796 the King of Sardinia renounced all his rights to the county of Nice, but following the defeat of Napoleon in 1815 he recovered all his territories and also acquired the Republic of Genoa. This was a terrible blow for the port of Nice, which till then had been a free port with a monopoly on movement of goods to Turin. This traffic was switched to the much larger and more convenient port of Genoa and Nice's free port status ended in 1853. The county of Nice was neglected by the government in Turin, ceased to be the preferred link between the Sardinian States and the Mediterranean and retreated into its own world, remote from the main social and economic developments which in the first half of the 19th century were to transform the whole of Europe. In Turin they were far more interested in the unifi-

cation of Italy. Napoleon III promised military aid to the Piedmontese leader Cavour in exchange for Savoy and the county of Nice, if the people agreed. On 15 and 16 April 1860 the populations of both areas voted to join France.

Tourism began slowly but surely to change the coast, but the real explosion of winter visitors came with the building of the railway in 1864. The English were in the majority, way ahead of the Russians who were overtaken in 1870 by the Americans. These wealthy visitors would arrive in September or October and leave again in April or May. The crowned heads of Europe were among them, most notably Queen Victoria, for whom the architect Biasini built the magnificent Regina Palace near the arena at Cimiez.

The tourist phenomenon also developed at Cannes. Between 1875 and 1900 the town built up its facilities and the winter season took off. Its regattas, horse and cycle races, archery competitions and cavalcades were a huge success and reports in the local newspapers give

Above: Flower market in the Cours Saleya in Nice. Right: The Côte d'Azur continues to inspire artists.

226

details of the dazzling evening receptions that were held. The surrounding hills and the Iles de Lérins were favorite places for walking. Around 1880 several hydrotherapy establishments began to offer climatic treatments. The foreign colony at this time consisted mainly of British people, with some Russians, Italians and Germans, while the French colony grew more slowly. Public works projects were initiated and 450 villas, 45 hotels and 1,449 houses were built during the five years from 1870-75 alone.

The landscape changed completely, due as much to the introduction of exotic flora as to the new buildings, which represented a complete break with Provençal tradition. Building took place in a mixture of eclectic styles and design expressed a preference for the new, the strange and the colossal. A villa at Cannes was meant to be both a status symbol and a haven of peace, so it had to impress and yet be comfortable. There were Moorish villas, English country houses, baronial castles with turrets and parapets, rustic cottages, Roman villas and Alpine chalets.

Although its climate and situation were ideal, Menton had no tourist hotels or infrastructure during this period, but everything changed in 1879 with the arrival of the railway which gave access to visitors from all over Europe. Menton became a fashionable resort with about 50 hotels and *pensions* and more than 200 villas. After that, the French Riviera reigned supreme; all it lacked was a name, and that was acquired in 1887 with the publication of a bestselling book by Stéphen Liégeard entitled *La Côte d'Azur.*

The reputation of the *Côte* was made by artists just as much as by the aristocracy and bourgeoisie of Europe and America. Painters were attracted by the uniquely pure, clear light of the Riviera and helped to spread its reputation, succeeding only in ruining its purity as they did so. Painters, writers, musicians and

actors flocked to the coast, including Monet, Nietzsche, Chéret, Chekhov and Offenbach. Claude Monet led the way when he stayed at Bordighera, across the border in Italy, in 1880. He was dazzled by the quality of the light, struggled to capture the blues in paint and found that the incredible blue of the sky, the purple of the sea, the gray-green olives and the exotic green of the palms were positively dangerous to attempt.

Sure enough, the coast soon became one vast artist's studio to which painters were attracted by the bright sunlight and the images of Paradise. Only the real masters managed to trap the seductive beauty and the dazzling light of this other Eden within the confines of their canvasses. One thinks of Renoir in Cagnes-sur-Mer and Signac in Saint-Tropez.

Alexis Mossa, the Nice painter, established *His Majesty King Carnival I* in 1873, reviving a tradition which had begun in Nice in 1294. In 1876 the first Battle of Flowers took place and the carnival became the highlight of the season.

At Le Cannet Bonnard painted his voluptuous Oriental pictures, in quite dramatic contrast to Picasso, to whom the Provençal sun appeared dark, a sun which "becomes horrifying when it is looked at" as Georges Bataille wrote.

Painters who celebrated the ever-present sea included Chagall, Vallotton and Dufy. Van Dongen and Picabia painted and took part in the society high-life, which also attracted the playwright and film-maker Jean Cocteau and many more. All were well known before they came to expand their perceptions in the light of the Côte d'Azur which they helped to make famous.

The *Belle Epoque* was the age of the casino – flourishing in Nice and rivaling the one in Monaco which had been run by its famous director François Blanc since 1863. They were patronized by celebrated artistes who loved to fool about

Above: Showing off the Harley Davidson at Mougins. Right: Temple of fortune – the casino in Monte Carlo.

and show off. The tone was set by the actress Sarah Bernhardt at Monte Carlo: Scandal is an art, and art that scandalizes is its highest form. Women added a special glitter to the legend of the casinos. The great courtesans of the early 1900s wore their beauty as a badge of success for gamblers, gambled with the men's money, set their own price if they won and seduced the lucky winners. It was also considered good form for princes and the rich and famous to gamble at the casino and prove they could lose gracefully.

The First World War put an end to all this frivolity. The palaces on the Côte d'Azur were converted into makeshift hospitals. Attempts were made to salvage the winter season, but foreigners stayed away. The Russians virtually disappeared after the Revolution and those visitors who did come had less money to spend than before 1914. The Côte d'Azur survived simply by replacing winter with summer. In 1917 all the hotels opened in July and August for the first time.

The ones on the seafront became more and more popular and those up in the hills were converted into apartments. Gradually, the Côte d'Azur took on the appearance we are familiar with today.

The Riviera began to attract a variety of immigrants: aristocrats, artists, businessmen and adventurers; country people from the Alpes-Maritimes hinterland and from Piedmont, and pensioners with enough money to retire to the sun; in the 1950s former colonial settlers from Indochina, in the 1960s refugees from Algeria after independence and more recently Lebanese and Iranians fleeing their countries; not to mention the many holidaymakers who come simply in search of summer sun.

In the 1950s Juan-les-Pins reminded the jazz musician Sydney Bechet of New Orleans with its incredible mixture of multimillionaires and ordinary tourists, princes and hitchhikers, the smell of sun tan lotion and hot dogs and the crowds in the evening filling the streets and dancing to juke-boxes. Bechet was so besotted with Juan-les-Pins that he decided to get married there in 1951, amid wild celebrations. Dixieland jazz bands played in the streets with the whole town swaying in time to the music, dressed in shorts and bikinis. So attached was Bechet to the place that he came back every summer. The whole coast was bitten by the bug, began to swing and the age of the jazz festivals was born.

At the height of the Cold War, the American Sixth Fleet was stationed in the Mediterranean and for two weeks every two months shiploads of sailors hungry for women and be-bop invaded the resorts along the coast from Villefranche to Cannes. The film industry was naturally lured by this fantastic backdrop and by 1930 Nice had six studios working at full capacity. The most famous studio, the Victorine, was set up with the latest equipment in 1925 and still exists. About 30 films were made there from 1940 to

1944, including a number of undisputed masterpieces of the French cinema like Marcel Carné's *Les Visiteurs du Soir* and *Les Enfants du Paradis*.

Stars made the name of the Côte d'Azur – at the Cannes Film Festival, at showpiece events or simply at home for a few months every year. Grace Kelly married Prince Rainier of Monaco, houses were bought by famous novelists, Colette at Saint-Tropez and Blaise Cendrars and Graham Greene at Villefranche. Rita Hayworth married Ali Khan and in the same year, 1949, Martine Carol married Steve Crane. Poet and songwriter Jacques Prévert was a witness at the wedding of Yves Montand to Simone Signoret. Van Dongen painted the beautiful people, Cocteau painted the chapel at Villefranche and Matisse the one in Vence, while Picabia cut a dash in Antibes and Douglas Fairbanks in Monte Carlo. The Côte d'Azur is still the colorful living legend it always was, like a dream which sometimes ends in disillusionment.

TRADITIONS OF PROVENCE

Provence, the Comtat Venaisson and the county of Nice have always maintained a strong tradition of local festivals. This is in part due to the efforts of the Félibrige society, started by the local writer Frédéric Mistral at the beginning of the century, with the aim of preserving Provençal traditions for posterity, notably through the creation of folklore clubs which would keep alive all the costumes, dances and songs in the Provençal language.

Today's Félibrige groups give concerts on the *tambourin*, the traditional musical instrument of Lower Provence. The *tambourin* is rather like a combination of a one-handed flute called a *galoubet* and a long drum. In the 18th and 19th centuries the *tambourin*, sometimes accompanied by a fiddle, was the instrument played for dancing at weddings and saints' day festivals. Although it was later replaced for dancing by the accordeon, the *tambourin* continued to be an accompaniment to processions.

Among the most important of the festivals during the year are the two **annual gypsy pilgrimages** on 24 and 25 May and again on the penultimate Sunday in October, when gypsies from all round the world flock to Les-Saintes-Maries-de-la-Mer to honor their patron saint, St. Sarah, and all the other "Saints of Provence" who according to legend landed on this coast after the death of Christ. Their relics are brought down from the church and among huge crowds their statues are borne in a long procession to the sea where they are used in a ceremonial blessing.

Unfortunately, many of the traditional old Provençal customs which were once common are only kept up in a few places, like the **bravade**, where a group of young

Right: Mass outside Notre-Dame during the Fête des Gardians in Arles.

men with weapons accompany processions and occasionally fire off salvoes and engage in simulated combat.

Bravades were a normal part of festive ritual in 18th century Provence, especially the ceremonials associated with welcoming important visitors to the town. They have only survived to the present day in a few places like Saint-Tropez, Fréjus, Castellane, Gréoux and Soleilhas, usually as part of a saint's day ceremony, in association with local legends.

Some festivals have retained their unique features, however, like the **Danse des Tripettes** at the Feast of Saint-Marcel in Barjols (16/17 January) when an energetic dance takes place in the church and every four years an ox is paraded through the streets to be blessed by the local priest and is then slaughtered, cooked and eaten by the participants.

Calendar of Religious Festivals

The calendar of Provençal traditions centers mainly around two dates which correspond approximately to the times of the winter and summer solstice – the Feast of St. John (24 June) and, not surprisingly, Christmas.

Other feast-days are spaced through the year. Thus **Candlemas** on 2 February forms a bridge between the Christmas season, which in Provence lasts forty days, and Easter, preceded by Lent. During the week of Candlemas thousands of the faithful make their way to the abbey of Saint-Victor in Marseilles.

The **Messe de l'Aube** (Dawn Mass) celebrated by the archbishop at 6 am on 2 February is preceded by the blessing of the fire in the Early Christian crypt and a procession of the Black Madonna in the church above. Green candles are lit by the congregation, and left burning in the church or taken home.

In Marseilles, Candlemas is the time for *navettes*. These are special biscuits which are decorated with cuts along their

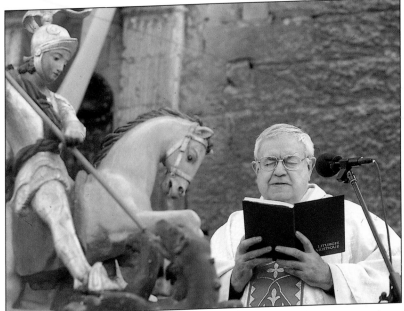

length. They can be bought at bakers and also at the *Four des Navettes* near the Basilica where they have been produced since 1781.

The **Carnival** in Nice is one of the highlights of the Riviera year. It begins traditionally during the third week-end before Shrove Tuesday and, after romantic masked balls and many religious and ceremonial processions, ends with the **Battle of Flowers** on the Promenade des Anglais.

Carnival is the time for letting your hair down before starting the rigorous privations of Lent (*Carême* in French). In some places around Nice the tradition is still maintained, of carrying a straw dummy, called a *caramentrant* , in procession and then burning it on Ash Wednesday in a ceremonial *brûlement*. At Aix-en-Provence, Carnival takes the more modest form of a *corso* or procession of waggons, which dates from the 19th century. In some small towns and suburbs there have been attempts to revive the old carnival traditions, drawing on written sources or based on models from neighbouring Languedoc, where the old folk-festivals have been better preserved.

On **Palm Sunday**, olive branches are blessed in all the churches. Children should traditionally carry *branches* that are made of wire covered with crepe paper and ribbons and hung with sweets and gifts from their godparents, but this charming tradition is now quite rare. In Nice the congregations have palms that have been woven to form the shape of a cross, in place of the traditional olive branches. During **Holy Week**, an altar of repose covered with floral decorations is set up and it has long been the custom of many of the devout elderly members of the congregation to kiss the stigmata on the statue of Christ in the center of this altar. At **Easter**, some confectioners still make gorgeous creations of chocolate and nougatine. In the old days these used to be raffled.

Every spring sees the return of **processions** through the countryside: up to

the Lady chapels on 25 March (the Annunciation), a procession of the winegrowers of the lower Durance valley on the feast of Saint Mark, a pilgrimage to the chapels of the Holy Cross on 3 May and a procession of farmers on Rogation Days, before Ascension, when the clergy bless the soil so that the next harvest will be plentiful and the farmers will prosper.

In Marseilles, the **Feast of the Sacred-Heart** is marked by the "Mass of the Vow," in memory of the time when the city was placed under the protection of the Sacred Heart during the great plague of 1720 which killed thousands of people and left many Provençal towns and villages deserted.

It is celebrated by the archbishop in the presence of the city council and the President of the Chamber of Commerce, who passes the archbishop the "three-pound candle" which the aldermen of 1720

vowed to offer up every year in thanks for their deliverance.

For one day, or occasionally the whole week, at **Whitsun**, pâtisseries sell the *colombier*, a confection containing a small charm worked in the shape of a dove. They say that *whoever gets the dove, will this year find their love*. At Tarascon, Whitsun is the time for the **Fêtes de la Tarasque**, a fabled dragon tamed by St. Martha, according to the legend. In one procession a wooden effigy of the dragon covered with cloth is carried through the streets. In former times this Pentecostal procession was a brutal affair, with the furious Tarasque knocking people down with its tail. This was intended to symbolize paganism.

On the **Feast of St. Martha** (29 July) Christian peace was symbolized instead, with a tame dragon held on a leash by a girl representing the saint.

Only the first of the two processions survives, stripped of its violent episodes and combined with the more recent feast of the "Return of Tartarin," the braggart

Above: Members of a tambourin group called "Lou Velout d'Arles."

hunter hero of a popular novel by Alphonse Daudet.

As already mentioned, the feast of St. John on 24 June each year is an important one in Provence. In many towns, there is a special ceremony when the mayor lights a bonfire and the festivities last well into the night. The **St. John's Fair** is held in the Cours Belsunce in Marseilles between 24 June and the end of July and the wares include bunches of garlic and *tarraiettes* (a diminutive form of *terraio*, a clay vessel), which are reproductions in miniature of pots used in former times, intended as toys for little girls. Most of them are made at Aubagne and Vallauris.

The **cavalcade of Saint-Eloi** is the feast of the *ménagers* or well-to-do farmers who were traditionally the only ones to own their own teams of horses. Saint-Eloi was the patron saint of blacksmiths and, by extension, of the *ménagers*. The farmers in the département of Bouches-du-Rhône celebrate every year with a procession on 25 June (and the weeks following). In the north-west of the département, each village runs its *carreto ramado*, a cart decorated with branches to which a line of horses and mules is harnessed. In the south-east, from the outskirts of Marseille to Gémenos, each owner decks out his own team and the *gaillardet* (bridle of honor) is put up for auction. The only "Saint-Eloi" celebrations to survive in eastern Provence are those organized by riding-clubs.

Apart from the Annunciation, the **Feasts of the Assumption** (15 August) and the **Birth of the Virgin** (8 September) are also celebrated at many sanctuaries in Provence dedicated to the Virgin Mary, especially those that have been built on a hill. All these chapels are the destination of the *roumavage* or *romeirage*, when the people of the villages go in pilgrimage to hear mass and the fruits of the earth are blessed. They bring food with them to eat and do not return until the evening.

All Saints and **All Souls** (1 and 2 November) is the time to visit the cemetery, when the graves have been cleaned and decorated and everything is made tidy and repaired – at considerable expense.

Christmas in Provence

On 4 December the planting of "St. Barbara's corn" marks the beginning of **Advent**. Seeds of corn, lentils and sometimes cress are germinated on wet cotton wool in saucers and the little plant shoots then decorate the table and the crib.

On the last Sunday in November the **Foire aux Santons** is opened in the Allées de Meilhan in Marseilles by the mayor preceded by *tambourin* players.

Christmas time is the most important of the festivals in Provence. A few days before Christmas Eve every house and church makes up its **crib** portraying the Nativity – a large confection of crumpled paper, cardboard houses and painted clay figurines called *santons* (Provençal for little saints). Jean-Louis Lagnel from Marseilles (1764-1822) appears to have had the splendid idea at the end of the 18th century of portraying the figures in the crib in the form of santons and also of adding many secular figures who are based on the inhabitants and tradesmen of the old parts of Marseilles. Thérèse Neveu (1866-1946), a potter from Aubagne, began firing the figurines in her kiln about seventy years ago. A priest named César Sumien (1858-1943) created the dressed *santon*, a small figure with fabric clothing which now has an important part to play.

On Christmas Eve everyone – young and old – stays up late to go to Midnight Mass. The long evening begins with the **Gros-Souper**, a plain but substantial meal, usually of fish and vegetables, then until it is time to go to Mass, everyone eats a wide variety of desserts – thirteen of them in all to symbolize Christ and the Twelve Apostles. They are accompanied

by a fortified wine, which is only sold at Christmas time. At this time also, bakers make the traditional *pompe*, a cake made with oil or butter. In many places, *tambourin* players and folk-singers take part in the Midnight Mass. Elsewhere, it is the time to sing the many *Noëls* or carols in the Provençal dialect that were composed between the 17th and 19th centuries. The clergy arrive in procession at midnight and carry the baby Jesus to the crib. In the churches around Les Baux and at Allauch near Marseilles, shepherds make an offering of a new-born lamb in a ceremony called the **pastrage**. Fishermen and fishmongers make a similar **offering of fish** at the Augustinian church in the port at Marseilles. On Christmas morning the children find their presents in their shoes beside the crib.

The two weeks around Christmas is the time for the **pastorales**, plays which combine religious and secular themes and portray the various figures in a Provençal town where the birth of Christ is supposed to take place. These *pastorales* were first performed in the 18th century. In 1842 Antoine Maurel, a mirror-cutter from Marseille, wrote the best-known version which is most frequently performed today.

On 6 January, the **Feast of Epiphany**, the *santons* of the Three Wise Men are added to the crib. Between Epiphany and Candlemas, pastry-cooks bake the "kings' crown," a pastry biscuit covered with candied fruits, and everyone "draws the kings" at parties at home and elsewhere. The crown contains a bean and a charm (often a pottery *santon*) and those who find them are king and queen for the day.

Provençal Sports

Among the various traditional sports which the Provençaux like to play, one of the most popular is the game of **boules**.

Above: Pétanque is a very popular game everywhere. Right: A sport for the daring – bullfighting.

Like the Italian *boccia*, the Provençal game seems to be derived from skittles and first began in the 18th century in the street cafés round Marseilles. The *Cercle de Boulemanes* (the Boules Enthusiasts Club) was founded in 1828, also in Marseilles, and this organization gradually defined the rules of the game known as *la longue*. *Pétanque*, which is played *à pié tanca* (with the feet still), first appeared at La Ciotat at the beginning of this century. Its advantage is that it can be played on smaller pitches than *la longue* and it has now become very popular throughout Provence.

Water jousting tournaments, called *joutes*, are organized by fishermen in the coastal ports. Two rival teams crew their own boats which are decorated in distinctive colors (blue or red) and which have a *tintaino* (something which "wobbles") in the stern – a narrow overhanging platform on which the *jouteur* stands. He is protected by a wooden shield *(targo)* and also holds a wooden lance nearly 9 ft (2.70m) long in one hand and a piece of wood in the other. When the two boats pass, the *jouteurs* try to knock each other's shields with their lances and push their opponent into the water. The winner must hold on to his piece of wood and remain on his *tintaino* in order to qualify. The one who beats all his opponents is the tournament winner. It is always an occasion of much laughter and fun.

Bull fights are only held now in the Lower Rhône area. Unlike the Spanish *corrida* where the bull is nearly always killed, in a Provençal bullfight *(course provençale)* the so-called *razeteur* only has to remove a rosette from between the bull's horns and the locally-reared animal is allowed to live. Some arenas in the distri ct put on Spanish-style bullfights.

Games, festivals and traditional crafts are an important part of the daily life of Provence, both for tourists and the locals themselves. They make a significant contribution to the sense of identity of the people of Provence, who set great store by maintaining them in their pure form, not just as a tourist attraction.

FOOD AND DRINK

Provençal Cooking

The rich reserves of natural produce have enhanced the quality and variety of Provençal cooking, which boasts no less than 420 different traditional dishes. Herbs and spices are available in abundance and play an enormously important role in Provençal recipes.

Provençal cuisine is based to a great extent on the products of the local area, using the natural ingredients from its balmy hills and warm Mediterranean shores – fresh vegetables, 20 kinds of herb, delicious olive oil, 16 species of shell-fish, 46 species of fish only caught off this coast, and the grapes of Châteauneuf-du-Pape, which produce such excellent vintages.

The Provençal cook tries above all to stay close to nature, but he likes to embel-

Above: A girl selling crêpes. Right: Seafood is an important part of Provençal cooking.

lish it a little with condiments whose flavors accompany and enhance every dish. They are just as vital to the Provençal cook as the rest of the ingredients.

The cuisine of Provence, with its blends of anchovy, garlic, herbs and spices, olive oil and saffron, bears no resemblance to that of the rest of France or even of Italy. It may have originated with the Phocaeans who landed on the coast of Provence around 600 B.C., but it has none the less become the archetypal Mediterranean cuisine, having been refined and experimented upon over the last two thousand years.

An essential element of Provençal cooking and the secret of its style is **olive oil** – pure, aromatic and fruity. Another necessity is **garlic**, which dates back to the ancient civilizations of the Mediterranean. But it must be used sparingly so that its flavor does not overpower and conceal the taste of the other ingredients, but intensifies and reinforces them. Provençal garlic, which is less strong than that grown in other regions, is a vital element in the famous olive oil mayonnaise called **aïoli** which is one of the most important local specialties.

Far more herbs and spices are used than just the ones commonly known in international cuisine as the **Herbes de Provence**. In addition to thyme, sage, savory, rosemary, marjoram, hyssop, fennel, tarragon and basil, there are saffron, mint, bay, cloves, garlic, onion, juniper and capers. Using all these ingredients in the right proportions is an art in itself: It requires both experience and intuition to combine and blend the contrasting flavours, knowing exactly what each one can contribute to the whole. Herbs are used in a very different way to spices, since they should do no more than enhance the flavours of a dish with their own subtle aroma.

Some of the aromatic local dishes are very well known, such as the soups made with fish or vegetables. The most famous

of these is **bouillabaisse**, which is rather like a thick fish soup or stew. It should contain at least three kinds of fish: scorpion-fish, gurnard and conger eel. Many others are usually added, together with shellfish. Marcel Pagnol celebrated *bouillabaisse* in his novel *Fanny* as follows: "Please be good enough to tell her not to forget my bouillabaisse every day, nor my shellfish. My normal diet is shellfish in the morning, bouillabaisse at lunchtime and aïoli in the evening. Don't forget, Mademoiselle Fanny!". Fish and seafood generally are very important parts of the diet in this region of France.

Anchovies, especially from Martigues, are often found in sauces and side-dishes. They appear in many different forms like t*apenade*, *pissala* and *anchoïade* (in this dish anchovies are sweated in olive oil with garlic, then spread on slices of bread and briefly grilled before serving).

Other popular types of seafood are mussels, clams, sea urchins, crabs and squid, all to be found around the Old Port in Marseilles. Apart from many small

varieties added to soups, the most common fish are sardines (cooked *à l'antiboise*, stuffed with spinach), bream, bass, mullet, angler fish and cod.

As far as meat is concerned, lamb from the Crau, Sisteron and the Préalpes is particularly good. Leg of lamb is roasted with garlic, and *noisettes* served with a sauce, while mutton stew is a traditional dish in Avignon and will feature on most restaurant menus.

Vegetables are available in abundance. The Vaucluse, called "the garden of France", has potatoes, cabbage, green beans, celery, turnips, carrots, marrows, leeks, radishes, Jerusalem artichokes (which are vital to the success of a good *aïoli*), tomatoes, peppers, aubergines, artichokes, fresh herbs, asparagus from Villelaure and garlic, with the Garlic Fair held in the streets of Marseilles. Chinese leaves and spinach are very popular in Nice, where they are often used to stuff ravioli and other pasta.

The purple artichokes of Provence can be eaten raw with *vinaigrette* before their

feathery heads form. Tomatoes, peppers and courgettes are not cooked in traditional Provençal cuisine, they are merely "sweated" with herbs and olive oil. In this way you retain the exquisite flavor that has developed from weeks of ripening in the warm sun. Last but not least are the wild mushrooms and truffles, which are gathered at Apt, Carpentras, Riz and Valréas.

Turning to **desserts**, fruits ripen beautifully in this land of sunshine and plenty and the peaches, apricots, cherries, melons and almonds are particularly good. The most popular fruit of all is the green or Marseilles fig, which is small, juicy and very sweet.

Some of the region's specialties are candied melons from Avignon, *calissons* (ground-almond sweets) from Aix, *berlingots* (striped sweets) from Carpentras,

black and white nougat from Sault and *croquets* (almond biscuits) from Allauch.

Wine

In ancient times, the Rhône valley was the route along which the Mediterranean civilization that flourished long before the Christian era spread inland to Gaul. The Phocaeans, who founded Massalia, probably introduced to the area a vine of levantine origin called the *Shyra*, or *Syrah* and thus originated the vineyards of the **Côtes-du-Rhône**.

The leading wine of this region, *Châteauneuf-du-Pape*, is a full, rich red with a high alcoholic content and a perfumed, raspberry bouquet.

Grown over an area of 3,700 acres (1,500 hectares), this great wine is unrivaled as an accompaniment to the aromatic cuisine of Provence. Also very popular are the *Gigondas* and their neighbors from the Gard, *Tavel* (a favorite with Louis XVI) and *Lirac,* both *rosé* wines, a delicate pink color.

Above: The famous Herbes de Provence.
Right: The brasserie Les Deux Garçons at Aix-en-Provence.

Turning to the wines of the **Coteaux d'Aix**, the whites are dry and scented, the *rosés* soft and fruity and the reds rich and full-bodied. A few miles from Aix is the **Palette** district, which has produced excellent wines since the age of good King René, in the 15th century. The most famous vintage wine of the area is *Château-Simone*. Matured naturally in underground cellars dug long ago by Carmelite monks, it is a wine with a superb flavor.

On the subject of the wines of **Cassis,** the writer Mistral-Calendal said: "Our wine is so famous that Marseilles asked us to send some so that it could be presented to the King. Oh, if you would just taste it! It glows like a clear diamond. It captures the scent of rosemary, heather and myrtle in the glass." The vineyard covers an area of 500 acres (200 hectares). It produces wonderful white wines which are the perfect accompaniment to seafood and *bouillabaisse*. The *rosés* and reds are at their best after a few years in the barrel and are served with grills, roasts and game.

The wines of **Bandol** are named after the small port that lies between Toulon and Marseilles. Although they are produced from grapes grown on the nearby hills, they used to be taken to Bandol for shipment. The whites are dry with a high alcohol content, the reds often have an amber tinge and the *rosés* have a distinctive flavor all of their own.

Côtes-de-Provence wines have been produced at least since the time of the Gauls and became widely known in the medieval and Renaissance period, when they were always served at the king's table. Today's wine-growers aim to maintain their reputation. The wines are matured for several years before being sold and are excellent with any Provençal dish. There are whites of the palest straw color, glowing reds and rosés with a hint of gold. They are exported far and wide.

The wines produced in the former county of Nice should definitely not be forgotten either. The most famous of the *vins niçois* is the pale golden, velvety and sparkling *Vin de Bellet*.

239

Nelles Maps ...the maps that get you going.

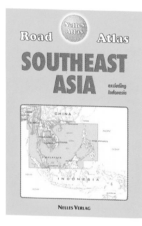

- Afghanistan
- Australia
- Bangkok
- Burma
- Caribbean Islands 1 / Bermuda, Bahamas, Greater Antilles
- Caribbean Islands 2 / Lesser Antilles
- China 1 / North-Eastern China
- China 2 / Northern China
- China 3 / Central China
- China 4 / Southern China
- Crete
- Egypt
- Hawaiian Islands
- Hawaiian Islands 1 / Kauai
- Hawaiian Islands 2 / Honolulu, Oahu

Nelles Maps

- Hawaiian Islands 3 / Maui, Molokai, Lanai
- Hawaiian Islands 4 / Hawaii
- Himalaya
- Hong Kong
- Indian Subcontinent
- India 1 / Northern India
- India 2 / Western India
- India 3 / Eastern India
- India 4 / Southern India
- India 5 / North-Eastern India
- Indonesia
- Indonesia 1 / Sumatra
- Indonesia 2 / Java + Nusa Tenggara
- Indonesia 3 / Bali
- Indonesia 4 / Kalimantan
- Indonesia 5 / Java + Bali
- Indonesia 6 / Sulawesi

- Indonesia 7 / Irian Jaya + Maluku
- Jakarta
- Japan
- Kenya
- Korea
- Malaysia
- West Malaysia
- Manila
- Mexico
- Nepal
- New Zealand
- Pakistan
- Philippines
- Singapore
- South East Asia
- Sri Lanka
- Taiwan
- Thailand
- Vietnam, Laos Cambodia

GUIDELINES

Preparation 242
   Entry Requirement 242
   Climate 242
   Currency and Exchange 242
   Health 243

Traveling to Provence 243
   By Plane 243
   By Train 243
   By Road 244
   By Sea 244

Traveling in Provence 244
   By Bus 244
   By Rail 245

Practical Tips 245
   Accommodation 245
   Consulates in France 246
   Driving 246
   Electricity 247
   Emergencies and Problems 247
   Festivals and Holidays 247
   Forest Fires 248
   Maps 248
   Media 248
   Postal Services 249
   Restaurants 249
   Shopping 249
   Telephone Services 250
   Tipping 250
   Time Differences 250
   Tourist Information 250

Authors 251
Photographers 251
Index 252

PREPARATION
Entry Requirements

All nationals need a valid passport and most also require a visa to enter France. Exceptions for visa obligations are citizens of the European Community (EC), Andorra, Monaco, Switzerland, United States and Canada. Three types of visas are currently issued:
- a transit visa, valid for three days;
- a short stay visa, valid for 90 days from date of issue, valid for multiple entries;
- the more popular multiple-stay *visa de circulation*, allowing multiple stays of 90 days over three years with a maximum of 180 days in any one-year period.

After a 3-month period EC nationals are officially supposed to apply for a *carte de séjour*. However, since EC passports are rarely stamped, it will only be in a working situation that this would be enforced. Applications are made to the *Prefecture* within the département of residence.

Monaco, an independent principality, has identical visa requirements to France, with no border controls.

Climate

This is characteristically Mediterranean with short winters and long, hot, dry summers. The day-time temperatures along the Côte d'Azur and in Central Provence range from an average of 12° C in January to 28°C in August, with the Rhône Valley only slightly cooler. Sea temperatures range from 17°C in May to 25°C in August along the Côte d'Azur and two degrees less between the Camargue and Toulon.

The coast and plains receive from 2,200 to over 3,000 sunshine hours a year, spread over 300 days. Sunbathing poses no problems from February through October. Winds are predominantly from the north to north-west, with the mistral sending violent gusts down the Rhône valley, occasionally as far east as Toulon, often for days at a time, particularly in winter.

Inland Provence can experience snow from early December to early April, but changing weather patterns have led to virtually snowless winters recently, except on the higher peaks, with desertification predicted by some for the south of France over the next century.

Weather forecasts may be obtained for the following regions 24 hours a day:
- All France: 36 650 101 or 36 650 909
- Coastal waters and the Mediterranean: 36 650 808
- Mountains (Alpes du Sud): 36 650 404 or by Minitel - 3615 or 3616 code MET.

Currency and Exchange

Banking hours can be unpredictable, but generally they are 8 or 9 a.m. to 4 or 5 p.m., with or without a lunch break around 12 until 2. Some branches open Saturday and close Monday.

Bureaux de Change operate a daily service at the international airports from 6.00 to 23.00 and in railway stations in the major cities at slightly reduced hours.

Rates of exchange and commission can vary from bank to bank, even more so with the Bureau du Change. BNP (*Banque National de Paris*) and *Credit Lyonnais* usually take the least commission and offer the best rates.

Travelers' cheques remain one of the safest ways of carrying money. An alternative are Eurocheques for those with European bank accounts or International Giro Cheques, which provide a cash service in any Post Office.

Credit cards (*Carte Bancaire*), particularly Visa, known as *Carte Bleue* in France, where it is almost universal, are probably the safest and most efficient means of settling shop, hotel and restaurant bills or for obtaining cash directly from a money machine. Access, Mastercard and American Express are accepted, but considerably less frequently.

Health

While the French health service is efficient and reliable it can be expensive if you're hospitalized or are taken there by ambulance unless you are covered by travel insurance. With the correct documentation, all EC citizens are entitled to take advantage of each other's health services under the same terms as residents of the country.

After consultation with a doctor or dentist you will receive a *feuille de soins* and upon collecting any prescription from the chemist you will receive a *volet de facturation* with little stickers or *vignettes* attached. Having paid the full fees these forms are then sent to the local *Caisse Primaire* for a 80% refund.

All pharmacies (designated by a green cross) are equipped with and obliged to give first aid on request, for which you will be charged unless it is minor. They can also provide you with the address of a doctor or dentist. In urgent cases you can contact *SOS Médecins* in most major towns. In the event of a pharmacy being closed a list of alternatives, including those open during the night (*pharmacie de garde*), will be displayed in the window and in the local newspaper.

TRAVELING TO PROVENCE

By Plane: Both Marseilles and Nice have international airports, with Marseilles frequently utilized as a passenger stopover for many flights originating in Paris and continuing onwards to Asian or African destinations.

With nearly 6 million passengers a year Nice International airport is France's second busiest after Paris. 35 airlines operate scheduled services here from 89 cities in 35 countries, including 15 to 20 flights daily from Paris.

Within France there is an extensive domestic network of flights between the regional airports like Bordeaux, Lyon, Montpellier, Mulhouse, Nantes and Strasbourg direct to Nice or Marseilles circumventing Paris. Reductions of up to 60% are available for groups, students, youths, senior citizens and regular users according to the day and flight time.

Airlines operating scheduled services to Nice include (with local contact numbers given for the busiest):

Aéromaritime and Air Algérie (93 832 416); Air France (93 839 100); Air India and Air Inter (93 148 484); Air Portugal and Alitalia (93 834 446); American Airlines (93 871 979); Austrian Airlines; British Airways (93 831 961); Danair (93 213 434); Garuda and Iberia (93 830 405); KLM (93 831 983); Lufthansa (93 974 663); Middle East Airlines and Minerve Air Liberte (93 710 444); Pan Am (93 160 116); Philippine Airlines and Royal Air Maroc (93 832 123); Sabena (93 830 390); SAS, Saudi Arabian Airlines, Thai, Tunis Air (93 886 691).

Airlines operating scheduled services to Marseilles include (with local contact numbers given for the busier airlines):

Aeroflot, Aéromaritime and Air Algérie (91 906 638); Air Afrique (91 911 000); Air France (91 549 292); Air Inter (91 919 090); Alitalia and British Airways (91 907 710); El Al Israeli Airlines and Iberia (91 919 225); Olympic Airways, Royal Air Maroc and Sabena (91 912 772); Swissair (91 904 283); Tunis Air, TWA and UTA (91 549 012).

By Train: From virtually any railway station in Europe tickets can be bought to any station in Provence. From Paris there is the choice of the high speed TGV (*train à grande vitesse*), sleepers and ordinary trains; via Lyon or the scenically renowned route between Clermont-Ferrand and Nîmes. Because all TGV passengers are seated a reservation must be made and for certain departures at peak hours a supplement will be demanded. Journey times by TGV have been more than halved from Paris; 3hr 45min to Avignon, 4hr 40min to Marseilles, 5hr

27min to Toulon and 7hr to Nice. For the coastal resorts not directly served by the TGV, changes can be made at Arles, Marseilles, Toulon, St.Raphaël, Cannes, Antibes, Cagnes-sur-Mer or Nice for local services. Many areas of northern Provence can be reached by TGV to Grenoble or Valence and ordinary train thereafter. All trains running south and south-east of Paris towards Provence depart and arrive from Gare du Lyon (info:1/45 8250; Res:1/45 656 060)

Tourists planning to visit other regions in France or to travel extensively in Provence should consider buying a *France Vacances* pass (unlimited travel for any 4 days during a period of 15 days or any 9 days in a month) or an *InterRail* (maximum age 26) pass giving one month's unlimited 2nd class travel. Both must be purchased outside of France. Once in France other discounts are available for couples with the *Carte Couple*, for families with a *Carte Kiwi*, for the over 65 with a *Carte Vermeille*, the *Carte Jeune* for the under-26s and for anyone traveling on *Période Bleue* days. As reductions do not apply on peak days or periods, users should ask for a *calendrier voyageurs* at any station which, by means of colour-coding, indicates when you can travel at a discount.

Remember you can be fined if your ticket is not date-stamped by one of the upright orange machines (*composteur*) that mark the entrance to the station platform. For up to 24 hours a rail journey may be broken anywhere, at any time, without revalidating your ticket.

Over 200 stations offer bicycle hire services and a number of major city stations coordinate car hire services.

By Road: The *Autoroute du Soleil* runs from Paris to Marseilles (the A6 to Lyon and the A7 thereafter) joining with the *Autoroute La Provençale* (the A8) to Nice (8 hours driving from Paris) and on to the Italian border. Bear in mind that toll fees (*péage*) from Paris to Nice will be around 400F.

Provence is also equally accessible by autoroute from Northern Italy, Switzerland via Geneva, Germany via Saarbrücken or Mulhouse and Lyon, Spain from Barcelona, and Bordeaux in Western France.

Integral to the French autoroute system you will find a service station, often with a restaurant and shops, every 24 miles (40km) open 24 hours around the clock; a rest area or *aire de repos*, often with picnic facilities, every 6 miles (10km) and every 2 kilometers (just over 1 mile) a free emergency telephone.

Alternative non-toll routes always run roughly parallel to the autoroutes but often pass through town centers.

Above all, if possible avoid traveling on the last weekend of July, the first and last weekend of August and the weekends closest to the national hoilidays of 14 July and 15 August.

By Sea: Regular maritime services are maintained between Marseilles and North Africa. Up to four weekly sailings to Tunis, Algiers and Oran, less frequently to Annaba and Skikda with a weekly sailing to Sardinia and 2-3 daily sailings to Corsica. Toulon and Nice have less frequent services to Corsica and Sardinia. Contact SNCM (*Société Nationale Maritime Corse Méditerranée*) 61 boulevard des Dames, Marseille (91 563 200); 3 av Gustave V, Nice (93 136 666).

TRAVELING IN PROVENCE

By Bus: Extensive travel within Provence by bus can prove to be both confusing and frustrating, but for those without private transport, there's no real choice as many small towns and villages are inaccessible by rail. Aside from limited numbers of SNCF buses along the rail network, the rest are operated by different private companies. As they don't all use the *gare routière* (bus station) it might be advisable to check with the local tourist office.

Bus station: Marseilles, place Victor-Hugo (91 081 640); Nice, boulevard Jean Jaures (93 856 181).

By Rail: Rail services in Provence are based around two major lines. A coastal line linking the Rhône Valley and Marseilles with Menton, and a line running along the Durance Valley from Marseilles to the Alps via Aix and Sisteron. A private narrow-gauge line *Chemin de Fer de la Provence* provides a spectacular link between Nice and Digne (3 hr 20 min).

SNCF: Avignon, bd St Roch (info: 90 825 050; res: 90 825 629); Digne (92 310 067); Marseille, Gare St Charles (info: 91 085 050; res: 91 088 412; train+auto: 91 951 167); Nice, av Thiers (info: 93 875 050; res: 93 888 993); Toulon, place Europe (info: 94 915 050; res: 94 223 919).

Chemins de Fer de Provence: Digne (92 310 158); Nice: Gare de Provence, 33 ave. Malausséna (93 882 856).

PRACTICAL TIPS

Accommodation

All forms and categories of accommodation can be found throughout the region. Those planning extensive traveling would be well advised to obtain one of the more reliable annual guides such as Michelin's *Red Guide, the Good Hotel Guide, Kléber, Gault-Millau, the Logis de France and the Guide des Relais Routiers;* the latter being unpretentious but usually providing a comfortable bed and good value for money.

During the tourist season, Easter and the course of exhibitions, festivals and trade fairs it would be prudent to book in advance. Problems arise mainly between 15 July and 15 August when the French take their own vacations *en masse*, with

the first weekend in August being the busiest time of all. Traveling during this period, hotel accommodation can be hard to come by – particularly in the coastal resorts – and you may well find yourself falling back on local tourist offices for help and ideas.

Hotels are officially classified by the *Direction de Tourisme* and their grading is shown by stars, depending on their amenities and the type of hotel, from 4-star (luxury) to 1-star (plain but comfortable). Hot and cold water will be found in all bedrooms, but only a proportion of hotels in the 1-, 2-, and 3-star categories have rooms with a private bath and WC en suite, although many more will provide a shower and bidet. Similarly, although many hotels have no restaurant, almost all will provide a continental breakfast.

Most hotels willingly provide extra beds to accommodate three or more people in the same room at fairly good discounts.

Charges vary, of course, according to the grade of hotel and the time of year, being at their highest from mid-June to mid-September. In many hotels 15% is now added to the bill for "service" – whether provided or not – and certainly when the bill is marked *services et taxes compris* no additional gratuity is expected.

Price more or less corresponds to the number of stars, though the system can be haphazard, having more to do with the existence of a television, en-suite bathroom or just simply the location, rather than genuine quality.

If you are planning to stay a week or more in one place it might be worth considering renting a house. This can be done through the official government service, the *Gîtes de France*; information and booking forms: 35, rue Godot de Mauroy, 75009 Paris (1/47 422 020). The cost varies, according to the season, from around 1000F to 2500F per week.

Practically every village and town in the region has at least one camp-site, whether it be a *camping municipal* or a luxury 4-star. North of the autoroute, camp-sites remain relatively calm even in peak season, whereas those with direct access to the sea or near a reputed resort will require a certain determination if you are to sruvive during the high season.

Consulates in France

Marseilles: **Austria**: 27 cours Pierre Puget, 6e (91 530 208); **Belgium**: 62 cours Pierre Pugot, 6e (91 332 526); **Canada**, 24 av du Prado, 6e (91 371 937); **Denmark**: 20 rue Henri Barbusse, 1e (91 908 023); **Germany**: 338 av Prado, 8e (91 776 090); **Ireland**: 148 rue Sainte, 1e (91 549 229); **Israel**: 454 rue Paradis, 8e (91 773 990)**; Italy:** 56 rue Alger, 5e (91 471 460); **Netherlands**: 139 av Toulon, 5e (91 256 664); **Norway + Sweden**: 376 av Prado, 8e (91 763 014); **South Africa**: 408 av Prado, 8e (91 226 690); **Spain**: 38 rue Edouard Delanglade, 6e (91 908 023); **Switzerland**: 7 rue Arcade, 6e (91 533 665); **UK**: 24 av du Prado, 6e (91 534 332); **USA**: 12 bd Paul Peytral, 6e (91 549 200).

Nice: **Austria**: 6 av de Verdun (93 870 131); **Belgium**: Bureau du Ruhl, av Gabriel Fauré (93 877 956); **Denmark**: Bureau 411, 30, av Jean Médecin (93 853 549); **Germany**: 22 av Notre-Dame (93 622 226); **Ireland**: 152 bd Kennedy, Antibes (93 615 063); **Italy**: 72 bd Gambetta (93 887 986); **Netherlands**: 14 rue Rossini (93 875 294); **Norway**: 20 quai Lunel (93 560 774); **Sweden**: 27-29 av Jean Médecin (93 881 440); **Switzerland**: 4 av G. Clémenceau (93 888 509); **UK**: (Honorary) 12 rue de France (93 823 204); **USA**: (Agence) 31 rue Maréchal Joffre (93 888 955).

Driving

Major roads (*routes nationales*, abbreviated to N or RN) are always of the highest standard; conditions of secondary roads (*routes départmentales*, denoted by the prefix D) vary but are usually good.

The speed limit in built-up areas is 60 kmph (36 mph). On toll motorways (autoroutes) the speed limit is 130 kmph (80 mph), on dual carriageways and motorways without tolls it is 110 kmph (68 mph) and on other roads 90 kmph (56 mph). Fines for driving violations are exacted on the spot and only cash or a French bank account cheque is accepted. The minimum fine for speeding is 1300F and for exceeding the drink driving level 2500 to 5000F.

Driving is on the right with overtaking on the left. The main rule of the road to remember when driving in France is that, unless there are signs to the contrary, you must always give way to traffic coming from your right, even when it is coming from a minor road. This is the law of *priorité à droite*.

All passengers, in both the front and back seats, must wear seat belts. Children under 10 years old are required to ride in the back seat. By law you must carry with you:

- a valid driving license
- car registration papers
- proof of insurance.

You are also required to carry a hazard warning triangle and headlights must be dipped towards the right and preferably changed to or painted yellow.

Suffice it to say in relation to parking, avoid leaving your car in an area marked *Zone Piétonne* (pedestrian precinct) and don't consider parking it if the sign says *Stationnement Gênant* (parking obstructive) or *Stationnement Interdit* (parking prohibited) if you expect to find it on your return. Cars with foreign number plates are rarely stolen, but radios, tape-decks and luggage are always tempting targets.

Recommended, particularly for those driving in the summer holiday season is the *Michelin* France N911 Route Planning Map or the free *Bison Fute* maps given out along the autoroutes with alternative roads, or *itinéraires bis*, and likely traffic jams delineated.

Constantly updated information regarding congestion, road works and alternative routes can be obtained for France as a whole on (1) 48 583 333 or for Provence on 91 787 878.

Car Hire: Internationally recognized agencies such as Avis, Budget, Eurocar, Hertz, along with a dizzying number of local agencies, will be found at the principal entry points (SNCF stations, airports) or through enquiry at the tourist office. Minimum age can vary from 18 to 30 depending on the company, engine size and model. A substantial deposit is usually required unless you hold a credit card.

However, due to the luxury-rate of TVA it may prove cheaper to bring your own vehicle along with you from Northern Europe or Britain than to hire for more than a few days.

Electricity

Virtually all France uses 220v (50-cycle) with double or triple round-pin wall sockets.

Emergencies and Problems

There are three important emergency phone numbers:

SAMU (ambulance service) 15
Police 17
Fire Brigade 18

In the event of sickness, pharmacies or chemists can provide addresses of local doctors and the nearest hospital casualty department.

In the case of theft or loss of personal belongings contact the nearest local or national police station, the *gendarmerie* or *Commissariat de Police*.

For loss or theft of passport or identity papers contact the nearest local or national police station, consulate or embassy, or administrative police headquarters, the *préfecture*.

For loss or theft of credit cards contact the nearest local or national police station and immediately notify:
- Carte Bleu (Barclaycard, Visa) 1/42 771 190
- Eurocard (Mastercard, Access) 1/45 678 484
- American Express 1/47 777 200
- Diner's Club 1/47 627 500.

Festivals and Holidays

The national holidays (*jours fériés*) in Provence and Côte d'Azur are:

January 1; Easter Sunday; Easter Monday; Ascension Day, (forty days after Easter); Pentecost, (seventh Sunday after Easter, with the Monday); May 1, (Workers' Day); May 8, (Armistice 1945); July 14, (Bastille Day); August 15, (Assumption); November 1, (All Saints' Day); November 11, (Armistice 1918); Christmas Day.

Banks are likely to shut at noon on days preceding public holidays. If any of these falls on a Sunday, the following day is taken as a holiday; if falling on a Tuesday or Friday, the intervening Monday or Saturday is often taken, making a "long weekend" or *pont* (bridge).

The following list outlines the main annual regional events. Details are given in the relevant regional chapters. Telephone numbers are given for reservations and program requests for those festivals with events of a short duration or limited seating capacity. Further details can be obtained through Minitel: 3615 RF Rubrique Festivals.
- *Aix-en-Provence:* Rock Festival, June; International Dance Festival, July; Classical Music, July (all: 42 630 675).
- *Antibes/Juan-les-Pins:* International Jazz Festival, July (93 339 564).
- *Arles:* International Photographic Meeting, July-August; Dance and Theater Festival, August (90 939 090).
- *Avignon:* International Theater and Dance Festival, July-August (90 826 708).

- *Cannes:* International Film Festival, May (93 390 101); Festival of Café-Théâtre, June (93 397 468).
- *Dignes-les-Bains:* Film Festivals, April + July + September + November.
- *Marseilles:* Santons, December-January; International Folklore Festival, July (91 051 565).
- *Menton:* Lemon Festival, February; Chamber Music Festival, July (93 358 222).
- *Monaco:* International Circus Festival, usually January; International Television Festival, February; Formula 1 Grand Prix, June; International Firework Festival, July-August.
- *Nice:* Mardi Gras Carnival, February; Jazz Festival, July (93 212 201).
- *Orange:* Chorégies, July (90 347 088).
- *Ramatuelle:* Gerard Philippe Festival, August (94 792 604).
- *Saintes-Maries-de-la-Mer:* Gypsy Festival, 24 May.
- *St-Rémy-de-Provence:* Fête de Transhumance, Whit Monday.
- *Tarascon:* Tarasque Festival, last Sunday in June.
- *Toulon:* Chateauvallon Dance Festival, July (94 241 176).

Forest Fires

Headline-grabbing forest fires every summer have devastated forests and homes, with frequent loss of life .

One cigarette is sufficient in Provence or along the Côte d'Azur to ignite this tinder-box. So always take the utmost care and never light fires or throw away glass bottles.

Maps

For a general coverage of France for driving, orientation and relief purposes the *Michelin* N989 is probably the best, with N914 providing a general France map with specific autoroute information (junctions, tolls, services, emergency telephones, etc). Once in Provence, the most convenient for driving is the *IGN*

red series N115 (1:250,000) or the *Michelin* 1:200,000 yellow series, sheet 245. The *Michelin* Côte d'Azur-Alpes Maritimes map N195 at 1:100,000 gives excellent coverage for this region.

Cyclists, walkers or drivers wishing to explore a particular area would be well advised to regard the *IGN* green series at 1:100,000 or the blue series at 1:25,000 and their excellent new Top 25 series covering areas of specific recreational interest. *Didier Richard* publish a series (1:50,000) using an IGN base, extensively updated with walking and skiing information.

City and town plans are often given free at tourist offices, but if more detailed maps and indexing are required the maps published by *Blay* or *Bleu et Or* can be recommended.

Media

Aside from the Paris-based *International Herald Tribune* with its American bias, many of the major English, German, Italian and Spanish newspapers and magazines are available at main newsagents and important transport terminus in resorts and larger towns.

A number of the *Syndicats d'Initiative* (tourist offices) publish similar, smaller periodicals to cover the events and news of the region during the high season for non-French readers.

If you're interested in brushing up your French the respected national daily *Le Monde* newspaper is written in unpretentious and correct French. With considerably higher circulation and less news content the regional dailies (*La Marseillaise*, *Midi Libre*, *Nice Matin*, and *Le Provençal*) provide good listings and local news.

France Inter broadcasts news and traffic information in English, usually at 8 a.m., 1 p.m. and 7 p.m. BBC programs are easily received on long and medium wave radios.

French television has five public channels - TF1, Antenne 2, FR3, La Cinq, M6 and the subscriber-only Canal+. All programs, except for a few late night foreign films (normally on Friday and Sunday) and some documentaries, are in French. For those in hotels offering cable and Canal+ many of the films screened will be in their original language.

Postal Services

Most post offices, indicated by the sign PTT or *Bureau de Poste*, are open from 8.00 to 19.00 on weekdays, and until 12.00 on Saturday for both postal and banking services.

Correspondence marked "poste restante" may be addressed to any post office and will be handed to the addressee on proof of identity. Letter-boxes are painted yellow and are emptied in all but the smallest towns daily. Postage stamps (*timbres*) are sold at all post offices and most tobacconists (*tabac*).

Restaurants

It should be noted that the conventional eating times in France are earlier than in many other countries. Most people lunch between 12.00 and 13.00 (hence the remarkably traffic-free roads) and many hotels will expect their guests to arrive by 19.30 should they wish to dine.

All restaurants are obliged by law to display prices, including service outside. Tipping is not obligatory, but if the service has been especially good, it is accepted practise to round off the bill with an extra 5 to 10%.

It should be remembered that in many provincial towns the main meal of the day is at noon and that any specialties which may have been available at midday are unlikely to be on the evening menu; nor are these specialties cooked every day, or prepared for you at a moment's notice.The following offers a brief outline of where to eat:

Bars and **cafés** – will serve snacks including sandwiches, tea (with little regard to English expectations), coffee, soft drinks, beer, wine and spirits. Some have a limited selection of cooked meals.

Bistrots – are small café-restaurants offering simple meals like omelets, steak and chips and dishes of the day (*plat du jour*) or other house specialties.

Brasseries – their distinctive feature is that meals are served throughout the day and more quickly than in restaurants, in a café-style ambience, even though there is little difference in price or quality.

Rôtisseries – for grilled meat dishes.

In the country **auberges**, **hostelleries** and **relais de campagne** all serve full meals at defined hours.

Excellent picnic and take-away food can be brought from the ubiquitous *boulangerie (*baker), *charcuterie* (cooked meats) and *fromagerie (cheese)* shops or from the supermarket counters. As in many regions world-wide with a heavy reliance on the tourist trade, it pays to ask for recommendations from locals, regard long menus with suspicion and to think twice if you're paying more than 100F for a regional specialty like *Bouillabaisse*.

Water, despite its abundance in a multitude of bottled formats, is, unless otherwise stated (*eau non potable*) perfectly drinkable from a tap.

Shopping

VAT or TVA (*taxe sur la valeur ajoutée*) as it is known in France runs at a standard 18.6%, rising to 22% for luxury items. Goods purchased by non-French residents, over a certain value (often 1000F) can have the TVA refunded either directly at the point of purchase or by leaving the *ventes en détaxe* form with Customs on departure for a refund at your home address.

Shopping hours can vary considerably, particuarly between types of shops. Groceries (*épicerie*), bakeries *(bou-*

langerie) and butchers *(boucherie)* are generally open 7/8.30 to noon and 2 until 6.30/7.30 p.m., Monday to Saturday and occasionally Sunday morning. Bakeries will often operate a rota system so that at least one is open in the neighborhood every day. Department stores and supermarkets are generally open from 9/9.30 a.m. to 7/7.30 p.m. without a break, Tuesday to Saturday. Most close Monday morning or the whole day but many open Sunday morning in the high season. If a shop remains open on a Sunday, it will be closed on Monday. These hours will be closely adhered to inland in Provence and less so along the coast. Museums and monuments are normally closed on Tuesdays and public holidays.

Telephone Services

Given the problems of finding a coin-operated booth or the usual demand that you buy a drink before using the telephone or toilets in a café, the simplest method of making telephone calls is with a *télécarte* card giving credits of 50 or 120 units. These are available from post offices, tobacconists, SNCF counters, and newspaper kiosks. Calls within France, other than to the Paris area, do not require a prefix. Calling *from* Paris, you must dial 16 before the required number, and to ring Paris from anywhere else in France, you dial 1 first.

Calls made from your hotel may be charged at a higher rate, but any additional charge must not exceed 30%. If it does, you may report the matter to France Telecom (dial 14, toll-free).

Tipping

However anachronistic this practise might appear, it is the difference between a minimal and a living wage for a diminishing number of services. Hotel porters will expect 5 to 10F per item; chamber maids 50 to 100F per week, hairdressers around 10% as will tour guides, taxi drivers around 10% of the fare, waiters in cafes and bars a small tip and hostesses at the cinema, 2F with the same for toilet attendants.

Time Differences

France follows Central European time (GMT+1) and from the last Sunday in March to the last Sunday in September, clocks are put one hour ahead (GMT+2) for daylight saving.

Tourist Information

Each region and *départment* has its own tourist office *(comité régional du tourisme)* and in addition, each town of any importance and many smaller places, as well, with specific sights of interest, have a local SI *(Syndicat d'Initiative)* or *office du tourisme*, or if not, you can usually get help from the *Mairie* (Town Hall). Telephone numbers and addresses are given in the Guideposts at the end of each chapter for the more important towns and resorts. They will all provide free maps and useful information with regard to accommodation (for a small refundable charge they will search and make the necessary bookings), local events, sporting facilities, national parks and nature reserves, times of admission to museums, castles etc. Many of the larger offices will have at least one person speaking English, German or Italian, as well as a selection of information in various languages.

Hours vary from town to town but generally during summer most will be open every day except Sunday from 9 a.m. to noon or 1 p.m. and 1 or 2 until 6 or 6.30 p.m. Many of the inland offices will be closed or work greatly reduced hours from late October through to early April.

AUTHORS

Catherine Bray kept herself going throughout her university years (History of Art, Philosophy and Modern Literature), with dreams of traveling the world.

Now she is a professional travel writer. She was project editor of the *Nelles Guides Provence* and *Brittany* and also worked on the articles in her specialist fields.

Isabelle du Boucher comes from the Basque country. As a journalist she contributes to a number of gourmet magazines, and has a deep knowledge of the characteristics of France's many regional cuisines. She wrote our feature on "Food and Drink".

Régis Bertrand has a Ph.D. in history and is a lecturer at the University of Provence. His special field is Provençal traditions, and his doctoral thesis was on this subject.

In addition he has contributed as a historian to many important books about Provence, and particulary about Marseilles.

Sophie Bogrow has worked for the *Almanach de l'Aventure et du Voyage* from its first edition, and since 1985 has been responsible for its coverage of France. She is particularly knowledgeable on the individual regions of France.

Maryline Desbiolles was born in the Savoie and grew up near Nice. Over the years she has become thoroughly acquainted with Provence, from the Côte d'Azur to the Alps.

After graduation she wants to make a career as an author or journalist, devoting herself to modern art.

Pierre Léonforté is a journalist who hails from the Midi and has lived for the last eight years in Marseille. He loves good food and architecture and works on the staff of *Max* magazine. He plans to spend the rest of his life in Provence, just sitting in the sun.

PHOTOGRAPHERS

Archiv für Kunst und Geschichte, Berlin 23, 26, 29, 31L, 33R, 33L, 34, 38, 39, 41, 42, 43, 50/51
Brosse, Werner 83
Fischer, Peter 28
Henninges, Heiner 74L, 210
Poblete, José F. 8/9, 12, 14, 17, 18, 19, 21, 24, 32, 45, 47, 48/49, 52, 56, 57, 61, 63, 64, 66, 68, 72, 74R,76, 77, 79L, 79R, 82, 88, 97L, 98, 100, 103, 104, 105, 107, 108L, 108R, 110, 112, 113, 114L, 115, 117, 118, 120, 121, 128/129, 130, 134, 135, 136, 137, 140, 141, 143, 146, 150, 156, 157, 163, 172, 185, 186, 187, 194, 202/203, 205, 216, 219, 220, 221, 223, 224, 226, 229, 231, 232, 234, 235, 236, 237, 238, 239
Thiele, Klaus 16, 22, 27, 81, 99, 161, 176, 212, 215
Thomas, Martin 1, 10/11, 31R, 36, 62, 73, 86/87, 93, 95, 97R, 109, 114R, 122, 123, 124, 125, 144/145, 151, 154, 158, 160, 162, 165, 166, 167, 170/171, 177, 178, 179, 180, 181, 183, 196, 197, 200/201, 204, 207, 208, 213L, 213R, 218, 227, 228

A

Agay 167
Aigues-Mortes 83
Aiguines 139
Aix-en-Provence 15, 16, 19, 30, 32, 33, 34, 35, 36, 40, 46, 65, **66-69**, 122, 125
  Cathédrale du Saint-Sauveur 68
  Cours Mirabeau 38, 66
  Eglise de la Madeleine 68
  Le Parvis des Prêcheurs 68
  Mazarin Quarter 68
  Musée des Tapisseries 68
  Musée du Vieil Aix 68
  Musée Granet 68
  Old Corn House 67
  Palais de Justice 68
  Pavillon Vendôme 69
  Place d'Albertas 67
  Town Hall 67
Alleins 75
Allemagne-en-Provence 141
Alpes d'Azur 184-186
  Clue du Riolan, gorge 186
  Col de la Cayolle 185
  Gorges de Daluis 185
  Gorges du Cians 184
  La Madone de Fenestre 184
  La Madone d'Utelle 184
  Notre-Dame-d'Entrevignes 186
  Notre-Dame-du-Bueyi 185
  Val d'Entraunes 185
Alpes-de-Haute-Provence 131
Alpes-Maritimes 173-196
Alphonse I, Count 24
Alphonse II, Count 24
Alphonse of Poitiers 24
Alpilles, Les **76-80**, 89, 98
Annot 137
Ansouis 125
Antibes 180-181
  Château Grimaldi 180
  Fort Carré 181
  Marché des Artisans 181
  Picasso Museum 180
  Port Vauban 181
Apt 117, **120-122**, 122
Argens, river 148, 164
Arles 17, 18, 19, 20, 22, 25, 26, 27, 40, 42, 44, 46, **70-71**
  Espace Van Gogh 71
  Les Alyscamps, necropolis 70
  Musée d'Art Chrétien 71
  Musée d'Art Païen 71
  Musée Réattu 41, 70
  Museon Arlaten 44, 71
  Roman Amphitheater 70
  Saint-Trophime, church 70
  Thermal Baths 70
  Van Gogh Bridge 70
Aubagne 65, 66

Augustus, Emperor 17, 18, 70, 81, 82, 101, 102
Aups 147
Aureille 78
Aurel 112
Avignon 13, 14, 25, 26, 27, 29, 33, 35, 37, 39, 40, 42, 46, **93-97**
  Livrée Ceccano 97
  Musée Calvet 97
  Musée Félibriges 97
  Musée Lapidaire 97
  Musée Louis-Voulard 97
  Musée Petit Palais 96
  Musée Requien 97
  Musée Théodore Aubanel 97
  Notre-Dame-des-Doms 96
  Palais des Papes 96
  Place des Carmes 97
  St. Baldou Area 98

B

Bagnols-en-Forêt 162
  Gorges du Blavet 162
  Notre-Dame-de-Selves 162
  Saint-Auxile, chapel 162
Banon 135
Barbegal, castle 77
Barbentane 80
  Maison des Chevaliers 80
  Petit Trianon du Soleil, castle 80
  Porte Calendrale 80
  Porte du Séquier 80
  Tour Anglica 80
Bargème 164
Bargemon 162
Barjols 147, 148
Baroque architecture 37, 67
Bar-sur-Loup 178
Bastides 221
Baudinard 140
Bauduen 140
Beaulieu 192
Beaumes-de-Venise 108
Bédoin 111
Bégo, Mount 14, 197
Bell-towers 216-217
Belvédère 184
Berre-des-Alpes 190
Berthemont-les-Bains 184
Beuil 185
Biot 181-182
  Biot Glassworks 181
  Chemin des Combes 181
  Musée Fernand Léger 181
  Saint-Julien, chapel 182
Black Death 29, 30, 101
Bollène-Vésubie 184
Bonaparte, Napoleon 40, 41, 136
Bonnard, Pierre 159, 227
Bonnieux 124
Bories 117-118, **220-221**

Bormes-les-Mimosas 157
Bosco, Henri 113, 119, 122, 123
Bouches-du-Rhône,département **53-85**
Boulouris 166
Brantes 111
Braque, Georges 44, 159
Bréa, Louis, painter 189
Breil-sur-Roya, lake 196
Bretoule 80
Brignoles 151
Brue-Auriac 148
Bull Fights 235

C

Cabannes 75
Cabasse 161
Cabrières-d'Avignon 116
Cabris 178
Cadenet 125
Caderousse 103
Caesar, Gaius Julius 16, 164
Cagnes-sur-Mer 182
Cairanne 109
Callas 162
Callian 163
Camargue 13, 53, **71-74**, 83
  Bird Sanctuary of Pont de Gau 73
  Château d'Avignon 73
  Plain of Crau 73-74
Camps-la-Source 152
Cannes 42, 46, **173-176**
  International Film Festival 174
  La Croisette 174
  Le Suquet, old town 174
  Musée de la Castre 174
  Notre-Dame de l'Espérance 174
  Notre-Dame-de-Vie, chapel 176
  Old Castle 174
  Tour du Suquet 174
  Villa Rothschild 176
Caparon, Roman ruins 77
Cap Canaille 65
Cap d'Ail 192
Cap d'Antibes 180
Cap Ferrat 191, 192
  Musée Ephrussi de Rothschild 191
  Pointe des Fourmis 192
  Pointe Saint-Hospice 192
  Villa Kerylos 192
Caromb 111
Carpentras 39, 97, **100-101**
  Bibliothèque Inguimbertine 101
  Cathedral of St. Siffrein 100
  Foire Saint-Siffrein 101
  Hôtel-Dieu 101
  Palais de Justice 100
  Place Inguimbert 101
Cassis 65

Castellane 138, 161
Castellar 195
Catalonian dynasty 23, 24, 25, 26
Caussols, Plateau de 178
Cavaillon 39, **97-100**
  Archaeological Museum 98
  Place François-Tourel 98
  St. Jacques, chapel 98
  Synagogue 99
Cavalaire-sur-Mer 159
Cavalière 159
Cécile-les-Vignes 109
Celto-Ligurian tribes 15, 16, 18
Celts 14, 15, 82
Ceramics 179
Cézanne, Paul 44, 60, 68, 69, 212
Chabert 136
Chagall, Marc 160
Chapelles du Calvaire 183
Charles I, Count of Anjou 27
Charles II, Count of Anjou 28
Charles the Bald, king 21
Château-Arnoux 35
Châteauneuf-de-Gadagne 109
Châteauneuf-du-Pape 109
Châteaurenard 74
Châteauvieux 164
Châteaux-Arnoux 136
Christianity 19-20, 25, 33
Cimiez 190
Clement V, Pope 92, 93
Coaraze 190
Cocteau, Jean 56
Col de Braus 191
Col de Murs 117
Col de Vence 184
Colmars-les-Alpes 138
Col Saint-Roch 190
Combe de Murs 117
Comps-sur-Artuby 164
Comtat Venaissin 13, 24, 33, 89,
  91, 92, 99
Corniche d'Esterel 164, **166-167**
  Massif de l'Esterel 166
  Menhir of Ayre-Peyronne 167
  Menhirs of Veyssière 167
  Pic de l'Ours 167
  Pic du Cap-Roux 167
  Pointe de l'Esquillon 167
Corniche d'Or
  see Corniche d'Esterel 166
Corniche Inférieure 192
Corniche Moyenne 192
Coronne 104
Coteaux du Tricastin 109
Côte d'Azur 45, 46, 156, 173,
  179, 185
Côtes du Rhône 108
Cotignac 147
Coursegoules 178
Courthézon 92
Crestet 107

Crillon-le-Brave 111
Cros-de-Cagnes 182
Cruis 135
Crusades 25, 27, 139
Cucuron 124

D

D'Aubignan 109
Daudet, Alphonse 70, 77, 80
Dentelles de Montmirail **106-109**
  Cirque de Saint-Amand 107
  Mont-St-Amand 107
  Turc, mountain 107
Derain, André 45
Digne 19, 137
  Centre Géologique de
    Saint-Benoît 137
  Cours Gassendi 38
  Notre-Dame-du-Bourg,
    cathedral 137
Domaine des Collettes 182
Draguignan 160, 161
Dufy, Raoul 44, 46
Dumas, Alexandre 45, 56
Durance, river 13, 14, 20, 24, 34,
  53, 74, 75, 78, 79, 89, 98, 109,
  121, 125, 133, 134, 135, 136

E

Entrages 137
Entrechaux 111
Entremont 15, 16
Entrevaux 186
En-Vau 65
Esparron 141
Esparron-sur-Verdon, lake 140
Estoublon, castle 77
Etang de Berre 13
Eygalières 79
Eyguières 78
  Fontaine Bormes-à-la-Coquille
    78
  Fontaine Croix-du-Prêche 78
  Gallo-Roman Tombs 78
  Maison Garcin 78
  Saint-Pierre-de-Vence, chapel 78
  Saint-Sauveur, chapel 78
  Saint-Vérédème, chapel 78
Eze-sur-Mer 192

F

Fabre, Jean-Henri 103, 110
Faubourg de La Baume 136
Fayence 163
Fayence, Pays de **162-164**
  Château de Beauregard 163
  Château de Borigaille 163
  La Roche Taillée, aqueduct 163
Festivals 204-209

Festivals, Religious **230-234**
Fitzgerald, Francis Scott 46, 173
Flassan 111
Flayose 161
Fontaine-de-Vaucluse 114, 115,
  116
Fontvieille 77
Food and Drink 236-239
Forcalqueiret 152
Forcalquier 133
Fos, Roman port 74
Fox-Amphoux 147
Frederick Barbarossa, Emperor
  24, 70
Fréjus 18, 19, 157, **164-165**
  Archaeological Museum 165
  Baptistry 165
  Cathedral 164
  Cloisters 164
French Revolution 13, 19, 40,
  60, 75, 78, 83, 96

G

Ganagobie, Plateau de 134
  Avenue of the Monks 134
  Benedictine Monastery 134
  Saint-Donat, church 134
Gardiole Massif 65
Garéout 152
Gargas 120
Gassendi, Pierre, philosopher 38
Gauls 17, 20, 98, 101, 102, 115
Giacometti, Alberto 160
Giens Peninsula 156, 157
Gignac 120
Gigondas 108
Gillette 186
Giono, Jean 118, 119, 131
Glacières de Fontfrège 150
Glanum, Gallo-Roman site 79
Gogh, Vincent van 44, 60, 79, 80
Golfe-Juan 179
Gorbio 196
Gordes 117, **118-119**
  Château des Simiane 119
  Musée Vasarély 119
Gothic architecture 29, 30, 96
Gourdon 178
Grande Corniche 192
  Belvédère d'Eze 192
  Nice Observatory 192
  Plateau Saint-Michel 192
  Point Capitaine 192
Grasse 39, **176-178**
  Musée d'Art et Histoire de
    Provence 178
  Musée int. de la Parfumerie 177
  Notre-Dame-de-Gratemoine 178
  Notre-Dame-du-Puy 177
  Place aux Aires 177
  Villa-Musée Fragonard 178

Greeks 15, 16, 53, 155, 156
Gregory VII, Pope 23, 26
Gréoux-les-Bains, Reservoir 140
Grillon 105
Grimaud 160
   Castle 160
   Pénitents Blancs, chapel 160
   Saint-Michel, church 160
Guillaumes 185

H

Haut-de-Cagnes 182
Henri IV, King of France 34, 35
Herbes de Provence 236
History, Art and Culture 13-46
Hugo, Victor 155
Hyères 42, **155-156**

I

Ile Gaby 56
Iles de Lérins 20, 164, 176
Iles d'Hyères 156
   Ile de Levant 156, 157
   Porquerolles 156
   Port-Cros 156, 157
Impressionism **44-45**
Inquisition 34

J

Jabron Valley 135
Jews 32, 33, 39, 99, 100
Joanna of Naples, Countess 30
Juan-les-Pins **179-180**
   Jardin Thuret 180
   La Garoupe, hill 180
   Notre-Dame-du-Bon-Port 180

K

Kelly, Grace 192, 229
Knights of St. John 26
Knights Templar 26, 92, 105, 109, 152, 164

L

La Bastide-d'Esclapon 164
La Brigue 196
Lac de Castillon 137, 138
Lac de l'Escale 136
La Celle, abbey 152
La Chartreuse de Bonpas 92
Lacoste 124
La Croix-Valmer 159
Lafare 107
La Garde-Freinet 158
   13th-century chapel 158
   Fort Freinet 158
   Medieval Village 158

Lagarde-Paréol 109
La Garonne 155
L'Almanarre 156
Lamanon 75
La Martre 164
La Napoule 173
Lantosque 184
La Palud-sur-Verdon 139
La Penne 186
La Roque-Alrie 107
La Roque-d'Anthéron 74, 75
La Roque-Esclapon 164
La Tour d'Aigues 125
La Turbie 192
Lavender 112, 114, 116, 122, 131, 138, 141, 176
Le Barroux 111
Le Beaucet 92, 115
Le Castellar du Thorenc 178
Le Corbusier,Charles-Edouard 62, 194
Le Lavandou 159
Le Maugué 139
L'Engarvin 190
Le Pradet 155
Les Arcs-sur-Argens 160
Les Baux, Château 65
Les Baux-de-Provence **76-77**
Les Beaumes 107
Les Mées 134
Les Oursinières 155
Le Thor 92
Le Thoronet, abbey 161
Lieuche 184
Ligurians 15, 16, 117
L'Isle-sur-la-Sorgue 92
Lorgues 161
Loube Mountains 152
Louis I of Anjou, Count 30
Louis II of Anjou, Count 30, 31
Louis III of Anjou, Count 31
Louis the Blind, king 21
Louis XIV, King of France 35, 36, 102, 153, 189
Lourmarin 35, 124
Lourmarin, gorge of 122
Lubéron **122-125**, 123
   Fort de Buoux 124
   Parc Naturel Régional 119, 122
   Prieuré de Saint-Symphorien 124
Lubéron, Monts de 89, 98
Lucéram 191
Lure Mountains 112, 135
Lurs 133

M

Maillane 74
Malaucène 107, 111
Malaussène 184
Malézieux, spring 107
Mallefougasse 135

Mallemort 75
Mandelieu 173
Mane 133
Manosque 131
Marseilles 14, 15, 16, 18, 19, 22, 25, 27, 28, 29, 31, 33, 36, 37, 38, 40, 44, 46, **53-65**
   Basilica Saint-Victor 56
   Catalans Quarter 62
   Château Borély 62
   Château d'If, prison island 56
   City Hall 59
   Corniche John F. Kennedy 56, 61-62
   Cours Belsunce 38
   Jardins des Vestiges 53
   Maison Diamantée 60
   Marché Castellane 59
   Marché de la Plaine 57
   Marché de Noailles 59
   Musée Cantini 60
   Musée de la Mode 57
   Musée Grobet Labadié 60
   Museum of Archaeology 60
   New Cathedral of La Major 55
   Notre-Dame-de-la-Garde 53, 55
   Old Harbor 53, 55-56, 60, 65
   Palais Longchamp 60
   Panier, town quarter 59
   Pointe Rouge, beach 63
   Prado Beaches 56, 62
   Parc Chanot 62
   Quai des Belges 59
   Quartier des Capucins 59
   Saint-Jean, fort 56
   Saint Nicolas, fort 56
   Saint Victor, Abbey 23
   Vieille Charité 60, 62
Martini, Simone, painter 30, 210
Massif de la Sainte-Baume 150
Massif des Maures 155, **157-158**, 166
Massif des Morières 153
Massif d'Esterel 165
Matisse, Henri 45, 159, 183, 189
Maussane-les-Alpilles 78
   Château de Monblan 78
   Fontaine des Quatre-Saisons 78
   Oratoire de Saint-Marc 78
   Saint-Croix 78
Mazan 109
Mazarin, Cardinal 35
Megaliths 14
Ménerbes 123
Menton 191, **194-195**
   Jardin Fontana Rosa 195
   Les Colombières, garden 195
   Oliveraie du Pian, park 195
   Saint-Michel, church 195
   Val Rameh, botanic garden 195
Méounes-les-Montrieux 152, 153

Mercantour, Parc National du
185
Mérindol 124
Méthamis 113, 115
Mistral, Frédéric 44, 70, 71, 74,
80, 108, 205
Modène 111
Monaco 41, **192-194**
Fontvieille Quarter 192
Jardin Exotique 192
Oceanographic Museum 192
Quartier de Monte Carlo 194
Mondragon 104
Monet, Claude 227
Mons 163, 164
Montauban, castle 77
Montbrun 112
Monteux 91
Montfort-sur-Argens 151
Montfuron 131
Montmajour Abbey 23, 71, 75
Montmirail 107
Montpezat 141
Montrieux-le-Jeune, monastery
152
Montrieux-le-Vieux 152
Mormoiron 111
Mornas 104
Mornieux 113
Mouriès 78
Mas de Beauregard 78
Mas de Brau 78
Mas de Malacercis 78
Mas de Servanes 78
Saint-Jacques-le-Majeur 78
Saint Symphorien, chapel 78
Moustiers-Sainte-Marie 139
Murs 113, 117
Museums 210-215

N

Narbonne 16
Neolithic Age 14, 117
Nesque, river 92, 112, 113
Nice 13, 42, 46, **186-190**
Baie des Anges 187
Chapelle de la Miséricorde 187
Château de l'Anglais 190
Cours Saleya 187
Galeries des Ponchettes 190
Marché d'Art et d'Antiquités 189
Musée Chagall 190
Musée des Beaux-Arts 190
Musée Masséna 190
Musée Matisse 190
Museum of Modern Art 190
Palais Lascaris 187
Place Garibaldi 190
Promenade des Anglais 187
Russian Church 189
Sainte-Réparate, cathedral 187

Theatine Church 37
Nîmes 81, **82-83**
Amphitheater 82
Jardin de la Fontaine 83
Maison Carrée 82
Musée des Antiques 82
Porte d'Auguste 82
Tour Magne, Roman tower 83
Nostradamus, astrologer 75, 79,
80
Noves 75

O

Ollioules 155
Ongles 135
Oppède-le-Vieux 123
Orange 13, 17, 18, 24, 34,
101-104, 109
Orgon 78

P

Pagnol, Marcel 45, 60, 66
Paradou
Pays d'Aigues 122, 124
Pays d'Apt 118-122
Chaussée des Géants 119
Falaises de Sang 119
Notre-Dame-des-Lumières,
church 121
Pont Julien 121
Val des Fées 119
Pays d'Aups 147-151
Péone 185
Perfume Industry 176
Pernes-les-Fontaines 92, 115
Château of the Counts of
Toulouse 92
Notre-Dame-de-Nazareth 92
Tower of Ferrande 92
Pertuis 125
Picasso, Pablo 46, 69, 70, 176,
179, 180, 181, 211, 213, 227
Pierrefeu 186
Pont Du Gard,Roman aquaeduct
81
Pont-Durandy 184
Ponty 121
Popes of Avignon 29, 30, 75, 93,
104, 210
Port-Grimaud 160
Port-Miou 65
Port-Pin 65
Port-Saint-Louis-du-Rhône 71,
73
Pramousquier 159
Protestants 34
Provençal Language 21
Provence, Haute **131-136**
Puget-Théniers 186

Q

Quinquonce 141
Quinson Reservoir 140

R

Rainier of Monaco, Prince 192,
229
Ramatuelle 159
Rasteau 108, 109
Rayol 159
Reillane 131
Religious Wars 33-34
René of Anjou, King 31, 32, 66,
70, 80
Renoir, Auguste 45, 182
Rhône, river 13, 17, 20, 24, 25,
46, 53, 71, 74, 75, 80, 89, 94,
95, 101, 103
Rhône Valley 13, 15, 16, 19, 21,
25
Richard the Lionheart, king 25
Richerenches 105
Riez 19, 141
Rigaud 185
Rochegude 109
Rocher de Cire 113
Rocquefur 121
Romanesque Art 26-27
Romans 13, **16-19**, 17, 18, 19,
20, 21, 53, 66, 70, 81, 82, 91,
101, 102, 106, 111, 151, 152,
153, 156, 164
Roquebillère 184
Roquebrune-Cap-Martin 194
Roquebrune-sur-Argens 165
Roquebrussanne 152
Roquepertuse 15
Roquesteron 186
Roussillon 119
Route Napoléon 136, 138, 173,
178
Rustrel 120

S

Sablet 107
Sade, Marquis de 40, 116, 124
Saint-André-les-Alpes 137
Saint-Barnabé 184
Saint-Cassien, lake 163
Saint-Cézaire 178
Saint-Chamas 18
Saint-Christol 114
Saint Clair 159
Saint-Dalmas-de-Tende 196
Sainte-Agnès 191, 195
Sainte-Baume 66
Sainte-Croix, lake 139, 140
Sainte-Croix, village 140
Sainte-Marguerite, island 176

Saintes-Maries-de-la-Mer 19, 71, 72
Saint-Etienne 135
Sainte-Victoire, Mont 69, 141, 167
Saint-Gilles 83
Saint-Jeannet 184
Saint-Jurs 141
Saint-Léger-de-Ventoux 111
Saint-Martin-de-Brômes 141
Saint-Martin-Vésubie 184
Saint-Maximin-la-Sainte-Baume 150, 150
Saint-Michel-l'Observatoire 131, 133
Saint-Paul 182
　Fondation Maeght 183
Saint-Raphaël 165-166
Saint-Rémy-de-Provence 18, 80
　Hôtel de Sade 79
　Hôtel Mistral de Mondragon 80
　Les Antiques, excavations 79
　Présence Van Gogh, museum 79
　Saint-Paul-de-Mausole, abbey 80
Saint-Saturnin-lès-Apt 120
Saint-Trinit 112
Saint-Tropez 45, 159-160
　Chapel of Sainte-Anne 159
　Citadel 159
　Musée de l'Annonciade 159
Saint-Tropez, Gulf of 158, 160
Salernes 147
Salon-de-Provence 75-76
　Château de l'Emperi 76
　Collégiale Saint-Laurent 76
　Festival de Juillet 76
Santons 60, 64, 65, 66, 105, 116, 138, 141
Saorge 196
Saracens 22, 134, 139, 156
Sault, Pays de 110, 111-113
Sault, village 112, 115
Saumane-de-Vaucluse 115
Savona 17
Séguret 107
Seillans 162
Sénanque, Abbey 117
Séranon 178
Sérignan-du-Comtat 103
Sigale 186
Signac, Paul 45, 159, 210, 213
Signes 153
Silvacane 75, 116
Simiane-la-Rotonde 131
Sisteron 135, 136
　Citadel 135
　Notre-Dame, chapel 136
　Notre-Dame-des-Pommiers, cathedral 135
Six-Fours-les-Plages 155
Sorgue, river 114, 115
Sports of Provence 234-235

Suze-la-Rousse 104
Suzette 107

T

Tarascon 46, 80-81
　Cloître des Cordeliers 80
　Hôpital Saint-Nicolas 80
　Maison de Tartarin 80
　Musée Charles Demery Souleiado 81
　Sainte-Marthe, church 80
　Saint-Michel-de-Frigolet 80
Tende 197
Théoule-sur-Mer 167
Thoronet 116
Touët-sur-Var 184
Toulon 18, 39, 42, 153-155
　Cap Brun 155
　Centre de Châteauvallon 155
　Corniche du Mourillon 155
　Cours Lafayette 154
　Fort de Balaguier 155
　Musée de Toulon 155
　Naval Museum 155
　Sainte-Marie-de-la-Seds 154
　Saint- François, church 154
　Saint-Louis, church 155
Tourism, History of 224-229
Tourrettes 163
Tourrettes-sur-Loup 178
Tourves 151
Traditions of Provence 230-234
Trans-en-Provence 160
Turini 191

U

Uchaux, castle 103

V

Vacqueyras 107
Vaison-la-Romaine 101
　Cathedral of Notre-Dame 106
　Haute-Ville 106
　Museum 106
Valberg 185
Valbonne 182
Valbonne-Sophia-Antipolis 182
Val d'Enfer 77
Valensole, Plateau de 13, 112, 131, 141
Vallauris 179
　Castle-Museum 179
　Picasso Museum 179
　Saint-Martin, church 179
Vallée Close 114
Vallée de la Roya 196
Vallée de l'Esteron 186
Vallée des Merveilles 14, 197
Vallée du Gapeau 152

Vallon des Auffes 61
Vallon de Souïras 108
Valréas 104-105, 105
　Château de Simiane 105
　Museum 105
　Notre-Dame-de-Nazareth 105, 106
Var, Central 151
Var, département 147-169
Var, Eastern 160-164
　Chapel of Sainte-Roseline 160
　Neolithic Dolmen 161
　Notre-Dame des Sablettes 161
　Pennafort Gorges 162
　Pennafort Waterfall 162
　Saut-du-Capelan 162
Vasarély, Victor 119
Vaucluse, département 89-127
Vaucluse, Monts de 89, 101, 110
Vaucluse, Plateau de 13, 113
Vauvenargues 69
Venanson 184
Venasque 92, 115
Vence 182
　Cathédrale de la Nativité 183
　Chapelle du Rosaire 183
Ventoux, Mont 13, 89, 98, 106, 109, 110, 112
Ventoux, Pays de 111
Verdon, Gorges du 138, 139
　Cirque de Vaumale 139
　Col d'Illoire 139
　Corniche Sublime 139
　Grand Canyon 138, 139
　Grotte du Styx 139
　Point Sublime 139
　Pont de l'Artuby, bridge 139
　Signal de Margès, waterfall 139
Verdon, river 139, 140
Vieux-Noyers 135
Villars-sur-Var 184
Villefranche-sur-Mer 191
Villemus 131
Villeneuve-les-Avignon 95
Villeneuve-Loubet 182
Vins-sur-Caramy 151
Visan 105
Volonne 136

W

Waldo, Pierre, mystic 89
Water Gardens 219
Wines of Provence 238-239
World War, First 44, 228
World War, Second 46, 59, 60, 154

Z

Zola, Emile 44